Guide to College Reading

FOURTH EDITION

GUIDE TO College Reading

KATHLEEN T. McWHORTER

Niagara County Community College

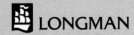 LONGMAN

An imprint of Addison Wesley Longman, Inc.

New York • Reading, Massachusetts • Menlo Park, California • Harlow, England
Don Mills, Ontario • Sydney • Mexico City • Madrid • Amsterdam

Acquisitions Editor: Ellen Schatz
Developmental Editor: Susan Messer
Project Coordination and Text Design: Ruttle, Shaw & Wetherill, Inc.
Cover Designer: Kay Petronio
Electronic Production Manager: Angel Gonzalez
Manufacturing Manager: Willie Lane
Electronic Page Makeup: Ruttle, Shaw & Wetherill, Inc.
Printer and Binder: R. R. Donnelley & Sons Company
Cover Printer: The Lehigh Press, Inc.

For permission to use copyrighted material, grateful acknowledgment is made to the copyright holders on p. 541–546, which are hereby made part of this copyright page.

Library of Congress Cataloging-in-Publication Data

McWhorter, Kathleen T.
    Guide to college reading / Kathleen T. McWhorter. —4th ed.
      p. cm.
    Includes bibliographical references and index.
    ISBN 0-673-52490-6. —ISBN 0-673-52491-4
    1. Reading (Higher education) 2. Developmental reading.
  3. College readers. I. Title.
  LB2395.3.M386 1997
  428.4'071'1—dc20   96-2358
                                   CIP

ISBN 0-673-52490-6 (student edition)
ISBN 0-673-52491-4 (instructor's edition)

12345678910—WOC—99989796

Contents

PART TWO　　　　*Reading as Thinking and Learning*　55

To the Instructor

Decreased spending for education and overcrowded classrooms are only two of the conditions that have contributed to the continuing decline of basic skill competencies. On a more positive note, the influx of nontraditional students has enriched the educational scene and made the preparation of these students for academic success of paramount importance. *A Guide to College Reading*, Fourth Edition, is written to equip students with the basic reading skills needed to cope with the demands of academic work.

This text uses approaches, methodology, and reading materials that address the learning characteristics, attitudes, and motivational levels of its target audience. This text adopts an encouraging, supportive, nonthreatening voice and an unassuming attitude toward learning. The text provides a variety of everyday examples and extensive exercises to encourage students to become involved and to apply the skills presented. The chapters are divided into numerous sections; exercises are frequent, but brief and explicit. The language and style are simple and direct; explanations are clear and often presented in step-by-step form. Reading topics and materials have been chosen carefully to relate to the students' interests and background, while exhibiting potential for broadening their range of experience. Many students have compensated for poor reading skills with alternate learning styles; they have become visual and auditory learners. To capitalize on this, a visual approach to learning, including drawings, diagrams, and visual aids to illustrate concepts, is used throughout.

Content Overview

The text is organized into six major sections, following the logical progression of skill development from words to sentences and then to paragraphs, articles, essays, and chapters. It also proceeds logically from literal comprehension to critical interpretation and reaction.

- **Part One presents basic approaches to vocabulary development.** It includes contextual aids, analysis of word parts, pronunciation, and the use of the dictionary and other reference sources.
- **Part Two emphasizes reading as a thinking process.** It emphasizes pre-reading. techniques that prepare and enable the student to comprehend and to recall content. Maintaining concentration, previewing, activating background knowledge, and using guide questions are emphasized. This unit also contains a chapter on comprehension monitoring and learning style. Students are shown how to recognize comprehension signals, how to assess their comprehension, and how to strengthen it. Students assess their learning style and develop a learning action plan for building on their strengths.
- **Part Three is concerned with the development of literal comprehension skills.** It provides extensive instruction and practice with sentence and paragraph comprehension and recognition of thought patterns.
- **Part Four deals with textbook reading skills.** Topics include textbook learning aids, chapter organization, ways to read graphics and technical material, and methods of organizing and retaining course content.
- **Part Five examines the interpretive and analytical skills.** It presents skills that enable students to interact with and evaluate written material, including essays and literature.
- **Part Six, "Reading Selections," contains 30 articles, essays, and textbook excerpts.** Each was chosen on the basis of interest and applicability to skills taught in the text. Each selection is prefaced by an interest-catching introduction, a vocabulary preview, and a previewing question. Literal and critical questions as well as a words-in-context exercise, vocabulary review, and a writing exercise follow each selection.

Special Features

The following features enhance the text's effectiveness and directly contribute to student success:

- **Integration of Reading and Writing.**   The text integrates reading and writing skills. Students respond to exercises by writing sentences and paragraphs. Answers to most questions for each reading selection also require composition. A writing exercise accompanies each reading selection.
- **Reading as Thinking.**   Reading is approached as a thinking process—a process in which the student interacts with textual material and sorts, evaluates, and reacts to its organization and content. Students, for example, are shown how to define their purpose for reading, ask questions, identify and use organization and structure as a guide to understanding, make inferences, and interpret and evaluate what they read.
- **Comprehension Monitoring.**   Comprehension monitoring is also addressed within the text. Through a variety of techniques, students are encouraged to be aware of and to evaluate and control their levels of comprehension of the material they read.
- **Skill Integration.**   Each part concludes with a unit titled "Making Your Skills Work Together" that integrates the skills taught in the section and provides reinforcement and application.
- **Instructor's Manual.**   An Instructor's Manual, including an Answer Key, accompanies the text. Chapter Review Quizzes, each consisting of ten multiple-choice items, are provided. The manual also describes in detail the basic features of the text and offers suggestions for structuring the course, for teaching developmental students, and for approaching each section of the text.

Changes in the Fourth Edition

Numerous changes and additions have been made in the fourth edition:

- Thirteen new reading selections have been added on topics of current interest, including acupuncture, television talk shows, lotteries, and ethnic naming.
- A collaborative exercise has been added to each chapter. These exercises encourage students to explore skill applications within a small-group setting.
- A learning style self assessment has been added to Chapter 4. A questionnaire enables students to identify their learning characteristics and develop a learning action plan which builds on individual strengths.
- Chapter 6 has been revised to focus on sentence meaning and is structured around a four-step approach to analyzing sentence meaning.
- New material on paraphrasing has been added to Chapters 6 and 7.

- Chapter 14 has been refocused to include approaches to reading essays (narrative, expository, and persuasive), as well as strategies for reading literature.
- Chapter summaries have been revised; the summaries now use an interactive, self-questioning format.

Acknowledgments

I wish to express my gratitude to my reviewers for their excellent ideas, suggestions, and advice on the revision of this text: Edith Alderson, Joliet Jr. College; Susan Schlough, U-Wisconsin, Whitewater; Mary Louise Holdway, College of DuPage; Kevin Hayes, Essex County College; Allan Carter, College of DuPage; Barbara Sullivan, Laramie County Community College; Ellen Bell, Manatee Community College; Virginia Reasor, Southeast Oklahoma State University; Miriam Kinard, Trident Technical College; Edwina Jordan, Illinois Central College; Bill Morris, College of the Redwoods; Lynn Roberts, Grand Rapids Community College; and Virginia Ann Stone Meyer, University of Akron. I am particularly indebted to Susan Messer, my developmental editor, for her patience and advice and to Ellen Schatz, Basic Skills Editor, for her enthusiastic support of this project.

K.T.M.

To the Student

■ ■ ■ ■ ■ ■ ■ ■ ■ ■ ■ ■ ■ ■ ■ ■

College is very different from any other type of educational experience. It is different from high school, job training programs, adult education, or technical training programs. New and different types of learning are demanded, and you need new skills and techniques to meet these demands.

Here are a few statements about college. Treat them like a quiz, if you wish. Decide whether each statement is true or false, and write *T* for True or *F* for False in the space provided. Each statement will make you think about the reading and study demands of college. Check your answers by reading the paragraph following each item. As you work through this quiz, you will find out a little about what is expected of you in college. You will see whether or not you have an accurate picture of what college work involves. You will also see how this text will help you to become a better, more successful student.

_____ 1. For every hour I spend in class, I should spend one hour studying outside of class.

False. Many students feel that even one hour for each class (or 15 hours per week for students carrying a 15 credit-hour load) is a lot. Actually, the rule of thumb used by many instructors is two hours of study for each class hour. So you can see that you are expected to do a great deal of reading, studying, and learning on your own time.

This text is written to help you read and learn in the easiest and best way.

_____ 2. I should expect to read about 80 textbook pages per week in each of my courses.

True. A survey of freshman courses at one college indicated that the average course assignment was roughly 80 pages per week. This may seem like a lot of reading—and it is.

This text will build your reading skills to handle this task. It will suggest techniques for understanding and remembering what you read, improving your concentration, and handling difficult reading assignments.

_____ 3. There are a lot of words I don't know, but my vocabulary is about as good as it needs to be.

False. For each college course you take, there will be new words to learn. Some will be everyday words; others will be specialized or technical.

Part One of this book will show how to develop your vocabulary by learning new words, figuring out words you don't know, and using reference sources.

_____ 4. College instructors will tell me exactly what to learn for each exam.

False. College instructors seldom tell you exactly what to learn or review. They expect you to decide what is important and to learn that information.

Part Three of this text will show you how to identify what is important in sentences and paragraphs and how to follow authors' thought patterns.

_____ 5. The more facts I memorize, the higher my exam grades will be.

False. Learning a large amount of facts is no guarantee of a high grade in a course. Some instructors and the exams they give are concerned with your ability to see how facts and ideas fit together, or to evaluate ideas, make comparisons, and recognize trends.

Parts Three and Four of this text will show you how to read textbook chapters, use graphic aids, and organize and remember information.

_____ 6. The only assignments that instructors give are readings in the textbook.

False. Instructors often assign readings in a variety of sources including periodicals, newspapers, and reference and library books. These readings are intended to add to the information presented in your text and by your instructor.

Part Six contains 30 reading selections from a variety of sources for practice and skill application.

7. Rereading a textbook chapter is the best way to prepare for an exam on that chapter.

   False. Reading is actually one of the poorest ways to review. Besides, it's often dull and time-consuming.

   Part Four of this text presents four more effective alternatives: Highlighting and marking, outlining, mapping, and summarizing.

8. College instructors expect me to react to, evaluate, and criticize what I read.

   True. Beyond understanding the content of textbooks, articles, and essays, instructors also want their students to be able to criticize and evaluate ideas.

   Part Five of this text will show you how to interpret what you read, find the author's purpose, and ask critical questions.

9. The best way to read a textbook assignment is to turn to the correct page, start reading, and continue until you reach the end of the assignment.

   False. There are numerous things you can do before you read, while you read, and after you read that can improve your comprehension and retention.

   Part Two of this text discusses how to build your concentration, preview and think about what you will read, and use questions to guide your reading. Part Four discusses techniques to use after you read to strengthen comprehension and recall.

10. You can never know whether you have understood a textbook reading assignment until you take an exam on the chapter.

    False. As you read, it is possible and important to keep track of and evaluate your level of understanding.

    Part Two of this text will show you how to monitor your comprehension. You will also learn to recognize comprehension signals and how to strengthen your comprehension.

By analyzing the above statements and the correct responses, you can see that college is a lot of work, much of which you must do on your own. However, college is also a new, exciting experience that will acquaint you with new ideas and opportunities.

This text is written to help you get the most out of college and to take advantage of the opportunities it offers. Its purpose is to equip beginning college students with the reading skills necessary for academic success.

The text is organized into five instructional units: Part One: Vocabulary; Part Two: Reading as Thinking; Part Three: Comprehension; Part Four: Textbook Reading Skills; and Part Five: Critical Reading and Thinking. A sixth unit, made up of 30 reading selections, gives you an opportunity to apply and practice skills using a wide range of articles, essays, and textbook excerpts.

The text contains numerous features to help you learn and to become a more successful student. These include:

- Numerous practical situations and everyday examples to explain techniques and to help you maintain interest
- Diagrams and drawings to help you visualize how reading material is organized
- Numerous exercises to enable you to try out new techniques
- A chapter on how to monitor (keep track of) your own comprehension and learning
- A learning style questionnaire to help you discover how you learn
- A special section at the end of each unit, "Making Your Skills Work Together," that helps you combine and apply your skills
- An emphasis on reading as a thinking process—as a way of processing and sorting information
- A chapter on reading literature and essays
- A chapter on reading graphics
- A section on "Reading Technical Material"
- An integration of reading and writing skills—as you learn skills for reading, you see how that can help you become a better writer
- A section on "Mapping"—a visual means of organizing information

The opportunity of college lies ahead of you. The skills this text provides, along with plenty of hard work, will make your college experience a meaningful and valuable one.

Kathleen T. McWhorter

PART 1

Vocabulary: The Key to Meaning

*L*eon and Joe are taking the same psychology course but have different instructors. Leon is feeling overwhelmed by the course. In particular, he's having trouble with the new vocabulary introduced in the first few chapters. He complains: "I've been out of school for six years. I've never *seen* some of these words before. And I know I don't have time to memorize them all." Joe agrees that the new vocabulary is a problem but he talked about it with his instructor, Mr. Rodriguez, who has given him some tips. Mr. Rodriguez explained that the meanings of some words can be figured out by the way each word is used in the sentence. Others can be broken down into parts: beginnings, middles, and endings. He said that this was true for new words in other courses, too. Once you learn the commonly used word parts, you can figure out the meanings of hundreds of other words that also contain these parts.

Building your vocabulary is well worth the effort. Vocabulary affects not only your reading skills, but your speaking, listening, and writing skills as well. In speaking, the words you choose affect how well you are understood, the impression you make, and how people react to you. In writing, your vocabulary determines how clearly and accurately you can express your ideas to others. In listening, your vocabulary influences how much you understand in class lectures, speeches, and class discussions.

THIS PART OF THE TEXT WILL HELP YOU

1. Use several types of context clues to figure out the meanings of words you do not know (Chapter 1)

2. Add words to your vocabulary by learning word parts (Chapter 2)

3. Use a dictionary easily and rapidly (Chapter 3)

4. Pronounce unfamiliar words (Chapter 3)

5. Develop a card system for learning new words (Chapter 3)

Using Context Clues

■ ■

THIS CHAPTER WILL SHOW YOU HOW TO

1. *Figure out the meanings of words from their use in a sentence*
2. *Use four types of context clues*

■ ■

What Is Context?

Read the following brief paragraph. Several words are missing. Try to figure out the missing words and write them in the blanks.

> Most Americans can speak only one _____. Europeans, however, _____ several. As a result, Europeans think _____ are unfriendly and unwilling to communicate with them.

Did you insert the word *language* in the first blank, *speak* or *know* in the second blank, and *Americans* in the third blank? Most likely, you correctly identified all three missing words. You could tell from the sentence which word to put in. The words around the missing words—the sentence context—gave you clues as to which word would fit and make sense. Such clues are called **context clues.**

While you probably won't find missing words on a printed page, you will often find words that you do not know. Context clues can help you to figure out the meanings of unfamiliar words.

3

Example:

Phobias, such as fear of heights, water, or confined spaces, are difficult to eliminate.

From the sentence, you can tell that *phobia* means "fear of specific objects or situations."

Here's another example:

The couple finally **secured** a table at the popular, crowded restaurant.

You can figure out that *secured* means "got or took ownership of" the table.

Types of Context Clues

There are four types of context clues to look for: (1) definition, (2) example, (3) contrast, and (4) inference.

Definition Clues

Many times a writer defines a word immediately following its use. The writer may directly define a word by giving a brief definition or a synonym (a word that has the same meaning). Such words and phrases as *means, is, refers to,* and *can be defined as* are often used. Here are some examples:

Corona refers to <u>the outermost part of the sun's atmosphere.</u>

A **soliloquy** is <u>a speech made by a character in a play that reveals his or her thoughts to the audience.</u>

At other times, rather than formally define the word, a writer may provide clues or synonyms. Punctuation is often used to signal that a definition clue to a word's meaning is to follow. Punctuation also separates the meaning clue from the rest of the sentence. Three types of punctuation are used in this way. In the examples below, notice that the meaning clue is separated from the rest of the sentence by punctuation.

1. Commas

   An **oligopoly,** <u>control of a product by a small number of companies,</u> exists in the long-distance phone market.

   Equity, <u>general principles of fairness and justice,</u> is used in law when existing laws do not apply or are inadequate.

2. Parentheses

A leading cause of heart disease is a diet with too much **cholesterol** (<u>a fatty substance made of carbon, hydrogen and oxygen</u>).

3. Dashes

Ancient Egyptians wrote in **hieroglyphics**—<u>pictures used to represent words.</u>

Facets—<u>small flat surfaces at different angles</u>—bring out the beauty of a diamond.

EXERCISE 1-1 *DIRECTIONS: Read each sentence and write a definition or synonym for each bold-faced word or phrase. Use the definition context clue to help you determine word meaning.*

1. **Glogg,** a Swedish hot punch, is often served at holiday parties.

   _____

2. The judge's **candor**—his sharp, open frankness—shocked the jury.

   _____

3. A **chemical bond** is a strong attractive force that holds two or more atoms together.

   _____

4. **Lithium** (an alkali metal) is so soft it can be cut with a knife.

   _____

5. Hearing, technically known as **audition,** begins when a sound wave reaches the outer ear.

   _____

6. Five-line rhyming poems, or **limericks,** are among the simplest forms of poetry.

   _____

7. Our country's **gross national product**—the total market value of its national output of goods and services—is increasing steadily.

   _____

8. A **species** is a group of animals or plants that share similar characteristics and are able to interbreed.

_____

9. Broad, flat noodles that are served covered with sauce or butter are called **fettucine.**

_____

10. Many diseases have **latent periods,** periods of time between the infection and the first appearance of a symptom.

_____

Example Clues

Writers often include examples that help to explain or clarify a word. Suppose you do not know the meaning of the word _toxic,_ and you find it used in the following sentence:

> **Toxic** materials, such as arsenic, asbestos, pesticides, and lead, can cause bodily damage.

This sentence gives four examples of toxic materials. From the examples given, which are all poisonous substances, you could conclude that _toxic_ means "poisonous."

Examples:

Forest floors are frequently covered with **fungi**—molds, mushrooms, and mildews.

Legumes, such as peas and beans, produce pods.

Arachnids, including tarantulas, black widow spiders, and ticks, often have segmented bodies.

Newsmagazines, like _Time_ or _Newsweek,_ provide more details about news events than newspapers because they focus on only a few stories.

DIRECTIONS: *Read each sentence and write a definition or synonym for each bold-faced word or phrase. Use the example context clue to help you determine meaning.*

1. Many **pharmaceuticals,** including morphine and penicillin, are not readily available in some countries.

   _____

2. The child was **reticent** in every respect; she would not speak, refused to answer questions, and avoided looking at anyone.

   _____

3. Most **condiments,** such as pepper, mustard, and catsup, are used to improve the flavor of foods.

   _____

4. Instructors provide their students with **feedback** through test grades and comments on papers.

   _____

5. **Physiological needs**—hunger, thirst, and sex—promote survival of the human species.

   _____

6. Clothing is available in a variety of **fabrics,** including cotton, wool, polyester, and linen.

   _____

7. In the past month, we have had almost every type of **precipitation**—rain, snow, sleet, and hail.

   _____

8. **Involuntary reflexes,** like breathing and beating of the heart, are easily measured.

   _____

9. The student had a difficult time distinguishing between **homonyms**—words such as *see* and *sea, wore* and *war,* and *deer* and *dear.*

   _____

10. Abstract paintings often include such **geometrics** as squares, cubes, and tri-angles.

_____

Contrast Clues

It is sometimes possible to determine the meaning of an unknown word from a word or phrase in the context that has an opposite meaning. Notice, in the following sentence, how a word opposite in meaning from the boldfaced word provides a clue to its meaning:

> One of the dinner guests **succumbed** to the temptation to have a second piece of cake, but the others resisted.

Although you may not know the meaning of _succumbed,_ you know that the one guest who succumbed was different from the others who resisted. The word _but_ suggests this. Since the others resisted a second dessert, you can tell that one guest gave in and had a piece. Thus, _succumbed_ means the opposite of _resist;_ that is, to give in to.

Examples:

The professor **advocates** testing on animals, but many of her students feel it is cruel.

Most of the graduates were **elated,** though a few felt sad and depressed.

The old man acted **morosely,** whereas his grandson was very lively.

The gentleman was quite **portly,** but his wife was thin.

| EXERCISE 1-3 | **DIRECTIONS:** _Read each sentence and write a definition or synonym for each bold-faced word. Use the contrast clue to help you determine meaning._ |

1. Some city dwellers are **affluent;** others live in or near poverty.

_____

2. I am certain that the hotel will hold our reservation; however, if you are **dubious,** call to make sure.

_____

3. Although most experts **concurred** with the research findings, several strongly disagreed.

   _____

4. The speaker **denounced** certain legal changes while praising other reforms.

   _____

5. The woman's parents **thwarted** her marriage plans though they liked her fiancé.

   _____

6. In medieval Europe, **peasants** led difficult lives, whereas the wealthy landowners lived in luxury.

   _____

7. When the couple moved into their new home they **revamped** the kitchen and bathroom but did not change the rest of the rooms.

   _____

8. The young nurse was **bewildered** by the patient's symptoms, but the doctor realized she was suffering from a rare form of leukemia.

   _____

9. Despite my husband's **pessimism** about my chances of winning the lottery, I was certain I would win.

   _____

10. The mayoral candidate praised the town council, while the mayor **deprecated** it.

   _____

Inference Clues

Many times you can figure out the meaning of an unknown word by using logic and reasoning skills. For instance, look at the following sentence:

Bob is quite **versatile;** he is a good student, a top athlete, an excellent car mechanic, and a gourmet cook.

You can see that Bob is successful at many different types of activities, and you could reason that *versatile* means "capable of doing many things competently."

Examples:

When the customer tried to pay with Mexican **pesos,** the clerk explained that the store accepted only U.S. dollars.

The potato salad looked so plain that I decided to **garnish** it with parsley and paprika to give it some color.

We had to leave the car and walk up because the **incline** was too steep to drive.

Since Reginald was nervous, he brought his rabbit's foot **talisman** with him to the exam.

EXERCISE 1-4

DIRECTIONS: *Read each sentence and write a definition or synonym for each bold-faced word. Try to reason out the meaning of each word using information provided in the context.*

1. The **wallabies** at the zoo looked like kangaroos.

   _____

2. The foreign students quickly **assimilated** many aspects of American culture.

   _____

3. On hot, humid summer afternoons, I often feel **languid.**

   _____

4. Some physical fitness experts recommend jogging or weight lifting to overcome the effects of a **sedentary** job.

   _____

5. The legal aid clinic was **subsidized** by city and county funds.

   _____

6. When the bank robber reached his **haven,** he breathed a sigh of relief and began to count his money.

   _____

7. The teenager was **intimidated** by the presence of a police officer walking the beat and decided not to spray-paint the school wall.

   _____

8. The vase must have been **jostled** in shipment because it arrived with several chips in it.

_____

9. Although she had visited the fortune teller several times, she was not sure she believed in the **occult.**

_____

10. If the plan did not work, the colonel had a **contingency** plan ready.

_____

EXERCISE 1-5 **DIRECTIONS:** _Read each sentence and write a definition or synonym for each bold-faced word. Use the context clue to help you determine meaning._

1. The economy was in a state of continual **flux;** inflation increased one month and decreased the next.

_____

2. The grand jury **exonerated** the police officer of any possible misconduct or involvement in illegal activity.

_____

3. Art is always talkative, but Ed is usually **taciturn.**

_____

4. Many **debilities** of old age, including poor eyesight and loss of hearing, can be treated medically.

_____

5. Police **interrogation,** or questioning, can be a frightening experience.

_____

6. The soap opera contained numerous **morbid** events: the death of a young child, the suicide of her father, and the murder of his older brother.

_____

7. After long hours of practice, Peter finally learned to type; Sam's efforts, however, were **futile.**

_____

8. Although the farm appeared **derelict,** we discovered that an elderly man lived there.

_____

9. The newspaper's error was **inadvertent;** the editor did not intend to include the victim's name.

_____

10. To save money, we have decided to **curtail** the number of tapes we buy each month.

_____

11. Steam from the hot radiator **scalded** the mechanic's hand.

_____

12. The businesswoman's **itinerary** outlined her trip and listed Cleveland as her next stop.

_____

13. **Theologies,** such as Catholicism, Buddhism, and Hinduism, are discussed at great length in the class.

_____

14. Steven had very good **rapport** with his father, but was unable to get along well with his mother.

_____

15. The duchess had a way of **flaunting** her jewels so that everyone could see and envy them.

_____

EXERCISE 1-6

DIRECTIONS: *Read each of the following passages and use context clues to figure out the meaning of each boldfaced word or phrase. Write a synonym or brief definition for each in the space provided.*

A. Can looking at a color affect your behavior or **alter** your mood? Some researchers are **skeptical,** but others believe color can influence how you act and feel. A number of experiments have been conducted that **demonstrate** the effects of color. In 1979 a psychologist named Schauss **evaluated** the effect of the color pink. He found that the color relaxed the subjects so much that they could not perform simple strength tests as well as they did when looking at other **hues.** The officer in charge of a U.S. Navy **brig** in Washington noticed Schauss's findings and allowed Schauss to test his calm–color **hypothesis** on inmates. Today, many **institutions,** such as jails, juvenile correction facilities, and holding centers, put individuals in pink rooms when their tempers **flare.**

No one is certain how color affects behavior. Schauss **conjectures** that a person's response to color is determined in the brain's **reticular formation,** a relay station for millions of the body's nerve impulses. Another researcher **speculates** that **perception** of color by the eye **spurs** the release of important chemicals in the body.

1. alter _____

2. skeptical _____

3. demonstrate _____

4. evaluated _____

5. hues _____

6. brig _____

7. hypothesis _____

8. institutions _____

9. flare _____

10. conjectures _____

11. reticular formation _____

12. speculates _____

13. perception _____

14. spurs _____

B. The most important set of symbols is language. **Language,** among humans, refers to the systemized use of speech and hearing to convey or express feelings and ideas. It is through language that our ideas, values, beliefs, and knowledge are **transmitted,** expressed, and shared. Other **media** such as music, art, and dance are also important means of communication, but language is uniquely flexible and precise. It permits us to share our experiences in the past and present, to **convey** our hopes for the future, and to describe dreams and fantasies that may bear little **resemblance** to reality. Some scientists have questioned whether thought is even possible without language. Although language can be used **imprecisely** and may seem hard to understand, it is the chief factor in our ability to transmit culture.

1. language _____

2. transmitted _____

3. media _____

4. convey _____

5. resemblance _____

6. imprecisely _____

C. Social norms are another element of culture. **Norms** are rules of conduct or social expectations for behavior. These rules and social expectations **specify** how people should and should not behave in various social situations. They are both **prescriptive** (they tell people what they should do) and **proscriptive** (they tell people what they should not do). . . .

An early American sociologist, William G. Sumner (1840–1910), identified two types of norms, which he labeled "folkways" and "mores." They are **distinguished** not by their content, but by the degree to which group members are **compelled** to conform to them, by their degree of importance, by the **severity** of punishment if they are violated, or by the intensity of feeling associated with adherence to them. Folkways are customs or conventions. They are norms in that they provide rules for conduct, but **violations** of folkways bring only mild censure. . . .

Mores are considered more important than folkways, and reactions to their violation are more serious. They are more likely than folkways to involve clear-cut distinctions between right and wrong, and they are more closely associated with the values a society considers important.

1. norms _____

2. specify _____

3. prescriptive _____

4. proscriptive _____

5. distinguished _____

6. compelled _____

7. severity _____

8. violations _____

The Limitations of Context Clues

There are two limitations to the use of context clues. First, context clues seldom lead to a complete definition. Second, sometimes a sentence does not contain clues to a word's meaning. In these cases you will need to draw on other vocabulary skills. Chapters 2 and 3 will help you with these skills.

■■■■■■■ *WORKING TOGETHER*

Directions: Bring a brief textbook excerpt, editorial, or magazine article that contains difficult vocabulary to class. Working in pairs with another student, locate and underline at least three words in your article that your partner can define by using context clues. Work together in reasoning out each word, checking a dictionary to verify meanings.

■■■■■■■ *SUMMARY*

What are context clues used for?

They are used to figure out the meaning of an unknown word used in a sentence or paragraph.

What are the four types of context clues?

The four types of context clues are

- DEFINITION—a brief definition of or synonym for a word
- EXAMPLE—specific instances or examples that clarify a word's meaning
- CONTRAST—a word or phrase of opposite meaning
- INFERENCE—the use of reasoning skills to figure out word meanings

■ ■

CHAPTER 2

Recognizing the Structure of Words

■ ■

THIS CHAPTER WILL SHOW YOU HOW TO

1. *Figure out the meaning of words you do not know*
2. *Use prefixes, roots, and suffixes*

■ ■

Using Word Parts to Expand Your Vocabulary

Suppose that you came across the following sentence in a human anatomy text-book:

Trichromatic plates are used frequently in the text to illustrate the position of body organs.

If you did not know the meaning of *trichromatic,* how could you determine it? There are no clues in the sentence context. One solution is to look up the word in a dictionary. An easier and faster way is to break the word into parts and analyze the meaning of each part. Many words in the English language are made up of word parts called **prefixes, roots, and suffixes.** These word parts have specific meanings that, when added together, can help you determine the meaning of the word as a whole.

The word *trichromatic* can be divided into three parts: its prefix, root, and suffix.

- Prefix—tri- ("three")
- Root—chrome ("color")
- Suffix—atic ("characteristic of")

You can see from this analysis that *trichromatic* means "having three colors."

Here are a few other examples of words that you can figure out by using prefixes, roots, and suffixes:

The parents thought the child was **unteachable.**

un- = not
teach = help someone learn
-able = able to do something
unteachable = not able to be taught

The student was a **nonconformist.**

non- = not
conform = go along with others
-ist = one who does something
nonconformist = someone who does not go along with others

The first step in using the prefix-root-suffix method is to become familiar with the most commonly used word parts. The prefixes and roots listed in Tables 2-1 and 2-2 will give you a good start in determining the meanings of thousands of words without looking them up in the dictionary. For instance, more than 10,000 words can begin with the prefix *non-*. Not all these words are listed in a collegiate dictionary, but they would appear in an unabridged dictionary (see Chapter 3). Another common prefix, *pseudo-*, is used in more than 400 words. A small amount of time spent learning word parts can yield a large payoff in new words learned.

Before you begin to use word parts to figure out new words, there are a few things you need to know:

1. In most cases, a word is built upon at least one root.
2. Words can have more than one prefix, root, or suffix.
   a. Words can be made up of two or more roots (geo/logy).
   b. Some words have two prefixes (in/sub/ordination).
   c. Some words have two suffixes (beauti/ful/ly).
3. Words do not always have a prefix and a suffix.
   a. Some words have neither a prefix nor a suffix (read).
   b. Others have a suffix but no prefix (read/ing).
   c. Others have a prefix but no suffix (pre/read).

4. The spelling of roots may change as they are combined with suffixes. Some common variations are included in Table 2-2.
5. Different prefixes, roots, or suffixes may have the same meaning. For example, the prefixes *bi-*, *di-*, and *duo-* all mean "two."
6. Sometimes you may identify a group of letters as a prefix or root but find that it does not carry the meaning of that prefix or root. For example, the letters *mis* in the word *missile* are part of the root and are not the prefix *mis-*, which means "wrong; bad."

Prefixes

Prefixes appear at the beginnings of many English words. They alter the meaning of the root to which they are connected. In Table 2-1, 39 common prefixes are grouped according to meaning.

EXERCISE 2-1

DIRECTIONS: *Use the list of common prefixes in Table 2-1 to determine the meaning of each of the following words. Write a brief definition or synonym for each. If you are unfamiliar with the root, you may need to check a dictionary.*

1. interoffice _____

2. supernatural _____

3. nonsense _____

4. introspection _____

5. prearrange _____

6. reset _____

7. subtopic _____

8. transmit _____

9. multidimensional _____

10. imperfect _____

TABLE 2-1
Common Prefixes

Prefix	Meaning	Sample Word
Prefixes referring to amount or number		
mono/uni	one	monocle/unicycle
bi/di/du	two	bimonthly/divorce/duet
tri	three	triangle
quad	four	quadrant
quint/pent	five	quintet/pentagon
deci	ten	decimal
centi	hundred	centigrade
milli	thousand	milligram
micro	small	microscope
multi/poly	many	multipurpose/polygon
semi	half	semicircle
equi	equal	equidistant
Prefixes meaning "not" (negative)		
a	not	asymmetrical
anti	against	antiwar
contra	against, opposite	contradict
dis	apart, away, not	disagree
in/il/ir/im	not	incorrect/illogical/irreversible/impossible
mis	wrongly	misunderstand
non	not	nonfiction
un	not	unpopular
pseudo	false	pseudoscientific
Prefixes giving direction, location, or placement		
ab	away	absent
ad	toward	adhesive
ante/pre	before	antecedent/premarital
circum/peri	around	circumference/perimeter
com/col/con	with, together	compile/collide/convene
de	away, from	depart
dia	through	diameter
ex/extra	from, out of, former	ex-wife/extra-marital
hyper	over, excessive	hyperactive
inter	between	interpersonal
intro/intra	within, into, in	introduction
post	after	posttest
re	back, again	review
retro	backward	retrospect
sub	under, below	submarine
super	above, extra	supercharge
tele	far	telescope
trans	across, over	transcontinental

DIRECTIONS: *Write a synonym for each word in boldface type.*

1. an **atypical** child _____

2. to **hyperventilate** _____

3. an **extraordinary** request _____

4. **semisoft** cheese _____

5. **antisocial** behavior _____

6. to **circumnavigate** the globe _____

7. a **triweekly** delivery _____

8. an **uneventful** weekend _____

9. a **disfigured** face _____

10. to **exhale** smoke _____

DIRECTIONS: *Read each of the following sentences. Use your knowledge of prefixes to fill in the blank and complete the word.*

1. A person who speaks two languages is _____ lingual.

2. A letter or number written beneath a line of print is called a _____ script.

3. The new sweater had a snag, and I returned it to the store because it was _____ perfect.

4. The flood damage was permanent and _____ reversible.

5. I was not given the correct date and time; I was _____ informed.

6. People who speak several different languages are _____ lingual.

7. A musical _____ lude was played between the events in the ceremony.

8. I decided the magazine was uninteresting, so I _____ continued my subscription.

9. Merchandise that does not pass factory inspection is considered _____ standard and sold at a discount.

10. The tuition refund policy approved this week will apply to last year's tuition as well; the policy will be _____ active to January 1 of last year.

11. The elements were _____ acting with each other when they began to bubble and their temperature rose.

12. _____ ceptives are widely used to prevent unwanted pregnancies.

13. All of the waitresses were required to wear the restaurant's _____ form.

14. The _____ viewer asked the presidential candidates unexpected questions about important issues.

15. The draperies were _____ colored from long exposure to the sun.

EXERCISE 2-4	**DIRECTIONS:** *Use your knowledge of prefixes to supply the missing word in each sentence. Write the word in the space provided.*

1. Our house is a duplex. The one next door with three apartments is a _____.

2. A preparation applied to the skin to reduce or prevent perspiration is called an _____.

3. A person who cannot read or write is _____.

4. I did not use my real name; instead I gave a _____.

5. If someone seems to have greater powers than do normal humans, he or she might be called _____.

6. A friend who criticizes you too often is _____.

7. If you plan to continue to take college courses after you graduate, you will be taking _____ courses.

8. Substances that fight bacteria are known as _____ drugs.

9. The branch of biology that deals with very small living organisms is _____.

10. In the metric system a(an) _____ is one one-hundredth of a meter.

11. One one-thousandth of a second is called a _____.

12. The tape showed an instant _____ of the touchdown.

13. A disabling physical handicap is often called a _____.

Roots

Roots carry the basic or core meaning of a word. Hundreds of root words are used to build words in the English language. Thirty-one of the most common and most useful are listed in Table 2-2. Knowledge of the meanings of these roots will enable you to unlock the meanings of many words. For example, if you know that the root *dic/dict* means "tell or say," then you would have a clue to the meanings of such words as *dictate* (to speak for someone to write down), diction (wording or manner of speaking), or *dictionary* (book that "tells" what words mean).

EXERCISE 2-5

DIRECTIONS: *Use the list of common roots in Table 2-2 to determine the meanings of the following words. Write a brief definition or synonym for each, checking a dictionary if necessary.*

1. dictaphone _____

2. biomedicine _____

3. photocopy _____

---

4. porter _____

5. visibility _____

6. credentials _____

7. speculate _____

8. terrain _____

9. audition _____

10. sentiment _____

11. astrophysics _____

12. capacity _____

13. chronicle _____

14. corporation _____

15. facile _____

16. autograph _____

17. sociology _____

18. phonometer _____

19. sensation _____

20. vocal _____

■■■■■

TABLE 2-2
Common Roots

Root	Meaning	Sample Word
aud/audit	hear	audible
aster/astro	star	asteroid/astronaut
bene	good, well	benefit
bio	life	biology
cap	take, seize	captive
chron(o)	time	chronology
corp	body	corpse
cred	believe	incredible
dict/dic	tell, say	predict
duc/duct	lead	introduce
fact/fac	make, do	factory
graph	write	telegraph
geo	earth	geophysics
log/logo/logy	study, thought	psychology
mit/miss	send	permit/dismiss
mort/mor	die, death	immortal
path	feeling	sympathy
phono	sound, voice	telephone
photo	light	photosensitive
port	carry	transport
scop	seeing	microscope
scrib/script	write	inscription
sen/sent	feel	insensitive
spec/spic/spect	look, see	retrospect
tend/tent/tens	stretch or strain	tension
terr/terre	land, earth	territory
theo	god	theology
ven/vent	come	convention
vert/vers	turn	invert
vis/vid	see	invisible/video
voc	call	vocation

EXERCISE 2-6	**DIRECTIONS:** *Complete each of the following sentences with one of the words listed below.*

apathetic	dictated	graphic	scriptures	tendon
captivated	extensive	phonics	spectators	verdict
deduce	extraterrestrial	prescribed	synchronized	visualize

1. The jury brought in its _____ after one hour of deliberation.

2. Religious or holy writings are called _____.

3. She closed her eyes and tried to _____ the license plate number.

4. The _____ watching the football game were tense.

5. The doctor _____ two types of medication.

6. The list of toys the child wanted for his birthday was _____.

7. The criminal appeared _____ when the judge pronounced sentence.

8. The runners _____ their watches before beginning the race.

9. The textbook contained numerous _____ aids, including maps, charts, and diagrams.

10. The study of the way different parts of words sound is called _____.

11. The athlete strained a(n) _____ and was unable to continue training.

12. The movie was about a(n) _____, a creature not from earth.

13. The district manager _____ a letter to her secretary, who then typed it.

14. Through his attention-grabbing performance, he _____ the audience.

15. By putting together the clues, the detective was finally able to _____ who committed the crime.

Suffixes

Suffixes are word endings that often change the part of speech of a word. For example, adding the suffix *y* to the noun *cloud* forms the adjective *cloudy*. Accompanying the change in part of speech is a shift in meaning (*cloudy* means "resembling clouds; overcast with clouds; dimmed or dulled as if by clouds").

Often, several different words can be formed from a single root word by adding different suffixes.

Examples:

Root: class

root + suffix = class/ify, class/ification, class/ic

Root: right

root + suffix = right/ly, right/ful, right/ist, right/eous

If you know the meaning of the root word and the ways in which different suffixes affect the meaning of the root word, you will be able to figure out a word's meaning when a suffix is added. A list of common suffixes and their meanings appears in Table 2-3.

You can expand your vocabulary by learning the variations in meaning that occur when suffixes are added to words you already know. When you find a word that you do not know, look for the root. Then, using the sentence the word is in (its context; see Chapter 1), figure out what the word means with the suffix added. Occasionally you may find that the spelling of the root word has been changed. For instance, a final *e* may be dropped, a final consonant may be doubled, or a final *y* may be changed to *i*. Consider the possibility of such changes when trying to identify the root word.

Examples:

The article was a **compilation** of facts.

root + suffix
compil(e) + -ation = something that has been compiled, or put together into an orderly form

We were concerned with the **legality** of our decision to change addresses.

root + suffix
legal + -ity = pertaining to legal matters

Our college is one of the most **prestigious** in the state.

root + suffix
prestig(e) + -ious = having prestige or distinction

TABLE 2-3
Common Suffixes

Suffix	Sample Word
Suffixes that refer to a state, condition, or quality	
able	touchable
ance	assistance
ation	confrontation
ence	reference
ible	tangible
ion	discussion
ity	superiority
ive	permissive
ment	amazement
ness	kindness
ous	jealous
ty	loyalty
y	creamy
Suffixes that mean "one who"	
an	Italian
ant	participant
ee	referee
eer	engineer
ent	resident
er	teacher
ist	activist
or	advisor
Suffixes that mean "pertaining to or referring to"	
al	autumnal
ship	friendship
hood	brotherhood
ward	homeward

EXERCISE 2-7

DIRECTIONS: *For each of the words listed, add a suffix so that the word will complete the sentence. Write the new word in the space provided. Check a dictionary if you are unsure of the spelling.*

1. converse

   Our phone _____ lasted ten minutes.

2. assist

   The medical _____ labeled the patient's blood samples.

3. qualify

   The job applicant outlined his _____ to the interviewer.

4. intern

   The doctor completed her _____ at Memorial Medical Center.

5. eat

   We did not realize that the blossoms of the plant could be _____.

6. audio

   She spoke so softly that her voice was not _____.

7. season

   It is usually very dry in July, but this year it has rained constantly. The weather isn't very _____.

8. permit

   The professor granted her _____ to miss class.

9. instruct

   The lecture on Freud was very _____.

10. remember

    The wealthy businessman donated the building in _____ of his deceased father.

11. mortal

    The _____ rate in Ethiopia is very high.

12. president

    The _____ race held many surprises.

13. feminine

    She called herself a _____, although she never actively supported the movement for equal rights for women.

14. hazard

    The presence of toxic waste in the lake is _____ to health.

15. destine

The young man felt it was his _____ to become a priest.

DIRECTIONS: *For each word listed below, write as many new words as you can create by adding suffixes.*

1. compare _____

2. adapt _____

3. right _____

4. identify _____

5. will _____

6. prefer _____

7. notice _____

8. like _____

9. pay _____

10. promote _____

How to Use Word Parts

Think of roots as being at the root or core of a word's meaning. There are many more roots than are listed in Table 2-2. You already know many of these, because they are used in everyday speech. Think of prefixes as word parts that are added before the root to qualify or change its meaning. Think of suffixes as add-ons that make the word fit grammatically into the sentence in which it is used.

When you come upon a word you do not know, keep the following pointers in mind:

1. **First, look for the root.** Think of this as looking for a word inside a larger word. Often a letter or two will be missing.

Examples:

un/utter/able	defens/ible
inter/colleg/iate	re/popular/ize
post/operat/ive	non/adapt/able
im/measur/ability	non/commit/tal

2. **If you do not recognize the root, then you will probably not be able to figure out the word.** The next step is to check its meaning in a dictionary. For tips on locating words in a dictionary rapidly and easily, see Chapter 3.

3. **If you did recognize the root word, look for a prefix.** If there is one, determine how it changes the meaning of the word.

   Examples:

un/utterable	un- = not
post/operative	post- = after

4. **Locate the suffix.** Determine how it further adds to or changes the meaning of the root word.

   Examples:

unutter/able	-able = able to
postoperat/ive	-ive = state or condition

5. **Next, try out the meaning in the sentence in which the word was used.** Substitute your meaning for the word and see whether the sentence makes sense.

   Examples: Some of the victim's thoughts were **unutterable** at the time of the crime.
   unutterable = that which cannot be spoken

   My sister was worried about the cost of **postoperative** care.
   postoperative = state or condition after an operation

EXERCISE 2-9

DIRECTIONS: Use the steps listed previously to determine the meaning of each bold-faced word. Circle the root in each word and then write a brief definition of the word that fits its use in the sentence.

1. The doctor felt the results of the X rays were **indisputable.**

   _____

2. The **dissimilarity** among the three brothers was surprising.

   _____

3. The **extortionist** demanded two payments of $10,000 each.

   _____

4. It is **permissible** to camp in most state parks.

   _____

5. The student had **retentive** abilities.

   _____

6. The **traumatic** event changed the child's attitude toward animals.

   _____

7. We were surprised by her **insincerity.**

   _____

8. The child's **hypersensitivity** worried his parents.

   _____

9. The English instructor told Peter that he had written a **creditable** paper.

   _____

10. The rock group's agent hoped to **repopularize** their first hit song.

    _____

11. The gambler was filled with **uncertainty** about the horse race.

    _____

12. The **nonenforcement** of the speed limit led to many deaths.

    _____

13. The effects of the disease were **irreversible.**

    _____

14. The mysterious music seemed to **foretell** the murder of the movie's heroine.

    _____

15. The **polyphony** filled the concert hall.

    _____

16. Sailors used to think the North Sea **unnavigable.**

    _____

17. She received a **dishonorable** discharge from the Marines.

_____

18. The criminal was **unapologetic** to the judge about the crimes he had committed.

_____

19. A systems analysis revealed that the factory was **underproductive**.

_____

20. He rotated the dial **counterclockwise**.

_____

■■■■■■■ WORKING TOGETHER

Directions: Your instructor will choose a reading selection from Part 6 and form groups. Locate and underline at least five words in the selection not included in its Vocabulary Preview or Words in Context that other group members can define by analyzing word parts. Work together with group members to determine the meaning of each word, checking a dictionary to verify meanings.

■■■■■■■ SUMMARY

When you can't figure out an unknown word by using context clues, what should you do?

Break the word into word parts and use your knowledge of prefixes, root words, and suffixes to figure out the word.

What are prefixes, roots, and suffixes?

Prefixes are beginnings of words, roots are middles of words, suffixes are endings of words.

Why is it useful to learn prefixes, roots, and suffixes?

They unlock the meaning of thousands of English words.

CHAPTER 3

■ ■

Learning New Words

■ ■

THIS CHAPTER WILL SHOW YOU HOW TO

1. Use the dictionary and the thesaurus

2. Pronounce unfamiliar words

3. Develop a system for learning new words

■ ■

Most people think they have just one level of vocabulary and that this can be characterized as large or small, strong or weak. Actually, everyone has at least four levels of vocabulary, and each varies in strength:

1. Words you use in everyday speech or writing

   Examples: decide, death, daughter, damp, date

2. Words you know but seldom or never use in your own speech or writing

   Examples: document, disregard, destination, demon, dense

3. Words you've heard or seen before but cannot fully define

   Examples: denounce, deficit, decadent, deductive, decisive

4. Words you've never heard or seen before

   Examples: doggerel, dogma, denigrate, deleterious, diatropism

In the spaces provided, list five words that fall under each of these four categories. It will be easy to think of words for Category 1. Words for Categories 2–4 may be taken from the following list:

contort	connive	fraught
continuous	congruent	gastronome
credible	demean	havoc
activate	liberate	impertinent
deletion	heroic	delicacy
focus	voluntary	impartial
manual	resistance	delve
garbanzo	alien	attentive
logic	meditate	osmosis

Category 1	*Category 2*	*Category 3*	*Category 4*
_____	_____	_____	_____
_____	_____	_____	_____
_____	_____	_____	_____
_____	_____	_____	_____
_____	_____	_____	_____

To build your vocabulary, try to shift as many words as possible from a less familiar to a more familiar category. However, this task is not easy. You start by noticing words. Then you question, check, and remember their meanings. Finally, and most important, you use these new words often in your speech and writing.

This chapter will help you improve your word awareness by (1) discussing the use of reference sources, (2) showing you how to pronounce difficult words, and (3) presenting an index card system for learning new words.

Word Information Sources

Three written sources are most useful in improving one's vocabulary: (1) the dictionary, (2) subject area dictionaries, and (3) the thesaurus.

The Dictionary

The Collegiate Dictionary The dictionary is an essential tool. If you do not already own a collegiate dictionary, buy one as soon as possible. You will need it to complete the exercises in this chapter.

Inexpensive paperback editions of the collegiate dictionary are available and recommended. Do not buy a condensed pocket dictionary. These do not contain enough words and will not give you enough information to suit your needs. Most college bookstores stock several collegiate dictionaries. Among the most widely used are *The American Heritage Dictionary of the English Language, Webster's New Collegiate Dictionary,* and *Webster's New World Dictionary of the American Language.*

The Unabridged Dictionary Libraries own large, complete dictionaries, called unabridged dictionaries. These often have thousands of pages. They contain much more information about each word than collegiate dictionaries. You may need to refer to an unabridged dictionary to find an unusual word, an unusual meaning of a word, or to check the various prefixes or suffixes that can be used with a particular word.

Subject Area Dictionaries

Many subject areas have specialized dictionaries that list most of the important words used in that field. These dictionaries give specialized meanings for words and suggest how and when to use them. For the field of nursing, for instance, there is *Taber's Cyclopedic Medical Dictionary.* Other subject area dictionaries include *A Dictionary of Anthropology, The New Grove Dictionary of Music and Musicians,* and *A Dictionary of Economics.*

Find out whether there is a subject area dictionary for the subjects you are studying. Most such dictionaries are available only in hardback and are likely to be expensive. However, many students find them worth the initial investment. You might find less expensive copies on sale at a used-book store. Most libraries have copies of specialized dictionaries in the reference section.

EXERCISE 3-1	**DIRECTIONS:** *Find the name of a subject area dictionary for each of the fields listed below.*

1. psychology _____

2. law _____

3. statistics _____

The Thesaurus

A thesaurus is a dictionary of synonyms. It groups words with similar meanings together. A thesaurus is particularly useful when you want to

- Locate the precise term to fit a particular situation
- Find an appropriate descriptive word
- Replace an overused or unclear word
- Convey a more specific shade of meaning

Suppose you are looking for a more precise word for the expression *will tell us about* in the following sentence:

In class today, our chemistry instructor **will tell us about** our next assignment.

The thesaurus lists the following synonyms for "tell—explain":

10 **explain, explicate, expound,** exposit; **give the meaning,** tell the meaning of; **spell out,** unfold; **account for,** give reason for; **clarify, elucidate,** clear up, **make clear,** make plain; **simplify,** popularize; **illuminate,** enlighten, **shed** *or* **throw light upon;** rationalize, euhemerize, demythologize, allegorize; tell *or* show how, show the way; **demonstrate, show, illustrate,** exemplify; decipher, crack, unlock, find the key to, unravel, **solve 487.2;** explain oneself; explain away.
11 **comment upon,** commentate, remark upon; **annotate,** gloss; **edit,** make an edition.
12 **translate, render,** transcribe, transliterate, put *or* turn into, transfuse the sense of; construe; English.
13 **paraphrase, rephrase, reword, restate,** rehash; give a free *or* loose translation.

Read the above entry and underline words or phrases that you think would be more descriptive than *tell about.* You might underline words and phrases such as *comment upon, illustrate, demonstrate,* and *spell out.*

The most widely used thesaurus is *Roget's Thesaurus.* Inexpensive paperback editions are available in most bookstores.

When you first consult a thesaurus, you will need to familiarize yourself with its format and learn how to use it. The following is a step-by-step approach:

1. Start with the extensive index in the back to locate the word you are trying to replace. Following the word, you will find the number(s) of the section(s) in the main part of the thesaurus that list the synonyms of that word.
2. Turn to those sections, scanning each list and jotting down all the words you think might work.
3. Test each of the words you selected in the sentence in which you will use it. The word should fit the context of the sentence.
4. Select the word that best expresses what you are trying to say.
5. Choose only words whose shades of meaning you know. Check unfamiliar words in a dictionary before using them. Remember, misusing a word is often a more serious error than choosing an overused or general one.

| EXERCISE 3-2 | **DIRECTIONS:** *Using a thesaurus, replace the boldfaced word or phrase in each sentence with a more precise or descriptive word. Write the word in the space provided. Rephrase the sentence, if necessary.* |

1. Although the movie was **good,** it lasted only an hour.

   _____

2. The judge **looked at** the criminal as she pronounced the sentence.

   _____

3. The accident victim was awarded a **big** cash settlement.

   _____

4. The lottery winner was **happy** to win the $100,000 prize, but he was surprised to learn that a sizable portion had already been deducted for taxes.

   _____

5. On the first day of class, the instructor **talked to** the class about course requirements.

   _____

Using Your Dictionary

The first step in using your dictionary is to become familiar with the kinds of information it provides. In the following sample entry, each kind of information is marked:

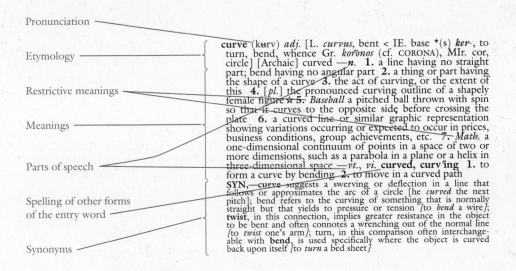

Pronunciation

Etymology

Restrictive meanings

Meanings

Parts of speech

Spelling of other forms
of the entry word

Synonyms

curve (kurv) *adj.* [L. *curvus*, bent < IE. base *(s) *ker-*, to turn, bend, whence Gr. *koronos* (cf. CORONA), MIr. cor, circle] [Archaic] curved —*n.* **1.** a line having no straight part; bend having no angular part **2.** a thing or part having the shape of a curve **3.** the act of curving, or the extent of this **4.** [*pl.*] the pronounced curving outline of a shapely female figure ☆**5.** *Baseball* a pitched ball thrown with spin so that it curves to the opposite side before crossing the plate **6.** a curved line or similar graphic representation showing variations occurring or expected to occur in prices, business conditions, group achievements, etc. **7.** *Math.* a one-dimensional continuum of points in a space of two or more dimensions, such as a parabola in a plane or a helix in three-dimensional space —*vt., vi.* **curved, curv'ing 1.** to form a curve by bending **2.** to move in a curved path **SYN.**—curve suggests a swerving or deflection in a line that follows or approximates the arc of a circle [he *curved* the next pitch]; bend refers to the curving of something that is normally straight but that yields to pressure or tension [to *bend* a wire]; **twist**, in this connection, implies greater resistance in the object to be bent and often connotes a wrenching out of the normal line [to *twist* one's arm]; turn, in this comparison often interchangeable with **bend**, is used specifically where the object is curved back upon itself [to *turn* a bed sheet]

You can see that a dictionary entry provides much more than the definition of a word. Information about the word's pronunciation, part of speech, history, and special uses can also be found.

EXERCISE 3-3

DIRECTIONS: *Use the sample dictionary entry above to complete the following items.*

1. Find three meanings for *curve* and write a sentence using each.

_____

2. Explain what *curve* means when used in baseball.

_____

3. Explain how the meaning of *curve* differs from the meaning of the word *bend*.

_____

In the past, you may have found parts of the dictionary confusing or difficult to use. Many students complain about the numerous symbols and abbreviations. Actually, once you are familiar with its format, you will see that the dictionary is systematic and highly organized. It provides a great deal of information about each word. The following is a brief review of the parts of a dictionary entry most often found confusing.

Abbreviations

All dictionaries provide a key to abbreviations used in the entry itself as well as some commonly used in other printed material. Most often this key appears on the inside front cover or on the first few pages of the dictionary.

EXERCISE 3-4

DIRECTIONS: *Find the meaning of each of the following symbols and abbreviations in a dictionary and write it in the space provided.*

1. v.t. _____

2. < _____

3. c. _____

4. Obs. _____

5. Fr. _____

6. pl. _____

Word Pronunciation

After each word entry, the pronunciation of the word is given in parentheses.

Examples:

helmet (hĕl'mĭt)   connection (kə-nĕk'shən)
apologize (ə-pŏl'ə-jīz)   orchestra (ôr'kĭ-strə)

This part of the entry shows how to pronounce a word by spelling it the way it

---

sounds. Different symbols are used to indicate certain sounds. Until you become familiar with this symbol system, you will need to refer to the pronunciation key. Most dictionaries include a pronunciation key at the bottom of every or every

ă pat/ā pay/â care/ä father/b bib/ch church/d deed/ĕ pet/ē be/f fife/g gag/ h hat/hw which/ĭ pit/ī pie/îr pier/j judge/k kick/l lid, needle/m mum/n no, sudden/ng thing/ŏ pot/ō toe/ô paw, for/oi noise/ou out/ŏŏ took/ōō boot/p pop/r roar/s sauce/sh ship, dish/ t tight/th thin, path/*th* this, bathe/ŭ cut/ûr urge/v valve/w with/y yes/z zebra, size/ zh vision/ə about, item, edible, gallop, circus/

other page. Here is a sample key from the *American Heritage Dictionary:*

The key shows the sound the symbol stands for in a word you already know how to pronounce. For example, suppose you are trying to pronounce the word *helix* (hē'lĭks). The key shows that the letter *e* in the first part of the word sounds the same as the *e* in the word *be*. The *i* in *helix* is pronounced the same way as the *i* in *pit*. To pronounce a word correctly, you must also accent (or put stress on) the appropriate part of the word. In a dictionary respelling, an accent mark (') usually follows the syllable, or part of the word, that is stressed most heavily.

Examples:

audience   ôd'ē-ən(t)s

football   fŏŏt'bôl

homicide   hŏm'ĭ-sīd

hurricane   hûr'ĭ-kān

literature   lĭt'ər-ə-chŏŏr

soporific   sŏp-ə-rĭf'ĭk

Some words have two accents—a primary stress and a secondary stress. The primary one is stressed more heavily and is printed in darker type than the secondary accent.

Example: interstate   ĭn'ter-stāt'

Try to pronounce each of the following dictionary respellings, using the pronunciation key:

dĭ-vûr'sə-fī   bŏŏsh'əl

chăl'ənj   bär'bĭ-kyoo

DIRECTIONS: *Use the pronunciation key above to sound out each of the following words. Write the word, spelled correctly, in the space provided.*

1. kə-mĭt′ _____

2. kăp′chər _____

3. bə-räm′ə-tər _____

4. sĕksh′ə-wəl _____

5. ī-dĕn′tə-fĭ-kā′shən _____

6. ĭn-dĭf′ər-əns _____

7. lûr′nĭd _____

8. lĭk′wĭd _____

9. noŏ′səns _____

10. fär′mə-sē _____

Etymology

Many dictionaries include information on each word's **etymology**—its origin and development. A word's etymology is its history, traced back as far as possible to its earliest use, often in another language. The sample dictionary entry on p. 39 shows that the word "curve" was derived from the Latin word *curvus* and the Greek word *koronos*.

Restrictive Meanings

Many dictionaries include restrictive meanings of words. These are definitions that apply only when the word is being used with respect to a specific topic or field of study. The sample entry on p. 39 gives two restrictive meanings for the word "curve"—one for baseball and another for math.

Multiple Meanings

Most words have more than one meaning. When you look up the meaning of a new word, you must choose the meaning that fits the way the word is used in the sentence context. The following sample entry for the word *green* contains many meanings for the word.

MEANINGS
GROUPED BY
PARTS OF SPEECH

green (grēn) *adj.* [ME. *grene* < OE., akin to G. *grün*, Du. *groen:* for IE. base see GRASS] **1.** of the color that is characteristic of growing grass **2.** overspread with or characterized by green plants or foliage [a *green* field] **3.** keeping the green grass of summer; snowless; a mild [a *green* December] **4.** sickly or bilious, as from illness, fear, etc. **5.** *a*) flourishing; active [to keep someone's memory *green*] *b*) of the time of one's youth [the *green* years] **6.** not mature; unripe [*green* bananas] **7.** not trained; inexperienced **8.** easily led or deceived; simple; naive **9.** not dried, seasoned, or cured; unprocessed [*green* lumber] **10.** fresh; new **11.** [cf. GREEN-EYED] [Colloq.] jealous —*n.* **1.** the color of growing grass; any color between blue and yellow in the spectrum: green can be produced by blending blue and yellow pigments **2.** any green pigment or dye **3.** anything colored green as clothing **4.** [*pl.*] green leaves, branches, sprigs, etc., used for ornamentation **5.** [*pl.*] green leafy plants or vegetables eaten cooked or raw, as spinach, turnip tops, lettuce, etc. **6.** an area of smooth turf set aside for special purposes [a village *green*, a bowling *green*] ★**7.** [Slang] money, esp. paper money: chiefly in **long green, folding green** **8.** *Golf a*) the plot of carefully tended turf immediately surrounding each of the holes to facilitate putting *b*) an entire golf course —*vt.*, *vi.* to make or become green —**green with envy** very envious —**green'ish** *adj.* —**green'ly** *adv.* —**green'ness** *n.*

MANY DIFFERENT
MEANINGS

Unripe fruit
Inexperienced person

Type of vegetable

Part of golf course

11 Adjectives

8 Nouns

1 Verb

The meanings are grouped by part of speech and are numbered consecutively in each group. Generally, the most common meanings of the word are listed first, with more specialized, less common meanings appearing toward the end of the entry. Now find the meaning that fits the use of the word *green* in the following sentence.

> The local veterans' organization held its annual fundraising picnic on the village **green.**

In this sentence, *green* refers to "an area of grass used for special purposes." Since this is a specialized meaning of the word, it appears toward the end of the entry.

Here are a few suggestions for choosing the correct meaning from among those listed in an entry:

1. If you are familiar with the parts of speech, try to use these to locate the correct meaning. For instance, if you are looking up the meaning of a word that names a person, place, or thing you can save time by reading only those entries given after *n.* (noun).

2. For most types of college reading, you can skip definitions that give slang and colloquial (abbreviated *colloq.*) meanings. Colloquial meanings refer to informal or spoken language.

3. If you are not sure of the part of speech, read each meaning until you find a definition that seems correct. Skip over restrictive meanings that are inappropriate.

4. Test your choice by substituting the meaning in the sentence with which you are working. Substitute the definition for the word and see whether it makes sense in the context (see Chapter 1).

Suppose you are looking up the word *oblique* to find its meaning in this sentence:

My sister's **oblique** answers to my questions made me suspicious.

Oblique is used in the above sentence as an adjective. Looking at the entries listed after *adj.* (adjective), you can skip over the definition under the heading *Geometry*, as it wouldn't apply here: Definition 2 (indirect, evasive) best fits the way *oblique* is used in the sentence.

o·blique (ō-blēk', ə-; *Military* ō-blīk', ə-) *adj. Abbr.* **obl. 1. a.** Having a slanting or sloping direction, course, or position; inclined. **b.** *Geometry.* Designating lines or planes that are neither parallel nor perpendicular. **2.** Indirect or evasive in execution, meaning, or expression; not straightforward. **3.** Devious, misleading, or dishonest; *oblique answers.* **4.** Not direct in descent; collateral. **5.** *Botany.* Having sides of unequal length or form: *an oblique leaf.* **6.** *Grammar.* Designating any noun case except the nominative or the vocative. **7.** *Rhetoric.* **Indirect** *(see).* —*n.* **1.** An oblique thing, such as a line, direction, or muscle. **2.** *Nautical.* The act of changing course by less than 90 degrees. —*adv. Military.* At an angle of 45 degrees: *Right oblique, march!* [Middle English *oblike*, from *Latin oblīquus†.*] —o·blique' ly *adv.* —o·blique' ness *n.*

EXERCISE 3-6 **DIRECTIONS:** *Use the dictionary to help you find an appropriate meaning for the boldfaced word in each of the following sentences.*

1. The last contestant did not have a **ghost** of a chance.

_____

2. The race car driver won the first **heat.**

_____

3. The police took all possible **measures** to protect the witness.

_____

4. The orchestra played the first **movement** of the symphony.

_____

5. The plane stalled on the **apron.**

_____

Spelling

The entry gives the correct spelling of a word. It also shows how the spelling changes when a word is made plural or endings (suffixes—see Chapter 2) are added, as in the following examples.

Word	Word + Ending
budget	budgetary
	budgeter
exhibit	exhibitor
	exhibition
fancy	fancily
	fanciness
	fancier

Other Aids

Many dictionaries (especially hardback editions) also contain numerous useful lists and tables. These are usually printed at the back of the dictionary. Frequently included are tables of weights and measures and of periodic elements in chemistry, biographical listings for famous people, a pronouncing gazetteer (a geographical dictionary), and lists of standard abbreviations, colleges, and signs and symbols.

EXERCISE 3-7

DIRECTIONS: *Use a dictionary to answer each of the following items. Write your answer in the space provided.*

1. What parts of speech can the word *interior* be used as?

2. How is the word *exacerbate* pronounced? Record its phonetic spelling.

3. Which part of the word *opinion* is stressed (accented)?

4. How many different meanings can you think of for the word *pitch?* Write as many as you can think of. Then check to see how many meanings are given in the dictionary.

Locating Words Rapidly

Most dictionaries include guide words to help you locate words rapidly. At the top of each dictionary page are two words in bold print, one on the left corner and one on the right. The guide word on the left is the first entry on that page. The right-hand guide word is the last entry. All the words on that page come between the two guide words in alphabetical order.

To check quickly whether a word is on a certain page, look at the guide words. If the word you are looking for falls alphabetically between the two guide words on the page, scan that page until you find the word. If the word does not come between those guide words, you need not look at that page at all.

Suppose you are looking up the word *loathsome*. The guide words on a particular page are *livid* and *lobster*. You know that the word *loathsome* will be on that page because, alphabetically, *loathsome* comes after *livid* and before *lobster*.

EXERCISE 3-8	**DIRECTIONS:** *Read each entry word and the pair of guide words that follows it. Decide whether the entry word would be found on the dictionary page with those guide words. Write* yes *or* no *in the space provided.*

Entry Word	Guide Words	
1. grotesque	gritty—ground	_____
2. stargaze	standard—starfish	_____
3. ridicule	ridgepole—rigid	_____
4. exponent	expletive—express	_____
5. dissident	displease—dissidence	_____

Pronouncing Unfamiliar Words

At one time or another, each of us comes across words that we are unable to pronounce. To pronounce an unfamiliar word, sound it out syllable by syllable. Here are a few simple rules for dividing words into syllables:

1. Divide compound words between the individual words that form the compound word.

Examples:

house/broken	house/hold	space/craft
green/house	news/paper	sword/fish

2. Divide words between prefixes (word beginnings) and roots (base words) and/or between roots and suffixes (word endings).

Examples:

Prefix + Root
pre/read   post/pone   anti/war
Root + Suffix
sex/ist   agree/ment   list/ing
(For a more complete discussion of prefixes, roots, and suffixes, see Chapter 2.)

3. Each syllable is a separate, distinct speech sound. Pronounce the following words and try to hear the number of syllables in each.

Examples:

expensive	ex/pen/sive = 3 syllables
recognize	rec/og/nize = 3 syllables
punctuate	punc/tu/ate = 3 syllables
complicated	com/pli/cat/ed = 4 syllables

4. Each syllable has at least one vowel and usually one or more consonants. (The letters *a, e, i, o, u,* and sometimes *y* are vowels. All other letters are consonants.)

Examples: as/sign re/act cou/pon gen/er/al

5. Divide words before a single consonant, unless the consonant is the letter *r*.

Examples: hu/mid pa/tron re/tail fa/vor mor/on ·

6. Divide words between two consonants appearing together.

Examples: pen/cil lit/ter lum/ber sur/vive

7. Divide words between two vowel sounds that appear together.

Examples: te/di/ous ex/tra/ne/ous

These rules will prove helpful but, as you no doubt already know, there will always be exceptions.

DIRECTIONS: *Use slash marks (/) to divide each of the following words into syllables.*

1. polka	6. innovative	11. tangelo	16. tenacity
2. pollute	7. obtuse	12. symmetry	17. mesmerize
3. ordinal	8. germicide	13. telepathy	18. intrusive
4. hallow	9. futile	14. organic	19. infallible
5. judicature	10. extoll	15. hideous	20. fanaticism

A System for Learning New Words

As you read textbook assignments and reference sources and while listening to your instructors' class presentations, you are constantly exposed to new words. Unless you make a deliberate effort to remember and use these words, many of them will probably fade from your memory. One of the most practical and easy-to-use systems for expanding your vocabulary is the index card system. It works like this:

1. Whenever you hear or read a new word that you intend to learn, jot it down in the margin of your notes or mark it some way in the material you are reading.
2. Later, write the word on the front of an index card. Then look up its meaning and write it on the back of the card. Also, record a phonetic key for the word's pronunciation, its part of speech, other forms the word may take, and a sam-

ostracize (ŏs´ trə sīz)	*to banish from social or political favor* *Ex.: A street gang will ostracize a member who refuses to wear the gang emblem.*
Front	Back

Figure 3-1 Sample index card.

ple sentence or example of how the word is used. Your cards should look like the one in Figure 3-1.

3. Once a day, take a few minutes to go through your pack of index cards. For each card, look at the word on the front and try to recall its meaning on the back. Then check the back of the card to see whether you were correct. If you were unable to recall the meaning or if you confused the word with another word, retest yourself. Shuffle the cards after each use.

4. After you have gone through your pack of cards several times, sort the cards into two piles—words you know and words you have not learned. Then, putting the known words aside, concentrate on the words still to be learned.

5. Once you have learned the entire pack of words, review them often to refresh your memory.

This index card system is effective for several reasons. First, it can be reviewed in the spare time that is often wasted waiting for a class to begin, riding a bus, and so on. Second, the system enables you to spend time learning what you do *not* know rather than wasting time studying what you already know. Finally, the system overcomes a major problem that exists in learning information that appears in list form. If the material to be learned is presented in a fixed order, you tend to learn it in that order and may be unable to recall individual items when they appear alone or out of order. By shuffling the cards, you scramble the order of the words and thus avoid this problem.

EXERCISE 3-10

DIRECTIONS: *Make a set of at least 20 word cards, choosing words from one of your textbooks or from one of the reading selections in the back of this book. Then study the cards using the method described in this chapter.*

■■■■■■■ **WORKING TOGETHER**

Directions: Locate ten words that you find difficult to pronounce. Sources may be a dictionary, a textbook, or one of the more difficult reading selections in Part 6 of this book. Write each of the ten words on a separate index card and then establish a list of the words and how they are pronounced. Your instructor will form groups. Pass the cards around the group. Each student attempts a pronunciation. The student who pronounces the word correctly keeps the card. Make a note of words that you were unable to pronounce; check their pronunciation in your dictionary.

▪▪▪▪▪▪▪▪ SUMMARY

What reference sources are useful in building a strong vocabulary?

Collegiate and unabridged dictionaries, subject area dictionaries, and the thesaurus are all useful.

How do you pronounce unfamiliar words?

To pronounce unfamiliar words, use the pronounciation key in the dictionary and apply the seven rules listed in this chapter.

Explain the index card system.

The index card system is a method of learning vocabulary. Write a word on the front of an index card and its meaning on the back. Study the cards by sorting the cards into two piles—known and unknown words.

Making Your Skills Work Together

A Combined Approach To Vocabulary

Throughout this unit you have learned several ways to approach words you do not know. In Chapter 1 you learned how to look for meaning clues in the sentence context. In Chapter 2 you saw that breaking a word into parts can help you discover its meaning. Finally, in Chapter 3 you learned how to use various information sources to unlock word meaning and a card system for learning new words.

While each of these skills is effective by itself, each becomes more useful when used in combination with others. You will find that various combinations of techniques work better than any one alone. The combination you use, however, depends on the situation. For instance, one time you might use context and then a dictionary. Another time you might use context and word parts. Context, however, is always the final test of whether you have correctly defined a word. To be correct, a definition must make sense in the context.

Let us consider an example in which combined skills are more effective than context alone. In figuring out the meaning of the word *unassuming* in the following sentence, both context and word parts are useful:

The bank executive's **unassuming** attitude toward her customers made them think of her as an ordinary person.

Context alone suggests that the executive had an attitude that made customers think of her as an ordinary person, but this still does not give you enough information. Using word parts, you can see the prefix *un-* (meaning "not") and the root word *assume*. By combining these clues, you can figure out that the executive did not assume too much about her position or herself. Thus, in the above context, *unassuming* means "not forward" or "modest."

Here's another example:

The security wall surrounding the building made it **impenetrable.**

Context tells you that *impenetrable* refers to a condition of the building. Using word parts, you know this:

prefix: im- = not
root: penetr(ate) = force a way through
suffix: -able = able to
impenetrable = not able to force a way through

In some situations it may be necessary to check a dictionary for an exact meaning once you have found a meaning clue in the context. Once you have a meaning clue, you will find that reading through the numerous definitions listed is much easier and faster than if you have no idea what you are looking for. Then, once you have used an effective combination of methods to determine a word's meaning, be sure not to forget it. Jot the new word onto an index card and use the card system to place that word in your permanent store of word meanings.

EXERCISE 1

DIRECTIONS: *Read each sentence and write a definition or synonym for each boldfaced word. Use a combination of skills to determine meaning.*

1. The class was **demoralized** when everyone failed the first exam.

   _____

2. The film we saw in class today was **noncontroversial.**

   _____

3. In spite of close **surveillance,** three inmates managed to escape.

   _____

4. The union leader **exculpated** himself from blame for the strike by saying he had encouraged members to return to work.

   _____

5. At eighty years of age, my grandmother still moves with **alacrity.**

   _____

6. There was no need to **recapitulate** the speaker's faults; they were clear to everyone.

   _____

7. The teenager's **puerile** remarks offended his parents' guests.

   _____

8. **Dehydrated** food often lacks flavor.

   _____

9. Sam's **maladroit** behavior surprised everyone at the concert.

   _____

10. The government **imposed** controls that froze prices and wages.

   _____

PART 2

Reading as Thinking and Learning

Rhonda is taking an anatomy and physiology course, one required in nursing. She reads all the assignments and spends long hours studying. She rereads assignments, underlines, and studies her notes. In fact, she spends more time preparing for each weekly quiz than most other students in the class. Before each quiz she is confident; she has studied and feels she knows the material. When the instructor returns the weekly quiz, Rhonda is always surprised and disappointed. She thinks she has done well, but receives a failing grade. She cannot understand why she fails the quizzes, since she has studied the material.

Rhonda decides to visit the college's learning center. The first thing the instructor asks her to do is to locate the correct answer to each quiz item in her textbook. When Rhonda has difficulty doing this, the instructor questions her on portions of the textbook. The instructor realizes that Rhonda has not thought about what she read so he asks Rhonda several questions about how she read the chapters and discovers that she did not use an active approach to studying. Rhonda did nothing before beginning to read to sharpen her mind and make reading easier. She read mechanically, from beginning to end, and she did not check her understanding of the material. She did not realize her comprehension was poor or incomplete. The instructor then suggests some strategies to help Rhonda get involved with what she is reading, and shows her how to keep track of her level of comprehension. He also suggested that Rhonda analyze how she learns best and begin to develop a plan of action for learning more effectively.

The purpose of this part of the book is to help you develop skills to approach reading as a thinking process. You will learn various techniques that will increase your comprehension. You will also learn how to keep track of your level of understanding and what to do if it is poor or incomplete.

THIS PART OF THE TEXT WILL HELP YOU

1. Start with a positive attitude (Chapter 4)
2. Maintain a high level of concentration (Chapter 4)
3. Learn what a chapter or article is about before you read it (Chapter 4)
4. Discover what you already know about a subject (Chapter 4)
5. Use questions to guide your reading (Chapter 4)
6. Keep track of your level of understanding (Chapter 5)
7. Correct weak or poor comprehension (Chapter 5)

Prereading Strategies

THIS CHAPTER WILL SHOW YOU HOW TO

1. *Start with a positive attitude*
2. *Control your concentration*
3. *Preview before reading*
4. *Activate your background knowledge*
5. *Develop questions to guide your reading*

Would you like to get more out of what you read in less time? Do you want to avoid spending unnecessary time rereading and reviewing? This chapter will discuss five techniques that can make an immediate, noticeable change in how well you understand and remember what you read. Because each is done *before* you actually begin reading, they are called *pre*reading strategies. As you work through this chapter you will see that there is more to reading an assignment than opening your book to the correct page, checking its length, and beginning to read.

Start with a Positive Attitude

Reading can open up worlds of new ideas, show you different ways of looking at things, and provide a welcome escape from day-to-day problems. Here are a few approaches that will make reading work for you:

1. *Actively search for key ideas as you read.* Try to connect these ideas with what your instructor is discussing in class. Think of reading as a way of sifting and sorting out what you need to learn from the less important information.
2. ***Think of reading as a way of unlocking the writer's message to you, the reader.*** Look for clues about the writer's personality, attitudes, opinions, and beliefs. This will put you in touch with the writer as a person and help you understand his or her message. Part 4 of this book will offer suggestions to help you do this.
3. ***Plan on spending time.*** Reading is not something you can rush through. The time you invest will pay off in increased comprehension.

Control Your Concentration

Do you have difficulty concentrating? If so, you are like many other college students who say that concentration is the main reason they cannot read or study effectively. Building concentration involves two steps: (1) controlling your surroundings and (2) focusing your attention.

Controlling Your Surroundings

Poor concentration is often the result of distractions caused by the time and place you have chosen to study. Here are a few ideas to help you overcome poor concentration.

1. ***Choose a place to read where you will not be interrupted.*** If people interrupt you at home or in the dormitory, try the campus library.
2. ***Find a place that is relatively free of distractions and temptations.*** Avoid places with outside noise, friends, a television set, or an interesting project close at hand.
3. ***Read in the same place each day.*** Eventually you will get in the habit of reading there and concentration will become easier, almost automatic.
4. ***Do not read where you are too comfortable.*** It is easy to lose concentration, become drowsy, or fall asleep when you are too relaxed.
5. ***Choose a time of day when you are mentally alert.*** Concentration is easier if you are not tired, hungry, or drowsy.

Focusing Your Attention

Even if you follow these suggestions, you still may find it difficult to become organized and stick with your reading. This takes self-discipline, but the following suggestions may help.

1. *Set goals and time limits for yourself.* Before you begin a reading assignment, decide how long it should take, and check to see that you stay on schedule. Before you start an evening of homework, write down what you plan to do and how long each assignment should take. Sample goals for an evening are shown in Figure 4-1 below.

12/20

Eng. paper—revise $\frac{1}{2}$ hr.

Math probs. 1–10   1 hr.

Sociology
   read pp. 70–82   1 hr.

Figure 4-1 Goals and time limits.

2. *Choose and reserve blocks of time each day for reading and study.* Write down what you will study in each time block each day/evening. Working at the same time each day establishes a routine and makes concentration a bit easier.
3. *Vary your reading.* For instance, instead of spending an entire evening on one subject, work for one hour on each of three subjects.
4. *Reward yourself for accomplishing things as planned.* Delay entertainment until after you have finished studying. Use such things as ordering a pizza, calling a friend, or watching TV as rewards after you have completed several assignments.
5. *Plan frequent breaks.* Do this at sensible points in your reading—between chapters or after major chapter divisions.
6. *Keep physically as well as mentally active.* Try highlighting, underlining, or making summary notes as you read (see Chapter 11). These activities will focus your attention on the assignment.

EXERCISE 4-1

DIRECTIONS: *Answer each of the following questions as honestly as you can. They will help you analyze problems with concentration. You may want to discuss your answers with others in your class.*

1. Where do you read and study? _____

What interruptions, if any, occur there? _____

2. Do you need to find a better place? _____

   If so, list a few alternatives. _____

3. What is the best time of day for you to read? (If you don't know, experiment with different times until you begin to see a pattern.)

   _____

4. How long do you normally read without a break?

   _____

5. What type of distraction bothers you the most?

   _____

6. On average, how many different assignments do you work on in one evening?

   _____

7. What types of rewards might work for you?

   _____

EXERCISE 4-2

DIRECTIONS: *As you read your next textbook assignment, either for this course or another, be alert for distractions. Each time your mind wanders, try to identify the source of distraction. List in the space provided the cause of each break in your concentration and a way to eliminate each, if possible.*

_____

_____

_____

EXERCISE 4-3

DIRECTIONS: *Before you begin your next study session, make a list in the space provided of what you intend to accomplish and how long you should spend on each task.*

Assignment   Time
   1. _____   _____

_____

2. _____ _____

3. _____ _____

Preview

Would you cross a city street without checking for traffic first? Would you pay to see a movie you had never heard of and knew nothing about? Would you buy a car without test driving it or checking its mechanical condition?

Most likely you answered "no" to each of these questions. Now answer a related question, one that applies to reading: Should you read an article or textbook chapter without knowing what it is about or how it is organized? You can probably guess that the answer is "no." This section explains a technique called previewing.

Previewing is a way of quickly familiarizing yourself with the organization and content of written material *before* beginning to read it. It is an easy method to use and will make a dramatic difference in how effectively you read.

How to Preview

When you preview, try to (1) find only the most important ideas in the material, and (2) note how they are organized. To do this, look only at the parts that state these important ideas and skip the rest. Previewing is a fairly rapid technique. Take only a few minutes to preview a 15- to 20-page textbook chapter. The portions to look at in previewing a textbook chapter are listed here.

1. **The Title and Subtitle** The title is a label that tells what the chapter is about. The subtitle, if there is one, suggests how the author approaches the subject. For example, an article titled "Brazil" might be subtitled "The World's Next Superpower." In this instance, the subtitle tells which aspects of Brazil the article discusses.
2. **Chapter Introduction** Read the entire chapter introduction if it is brief. If it is lengthy, read only the first few paragraphs.
3. **The First Paragraph** The first paragraph, or introduction, of each section of the chapter may provide an overview of the section and/or offer clues about its organization.
4. **Boldfaced Headings** Headings, like titles, serve as labels and identify the topic of the material. By reading each heading, you will be reading a list of the important topics the chapter covers. Together, the headings form a mini-outline of the chapter.
5. **The First Sentence Under Each Heading** The first sentence following the heading often further explains the heading. It may also state the central

thought of the entire selection. If the first sentence is purely introductory, read the second as well.

6. **Typographical Aids** Typographical aids are those features of a page that help to highlight and organize information. These include *italics,* **boldfaced type,** marginal notes, colored ink, <u>underlining</u>, and enumeration (listing). A writer frequently uses typographical aids to call attention to important key words, definitions, and facts.

7. **Graphs, Charts, and Pictures** Graphs, charts, and pictures will point you toward the most important information. Glance at these to determine quickly what information is being emphasized or clarified.

8. **The Final Paragraph or Summary** The final paragraph or summary will give a condensed view of the chapter and help you identify key ideas. Often, a summary outlines the key points of the chapter.

9. **End-of-Chapter Material** Glance through any study or discussion questions, vocabulary lists, or outlines that appear at the end of the chapter. These will help you decide what in the chapter is important.

Demonstration of Previewing

The following article was taken from a chapter of a sociology textbook on group behavior. It discusses the reasons people form groups and has been included to demonstrate previewing. Everything that you should look at or read has been shaded. Preview this excerpt now, reading only the shaded portions.

Why Do People Form Groups?

The most basic question about groups is why people form them in the first place. Exploring this question fully require a study of the psychological and biological bases of bonding among humans and primates. Such a study is beyond the scope of this book. Here it is enough to point out that many types of monkeys, some apes, and humans—the three most complex primates—all tend to live in groups. In fact, the group is a key to their survival. By playing different roles—lookout, dominant male, group defender, forager, and so on—group members can seek food and defend themselves against enemies more effectively than an individual acting alone.

To humans, group life is vital. As mentioned in Chapter 4, infants are dependent on adults for a long period. During this time they learn some of the skills and many of the attitudes needed to live in groups. As they grow older, they absorb some of the knowledge, ideas, values, and rules of their group. Socialization makes them fit for social life and helps preserve the group beyond the life span of any of its members. But groups serve many other functions besides socialization.

The Instrumental Role of Groups

Many groups are formed in order to get a specific job done. These **instrumental groups** are needed to perform tasks that would be hard or impossible for a person acting alone. A construction gang, a surgical team, an assembly line, and a football team are all formed to achieve certain desired goals.

Expression in Groups

Some kinds of groups are termed **expressive groups.** In these the goal is to satisfy the members' needs for acceptance, esteem, and independence.* Such groups form spontaneously, with little outside influence. Examples include friendship groups and groups of teenagers that go out simply to have fun bowling, skating, or partying. There is no clear boundary between instrumental and expressive groups, however. Instrumental groups often perform expressive functions. The members of a military battle unit form deep emotional ties that go well beyond what is needed to fight effectively in battle. On the other hand, expressive groups can be viewed as instrumental because they have a purpose: the pleasure of human company. Sometimes an expressive group is more clearly instrumental, as when a group of neighbors organize a tenants' association.

The Supportive Role of Groups

People band together not only to perform tasks and meet social needs but also to relieve unpleasant feelings. In a classic set of experiments, Schachter (1959) used undergraduate students in a "waiting room" as subjects. Some of the subjects were given anxiety-producing information about the fictitious experiment that was about to take place. They were told that they were going to take part in an experiment dealing with the effects of electric shock and then were asked to wait until the experimenters were ready to begin. . . .[1]

Although you may not realize it, you have gained a substantial amount of information from the minute or so that you spent previewing. You have become familiar with the key ideas in this section. To demonstrate, read each of the following statements and mark them *T* for "True" or *F* for "False" based on what you learned by previewing.

_____ 1. Humans are the only ones who form groups.

_____ 2. All members in a group perform the same function.

*Second sentence included here because the first in this paragraph is introductory.

_____ 3. Instrumental groups are formed to perform a specific task.

_____ 4. Expressive groups are formed, in part, to meet the members' need for acceptance.

_____ 5. Supportive groups meet social needs.

This quiz tested your recall of some of the more important ideas in the article. Check your answers by referring back to the article. Did you get most or all of the above items correct? You can see, then, that previewing acquaints you with the major ideas contained in the material before you read it.

EXERCISE 4-4

DIRECTIONS: *Preview Chapter 6 in this book. After you have previewed it, complete the items below.*

1. What is the subject of Chapter 6?

   _____

2. List the four major topics Chapter 6 covers.

   a. _____

   b. _____

   c. _____

   d. _____

EXERCISE 4-5

DIRECTIONS: *Preview a chapter from one of your other textbooks. After you have previewed it, complete the items below.*

1. What is the chapter title?

   _____

2. What subject does the chapter cover?

   _____

3. List some of the major topics covered.

   _____

Discover What You Already Know

Once you have previewed an assignment, the next step is to discover what you already know about the topic. Regardless of the topic, you probably know *something* about it. We will call this your **background knowledge.** Here is an example.

A student was about to read an article entitled "Growing Urban Problems" for a sociology class. At first she thought she knew very little about urban problems since she lived in a small town. Then she began thinking about her recent trip to a nearby city. She remembered seeing homeless people and overcrowded housing. Then she recalled reading about drug problems, drive-by shootings, and muggings.

Now let's take a sample chapter from a business textbook, titled *Small Business Management.* The headings are listed below. Spend a moment thinking about each one; then make a list of things you already know about each.

- Characteristics of Small Businesses
- Small-Business Administration
- Advantages and Disadvantages of Small Businesses
- Problems of Small Businesses

Discovering what you already know is useful for three important reasons. First, it makes reading easier because you have already thought about the topic. Second, the material is easier to remember because you can connect the new information with what you already know. Third, topics become more interesting if you can link them to your own experiences. You can discover what you know by using one or more of the following techniques.

1. *Ask questions and try to answer them.* For the above business textbook headings, you might ask and try to answer questions such as: Would or wouldn't I want to own a small business? What problems could I expect?
2. *Draw upon your own experience.* For example, if a chapter in your business textbook is titled "Advertising: Its Purpose and Design," you might think of several ads you have seen on television, in magazines, and in newspapers and analyze the purpose of each and how it was constructed.
3. *Brainstorm.* On a scrap sheet of paper, jot down everything that comes to mind about the topic. For example, suppose you are about to read a chapter on domestic violence in your sociology textbook. You might list types of violence—child abuse, rape, and so on. You could write questions such as: "What

causes child abuse?" or "How can it be prevented?" Or you might list incidents of domestic violence you have heard or read about. Any of these approaches will help to make the topic interesting.

EXERCISE 4-6

DIRECTIONS: *Assume you have just previewed a chapter in your American government text on freedom of speech. Discover what you already know about freedom of speech by using each of the techniques suggested above. Then answer the questions below.*

1. Did you discover you knew more about freedom of speech than you initially thought?

2. Which technique worked best? Why?

Develop Guide Questions

Did you ever read an entire page or more and not remember anything you read? Have you found yourself going from paragraph to paragraph without really thinking about what the writer is saying? Most likely you are not looking for anything in particular as you read. As a result, you do not notice or remember anything specific either. The solution is a relatively simple technique that takes just a few seconds: develop questions that will guide your reading and hold your attention.

How to Ask Guide Questions

Here are a few useful suggestions to help you form questions to guide your reading:

1. *Preview before you try to ask questions.* Previewing will give you an idea of what is important and indicate which questions you should ask.
2. *Turn each major heading into a series of questions.* The questions should ask something that you feel is important to know.
3. *As you read the section, look for the answer to your questions.*
4. *When you finish reading a section, stop and check to see whether you have found the answers.*
5. *Avoid asking questions that have one-word answers.* Questions that begin with *what, why,* or *how* are more useful.

Here are a few headings and some examples of questions you could ask:

Heading	Questions
1. Reducing Prejudice	1. How can prejudice be reduced? What type of prejudice is discussed?
2. The Deepening Recession	2. What is a recession? Why is it deepening?
3. Newton's First Law of Motion	3. Who is or was Newton? What is his First Law of Motion?

EXERCISE 4-7

DIRECTIONS: *Write at least one question for each of the following headings.*

Heading	Question(s)
1. World War II and Black Protest	1. _____
2. Foreign Policy under Reagan	2. _____
3. The Increase of Single-Parent Families	3. _____
4. Changes in Optical Telescopes	4. _____
5. Causes of Violent Behavior	5. _____

EXERCISE 4-8

DIRECTIONS: *Preview Chapter 8 of this book. Then write a question for each heading.*

_____

_____

_____

_____

_____

_____

EXERCISE 4-9

DIRECTIONS: *Turn back to the textbook excerpt on p. 62. You have already pre-viewed it. Without reading the article, write four important questions to be answered after finishing it.*

_____

_____

_____

_____

_____

EXERCISE 4-10

DIRECTIONS: *Select a textbook from one of your other courses. Preview a 5-page por-tion of a chapter that you have not yet read. Then write questions for each heading.*

_____

_____

_____

_____

_____

■■■■■■■ **WORKING TOGETHER**

Directions: Bring two brief magazine or newspaper articles or two 2-page texbook excerpts on interesting subjects to class. You should preview and then read both articles before class. Working in pairs with another student, exchange and preview each other's articles. Take turns predicting each article's content and organization. The student who has read the article verifies or rejects the predictions. Alternately, the "reader" may ask the "previewer" about the article's content or organization. Then work together to generate a list of guide questions that could be used when reading the material.

■■■■■■■■ *SUMMARY*

What techniques can you use *before* reading to read efficiently?

There are five techniques you can use *before* you even begin to read which will help you to read more efficiently. These five techniques are:

1. Start with a positive attitude. Think of reading as an active process in order to approach difficult assignments.

2. Control your concentration. Control time, place, and distractions and focus your attention on the assignment.

3. Preview. Become familiar with the material before you read it.

4. Activate your background knowledge. Bring to mind what you already know about a topic.

5. Use Guide Questions. Formulate a series of questions that you expect to answer as you read. These questions guide your reading and increase your recall.

Monitoring Your Comprehension and Learning

■ ■

THIS CHAPTER WILL SHOW YOU HOW TO

1. *Recognize comprehension signals*
2. *Monitor your comprehension*
3. *Improve your comprehension*
4. *Discover how you learn*

■ ■

In many daily activities you maintain an awareness or "check" on how well you are performing. You also try to correct or improve your performance whenever possible. In sports such as racquetball, tennis, or bowling, you know if you are playing poorly; you actually keep score and deliberately try to correct errors and improve your performance. When preparing a favorite food, you often taste it and correct the seasonings. You can check to see whether your car is clean after taking it through the car wash and touch up any spots that were missed.

A similar type of checking should occur as you read. You should be aware of, or *monitor,* your performance. You need to "keep score" of how effectively and efficiently you are understanding what you read. This is called *comprehension monitoring.* As you monitor you also need to take *action* to correct poor comprehension. This chapter will show you how to monitor your comprehension and assess your learning style.

Recognizing Comprehension Signals

Think for a moment about how you feel when you read material you can easily understand. Now compare that to what happens when you read something difficult and complicated. When you read easy material, does it seem that everything "clicks"? That is, do ideas seem to fit together and make sense? Is that "click" noticeably absent in difficult reading?

Read each of the following paragraphs. As you read, be aware of how well you understand each of them.

Paragraph 1

The **spinal cord** is actually an extension of the brain. It runs from the base of the brain down the center of the back, protected by a column of bones. The cord acts as a sort of bridge between the brain and the parts of the body below the neck. But the spinal cord is not merely a bridge. It also produces some behaviors on its own, without any help from the brain. These behaviors, called spinal **reflexes,** are automatic, requiring no conscious effort. For example, if you accidentally touch a hot iron, you will immediately pull your hand away, even before the brain has had a chance to register what has happened. Nerve impulses bring a message to the spinal cord (HOT!), and the spinal cord immediately sends out a command via other nerve impulses, telling muscles in your arm to contract and pull your hand away from the iron. (Reflexes above the neck, such as sneezing and blinking, involve the lower part of the brain rather than the spinal cord.)[1]

Paragraph 2

In the HOSC experiment, two variables were of sufficient importance to include as stratification (classification) variables prior to the random assignment of class sections to treatments. These two stratification variables were science subject (biology, chemistry, or physics) and teacher's understanding of science (high or low). Inclusion of these two variables in the HOSC design allowed the experimenter to make generalizations about the HOSC treatment in terms of science subject matter and the teacher's understanding of science. Even if the HOSC experiments had selected a completely random sample of American high school science teacher-class sections, generalizations regarding the effectiveness of the HOSC treatment would only be possible in terms of the factors included in the experimental design. . . .[2]

Did you feel comfortable and confident as you read Paragraph 1? Did ideas seem to lead from one to another and make sense? How did you feel while reading Paragraph 2? Most likely you sensed its difficulty and felt confused. Some words were unfamiliar, and you could not follow the flow of ideas.

■ ■ ■ ■ ■

TABLE 5-1
Comprehension Signals

Positive Signals	Negative Signals
Everything seems to fit and make sense; ideas flow logically from one to another. You are able to understand what the author is saying.	Some pieces do not seem to belong; the ideas do not fit together or make sense. You feel as if you are struggling to stay with the author.
You can see where the author is leading.	You cannot think ahead or predict what will come next.
You are able to make connections among ideas.	You are unable to see how ideas connect.
You read at a regular comfortable pace.	You often slow down or lose your place.
You understand why the material was assigned.	You do not know why the material was assigned and cannot explain why it is important.
You can understand after reading the material once.	You need to reread sentences or paragraphs frequently.
You recognize most words or can figure them out from context.	Many words are unfamiliar.
You can express the key ideas in your own words.	You must reread and use the author's language to explain an idea.
You feel comfortable with the topic; you have some background knowledge.	The topic is unfamiliar; you know nothing about it.

As you read Paragraph 2, did you know that you were not understanding it? Did you feel lost and confused? Table 5-1 lists and compares some common signals that are useful in monitoring your comprehension. Not all signals appear at the same time, and not all signals work for everyone. As you study the list, identify those positive signals you sensed as you read Paragraph 1 on the spinal cord. Then identify those negative signals that you sensed when reading about the HOSC experiment.

Once you are able to recognize negative signals while reading, the next step is to take action to correct the problem. Specific techniques are given in the last section of this chapter.

In 1912, Alfred Wegener published a paper that was triggered by the common observation of the good fit between South America's east coast and Africa's west coast. Could these great continents ever have been joined? Wegener coordinated this jigsaw-puzzle analysis with other ecological and climatological data and proposed the theory of continental drift. He suggested that about 200 million years ago, all of the earth's continents were joined together into one enormous land mass, which he called Pangaea. In the ensuing millennia, according to Wegener's idea, Pangaea broke apart, and the fragments began to drift northward (by today's compass orientation) to their present location.

Wegener's idea received rough treatment in his lifetime. His geologist contemporaries attacked his naivete as well as his supporting data, and his theory was neglected until about 1960. At that time, a new generation of geologists revived the idea and subjected it to new scrutiny based on recent findings.

The most useful data have been based on magnetism in ancient lava flows. When a lava flow cools, metallic elements in the lava are oriented in a way that provides permanent evidence of the direction of the earth's magnetic field at the time, recording for future geologists both its north-south orientation and its latitude. From such maps, it is possible to determine the ancient positions of today's continents. We now believe that not only has continental drift occurred, as Wegener hypothesized, but that it continues to occur today. . . .

The disruption of Pangaea began some 230 million years ago in the Paleozoic era. By the Mesozoic era, the Eurasian land mass (called Laurasia) had moved away to form the northernmost continent. Gondwanaland, the mass that included India and the southern continents, had just begun to divide. Finally, during the late Mesozoic era, after South America and Africa were well divided, what was to be the last continental separation began, with Australia and Antarctica drifting apart. Both the North and South Atlantic Oceans would continue to widen considerably up to the Cenozoic era, a trend that is continuing today. So we see that although the bumper sticker "Reunite Gondwanaland" has a third-world, trendy ring to it, it's an unlikely proposition.[3]

1. How would you rate your overall comprehension? What positive signals did you sense? Did you feel any negative signals?

2. Test the accuracy of your rating in Question 1 by answering the following questions based on the material you read.
   a. Explain Wegener's theory of continental drift.
   b. Which two continents led Wegener to develop his theory?
   c. What recent findings have supported Wegener's theory?
   d. Describe the way in which Pangaea broke up and drifted to become the continents we know today.

3. In which sections was your comprehension strongest?

4. Did you feel at any time that you had lost, or were about to lose comprehension? If so, go back to that paragraph now. What made that paragraph difficult to read?

5. Would it have been useful to refer to a world map?

6. Underline any difficult words that interfered with your comprehension.

Monitoring Techniques

At times signals of poor comprehension do not come through clearly or strongly enough. In fact, at times you may think you understood what you read until you are questioned in class or take an exam. Only then do you discover that your comprehension was incomplete. Or you may find that you understand facts, but do not recognize more complicated relationships and implied meanings. Use the following monitoring techniques to determine if you are *really* understanding what you are reading.

Establish Checkpoints

Race car drivers make pit stops during races for quick mechanical checks and repairs; athletes are subject to frequent physical examinations. These activities evaluate or assess performance and correct any problems or malfunctions. Similarly, when reading it is necessary to stop and evaluate.

As you preview a textbook assignment, identify reasonable or logical checkpoints: points at which to stop, check, and, if necessary, correct your performance before continuing. Make a checkmark in the margin to designate these points. These checkpoints should be logical breaking points, where one topic ends and another begins or where a topic is broken down into several subtopics. As you reach each of these points, stop and assess your work using the techniques described below.

Use Your Guide Questions

In Chapter 4 you learned how to form guide questions using boldfaced headings. These same questions can be used to monitor your comprehension. When you finish a section with a bold heading, stop and take a moment to recall your guide questions and answer them mentally or on paper. Your ability to answer your questions is a strong indication of your level of comprehension.

Ask Connection Questions

To be certain that your comprehension is complete and that you are not *only* recalling facts, ask connection questions. **Connection questions** are those that require you to think about content. They force you to draw together ideas and to interpret and evaluate what you are reading. Ask such questions as:

> What does this topic have to do with topics discussed earlier in the article or chapter?
> Why is this material important?
> How can I use this information?

Connection questions help you to decide whether you are simply taking in information or whether you can actually use and apply the information.

EXERCISE 5-2

DIRECTIONS: *The following excerpt is from a business marketing textbook. Preview the excerpt and then write several guide questions in the spaces provided. As you read, monitor your comprehension and answer your guide questions. After you have read the material, answer the connection questions listed after the excerpt.*

Consumer Products

The most widely accepted approach to classifying consumer products relies on the common characteristics of consumer buying behavior. It divides products into four categories: convenience, shopping, specialty, and unsought products. However, not all buyers behave in the same way when purchasing a specific type of product. Thus a single product can fit into all four categories. To minimize this problem, marketers think in terms of how buyers *generally* behave when purchasing a specific item. In addition, they recognize

---

that the "correct" classification can be determined only by considering a particular firm's intended target market. With these thoughts in mind, let us examine the four traditional categories of consumer products.

Convenience Products

Convenience products are relatively inexpensive, frequently purchased items for which buyers exert only minimal purchasing effort. They range from bread, soft drinks, and chewing gum to gasoline and newspapers. The buyer spends little time planning the purchase or comparing available brands or sellers. Even a buyer who prefers a specific brand will readily choose a substitute if the preferred brand is not conveniently available.

Classifying a product as a convenience product has several implications for a firm's marketing strategy. A convenience product is normally marketed through many retail outlets. Because sellers experience high inventory turnover, per-unit gross margins can be relatively low. Producers of convenience products such as Lay's potato chips and Crest toothpaste expect little promotional effort at the retail level and thus must provide it themselves in the form of advertising and sales promotion. Packaging is also an important element of the marketing mix for convenience products. The package may have to sell the product because many convenience items are available only on a self-service basis at the retail level.

Shopping Products

Shopping products are items for which buyers are willing to expend considerable effort in planning and making the purchase. Buyers allocate much time for comparing stores and brands with respect to prices, product features, qualities, services, and perhaps warranties. Appliances, furniture, bicycles, stereos, and cameras are examples of shopping products. These products are expected to last a fairly long time and thus are purchased less frequently than convenience items. Even though shopping products are more expensive than convenience products, few buyers of shopping products are particularly brand loyal. If they were, they would be unwilling to shop and compare among brands.

To market a shopping product effectively, a marketer considers several key issues. Shopping products require fewer retail outlets than convenience products. Because shopping products are purchased less frequently, inventory turnover is lower, and middlemen expect to receive higher gross margins. Although large sums of money may be required to advertise shopping products, an even larger percentage of resources is likely to be used for personal selling. Usually, the producer and the middlemen expect some cooperation from one another with respect to providing parts and repair services and performing promotional activities.

Specialty Products

Specialty products possess one or more unique characteristics, and a significant group of buyers is willing to expend considerable effort to obtain them. Buyers actually plan the purchase of a specialty product; they know exactly what they want and will not accept a substitute. An example of a specialty product is a Jaguar automobile or a painting by Andy Warhol. When searching for specialty products, buyers do not compare alternatives; they are concerned primarily with finding an outlet that has a preselected product available. The fact that an item is a specialty product can affect a firm's marketing efforts several ways. Specialty products are often distributed through a limited number of retail outlets. Like shopping goods, they are purchased infrequently, causing lower inventory turnover and thus requiring relatively high gross margins.

Unsought Products

Unsought products are purchased when a sudden problem must be solved or when aggressive selling is used to obtain a sale that otherwise would not take place. In general, the consumer does not think of buying these products regularly. Emergency automobile repairs and cemetery plots are examples of unsought products. Life insurance and encyclopedias, in contrast, are examples of products that need aggressive personal selling. The salesperson tries to make consumers aware of benefits that can be derived from buying such products.[4]

Guide Questions	Answers
1. _____	_____
_____	_____
2. _____	_____
_____	_____
3. _____	_____
_____	_____

Connection Questions	Answers
1. Think of a product that you purchase in each of the four categories.	_____ _____
2. What type of product do you purchase most often?	_____
3. For which type do you spend the most time shopping?	_____ _____

Use Internal Dialogue

Internal dialogue, or mentally talking to yourself, is another excellent means of monitoring your comprehension. It involves rephrasing the message the author is expressing. You might think of internal dialogue as explaining what you are reading to someone who has not read the material. Try to briefly and accurately express each idea in your own words. If you are unable to do so, your understanding is incomplete. Here are a few examples of how internal dialogue can be used:

1. While reading a section in a math textbook, you mentally outline the steps to follow in solving a sample problem.
2. You are reading an essay that argues convincingly that nuclear power plants are unsafe. As you finish reading each stage of the argument, you rephrase it in your own words. You will learn more about how to express ideas in your own words in the next chapter in the section titled "Paraphrase," p. 109.
3. As you finish each boldfaced section in a psychology chapter, you summarize the key points.

EXERCISE 5-3	**DIRECTIONS:** *Complete each item as directed.*

1. *Read the following excerpt from a nursing textbook describing how to take a person's pulse. As you read the description, use internal dialogue to express each step in your own words. Then test your understanding by taking a classmate's pulse.*

Technique for Evaluating Pulses

If the pattern of a pulse rate is regular, you can count it for fifteen seconds and multiply by four to determine the person's pulse rate per minute. If it is not regular, you must count the rate for a full minute. Before you begin to take a pulse, be certain that the person is in a comfortable position since you do not know how long you will need to count. If he is lying supine, place his forearm across his chest and his palm downward; if he is sitting, bend his elbow ninety degrees and rest the elbow on the chair armrest. Gently place three of your fingertips on the designated pulse point with very light pressure. If you press on the artery too strongly, you will obscure blood flow and so not be able to feel a pulse any longer. Never palpate for a pulse with your thumb, which has such a strong pulse that it is possible to feel your own pulse when you press with it.[5]

2. *Read the following description of the elasticity of demand taken from an economics textbook. Use internal dialogue to explain to yourself how this principle of economics works.*

Elasticity of Demand

We have seen some of the factors that influence consumer response to price changes. Purchases of some goods change much more than purchases of others when their prices rise or fall. For instance, a price change for monogrammed T-shirts is likely to change sales substantially. On the other hand, a price change for calculus textbooks is not likely to have much effect on students' purchases. Economists say that the demand for T-shirts is more elastic than the demand for calculus textbooks. Elasticity measures the response of consumer demand to a change in price. More precisely, demand elasticity is the percentage change in quantity demanded for some good relative to the percentage change in price for that good. This relationship is described by a simple equation:

$$\text{Elasticity} = \frac{\%\ \text{change in quantity demanded}}{\%\ \text{change in price}}$$

Elasticity is a number without units. It doesn't tell us the level of price or quantity but shows how quantity demanded changes when price changes.[6]

Improving Your Comprehension

As you monitor your comprehension, you will at times realize that it is poor or incomplete. When this occurs, take immediate action to improve it. Begin by identifying, as specifically as possible, the cause of the problem. Do this by answering the following question: "Why is this not making sense?" Determine if it is your lack of concentration, difficult words, complex ideas, or organization that is bothering you. Next, make changes in your reading to correct or compensate for it. Table 5-2 lists common problems and offers strategies to correct them.

**EXERCISE
5-4**

DIRECTIONS: *Read each of the following difficult paragraphs, monitoring your comprehension as you do so. After reading each passage, identify and describe any problems you experienced. Then indicate what strategies you would use to correct these.*

1. A word about food—in the simplest of terms, there are two kinds of organisms: those that make their own food, usually by photosynthesis (autotrophs, "self-

■ ■ ■ ■ ■

TABLE 5-2
How to Improve Your Comprehension

Problems	Strategies
Poor concentration	1. Take limited breaks. 2. Tackle difficult material when your mind is fresh and alert. 3. Use guide questions (see Chapter 4). 4. Choose an appropriate place to study. 5. Focus your attention.
Words are difficult or unfamiliar	1. Use context and analyze word parts. 2. Skim through material before reading. Mark and look up meanings of difficult words. Jot meanings in the margin.
Sentences are long or confusing	1. Read aloud. 2. Locate the key idea(s). 3. Check difficult words. 4. Express each sentence in your own words.
Ideas are hard to understand; complicated	1. Rephrase or explain each in your own words. 2. Make notes. 3. Locate a more basic text that explains ideas in simpler form. 4. Study with a classmate; discuss difficult ideas.

Ideas are new and unfamiliar; you have little or no knowledge about the topic and the writer assumes you do	1. Make sure you didn't miss or skip introductory information.
	2. Get background information by
	  a. referring to an earlier section or chapter in the book.
	  b. referring to an encyclopedia.
	  c. referring to a more basic text.

The material seems disorganized or poorly organized	1. Pay more attention to headings. 2. Read the summary, if available. 3. Try to discover organization by writing an outline or drawing a map as you read (refer to Chapter 11).
You don't know what is and is not important	1. Preview 2. Ask and answer guide questions. 3. Locate and underline topic sentences (see Chapter 7).

feeders") and those that depend upon an outside-the-cell food source (heterotrophs, "other-feeders"). The autotrophs include a few kinds of bacteria, some one-celled eukaryotes (protistans), and all green plants. The heterotrophs encompass most bacteria, many protistans, all fungi, and all animals. Because this chapter is about animal nutrition, attention first will be given to examining the nature of food, then to how food is made available to cells.[7]

- Problem: _____

- Strategies: _____

2. There is reason to think that some tranquilizers owe their effects in reducing anxiety to interfering with dopamine. Heavy tranquilizers, such as chlorpromazine (Thorazine) and trifupromazine (Stelazine), used to treat schizophrenics, can lower dopamine levels, which appear to be abnormally high in some types of schizophrenia. Conversely, individuals who have taken heavy tranquilizers to reduce anxiety may develop temporary schizophrenia-like symptoms when they stop using them. Reserpine, the first of the heavy tranquilizers to be put into use in mental hospitals, apparently owes its effectiveness to its ability to reduce the output of norepinephrine in the central nervous system. The effectiveness of milder tranquilizers also is due to interactions with NTs or their receptors. Valium, the most widely prescribed tranquilizer, blocks GABA-receptor sites in postsynaptic membranes of brain neurons. Gamma aminobutyric acid (GABA) is the most abundant NT in the brain.[8]

- Problem: _____

- Strategies: _____

3. The objective of some tariffs is to protect an industry that produces goods vital to a nation's defense. In the case of a strategic industry, productive efficiency relative to that of other nations may not be an important consideration. The domestic industry—oil, natural gas, shipping, or steel, for example—may require protection because of its importance to national defense. Without protection, such industries might be weakened by foreign competition. Then, in an international crisis, the nation might find itself in short supply of products essential to national defense.[9]

- Problem: _____

- Strategies: _____

Discovering How You Learn

Reading assignments are the primary focus of many college classes. Instructors make daily or weekly textbook assignments. You are expected to read the material, learn it, and pass tests on it. Class lectures and discussions are often based on textbook assignments. An important part of many college classes, then, is completing reading assignments. So far in this chapter you have learned how to monitor and strengthen your understanding of an assignment.

Reading and understanding an assignment, however, does not mean you have learned it. In fact, if you have read an assignment once, you probably have *not* learned it. You need to do more than read to learn an assignment. Your question, then, is "What else should I do?" The answer is not a simple one.

Not everyone learns in the same way. In fact, everyone has his or her own individual way of learning, which is called *learning style*. The following section contains a brief Learning Style Questionnaire that will help you analyze how you learn and how to prepare an action plan for learning what you read.

Learning Style Questionnaire

DIRECTIONS: *Each item presents two choices. Select the alternative that best describes you. In cases in which neither choice suits you, select the one that is closer to your preference. Write the letter of your choice in the blank to the right of each item.*

Part One

_____ 1. I would prefer to follow a set of
    a. oral directions.
    b. written directions.

_____ 2. I would prefer to
    a. attend a lecture given by a famous psychologist.
    b. read an article written by the psychologist.

_____ 3. When I am introduced to someone, it is easier for me to remember the person's
    a. name.
    b. face.

_____ 4. I find it easier to learn new information using
    a. language (words).
    b. images (pictures).

_____ 5. I prefer classes in which the instructor
     a. lectures and answers questions.
     b. uses films and videos.

_____ 6. To follow current events, I would prefer to
     a. listen to the news on the radio.
     b. read the newspaper.

_____ 7. To learn how to operate a fax machine, I would prefer to
     a. listen to a friend's explanation.
     b. watch a demonstration.

Part Two

_____ 8. I prefer to
     a. work with facts and details.
     b. construct theories and ideas.

_____ 9. I would prefer a job involving
     a. following specific instructions.
     b. reading, writing, and analyzing.

_____ 10. I prefer to
     a. solve math problems using a formula.
     b. discover why the formula works.

_____ 11. I would prefer to write a term paper explaining
     a. how a process works.
     b. a theory.

_____ 12. I prefer tasks that require me to
     a. follow careful, detailed instructions.
     b. use reasoning and critical analysis.

_____ 13. For a criminal justice course, I would prefer to
     a. discover how and when a law can be used.
     b. learn how and why it became law.

_____ 14. To learn more about the operation of a high-speed computer
printer, I would prefer to
     a. work with several types of printers.
     b. understand the principles on which they operate.

Part Three

_____15. To solve a math problem, I would prefer to
    a. draw or visualize the problem.
    b. study a sample problem and use it as a model.

_____16. To best remember something, I
    a. create a mental picture.
    b. write it down.

_____17. Assembling a bicycle from a diagram would be
    a. easy.
    b. challenging.

_____18. I prefer classes in which I
    a. handle equipment or work with models.
    b. participate in a class discussion.

_____19. To understand and remember how a machine works, I would
    a. draw a diagram.
    b. write notes.

_____20. I enjoy
    a. drawing or working with my hands.
    b. speaking, writing, and listening.

_____21. If I were trying to locate an office on an unfamiliar campus, I would prefer
    a. a map.
    b. written directions.

Part Four

_____22. For a grade in biology lab, I would prefer to
    a. work with a lab partner.
    b. work alone.

_____23. When faced with a difficult personal problem I prefer to
    a. discuss it with others.
    b. resolve it myself.

_____24. Many instructors could improve their classes by
    a. including more discussion and group activities.
    b. allowing students to work on their own more frequently.

_____25. When listening to a lecture or speaker, I respond more to the
      a. person presenting the idea.
      b. ideas themselves.

_____26. When on a team project, I prefer to
      a. work with several team members.
      b. divide the tasks and complete those assigned to me.

_____27. I prefer to shop and do errands
      a. with friends.
      b. by myself.

_____28. A job in a busy office is
      a. more appealing than working alone.
      b. less appealing than working alone.

Part Five

_____29. To make decisions I rely on
      a. my experiences and gut feelings.
      b. facts and objective data.

_____30. To complete a task, I
      a. can use whatever is available to get the job done.
      b. must have everything I need at hand.

_____31. I prefer to express my ideas and feelings through
      a. music, song, or poetry.
      b. direct, concise language.

_____32. I prefer instructors who
      a. allow students to be guided by their own interests.
      b. make their expectations clear and explicit.

_____33. I tend to
      a. challenge and question what I hear and read.
      b. accept what I hear and read.

_____34. I prefer
      a. essay exams.
      b. objective exams.

_____35. In completing an assignment, I prefer to
     a. figure out my own approach.
     b. be told exactly what to do.

To score your questionnaire, record the total number of *a*'s you selected and the total number of *b*'s for each part of the questionnaire. Record your totals in the scoring grid provided below.

Scoring Grid

Parts	Choice A Total	Choice B Total
Part One	_____ Auditory	_____ Visual
Part Two	_____ Applied	_____ Conceptual
Part Three	_____ Spatial	_____ Verbal
Part Four	_____ Social	_____ Independent
Part Five	_____ Creative	_____ Pragmatic

Now, circle your higher score for each part of the questionnaire. The word below the score you circled indicates a strength of your learning style. The next section explains how to interpret your scores.

Interpreting Your Scores

The questionnaire was divided into five parts; each part identifies one aspect of your learning style. Each of these five aspects is explained below.

Part One: Auditory or Visual Learners This score indicates whether you learn better by listening (auditory) or by seeing (visual). If you have a higher score on auditory than visual, you tend to be an auditory learner. That is, you tend to learn more easily by hearing than by reading. A higher score in visual suggests strengths with visual modes of learning—reading, studying pictures, reading diagrams, and so forth.

Part Two: Applied or Conceptual Learners This score describes the types of learning tasks and learning situations you prefer and find easiest to handle. If you are an applied learner, you prefer tasks that involve real objects and situations. Practical, real-life examples are ideal for you. If you are a conceptual learner, you prefer to work with language and ideas; you do not need practical applications for understanding.

Part Three: Spatial or Nonspatial Learners   This score reveals your ability to work with spatial relationships. Spatial learners are able to visualize or mentally see how things work or how they are positioned in space. Their strengths may include drawing, assembling, or repairing things. Nonspatial learners lack skills in positioning things in space. Instead they rely on verbal or language skills.

Part Four: Social or Independent Learners   This score reveals whether you like to work alone or with others. If you are a social learner, you prefer to work with others—both classmates and instructors—closely and directly. You tend to be people-oriented and enjoy personal interaction. If you are an independent learner, you prefer to work alone and study alone. You tend to be self-directed or self-motivated and often goal oriented.

Part Five: Creative or Pragmatic Learners   This score describes the approach you prefer to take toward learning tasks. Creative learners are imaginative and innovative. They prefer to learn through discovery or experimentation. They are comfortable taking risks and following hunches. Pragmatic learners are practical, logical, and systematic. They seek order and are comfortable following rules.

If you disagree with any part of the Learning Style Questionnaire, go with your own instincts, rather than the questionnaire results. The questionnaire is just a quick assessment; trust your knowledge of yourself in areas of dispute.

Developing a Learning Action Plan

Now that you know more about *how* you learn, you are ready to develop an action plan for learning what you read. Suppose you discovered that you are an auditory learner. You still have to read your assignments, which is a visual task. However, to learn the assignment you should translate the material into an auditory form. For example, you could repeat aloud, using your own words, information that you want to remember, or you could tape record key information and play it back. If you also are a social learner, you could work with a classmate, testing each other out loud. Such activities not only translate ideas from visual to auditory form, but also give you practice in internal dialogue (see p. 78).

■ ■ ■ ■ ■
TABLE 5-3
Learning Styles and Reading/Learning Strategies

If your learning style is . . .	*Then the reading/learning strategies to use are . . .*
Auditory	• discuss/study with friends • talk aloud when studying • tape record self-testing questions and answers
Visual	• draw diagrams, charts, tables (Chapter 10) • try to visualize events • use films, videos, when available • use computer-assisted instruction if available
Applied	• think of practical situations to which learning applies • associate ideas with their application • use case studies, examples, and applications to cue your learning
Conceptual	• organize materials that lack order • use outlining (Chapter 11) • focus on organizational patterns (Chapter 8)
Spatial	• use mapping (Chapter 11) • use outlining (Chapter 11) • draw diagrams, make charts, and sketches • use visualization
Verbal	• translate diagrams and drawings into language • record steps, processes, procedures in words • write summaries (Chapter 11) • write your interpretation next to textbook drawings, maps, graphics
Social	• form study groups • find a study partner • interact with instructor • work with a tutor
Independent	• use computer-assisted instruction, if available • purchase review workbooks or study guides if available
Creative	• ask and answer questions • record your own ideas in margins of textbooks
Pragmatic	• study in an organized environment • write lists of steps, procedures and processes • paraphrase difficult material (Chapter 6)

Table 5-3 lists each aspect of learning style and offers suggestions for how to learn from a reading assignment. To use the table

1. Circle the five aspects of your learning style in which you received higher scores. Disregard the others.
2. Read through the suggestions that apply to you.
3. Place a checkmark in front of suggestions that you think will work for you. Choose at least one from each category.
4. List the suggestions that you chose in the box labeled Action Plan for Learning.

ACTION PLAN FOR LEARNING

Learning Strategy 1. _____

_____

Learning Strategy 2. _____

_____

Learning Strategy 3. _____

_____

Learning Strategy 4. _____

_____

Learning Strategy 5. _____

_____

Learning Strategy 6. _____

_____

In the Action Plan for Learning box you listed four or more suggestions to help you learn what you read. The next step is to experiment with these techniques, one at a time. (You may need to refer to chapters listed in parentheses in Table 5-3 to learn or review how a certain technique works.) Use one technique for a while, then move to the next. Continue using the techniques that seem to work; work on revising or modifying those that do not. Do not hesitate to experiment with other techniques listed in the table as well. You may find other techniques that work well for you.

Developing Strategies to Overcome Limitations

You should also work on developing styles in which you are weak. Your learning style is not fixed or unchanging. You can improve areas in which you scored lower. Although you may be weak in auditory learning, for example, many of your professors will lecture and expect you to take notes. If you work on improving your listening and notetaking skills, you can learn to handle lectures effectively. Make a conscious effort to work on improving areas of weakness as well as taking advantage of your strengths.

DIRECTIONS: *For each learning strategy you listed in your Action Plan for Learning, write a brief evaluation of the strategy. Explain which worked; which, if any, did not; and what changes you have noticed in your ability to learn from reading.*

■■■■■■■■ WORKING TOGETHER

Directions: Bring to class a difficult paragraph or brief excerpt. Working in groups, each group member reads each piece and then together (1) discuss why the material was difficult and (2) compare negative and positive signals they received (refer to Table 5-1). Each student then selects strategies to overcome their difficulties.

■■■■■■■ SUMMARY

What is previewing?	Previewing is a method of discovering what an article will be about and how it will be organized before reading it.
What does monitoring your comprehension mean?	It means keeping track of your comprehension as you read and deciding whether or not you are understanding what you are reading.
How can you monitor or keep track of your comprehension?	There are four monitoring strategies you can use. They are:

1. Establishing checkpoints

2. Using guide questions

3. Asking connections questions

4. Using Internal dialogue

What is learning style?	Learning style refers to your profile of relative strengths as a learner. Its five components are:

1. Auditory or visual learner

2. Applied or conceptual learner

3. Spatial or verbal learner

4. Social or independent learner

5. Creative or pragmatic learner

Making Your Skills Work Together

Part Two focused on techniques to help you read actively—to get involved with what you are reading. In Chapter 4 you learned five techniques to use before you read to build your comprehension. In Chapter 5 you learned to monitor your comprehension and to take action when it is poor or incomplete. Now let's apply these skills and see how together they affect your comprehension.

EXERCISE 1

DIRECTIONS: *Read the following article on testing the effectiveness of advertising. Use the following steps.*

1. Assess your attitude. Are you approaching this assignment as busywork or are you doing it to learn how the skills in Chapters 4 and 5 work together?

2. Assess where you are working. Are your surroundings conducive to concentration? Set a time limit for the completion of this assignment.

3. Preview the article.

4. Activate what you already know about advertising. What makes it effective?

5. Develop three to four guide questions and write them below:

   a. _____

   b. _____

   c. _____

   d. _____

6. Read the article and monitor your comprehension.

7. Answer each of your guide questions.

   a. _____

   b. _____

c. _____

d. _____

8. Use the following questions to evaluate how well you monitored your compre-
    hension and how well you understood the article.

    a. Why do some advertisers want to test an ad's effectiveness?

    b. Why do other advertisers say it is unnecessary to test ads?

    c. Explain each of the five testing procedures described in the reading.

9. Taking into account your learning style, what strategies would you use to learn
    this material?

Measuring Advertising Effectiveness

While it is difficult to approach the creative component of advertising scientif-
ically, the amount of money involved in an ad's production and the cost of
the media time still require that this process be subject to research evaluation.
A 30-second television commercial costs about $75,000 to produce. Ads us-
ing special effects can cost far more than that. Some advertising agencies
have begun using personal computers and commercial software to produce
"rough" versions of ads. This approach can save a client thousands of dollars
over the traditional approach of having a production house produce several
interim versions of an advertisement. Despite such innovations, however, ad
production is still expensive. Media time is equally expensive. A 30-second
spot on the Super Bowl in 1994 cost advertisers $900,000!
Despite these costs, some advertisers argue that it is inappropriate or unnecessary to attempt to measure the effectiveness of advertising. The cost of testing, the imprecise nature of available testing methods, and the time it requires have all been cited as reasons not to test. Even determining what to
test can be a problem. Finally, some advertisers believe that testing stifles the
creative process.
    While there may be some truth to these concerns, we take the position
that good advertisers put considerable effort into testing an ad's effectiveness. Though measuring advertising effectiveness is important, what constitutes a good test of effectiveness is not always clear. First and foremost, any
test of effectiveness should attempt to measure the extent to which the ad
succeeded in accomplishing its objectives. This seems obvious, but many
times ads have been judged ineffective when sales did not rise despite the
fact that the ad was intended to build interest, liking, or desire.

Testing Methods

Ads may be tested at any one of a number of stages—as a concept, as a set of rough drawings, or as a finished ad, both before and after media exposure. An ad is pretested if the test occurs before media dollars are committed; tests after commitment of funds are designated as post-tests.

Pretesting. Several testing procedures are available for this stage.

- *Focus-group interviews.* In this procedure, about six to ten target audience consumers are brought together with a group leader. They are then exposed to an ad or a part of an ad. The leader encourages group members to interact and asks probing questions about the ad. What do they understand from the ad? Does it interest them? Do they believe it? Would they try the product? This technique is most commonly used when an ad is being developed.
- *Folio tests.* This procedure takes place at the consumer's home. An interviewer shows the consumer a loose-leaf binder containing the test ad and others and asks the consumer to look through the ads, noting what he or she remembers or finds interesting. This technique is designed exclusively for testing print ads, usually when the ad is in a finished or nearly finished form. It measures an ad's attention-getting abilities. In addition, it provides insights into motivational and comprehensibility aspects and measures potential attitude changes.
- *In-home projector tests.* A rough or finished version of a television commercial is shown, in a consumer's home, as part of a short sequence from a television program or film. This procedure does not measure attention-getting aspects, but it does give a measure of comprehension, motivation, credibility, and possible consumer attitude change, if attitude measures are taken before and after the ads are shown.
- *Trailer tests.* Trailer tests are less expensive ways to evaluate television commercials. A trailer is parked in a shopping center parking lot, and people are asked to take part in a marketing research study. They are put in a waiting room with magazines and a television set. The set shows a closed circuit version of a prerecorded program in which the test ad is aired. The subject is then interviewed to determine the attention-getting impact of the ad, plus comprehension, credibility, and motivation. Alternatively, respondents may be shown an ad directly and asked for their reactions, but this procedure would not yield information about the attention-getting aspect of the ad.
- *Theater tests.* An audience is recruited to view a few test television programs. On arrival the participants fill out questionnaires about their opinions and preferences for the product categories and brands of interest. Then they see television shows into which the relevant commercials have been inserted. Following this, they complete another questionnaire. Comparing the before and after questionnaires gives measures of attention-getting power, credibility, motivation, and preference.

PART 3 *Comprehension Skills*

James was taking a business management course and was finding the textbook hard to understand. After receiving a grade of C- on the first exam, he decided to talk to his instructor. James began by explaining that he found the text difficult and felt this was his major problem in the course. He said that he spent several hours reading and rereading each chapter, but still didn't feel as if he knew the material.

When he finished, his instructor said: "Many students have the same problem, especially during their first semester. You're right. The textbook *is* difficult, but it's a good sign that you're concerned." Then she suggested these three helpful strategies: (1) Take the time to decipher difficult sentences, (2) be sure to identify and underline the main idea of each paragraph, and (3) pay attention to how the author organizes ideas. This will help you stay with the text and remember what you read.

The purpose of this part of the book is to explain these three strategies so that you will be able to understand the textbooks you are using.

THIS PART OF THE TEXT WILL HELP YOU

1. Read complicated sentences more easily
2. Understand how paragraphs are structured (Chapters 6 and 7)
3. Become familiar with the various organizational patterns that writers commonly use (Chapter 8)

Understanding and Paraphrasing Sentences

■ ■

THIS CHAPTER WILL SHOW YOU HOW TO

1. *Identify the parts of a sentence that express its basic meaning*
2. *Recognize sentences that combine ideas*
3. *Read complicated sentences*

■ ■

Suppose you read the following sentence in a United States government textbook:

> The president is the party's leader, not by any authority of the Constitution, whose authors abhorred parties, but by strong tradition and practical necessity.

Try to explain what this sentence means. The real test of whether you understand an idea is whether you can express it in your own words.

Basically, the sentence explains why the president is the leader of his or her political party. Although less important, the sentence also explains that this is not a rule stated in the Constitution. Finally, the sentence contains the additional information that the authors of the Constitution abhorred, or hated, political parties.

Now let us look at how you might have arrived at this meaning. Answer each of the following questions:

1. Did you search for the most important information in the sentence?
2. Did you try to discover how various parts of the sentence were connected?
3. Did you check the meaning of any unfamiliar words such as *abhorred*?
4. Did you put the meaning of the sentence in your own words?

If you answered "yes" to each of these questions, you are well on your way to reading sentences effectively. Together, these questions suggest a four-step approach to sentence reading.

Step 1: Locate the key ideas
Step 2: Study the modifiers
Step 3: Check unknown words
Step 4: Paraphrase, or use your own words to express ideas

This chapter will show you how to find important information in sentences, sort or sift out less important ideas, see how ideas are connected, and paraphrase sentences.

Step 1: Locating Key Ideas

Every sentence expresses at least one key idea, or main point. This main idea is a statement about someone or something. You can identify the main point by finding the subject and the predicate. Both are discussed in more detail below.

Finding the Subject and Predicate

Every sentence is made up of at least two parts, a simple subject and a simple predicate. The **simple subject,** often a noun, identifies the person or object the sentence is about. The main part of the predicate—the **simple predicate**—is a verb, which tells what the person or object is doing or has done. Usually a sentence contains additional information about the subject and/or the predicate.

Example:

The average <u>American</u> <u>consumed</u> six gallons of beer last year.

The key idea of this sentence is "American consumed." It is expressed by the simple subject and simple predicate. The simple subject of this sentence is *American;* it explains who the sentence is about. The words *the* and *average* give more information about the subject, American, by explaining which one. The main part of the predicate is the verb *consumed;* this tells what the average American did. The rest of the sentence gives more information about the verb by telling what (beer) and how much (six gallons last year) was consumed. Here are a few more examples:

The <u>ship</u> <u>entered</u> the harbor early this morning.

<u>Lilacs</u> <u>bloom</u> in the spring.

<u>Jeff</u> <u>cooks</u> dinner for the family every night.

In many long and complicated sentences, the key idea is not as obvious as in the previous examples. To find the key idea, ask these questions:

1. Who or what is the sentence about?
2. What is happening in the sentence?

Here is an example of a complicated sentence that might be found in a psychology textbook:

Intelligence, as measured by IQ, depends on the kind of test given, the skill of the examiner, and the cooperation of the subject.

In this sentence, the answer to the question, "Who or what is the sentence about?" is *intelligence.* The verb is *depends,* and the remainder of the sentence explains the factors upon which intelligence depends. Let us look at a few more examples:

<u>William James</u>, often thought of as the father of American psychology, <u>tested</u> whether memory could be improved by exercising it.

<u>Violence</u> in sports, both at amateur and professional levels, <u>has</u> <u>increased</u> dramatically over the past ten years.

Some sentences may have more than one subject and/or more than one verb in the predicate.

Example:

subject   subject
Poor <u>diet</u> and <u>lack</u> of exercise can cause weight gain.

verb   verb
My brother always <u>worries</u> and <u>complains</u> about his job.

subject subject verb verb
Many <u>homes</u> and <u>businesses</u> <u>are</u> <u>burglarized</u> or <u>vandalized</u> each year.

subject verb verb verb
The angry <u>customer</u> <u>was screaming</u>, <u>cursing</u>, and <u>shouting</u>.

DIRECTIONS: *Find the key idea in each of the following sentences. Draw one line under the subject and two lines under the verb.*

Example: The <u>instructor</u> <u><u>assigned</u></u> a fifteen-page article to read.

1. Every summer my parents travel to the eastern seacoast.

2. Children learn how to behave by imitating adults.

3. William Faulkner, a popular American author, wrote about life in the South.

4. Psychologists are interested in studying human behavior in many different situations.

5. Terminally ill patients may refuse to take their prescribed medication.

6. The use of cocaine, although illegal, is apparently increasing.

7. The most accurate method we have of estimating the age of the earth is based on our knowledge of radioactivity.

8. Elements exist either as compounds or as free elements.

9. Attention may be defined as a focusing of perception.

10. The specific instructions in a computer program are written in a computer language.

Finding Combined Ideas Within A Sentence

Sentences always express at least one complete idea. However, a sentence may combine several ideas. Two common types of sentences combine ideas:

1. Coordinate Sentences
2. Subordinate Sentences

Each type gives you clues about how the ideas are connected and whether one is more important than the other.

Coordinate Sentences Coordinate sentences express ideas that are equally important. They got that name because they coordinate, or tie together, two or more ideas. This is done for three reasons: (1) to emphasize the relationship between ideas, (2) to indicate their equal importance, and/or (3) to make the material more concise and easier to read. In the following example notice how two related ideas can be combined.

Two related ideas:

1. Marlene was in obvious danger.
2. Joe quickly pulled Marlene from the street

Combined sentence:

Marlene was in obvious danger, and Joe quickly pulled her from the street.

In this case the combined sentence establishes that the two equally important events are parts of a single incident.

As you read coordinate sentences, be sure to locate both subjects and predicates. If you do not read carefully or if you are reading too fast, you might miss the second idea. Often you can recognize a sentence that combines two or more ideas by its structure and punctuation. Coordinate ideas are combined in one of two ways:

1. Use a semicolon.

    The union members wanted to strike; the company did nothing to discourage them.

2. Use a comma and one of the following words: *and, or, but, nor, so, for, yet* these words are called coordinating conjunctions. See Table 6-1 for the meaning clues each provides.

    Some students decided to take the final exam, *and* others chose to rely on their semester average.

    The students wanted the instructor to cancel the class, *but* the instructor decided to reschedule it.

Subordinate Sentences Subordinate sentences contain one key idea and one or more less important, or subordinate, ideas that explain the key idea. These less important ideas each have their own subject and predicate, but they depend on the main sentence to complete their meaning. For example, in the following sentence you cannot understand fully the meaning of the underlined portion until you read the entire sentence.

<u>Because Stewart forgot to make a payment</u>, he had to pay a late charge on his loan.

In this sentence, the more important idea is that Stewart had to pay a late charge since that portion of the sentence could stand alone as a complete sentence. The

■ ■■ ■

TABLE 6-1
The Meaning of Coordinating Conjunctions

Coordinating Conjunctions	Meaning Clues	Example
and	links similar and equally important ideas	Jim is in my biology class, <u>and</u> Pierce is in my psychology class.
but, yet	connects opposite ideas or change in thought	Professor Clark gave a homework assignment, <u>yet</u> she did not collect it.
for, so	indicates reasons or shows that one thing is causing another	Most English majors in our college take a foreign language, <u>for</u> it is a requirement.
or, nor	suggests choice or options	We could make a fire in the fireplace, <u>or</u> we could get out some extra blankets.

reason for the late charge is presented as background information that amplifies and further explains the basic message.

As you read subordinate sentences, be sure to notice the relationship between the two ideas. The less important idea may describe or explain a condition, cause, reason, purpose, time, or place set out in the more important idea. Here are a few additional examples of sentences that relate two or more ideas. In each the base idea is underlined and the function of the less important idea is indicated in parentheses above it.

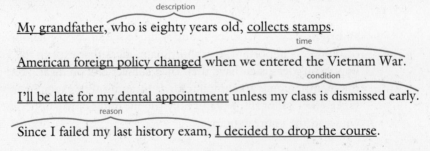

description
<u>My grandfather</u>, who is eighty years old, <u>collects stamps</u>.

time
<u>American foreign policy changed</u> when we entered the Vietnam War.

condition
<u>I'll be late for my dental appointment</u> unless my class is dismissed early.

reason
Since I failed my last history exam, <u>I decided to drop the course</u>.

Notice that if the subordinate idea comes first in the sentence, a comma follows it. If the key, complete idea comes first, a comma is not used.

As you read subordinate sentences, pay attention to the connecting word used. It should signal the relationship of ideas. You must be sure to pick up the

■ ■ ■ ■ ■

TABLE 6-2
The Meaning of Subordinating Conjunctions

Subordinating Conjunctions	Meaning Clues	Example
before, after, while, during, until, when, once	indicates time	<u>After</u> taking the test, Leon felt relieved.
because, since, so that	gives reasons	<u>Because</u> I was working, I was unable to go bowling.
if, unless, whether, even if	explains conditions	<u>Unless</u> I leave work early, I'll miss class.
although, as far as, in order to, however	explains circumstance	<u>Although</u> I used a dictionary, I still did not fully understand the word.

signal. You should know *why* the two ideas have been combined and *what* they have to do with each other. Table 6-2 lists some common connecting words, called subordinating conjunctions, and tells you what each signals.

EXERCISE 6-2

DIRECTIONS: *Read each of the following sentences. In the space provided describe how the underlined idea is related to the rest of the sentence. For example, does it indicate time, give reasons, or explain a condition or circumstance?*

1. I will probably transfer to a four-year school next year <u>unless I find a good job.</u>

   _____

2. <u>Although I broke my leg,</u> I am still able to drive a car.

   _____

3. Peter will become a truck driver, unless <u>he decides to go back to school for further training.</u>

   _____

4. She always picks up her mail <u>after she eats lunch.</u>

   _____

5. Since Arturio was a student, he was not drafted to go to Vietnam.

   _____

6. Since the corporation is community-oriented, it donates large amounts to local charities.

   _____

7. Because violence is regularly shown on television, children accept it as an ordinary part of life.

   _____

8. As far as scientists can tell from available research, some types of cancer may be caused by a virus.

   _____

9. Because a vaccine was developed, polio has practically been eliminated.

   _____

10. Since comparison shopping is a necessary part of the buying process, wise consumers look for differences in quality as well as price.

   _____

EXERCISE 6-3

DIRECTIONS: *Complete each of the following sentences by supplying a complete thought. Pay close attention to the connecting word.*

1. Because I ran out of time on my exam _____

2. After I took my psychology exam _____

3. Although the library is open weekends _____

4. Unless I get an "A" on my next paper in English _____

5. After a car runs out of gas _____

6. The poverty rate in the United States is low, but _____

7. Bad eating habits have been found to lead to cancer, so _____

8. Handguns may be made illegal, or _____

9. China has agreed to limit nuclear weapons, and _____

10. People have become very health conscious, yet _____

EXERCISE 6-4

DIRECTIONS: *Read each of the following and decide whether it is a coordinate or a subordinate sentence. Mark* C *in the space to the left if the sentence is coordinate and underline both sets of subjects and predicates. Mark* S *if it is subordinate, and underline the more important idea.*

_____ 1. The personnel office eagerly accepted my application for a job, and I expect to receive an offer next week.

_____ 2. Since it is difficult to stop smoking, the individual who wants to quit may find group therapy effective.

_____ 3. Birth control is interference with the natural rhythms of reproduction; some individuals object to it on this basis.

_____ 4. Computers have become part of our daily lives, but their role in today's college classrooms has not yet been fully explored.

_____ 5. Marriage consists of shared experiences and ambitions, and both are influenced by the values of each partner.

_____ 6. As far as we can tell from historical evidence, humankind has inhabited this earth for several million years.

_____ 7. Because sugar is Cuba's main export, the Cuban economy depends upon the worldwide demand for sugar.

_____ 8. The personnel manager who accepted my application is well known for interviewing all likely candidates.

_____ 9. Even though a feather and a brick will fall equally fast in a vacuum, they fall quite differently in the presence of air.

_____ 10. We never learn anything in a vacuum; we are always having other experiences before and after we learn new material.

Step 2: Studying Modifiers

After you have identified the key ideas, the next step in understanding a sentence is to see how the modifiers affect its meaning. **Modifiers** are words that change, describe, qualify, or limit meaning of another word or sentence part. Most modifiers either add to or change the meaning of the key idea. Usually they answer such questions about the subject or predicate as what, where, which, when, how, or why. For example:

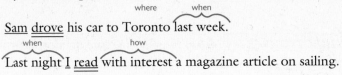

Sam drove his car to Toronto last week.

Last night I read with interest a magazine article on sailing.

As you read a sentence, be sure to notice how the details change, limit, or add to the meaning of the key idea. Decide, for each of the following examples, how the underlined portion affects the meaning of the key idea.

Maria took her dog to the pond yesterday.

Recently, I selected with great care a wedding gift for my sister.

The older Cadillac with the convertible top belongs to my husband.

In the first example, the underlined detail explains *when* Maria took her dog to the pond. In the second example, the underlined words tell *how* the gift was selected. In the last example, the underlined phrase indicates *which* Cadillac.

EXERCISE 6-5

DIRECTIONS: *Read each of the following sentences. Circle the subject and predicate, and decide what the underlined part of the sentence tells about the key idea. Write* which, when, where, how, *or* why *in the space provided.*

1. You can relieve tension through exercise. _____

2. The English instructor who teaches a modern fiction course expects students to submit plot summaries. _____

3. Many students in computer science courses can use the computer terminals only late at night. _____

4. Many shoppers clip coupons to reduce their grocery bills. _____

---

5. <u>After class</u> I am going to talk to my instructor. _____

6. Astronomers have learned about stars and galaxies <u>by analyzing radiation they emit.</u> _____

7. The world's oil supply is concentrated <u>in only a few places around the globe.</u>

8. Light <u>traveling through empty space</u> will move in a straight line. _____

9. Cobalt, <u>essential for the manufacture of jet aircraft engines,</u> is a valuable resource. _____

10. Ebbinghaus, <u>one of psychology's pioneers,</u> studied learning and memory processes. _____

Step 3: Checking Unfamiliar Vocabulary

If a word (or words) interferes with your comprehension of the sentence, you will need to figure out its meaning. Try the following steps until you have figured out the word's meaning.

1. *Pronounce it.* Often hearing the word will help you recognize it and recall its meaning.
2. *Use context.* Try to figure out the meaning of the word from the way it is used in a sentence (see Chapter 1 for specific techniques). In the following sentence, you can figure out the meaning of *nonverbal communication* from context.

   Nonverbal communication, or communication using the body rather than words, can be easily misinterpreted.

   Here nonverbal means "communication using the body rather than words."
3. *Analyze word parts.* Look for prefixes, roots, and suffixes that you are familiar with (refer to Chapter 2). In the following sentence word parts can help you figure out the meaning of *misdiagnosis.*

   The lawsuit was based on the doctor's misdiagnosis of the patient's symptoms.

   mis = wrong
   diagnose = to identify a disease

misdiagnosis = incorrect identification of a disease

4. **Check the glossary.** Many textbooks include glossaries to define words used in that particular subject matter.
5. **Check the dictionary.** Some words do have several meanings. Be sure to find the meaning that fits the way the word is used in the sentence you are working with.

DIRECTIONS: *Read each of the following paragraphs and determine the meaning of each underlined word. Write a brief definition or synonym in the space provided.*

1. A <u>rumor</u> is an <u>unverified</u> story that is spread from one person to another. As the story is <u>circulating</u>, each person <u>distorts</u> the account by dropping some items and adding his or her own interpretation. But a rumor is not necessarily false. It may turn out to be true. It is unverified *not* because it is necessarily a <u>distortion</u> but because people do not bother to check it against facts.[1]

   a. rumor _____

   b. unverified _____

   c. circulating _____

   d. distorts _____

   e. distortion _____

2. Compared with crowds, fashions are more subject to traditional norms. Practically all aspects of human life—clothes, hairstyles, architecture, philosophy, and the arts—are influenced by fashions. A <u>fashion</u> is a great though brief enthusiasm among a relatively large number of people for a particular <u>innovation</u>. Because their <u>novelty</u> wears off quickly, fashions are very short-lived. Most are related to clothes, but as long as there is something new about any <u>artifact</u> that strikes many people's fancy, it can become a fashion.[2]

   a. fashion _____

   b. innovation _____

   c. novelty _____

   d. artifact _____

Step 4: Paraphrasing

Paraphrasing means putting an author's thoughts in your own words. Paraphrasing is the true test of whether you have understood an author's ideas. It provides a useful way to figure out what difficult and confusing sentences mean and it helps you remember what you read. By taking time with and thinking through an idea in order to paraphrase it, you'll find you'll be able to remember it.

Paraphrasing involves two skills:

1. Using synonyms (words that mean the same thing) to replace the author's words
2. Rearranging the order of ideas

Substituting Synonyms

A **synonym** is a word that has the same general meaning as another word. The following pairs of words are synonyms:

ruin—destroy	rich—affluent
rough—harsh	repeat—reiterate
real—actual	quibble—nit-pick

Now, let's try substituting synonyms in a sentence from the U.S. Constitution:

The Congress shall have power to . . . regulate commerce with foreign nations, and among the several States and with the Indian tribes. . . .

Notice how the following underlined synonyms have been substituted.

Congress is <u>allowed</u> to <u>control</u> <u>trade</u> with foreign <u>countries</u>, among states, and with Indian tribes.

When selecting synonyms use the following guidelines.

1. **Choose words close in meaning to the original**.

   Prehistoric people worshipped animate objects.

The words *living, alive,* and *vital* are synonyms for *animate,* but in the previous sentence, *living* is closest in meaning to *animate.*

2. **Make sure the synonym you choose fits the context (overall meaning) of the sentence.**

   The physician attempted to *neutralize* the effects of the drug overdose.

   All the following words are synonyms for *neutralize: negate, nullify, counteract.* However, *counteract* fits the context, while *negate* and *nullify* do not. *Negate* and *nullify* suggest the ability to cancel, and a drug overdose, once taken, cannot be canceled. It can, however, be *counteracted.*

3. **Use a dictionary, if necessary.** If you get stuck, check a dictionary. You don't have to replace every word in a sentence with a synonym. Often, the word the author used is the clearest or most accurate word choice.

   A riot is an extended outbreak of *violent behavior.*

   The phrase *violent behavior* clearly and accurately describes what happens in a riot, so it's fine to use that phrase in your paraphrase.

   A riot involves frequent and long-lasting occurrences of violent behavior.

4. When the author is introducing or defining a new term, be sure to use that term in your paraphrase. Specialized terminology is the basic language of a course, and it is often the best and most concise word to use.

   Sentence: A *panic* is characterized by a massive flight from something that is feared.[3]

   Paraphrase: A panic occurs when people run away from something they fear.

EXERCISE 6-7

DIRECTIONS: *Write synonyms above each of the underlined words.*

1. Homeless people are in <u>desperate</u> need of <u>sustenance.</u>

2. The Constitution <u>limits</u> the presidential <u>term</u> of office to four years.

3. The politician's speech, which was full of <u>witticisms,</u> <u>elicited</u> much laughter from the audience.

4. The <u>convivial</u> group of business leaders agreed to <u>establish</u> a <u>consortium</u> to <u>regulate</u> international trade agreements.

5. The musician <u>performed</u> a <u>complex</u> set of musical variations.

Rearranging Sentence Parts, if Necessary

In a paraphrase you often change or rearrange the order of ideas to make the ideas clearer or simpler. Here are a few obvious rearrangements without the use of synonyms:

Last night a robbery occurred.

A robbery occurred last night.

Because the first set of results was inconclusive, the researcher repeated the experiment.

The researcher repeated the experiment because the first set of results was inconclusive.

When rearranging sentence parts, use the following guidelines:

1. Split lengthy, complicated sentences into two or more shorter sentences.

   Lengthy:
   Especially since the rise of television, modern presidents have enhanced their power to shape public opinion, as Reagan did in mobilizing support for his tax and budget cuts in 1981, as Kennedy did when he dramatically called up the reserves during the Berlin crisis in 1961, and as Bush did in building support for the Persian Gulf war.[4]

   Split Paraphrase:
   a. Television has increased the ability of modern presidents to influence public opinion.
   b. Examples of this influence include Reagan building public support for tax and budget reductions in 1981, Kennedy calling up the reserves in 1961 during the Berlin crisis, and Bush shaping public opinion during the Persian Gulf War.

2. Identify the author's key ideas and related ideas; emphasize these in your paraphrase.

   Sentence:
   Some analysts argue that the federal government should provide money to deal with urban problems, because a national solution is possible for such nationwide problems.[5]

   Incomplete paraphrase:
   The federal government should pay for urban problems.

   Correct paraphrase:
   The federal government should pay for urban problems, since national solutions are needed for such widespread problems.

The incomplete paraphrase does not include the reason *why* (a related idea) the federal government should pay for them.

Sentence:

Fads—temporary, highly imitated outbreaks of unconventional behavior—are particularly common in popular music, where the desire to be "different" continually fosters the emergence of new looks and sounds.[6]

Incorrect paraphrase:

Fads are occurrences of nontraditional behaviors that are imitated by others, especially in the field of music.

Correct paraphrase:

Fads are occurrences of nontraditional behavior. Fads are especially common in popular music because the need to set oneself apart from others encourages the development of new looks and sounds.

The incorrect paraphrase does not convey fully the idea of popular music creating fads.

EXERCISE 6-8

DIRECTIONS: *Read each of the following sentences. Using the procedure suggested in this chapter, paraphrase each sentence.*

1. There has been an increase in female sports participation since the early 1970s.

   _____

   _____

2. A distinction still exists between what are traditionally considered to be male and female sports.

   _____

   _____

3. Two primary motivations for shoplifting are being poor or unemployed and desiring fashionable clothes like those worn by peers.

   _____

   _____

4. The right of citizens of the United States, who are 18 years of age or older, to vote shall not be denied or abridged by the United States or any state on account of age. (Amendment XXIV to the U.S. Constitution)

_____

_____

5. In armed robberies, potential violence—violence that is rarely carried out—enables the robber to achieve his or her material goal, usually money.

_____

_____

6. There are two opposing views of what constitutes mental illness. The medical view holds that mental illness is biological, similar to a physical disease, while the psychosocial view defines mental illness as an emotional problem.

_____

_____

7. In trying to identify the causes of problem drinking, some researchers have stressed the role of genetic factors, while others have viewed it as an inability to adjust to the stress of life.

_____

_____

8. Much of the progress has been effected by the Supreme Court, but the Court has mainly done this, we have found, when it was pushed by popular pressures: elections, public opinion, civil liberties and civil rights organizations, and social movements.

_____

_____

9. Organized crime is not unique to contemporary America: in the last century, there were already a number of criminal groups in other parts of the world, including the Thugs of India, who were well known for killing travelers for possessions, and the Assassins in the Middle East, who held a reputation for murdering Christians.[7]

_____

_____

10. American history has witnessed an expansion of the boundaries of rights and liberties, especially during the present century, though much remains to be achieved.

_____

_____

■■■■■■■ WORKING TOGETHER

Directions: Bring a difficult sentence to class. Working in groups, each group member should write a statement to paraphrase each sentence.

■■■■■■■ SUMMARY

What are the four steps in understanding complicated sentences?

Understanding difficult sentences involves four steps:

Step 1: Locate key ideas

Step 2: Study the modifiers

Step 3: Check unknown words

Step 4: Paraphrase

Explain the terms *subject* and *predicate*.

The *subject* of a sentence is usually a noun that identifies the person or object that the sentence is about. The *predicate* of a sentence tells what the person or object is doing, has done, or will do.

Explain the two common types of sentences that combine ideas. How are the ideas connected?

Coordinate sentences express two ideas that are equally important. They are connected by using a semicolon or a comma and a coordinating conjunction. Subordinate sentences contain one key idea and at least one less important subordinate idea. They are connected with a comma if the subordinating idea appears first in the sentence.

What steps should you follow in figuring out the meaning of an unknown word?	1. Pronounce it.
	2. Use context.
	3. Analyze word parts.
	4. Check the glossary.
	5. Check the dictionary.
How do you paraphrase a sentence?	1. Substitute synonyms (words that have the same general meaning as another word).
	2. Rearrange sentence parts, if needed. Split lengthy sentences into two or more shorter sentences. Identify the author's key ideas and related ideas and emphasize these in your paraphrase.

Understanding Paragraphs

■ ▪ ■ ▪ ■ ▪ ■ ▪ ■ ▪ ■ ▪ ■ ▪ ■ ▪ ■ ▪ ■ ▪ ■ ▪ ■ ▪ ■ ▪ ■ ▪ ■

THIS CHAPTER WILL SHOW YOU HOW TO

1. *Identify main ideas in paragraphs*
2. *Pick out the key details*
3. *Use transitions to make reading easier*

■ ▪ ■ ▪ ■ ▪ ■ ▪ ■ ▪ ■ ▪ ■ ▪ ■ ▪ ■ ▪ ■ ▪ ■ ▪ ■ ▪ ■ ▪ ■ ▪ ■

When you plan to go to see a movie, the first thing you ask is: "What is it about?" As the movie begins, various characters interact. To understand this interaction, you have to know who the characters are and understand what they are saying. Then you have to note how the characters relate to one another. To grasp the point the film is making, you have to realize what all the conversations and action, taken together, mean.

Understanding a paragraph is similar. The first thing you need to know is what the paragraph is about. Then you have to understand each of the sentences and what it is saying. Next, you have to see how the sentences relate to one another. Finally, to understand the main point of the paragraph, you have to consider what all the sentences, taken together, mean.

The one subject the whole paragraph is about is called the **topic.** The point that the whole paragraph makes is called the **main idea.** The sentences that explain the main idea are called **details.** To connect their ideas, writers use words and phrases known as **transitions.**

A paragraph, then, is a group of related sentences about a single topic. It has four essential parts: (1) topic, (2) main idea, (3) details, and (4) transitions. To read paragraphs most efficiently, you will need to become familiar with each part of a paragraph and be able to identify and use these parts as you read.

General and Specific Ideas

To identify topics and main ideas in paragraphs, it will help you to understand the difference between **general** and **specific.** A general idea is a broad idea that applies to a large number of individual items. The term *clothing* is general because it refers to a large collection of individual items—pants, suits, blouses, shirts, scarves, and so on. A specific idea or term is more detailed or particular. It refers to an individual item. The word *scarf*, for example, is a particular term. The phrase *red plaid scarf* is even more specific.

Examples:

General: pies
Specific: chocolate cream
apple
cherry

General: countries
Specific: Great Britain
Finland
Brazil

General: fruit
Specific: grapes
lemons
pineapples

General: types of context clues
Specific: definition
example
contrast

General: word parts
Specific: prefix
root
suffix

DIRECTIONS: *Read each of the following items and decide what term(s) will complete the group. Write the word(s) in the spaces provided.*

1. General: college courses

    Specific: math

    _____

    _____

    _____

2. General: _____

    Specific: roses

    tulips

    narcissus

3. General: musical groups

    Specific: _____

    _____

    _____

4. General: art

    Specific: sculpture

    _____

    _____

    _____

5. General: types of movies

    Specific: comedies

    _____

    _____

EXERCISE 7-2

DIRECTIONS: *Underline the most general term in each group of words.*

1. pounds, ounces, kilograms, weights

2. soda, coffee, beverage, wine

3. soap operas, news, TV programs, sports special

4. home furnishings, carpeting, drapes, wall hangings

5. sociology, social sciences, anthropology, psychology

Now we will apply the idea of general and specific to paragraphs. The main idea is the most general statement the writer makes about the topic. Pick out the most general statement among the following sentences.

1. People differ according to height.
2. Hair color distinguishes some people from others.
3. People differ in a number of ways.
4. Each person has his or her own personality.

Did you choose item 3 as the most general statement? Now we will change this list into a paragraph by rearranging the sentences and adding a few facts.

People differ in numerous ways. They differ according to physical characteristics, such as height, weight, and hair color. They also differ in personality. Some people are friendly and easygoing. Others are more reserved and formal.

In this brief paragraph, the main idea is expressed in the first sentence. This sentence is the most general statement expressed in the paragraph. All the other statements are specific details that explain this main idea.

Identifying the Topic

The **topic** is the subject of the entire paragraph. Every sentence in a paragraph in some way discusses or explains this topic. If you had to choose a title for a paragraph, the one or two words you would choose are the topic.

To find the topic of a paragraph, ask yourself: What is the one thing the author is discussing throughout the paragraph?

Now read the following paragraph with that question in mind:

Flextime, which began in the mid-1960s as an alternative work schedule experiment, will be a fact of life in many industries in the 21st century. We'll work not according to traditional work schedules but according to our biological and emotional rhythms. The night owls among us will be delighted to work the lobster shifts and let the rest of us work during the day. The number of hours worked won't be as significant as what you accomplish when you work. The advantage of flextime is that it permits flexible, cost-effective work arrangements.[1]

In this example, the author is discussing one topic—flextime—throughout the paragraph. Notice that the words *flexible* and *flextime* are used several times. Often the repeated use of a word can serve as a clue to the topic.

**EXERCISE
7-3**

DIRECTIONS: *Read each of the following paragraphs. Write the topic of each paragraph in the space provided.*

1. Discrimination doesn't go away: it just aims at whatever group appears to be out of fashion at any given moment. One expert feels that *age* is the major factor in employment discrimination today, although studies have shown older workers may be more reliable than young workers and just as productive. The Age Discrimination in Employment Act gives protection to the worker between forty and sixty-five. If you're in this age range, your employer must prove that you have performed unsatisfactorily before he can legally fire you. This act also prohibits age discrimination in hiring, wages, and benefits. To report age discrimination, call your local office of the Wage and Hours Division of the U.S. Labor Department, or the Human Relations Commission in your state. If local offices are unable to help, try the national Equal Employment Opportunity Commission, Washington, D.C. 20460.[2]

   Topic:_____

2. Traditionally for men, and increasingly for women, one's job or career is tied in intimately with the way one regards oneself. Thus, loss of job becomes in part a loss of identity, and in part a seeming criticism of oneself as a total being, not merely as a worker. Even people who have lost jobs in mass layoffs through no fault of their own often feel guilty, especially if they are in the role of provider and no longer feel competent in fulfilling that role.[3]

   Topic:_____

3. The words "effortless exercise" are a contradiction in terms. Muscles grow in strength only when subjected to overload. Flexibility is developed only by extending the normal range of body motion. Endurance is developed only through exercise that raises the pulse rate enough to achieve a training effect on the heart, lungs, and circulatory system. In all cases, the benefits from exer-

cise come from extending the body beyond its normal activity range. What this requires is, precisely, effort.[4]

Topic:_____

4. Mental illness is usually diagnosed from abnormal behavior. A woman is asked the time of day, and she begins to rub her arms and recite the Apostles' Creed. A man is so convinced that someone is "out to get him" that he refuses to leave his apartment. Unusual behaviors like these are taken as evidence that the mental apparatus is not working quite right, and mental illness is proclaimed.[5]

Topic:_____

5. How, exactly, does sleep replenish your body's fund of energy? Despite much interesting recent research on sleep, we still don't know. Certainly the metabolic rate slows during sleep (down to a level of about one met). Respiration, heartbeat, and other body functions slow down; muscular and digestive systems slow or cease their activity, allowing time for tissue repair. But the precise mechanisms by which sleep restores and refreshes us remain a mystery.[6]

Topic:_____

Finding the Main Idea

The main idea of a paragraph is the most important idea; it is the idea that the whole paragraph explains or supports. Usually it is expressed in one sentence called the **topic sentence.** To find the main idea, use the following suggestions.

Locate the Topic

You have learned that the topic is the subject of a paragraph. The main idea is the most important thing the author wants you to know about the topic. To find the main idea, ask yourself, "What is the one most important thing to know about the topic?" Read the following paragraph and then answer this question:

The earth's water environments may be classified roughly as fresh water or marine, although not all bodies of water fall neatly into one category or the other. For example, Lake Pontchartrain, near New Orleans, is *brackish,* or a mixture of salt and fresh water. So are *estuaries,* the places where rivers flow into seas. Fresh water has about 0.1 percent salt; seawater has about 3.5 percent salt; and, as we will see, each has its importance in the earth's drama.[7]

In this example, the topic is water classification. The most important point the author is making is that water can be classified as either fresh or marine, although exceptions do exist.

Locate the Most General Sentence

The most general sentence in the paragraph expresses the main idea. This sentence is called the topic sentence. This sentence must be broad enough to include or cover all the other ideas (details) in the paragraph. In the above paragraph, the first sentence makes a general statement about the earth's water—that most of it can be classified as fresh or marine. The rest of the sentences provide specifics about this classification.

Study the Details

The main idea must connect, draw together, and make the rest of the paragraph meaningful. You might think of the main idea as the one that all the details, taken together, add up to, explain, or support. In the above paragraph, sentences 2, 3, and 4 each give details about water classification. Sentences 2 and 3 give examples of exceptions to the fresh/marine categories. Sentence 5 defines the salt content of each category.

Where to Find the Topic Sentence

The topic sentence can be located anywhere in the paragraph. However, there are several positions where it is most likely to be found.

Topic Sentence First Most often the topic sentence is placed first in the paragraph. In this type of paragraph, the author first states his or her main point and then explains it.

Example:

Another important event in the early 1970s was the Watergate scandal, which affected the public on the same level psychologically as the Vietnam War. The Vietnam conflict had ended and we lost face as a result of it. However, Watergate was to drop a great blanket on our trust in government. Everything ugly in American society was reflected in Watergate, which was devastating in its impact. Society had changed, and the result was massive depression. The American people had lost faith in our government; it does not seem as if we got it back during the 1970s.[8]

Here the writer first states that the Watergate scandal had a psychological effect on the public. The rest of the paragraph explains this effect.

Topic Sentence Last The second most likely place for a topic sentence to appear is last in the paragraph. When using this arrangement, a writer leads up to the main point and then directly states it at the end.

Example:

At the beginning of this century, only eight percent of marriages ended in divorce. In 1976, just over fifty percent did. The dramatic change doesn't necessarily mean that people were happy in marriage in the old days and are unhappy today. Expectations have changed, and divorces are now much easier to come by. People who years ago might have suffered along now sever the marriage bond. <u>Yet, however the statistics are interpreted, it is clear that there is a reservoir of dissatisfaction in many marriages.</u>[9]

This paragraph first provides statistics on the increasing rate of divorce. Then possible reasons for the increase are given. The paragraph ends with a general statement of what the statistics do show—that there is much dissatisfaction in many marriages.

Topic Sentence in the Middle If it is placed neither first nor last, then the topic sentence appears somewhere in the middle of the paragraph. In this arrangement, the sentences before the topic sentence lead up to or introduce the main idea. Those that follow the main idea explain or describe it.

Example:

You could be the greatest mechanical genius since Thomas Edison, but if no one knows about your talent or is in a position to judge it, you're wasting your time. Being in the right field is important. <u>But within that field, it's also a good idea to maintain a high degree of visibility.</u> If you've got the potential to be a brilliant corporate strategist, you may be wasting your time working for a small company employing a dozen or so workers. You'd be better off working for a large corporation where you have the opportunity to take off in any number of directions, learn how the different departments interface, and thus have a larger arena to test your skills.[10]

In this paragraph, the writer begins with an example using Thomas Edison. He then states his main point and continues with examples that illustrate the importance of visibility in career advancement.

Topic Sentence First and Last   Occasionally the main idea will appear at the beginning of a paragraph and again at the end. Writers may use this organization to emphasize an important idea or to explain an idea that needs clarification.

Example:

<u>Burger King Corporation offers both a service and a product to its customers.</u> Its service is the convenience it offers the consumer—the location of its restaurants and its fast food service—in catering to his or her lifestyle. Its product, in essence, is *the total Burger King experience,* which starts from the time you drive into the restaurant's parking lot and ends when you drive out. It includes the speed of service, the food you order, the price you pay, the friendliness and courtesy you are shown, the intangible feeling of satisfaction—in short, an experience. <u>Burger King, then, is marketing a positive experience, as promised by its advertising and promotional efforts and delivered by its product.</u>[11]

The first and last sentences both state, in slightly different ways, that Burger King provides a desirable product and service that results in a positive experience.

EXERCISE 7-4

DIRECTIONS: *Underline the topic sentence in each of the following paragraphs.*

1. Leadership can assume any one of three basic styles: authoritarian, democratic, and laissez-faire. *Authoritarian* leaders give orders and direct activities with minimal input from followers. In extreme cases, they may be said to rule with an iron fist that crushes all dissent. In cultures where it is customary for authoritarian leaders to make decisions in both the political and domestic spheres, this leadership style may be preferred. In egalitarian societies, authoritarian leaders may be tolerated, but members of small groups typically prefer democratic leaders, who attempt to involve others in the decision-making process. *Laissez-faire* leaders take a "hands-off" approach; they neither set the agenda nor try

---

to direct followers in any obvious way. Instead, they allow group members the freedom to choose whatever direction they think is best.[12]

2. Dirty words are often used by teenagers in telling off-color stories and this can be considered part of their sex education. As their bodies grow and change, both boys and girls wonder and worry. To keep from being overwhelmed by these fears, they turn them into jokes or dirty-word stories. By telling and retelling off-color stories, they gain a little information, more misinformation and a lot of reassurance. They learn that they aren't the only ones in the group disturbed about their future roles in courtship and marriage. Using dirty words and stories to laugh at sexual doubts and fears may diminish their importance and make them less frightening.[13]

3. Deciding to buy a product or service takes preparation. Since time has already been spent to gather information and compare what is available, money managers should spend a little more time prior to arriving at a final decision. In this respect it is best if prospective buyers go home before making a selection. At home it is easier to evaluate all of the accumulated information while not under any sales or time pressure to make a purchase. In addition, at home it is possible to take a final look at financial plans to be sure the purchase will mesh with these plans.[14]

4. It is important to realize that the 1950s were to most Americans a time of great security. After World War II, the people prospered in ways they had never known before. Our involvement in the Korean War was thought to be successful from the point of view of national image. We saw ourselves as *the* world power, who had led the fight for democracy. When Dwight D. Eisenhower was elected president, we entered a period in American history where everything was all right, everyone was getting richer, and tomorrow would always be better than today.[15]

5. The other day a good friend, senior executive of a large company and in his early forties, dropped by for a visit. He told me he had been thinking of divorce after sixteen years of marriage. The couple have a boy, twelve, and two girls, one of whom is ten, the other eight. "We've grown apart over the years, and we have nothing in common left anymore other than the children. There are at least twenty years of enjoying life still ahead of me. I was worried about the children until we discussed it with them. So many of their schoolmates have had divorced parents or parents who had remarried, they are accustomed to the idea. It's part of life. Of course, if the older ones need help, I want them to see a good psychiatrist while we go through with this. My wife is still a good-looking woman, younger than I, and probably will remarry. I'm not thinking of

it now, but I'll probably remarry someday." This situation illustrates an attitude and the climate of the times. Divorce has become as much an institution as marriage.[16]

Inferring Unstated Main Ideas

Although most paragraphs do have a topic sentence, some do not. This type of paragraph contains only details or specifics that, taken together, point to the main idea. In paragraphs in which no one sentence clearly expresses the main idea, you must figure it out. Reading a paragraph in which the main idea is unstated is similar to doing a math problem. It is a process of adding up the facts and deciding what they mean together. To solve this math problem you add the numbers and come up with a total sum.

46	fact
74	fact
89	fact
22	fact
+ 10	+ fact
241	main idea

Think of a paragraph without a topic sentence in a similar way. It is a list of facts or details that you add up or put together to determine the meaning of the paragraph as a whole.

Use the following steps as a guide to finding unstated main ideas:

1. Find the topic. Ask yourself: "What is the one thing the author is discussing throughout the paragraph?"
2. Decide what the writer wants you to know about the topic. Look at each detail and decide what larger idea each explains.
3. Express this idea in your own words.

Read the following paragraph; then follow the three steps listed above.

In the past, most individuals were educated during a specific period of their lives. By the time they reached their mid-20s, they could retire their notebooks, textbooks, carbon paper, scratch pads, and pencils and pens and concentrate on building their careers. Tomorrow's workers will have to hold on to their training paraphernalia because they can expect to be retrained throughout their working lives. It may mean taking company-sponsored courses every few months, after-work seminars, or spending a number of days or weeks in a nearby university attending lectures at different points during the year.[17]

The topic of this paragraph is education. The writer begins by explaining that in the past, education took place during a certain time period in our lives. Then the writer predicts that in the future, education will continue throughout a person's life. The main point the writer makes is that the idea of education is changing. Notice, however, that no single sentence states this idea clearly. The reader had to infer this idea from the way all the sentences in the paragraph worked together.

EXERCISE 7-5

DIRECTIONS: None of the following paragraphs has a topic sentence. Read each paragraph and, in the space provided, write a sentence that expresses the main idea.

1. Immigration has contributed to the dramatic population growth of the U.S. over the past 150 years. It has also contributed to the country's shift from a rural to an urban economy. Immigrants provided inexpensive labor which allowed industries to flourish. Native-born children of immigrants, benefitting from education, moved into professional and white collar jobs, creating a new middle class. Immigration also increased the U.S. mortality rate. Due to crowded housing and unhealthy living conditions, disease and fatal illness were common.

   Main Idea:_____

   _____

2. Jack Schultz and Ian Baldwin found last summer that trees under attack by insects or animals will release an unidentified chemical into the air as a distress signal. Upon receiving the signal, nearby trees step up their production of tannin—a poison in the leaves that gives insects indigestion. The team learned, too, that production of the poison is in proportion to the duration and intensity of the attack.[18]

   Main Idea:_____

   _____

3. When President Lincoln was shot, the word was communicated by telegraph to most parts of the United States, but because we had no links to England, it was five days before London heard of the event. When President Reagan was shot, journalist Henry Fairlie, working at his typewriter within a block of the shooting, got word of it by telephone from his editor at the *Spectator* in London, who had seen a rerun of the assassination attempt on television shortly after it occurred.[19]

   Main Idea:_____

   _____

4. Suppose you wanted to teach your pet chimpanzee the English language. How would you go about it? Two psychologists raised Gua, a female chimpanzee, at home with their son, Donald. Both boy and chimp were encouraged to speak, but only Donald did. Gua indicated she could comprehend some language, for she could respond appropriately to about 70 different utterances, but she never *produced* a single word. A second attempt involved more intensive training in speech, and Viki, another chimpanzee, was eventually able to pronounce three recognizable words: "Mama," "Papa," and "cup."[20]

   Main Idea:_____

   _____

5. Traffic is directed by color. Pilot instrument panels, landing strips, road and water crossings are regulated by many colored lights and signs. Factories use colors to distinguish between thoroughfares and work areas. Danger zones are painted in special colors. Lubrication points and removable parts are accentuated by color. Pipes for transporting water, steam, oil, chemicals, and compressed air are designated by different colors. Electrical wires and resistances are color coded.[21]

   Main Idea:_____

   _____

Recognizing Supporting Details

Supporting details are those facts and ideas that prove or explain the main idea of a paragraph. While all the details in a paragraph do support the main idea, not all details are equally important. As you read, try to identify and pay attention to the most important details. Pay less attention to details of lesser importance. The key details directly explain the main idea. Other details may provide additional information, offer an example, or further explain one of the key details.

The following diagram shows how details relate to the main idea and how details range in degree of importance. In the diagram, more important details are placed toward the left; less important details are closer to the right.

Most Important → *Less Important* → *Least Important*

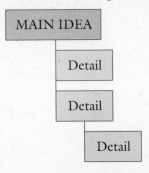

Read the following paragraph and study the diagram that follows.

The skin of the human body has several functions. First, it serves as a protective covering. In doing so, it accounts for 17 percent of the body weight. Skin also protects the organs within the body from damage or harm. The skin serves as a regulator of body functions. It controls body temperature and water loss. Finally, the skin serves as a receiver. It is sensitive to touch and temperature.

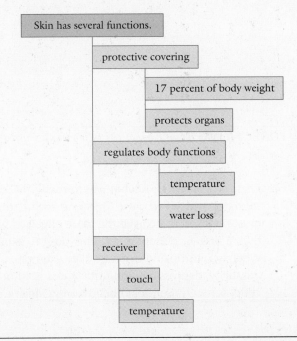

From this diagram you can see that the details that state the three functions of skin are the key details. Other details, such as "protects the organs," provide further information and are at a lower level of importance.

Read the following paragraph and try to pick out the more important details.

By contrast, the modern census, which started to evolve in the seventeenth century, is designed to count all people within a country for governmental, scientific, and commercial purposes. A good example is the U.S. census, which has been taken every 10 years since 1790. It is used for determining the number of congressional seats for each state and allocating federal and state funds to local governments. It is also used for scientific analysis of the nation's demographic traits and trends, economic development, and business cycles. As for its commercial use, an orthodontist, for example, would find the census data worthwhile, because they can show where there are a lot of teenagers in high-income households.

This paragraph could be diagrammed as follows (key details only):

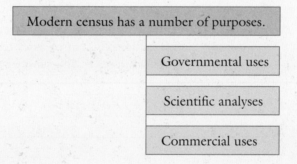

EXERCISE 7-6

DIRECTIONS: *Read each of the following paragraphs and underline only the most important details.*

1. *Physical dependence* is what was formerly called addiction. It is characterized by *tolerance* and *withdrawal*. *Tolerance* means that more and more of the drug must be taken to achieve the same effect, as use continues. *Withdrawal* means that if use is discontinued, the person experiences unpleasant symptoms. When I quit smoking cigarettes, for example, I went through about five days of irritability, depression, and restlessness. Withdrawal from heroin and other narcotics is much more painful, involving violent cramps, vomiting, diarrhea, and

other symptoms that continue for at least two or three days. With some drugs, especially barbiturates, cold-turkey (sudden and total) quitting can result in death, so severe is the withdrawal.[22]

2. The two most common drugs that are legal and do not require a prescription are caffeine and nicotine. *Caffeine* is the active ingredient in coffee, tea, and many cola drinks. It stimulates the central nervous system and heart and therefore is often used to stay awake. Heavy use—say, seven to ten cups of coffee per day—has toxic effects, that is, it acts like a mild poison. Prolonged heavy use appears to be addicting. *Nicotine* is the active ingredient in tobacco. One of the most addicting of all drugs and one of the most dangerous, at least when obtained by smoking, it has been implicated in lung cancer, emphysema, and heart disease.[23]

3. Hypnosis today is used for a number of purposes, primarily in psychotherapy or to reduce pain, and it is an acceptable technique in both medicine and psychology. In psychotherapy, it is most often used to eliminate bad habits and annoying symptoms. Cigarette smoking can be treated, for example, by the suggestion that the person will feel nauseated whenever he or she thinks of smoking. Sufferers of migraine headaches treated with hypnotic suggestions to relax showed a much greater tendency to improve than sufferers treated with drugs; 44 percent were headache-free after 12 months of treatment, compared to 12 percent of their drug-treated counterparts.[24]

4. There are four main types of sunglasses. The traditional *absorptive* glasses soak up all the harmful sun rays. *Polarizing* sunglasses account for half the market. They're the best buy for knocking out glare, and reflections from snow and water, but they may admit more light rays than other sunglasses. *Coated* sunglasses usually have a metallic covering that itself reflects light. They are often quite absorptive, but a cheap pair of coated glasses may have an uneven or nondurable coating that could rub off after a short period of time. New on the market are the somewhat more expensive *photochromatic* sunglasses. Their chemical composition causes them to change color according to the brightness of the light: in the sun, they darken; in the shade, they lighten. This type of sunglasses responds to ultraviolet light only, and will not screen out infrared rays, so they're not the best bet for continual exposure to bright sun.[25]

5. In simplest outline, how is a President chosen? First, a candidate campaigns within his party for nomination at a national convention. After the convention comes a period of competition with the nominee of the other major party and perhaps the nominees of minor parties. The showdown arrives on Election Day. The candidate must win more votes than any other nominee in enough states and the District of Columbia to give him a majority of the electoral votes.

If he does all these things, he has won the right to the office of President of the United States.[26]

Types of Supporting Details

There are many types of details that a writer can use to explain or support a main idea. As you read, be sure you know *how* or what types of detail a writer uses to support his or her main idea. As you will see in later chapters, the way a writer explains and supports an idea may influence how readily you accept or agree with it. The most common types of supporting details are (1) examples, (2) facts or statistics, (3) reasons, (4) descriptions, and (5) steps or procedures. Each will be briefly discussed here.

Examples

One way a writer may support an idea is by using examples. Examples make ideas and concepts real and understandable. A writer may explain stress by giving examples of it. In the following paragraph, an example is used to explain instantaneous speed.

> The speed that a body has at any one instant is called instantaneous speed. It is the speed registered by the speedometer of a car. When we say that the speed of a car at some particular instant is 60 kilometers per hour, we are specifying its instantaneous speed, and we mean that if the car continued moving as fast for an hour, it would travel 60 kilometers. So the instantaneous speed, or speed at a particular instant, is often quite different from average speed.[27]

In this paragraph the author uses the speed of a car to explain instantaneous speed. As you read illustrations and examples, try to see the relationship between the example and the concept or idea it illustrates.

Facts and Statistics

Another way a writer supports an idea is by including facts and/or statistics. The facts and statistics may provide evidence that the main idea is correct. Or the facts may further explain the main idea. For example, to prove that the divorce rate is high, the author may give statistics about the divorce rate and percentage of the population that is divorced. Notice how, in the following paragraph, the main idea stated in the first sentence is explained using statistics.

An increasing number of minority workers will join the work force by the year 2000. The United States Bureau of Labor Statistics estimates that white males, who have dominated the work force for several generations, will make up only 15 percent of the new entrants into the labor force between 1990 and 2000. Meanwhile, women, African Americans, Hispanics, and Asians will account for about 84 percent of the new entrants into the world of work. Of these categories, women, many of whom will be members of racial and ethnic minorities, will represent the largest proportion of new workers, accounting for approximately 64 percent.[28]

In this paragraph, the main idea that the number of minority workers will increase by the year 2000 is supported using statistics.

Reasons

A writer may support an idea by giving reasons *why* a main idea is correct. A writer might explain *why* nuclear power is dangerous or give reasons *why* a new speed limit law should be passed by Congress. In the following paragraph, the author explains why warm air rises.

We all know that warm air rises. From our study of buoyancy we can understand why this is so. Warm air expands and becomes less dense than the surrounding air and is buoyed upward like a balloon. The buoyancy is in an upward direction because the air pressure below a region of warmed air is greater than the air pressure above. And the warmed air rises because the buoyant force is greater than its weight.[29]

Description

When the topic of a paragraph is a person, object, place, or process, the writer may develop the paragraph by describing the object. Descriptions are details that help you create a mental picture of the object. In the following paragraph, the author describes a sacred book of the Islamic religion, by telling what it contains.

The *Koran* is the sacred book of the Islamic religion. It was written during the lifetime of Mohammed (570–630) during the years in which he recorded divine revelations. The *Koran* includes rules for family relationships, including marriage and divorce. Rules for inheritance of wealth and property are specified. The status of women as subordinate to men is well-defined.

Steps or Procedures

When a paragraph explains how to do something, the paragraph details are often lists of steps or procedures to be followed. For example, if the main idea of a paragraph is how to prepare an outline for a speech, then the details would list or explain the steps in preparing an outline. In the following paragraph the author explains how fog is produced.

> Warm breezes blow over the ocean. When the moist air moves from warmer to cooler waters or from warm water to cool land, it chills. As it chills, water vapor molecules begin coalescing rather than bouncing off one another upon glancing collisions. Condensation takes place, and we have fog.[30]

EXERCISE 7-7

DIRECTIONS: *For each paragraph listed in Exercise 7-6, identify the type or types of details used to support the main idea. Write your answers in the margin of Exercise 7-6.*

Transitions

Transitions are linking words or phrases used to lead the reader from one idea to another. If you get in the habit of recognizing transitions, you will see that they often guide you through a paragraph, helping you to read it more easily.

In the following paragraph, notice how the underlined transitions lead you from one important detail to the next.

> The principle of rhythm and line also contributes to the overall unity of the landscape design. This principle is responsible for the sense of continuity between different areas of the landscape. <u>One</u> way in which this continuity can be developed is by extending planting beds from one area to another. <u>For example</u>, shrub beds developed around the entrance to the house can be continued around the sides and into the backyard. Such an arrangement helps to tie the front and rear areas of the property together. <u>Another</u> means by which rhythm is given to a design is to repeat shapes, angles, or lines between various areas and elements of the design.[31]

Not all paragraphs contain such obvious transitions, and not all transitions serve as such clear markers of major details. Transitions may be used to alert you to what will come next in the paragraph. If you see the phrase *for instance* at the beginning of a sentence, then you know that an example will follow. When you see the phrase *on the other hand,* you can predict that a different, opposing idea will follow. Table 7-1 lists some of the most common transitions used within a paragraph and indicates what they tell you.

TABLE 7-1
Common Transitions

Type of Transition	Example	What They Tell the Reader
Time—Sequence	first, later, next, finally	The author is arranging ideas in the order in which they happened.
Example	for example, for instance, to illustrate, such as	An example will follow.
Enumeration	first, second, third, last, another, next	The author is marking or identifying each major point (sometimes these may be used to suggest order of importance).
Continuation	also, in addition, and, further, another	The author is continuing with the same idea and is going to provide additional information.
Contrast	on the other hand, in contrast, however	The author is switching to a different, opposite, or contrasting idea than previously discussed.
Comparison	like, likewise, similarly	The writer will show how the previous idea is similar to what follows.
Cause—Effect	because, thus, therefore, since, consequently	The writer will show a connection between two or more things, how one thing caused another, or how something happened as a result of something else.

EXERCISE 7-8

DIRECTIONS: *Turn back to Exercise 7-6 on pp. 130–132. Reread each paragraph and underline any transitions that you find.*

EXERCISE 7-9

DIRECTIONS: *Each of the following beginnings of paragraphs on p. 136 uses a transitional word or phrase to tell the reader what will follow in the paragraph. Read each, paying particular attention to the underlined word or phrase. Then, in* *the space provided, describe as specifically as you can what you would expect to find next in the paragraph.*

1. Price is not the only factor to consider in choosing a pharmacy. Many provide valuable services that should be considered. <u>For instance</u> . . .

    _____

2. There are a number of things you can do to prevent a home burglary. <u>First,</u> . . .

    _____

3. Most mail order businesses are reliable and honest. <u>However,</u> . . .

    _____

4. One advantage of a compact stereo system is that all the components are built into the unit. <u>Another</u> . . .

    _____

5. Taking medication can have an effect on your hormonal balance. <u>Consequently,</u> . . .

    _____

6. To select the presidential candidate you will vote for, you should examine his or her philosophy of government. <u>Next</u> . . .

    _____

7. Eating solely vegetables drastically reduces caloric and fat intake, two things on which most people overindulge. <u>On the other hand</u> . . .

    _____

8. Asbestos, a common material found in many older buildings in which people have worked for decades, has been shown to cause cancer. <u>Consequently,</u> . . .

    _____

9. Cars and trucks are not designed randomly. They are designed individually for specific purposes. <u>For instance</u> . . .

    _____

10. Jupiter is a planet surrounded by several moons. <u>Likewise</u> . . .

    _____

DIRECTIONS: *Read each of the following sentences. In each blank, supply a transitional word or phrase that makes sense in the sentence.*

1. As a young poet, e e cummings was traditional in his use of punctuation and capitalization. _____, he became much more experimental and began to create his own grammatical rules.

2. Some metals, _____ gold and silver, are represented by symbols derived from their Latin names.

3. In order to sight read music, you should begin by scanning it. _____, you should identify the key and tempo.

4. The *Oxford English Dictionary,* by giving all present and past definitions of words, shows how word definitions have changed with time. _____, it gives the date and written source where each word appears to have first been used.

5. Some scientists believe intelligence to be determined equally by heredity and environment. _____, other scientists believe heredity to account for about sixty percent of it and environment for the other forty percent.

6. Tigers tend to grow listless and unhappy in captivity. _____, pandas grow listless and have a difficult time reproducing in captivity.

7. Touching the grooves on a record is not advisable _____ oils and minerals in the skin get into the grooves and reduce the quality of sound.

8. Many rock stars have met with tragic ends. _____, John Lennon was gunned down, Buddy Holly and Ritchie Valens were killed in a plane crash, and Janis Joplin died of a drug overdose.

9. American voters tend to vote according to the state of the economy. _____, if the economy is good, they tend to vote for the party in power and if the economy is poor, they tend to vote for the party not in power.

10. Buying smaller sized clothing generally will not give an overweight person the incentive to lose weight. People with weight problems tend to eat when they're upset or disturbed, and _____ wearing smaller clothing is frustrating and upsetting, overweight people will generally gain weight by doing so.

Paraphrasing Paragraphs

Paraphrasing paragraphs is a useful technique for both building and checking on your comprehension. By taking a paragraph apart sentence by sentence, you are forced to understand the meaning of each sentence and see how ideas relate to one another. Paraphrasing paragraphs is similar to paraphrasing sentences. It involves the same two steps:

1. Rewording using synonyms
2. Rearranging the order of ideas

Refer to Ch. 6, p. 109, for a review of these two steps.

Here are some additional guidelines for paraphrasing paragraphs.

1. Concentrate on maintaining the author's focus and emphasis. Ideas that seem most important in the paragraph should appear as most important in your paraphrase.
2. Work sentence-by-sentence, paraphrasing the ideas in the order in which they appear in the paragraph.

Here is a sample paraphrase of a paragraph:

Paragraph

For the most part, the American media share one overriding goal: to make a profit. But they are also the main instruments for manipulating public opinion. Politicians want to win our hearts and minds, and businesses want to win our dollars. Both use the media to try to gain mass support by manipulating public opinion. In other words, they generate **propaganda**—communication tailored to influence opinion. Propaganda may be true or false. What sets it apart from other communications is the intent to change opinion.[32]

Paraphrase

American media (newspapers, TV, and radio) have one common purpose, which is to make money. Media are also vehicles for controlling how the public thinks. Politicians want us to like them; businesses want our money. Both use media to get support by controlling how people think. Both use propaganda. Propaganda is words and ideas that are used to affect how people think. Propaganda can be either true or false. It is different from other forms of communication because its purpose is to change how we think.

DIRECTIONS: *Write a paraphrase of paragraphs 1, 2, and 3 in Exercise 7-3.*

■■■■■■■■ **WORKING TOGETHER**

Directions: Separate into groups. Using a reading selection from Part 6, work with your group to identify and underline the topic sentence of each paragraph. Try to identify key supporting details and/or type of supporting details. When all the groups have completed the task, the class will compare the findings of the various groups.

■■■■■■■■ **SUMMARY**

Name and describe the four essential parts of a paragraph?	1. Topic. The topic is the one thing the entire paragraph is about.
	2. Main idea. The main idea is the most important idea the writer wants the reader to know about the topic.
	3. Details. Details are facts and ideas that support the main idea.
	4. Transitions. Transitions are words and phrases that lead the reader from one idea to another.
What sentence states the main idea of a paragraph?	The topic sentence states the main idea of a paragraph.
Where is the topic sentence located?	The topic sentence can be located anywhere in the paragraph, but the most common positions are first, last, in the middle, or first and last.
What are the five types of details used to support the main idea?	The types of details are facts and statistics, reasons, description, and steps and procedures.

Following the Author's Thought Patterns

▪▪▪▪▪▪▪▪▪▪▪▪▪▪▪▪▪▪▪▪▪▪▪▪▪▪▪▪▪▪▪

THIS CHAPTER WILL SHOW YOU HOW TO

1. *Improve your understanding and recall by recognizing thought patterns*

2. *Identify six commonly used thought patterns*

▪▪▪▪▪▪▪▪▪▪▪▪▪▪▪▪▪▪▪▪▪▪▪▪▪▪▪▪▪▪▪

As a way of beginning to think about authors' thought patterns, complete each of the following steps:

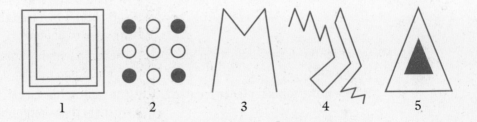

1. Study each of these drawings for a few seconds (count to ten as you look at each one):
2. Cover up the drawings and try to draw each from memory.
3. Check to see how many you had exactly correct.

Most likely you drew all but the fourth correctly. Why did you get that one wrong? How does it differ from the others?

Drawings 1, 2, 3, and 5 have patterns. Drawing 4, however, has no pattern; it is just a group of randomly arranged lines.

From this experiment you can see that it is easier to remember drawings that have a pattern, some understandable form of organization. The same is true of written material. If you can see how a paragraph is organized, it will be easier to understand and remember. Writers often present their ideas in a recognizable order. Once you can recognize the organizational pattern, you will remember more of what you read.

This chapter briefly reviews some of the more common patterns that writers use and shows how to recognize them: (1) illustration/example, (2) definition, (3) comparison/contrast, (4) cause/effect, (5) classification, and (6) chronological order/process.

Illustration/Example

One of the clearest, most practical, and most obvious ways to explain something is to give an example. Suppose you had to explain what anthropology is. You might give examples of the topics you study. By using examples, such as the study of apes and early humans, and the development of modern humans, you would give a fairly good idea of what anthropology is all about. When a subject is unfamiliar, an example often makes it easier to understand.

Usually a writer will state the idea first and then follow with examples. Several examples may be given in one paragraph, or a separate paragraph may be used for each example. It may help to visualize the illustration/example pattern this way:

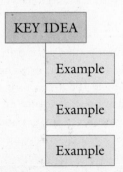

Notice how this thought pattern is developed in the following passage.

> Electricity is all around us. We see it in lightning. We receive electric shocks when we walk on a nylon rug on a dry day and then touch something (or someone). We can see sparks fly from a cat's fur when we pet it in the dark. We can rub a balloon on a sweater and make the balloon stick to the wall or the ceiling. Our clothes cling together when we take them from the dryer.
>
> These are all examples of *static electricity*. They happen because there is a buildup of one of the two kinds of electrical charge, either positive or negative. . . .[1]

In the preceding passage, the concept of static electricity was explained through the use of everyday examples. You could visualize the selection as follows:

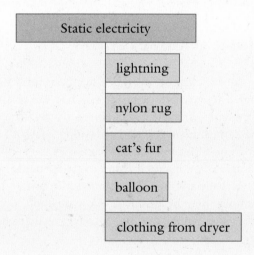

Here is another passage in which the main idea is explained through example:

> It is a common observation that all bodies do not fall with equal accelerations. A leaf, a feather, or a sheet of paper, for example, may flutter to the ground slowly. That the air is the factor responsible for these different accelerations can be shown very nicely with a closed glass tube containing a light and heavy object, a feather and a coin, for example. In the presence of air, the feather and coin fall with quite unequal accelerations. But if the air in the tube is evacuated by means of a vacuum pump, and the tube is quickly inverted, the feather and coin fall with the same acceleration. . . . Although air

resistance appreciably alters the motion of falling feathers and the like, the motion of heavier objects like stones and baseballs is not appreciably affected by the air. The relationships $v = gt$ and $d = \frac{1}{2} gt^2$ can be used to a very good approximation for most objects falling in air.[2]

The author explains that objects do not fall at equal rates by using the examples of a leaf, a feather, and a sheet of paper.

EXERCISE 8-1 **DIRECTIONS:** *For each of the following paragraphs, underline the topic sentence and list the examples used to explain it.*

1. Perception is the process of gathering information and giving it meaning. You see a movie and you give meaning to it: "It's one of the best I've seen." You come away from class after the third week and you give meaning to it: "It finally makes sense." We gather information from what our senses see, hear, touch, taste, and smell, and we give meaning to that information. Although the information may come to us in a variety of forms, it is all processed, or *perceived,* in the mind.[3]

   Examples: _____

   _____

2. The action and reaction forces make up a *pair* of forces. Forces always occur in pairs. There is never a single force in any situation. For example, in walking across the floor, we push against the floor, and the floor in turn pushes against us. Likewise, the tires of a car push against the pavement, and the pavement pushes back on the tires. When we swim, we push the water backward, and the water pushes us forward. The reaction forces, those acting in the direction of our resulting accelerations, are what account for our motion in these cases. These forces depend on friction; a person or car on ice, for example, may not be able to exert the action force to produce the needed reaction force by the ice.[4]

   Examples: _____

   _____

3. Have you ever noticed that some foods remain hotter much longer than others? Boiled onions and squash on a hot dish, for example, are often too hot to

eat when mashed potatoes may be eaten comfortably. The filling of hot apple pie can burn your tongue while the crust will not, even when the pie has just been taken out of the oven. And the aluminum covering on a frozen dinner can be peeled off with your bare fingers as soon as it is removed from the oven. A piece of toast may be comfortably eaten a few seconds after coming from the hot toaster, but we must wait several minutes before eating soup from a stove no hotter than the toaster. Evidently, different substances have different capacities for storing internal energy.[5]

Examples: _____

_____

EXERCISE 8-2

DIRECTIONS: *Choose one of the following topics. On a separate sheet, write a paragraph in which you use illustration/example to organize and express your ideas on the topic. Then draw a diagram showing the organization of your paragraph.*

1. Parents or friends are helpful (or not helpful) in making decisions.

2. Attending college has (has not) made a major change in my life.

Definition

Another way to provide an explanation is to offer a definition. Let's say that you see an opossum while driving in the country. You mention this to a friend. Since your friend does not know what an opossum is, you have to give a definition. Your definition should describe an opossum's characteristics or features. The definition should have two parts: (1) Tell what general group or class an opossum belongs to—in this case, animals. (2) Explain how an opossum is different or distinguishable from other items in the group. For the term *opossum,* you would need to describe features of an opossum that would help someone tell the difference between it and other animals, such as dogs, raccoons, and squirrels. Thus, you could define an opossum as follows:

An opossum is an animal with a ratlike tail that lives in trees. It carries its young in a pouch. It is active at night and pretends to be dead when trapped.

This definition can be diagrammed as follows:

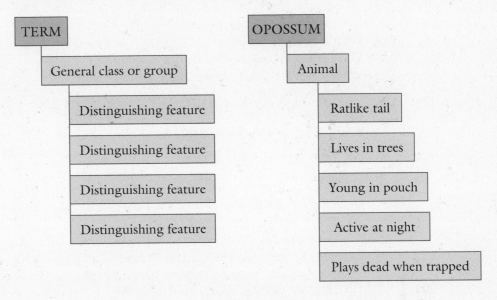

The following passage was written to define the term *ragtime music*.

Ragtime music is a piano style that developed at the turn of the twentieth century. Ragtime music usually has four themes. The themes are divided into four musical sections of equal length. In playing ragtime music, the left hand plays chords and the right hand plays the melody. There is an uneven accenting between the two hands.

The thought pattern of this passage might be diagrammed as follows:

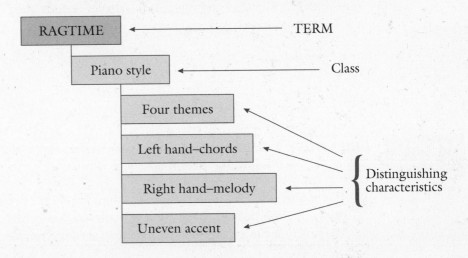

As you read passages that use the definition pattern, keep these questions in mind:

1. What is being defined?
2. What general group or class does it belong to?
3. What makes it different from others in the group?

Read the following passage and apply the above questions.

Nez Percé Indians are a tribe that lives in north-central Idaho. The rich farm-lands and forests in the area form the basis for the tribe's chief industries, agriculture and lumber.

The name *Nez Percé* means *pierced nose,* but few of the Indians ever pierced their noses. In 1805, a French interpreter gave the name to the tribe after seeing some members wearing shells in their noses as decorations.

The Nez Percé originally lived in the region where the borders of Idaho, Oregon, and Washington meet. Prospectors overran the Nez Percé reserva-tion after discovering gold there in the 1860's.

The Nez Percé resisted the efforts of the government to move them to a smaller reservation. In 1877, fighting broke out between the Nez Percé and U.S. troops. Joseph, a Nez Percé chief, tried to lead a band of the Indians into Canada. But he surrendered near the United States-Canadian border.[6]

This passage was written to define the Nez Percé. The general group or category is "Indian tribe." The distinguishing characteristics include their original location, their fight against relocation, and the source of their name.

EXERCISE 8-3

DIRECTIONS: Read each of the following paragraphs. Then identify the term being defined, its general class, and its distinguishing features.

1. The partnership, like the sole proprietorship, is a form of ownership used pri-marily in small business firms. Two or more owners comprise a partnership. The structure of a partnership may be established with an almost endless varia-

---

tion of features. The partners establish the conditions of the partnership, contribution of each partner to the business, and division of profits. They also decide on the amount of authority, duties, and liability each will have.[7]

Term: _____

General class: _____

Distinguishing features: _____

_____

2. A language is a complex system of symbols with conventional meanings, used by members of a society for communication. The term *language* is often thought to include only the spoken word, but in its broadest sense language contains verbal, nonverbal, and written symbols. Whereas complex cultures employ all three kinds of symbols in communication, simple and preliterate cultures typically lack written symbols.[8]

Term: _____

General class: _____

Distinguishing features: _____

_____

3. The Small Business Administration (SBA) is an independent agency of the federal government that was created by Congress when it passed the Small Business Act in 1953. Its administrator is appointed by and reports to the President. Purposes of the SBA are to assist people in getting into business, to help them stay in business, to help small firms win federal procurement contracts, and to act as a strong advocate for small business.[9]

Term: _____

General class: _____

Distinguishing features: _____

_____

DIRECTIONS: *Choose one of the topics listed below. On a separate sheet, write a paragraph in which you define the topic. Be sure to include both the general group and what makes the item different from other items in the same group. Then draw a diagram showing the organization of your paragraph.*

1. A type of music

2. Soap operas

3. Junk food

Comparison/Contrast

Often a writer will explain something by using **comparison** or **contrast**—that is, by showing how it is similar to or different from a familiar object or idea. Comparison treats similarities, while contrast emphasizes differences. For example, an article comparing two car models might mention these common, overlapping features: radial tires, clock, radio, power steering, power brakes. The cars may differ in gas mileage, body shape, engine power, braking distance, and so forth. When comparing the two models, the writer would focus on shared features. When contrasting the two cars the writer would focus on individual differences. Such an article might be diagrammed as follows:

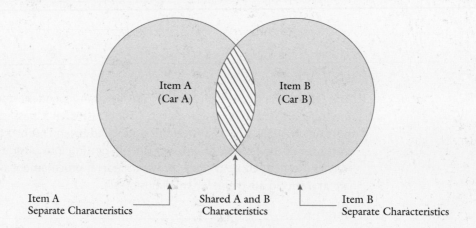

In this diagram, Items A and B are different except where they overlap and share the same characteristics.

In most articles that use the comparison/contrast method, you will find some passages that only compare, some that only contrast, and others that both compare and contrast. To read each type of passage effectively, you must follow the pattern of ideas. Passages that show comparison and/or contrast can be organized in a number of different ways. The organization depends on the author's purpose.

Comparison

If a writer is concerned only with similarities, he or she may identify the items to be compared and then list the ways in which they are alike. The following paragraph shows how chemistry and physics are similar.

> Although physics and chemistry are considered separate fields of study, they have much in common. First, both are physical sciences and are concerned with studying and explaining physical occurrences. To study and record these occurrences, each field has developed a precise set of signs and symbols. These might be considered a specialized language. Finally, both fields are closely tied to the field of mathematics and use mathematics in predicting and explaining physical occurrences.[10]

Such a pattern can be diagrammed as follows:

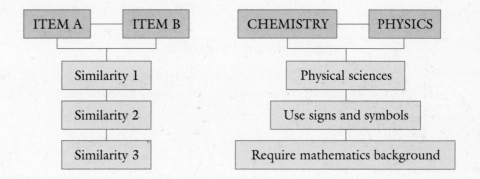

Contrast

A writer concerned only with the differences between sociology and psychology might write the following paragraph:

> Sociology and psychology, although both social sciences, are very different fields of study. Sociology is concerned with the structure, organization, and behavior of groups. Psychology, on the other hand, focuses on individual behavior. While a sociologist would study characteristics of groups of people, a

psychologist would study the individual motivation and behavior of each group member. Psychology and sociology also differ in the manner in which research is conducted. Sociologists obtain data and information through observation and survey. Psychologists obtain data through carefully designed experimentation.

Such a pattern can be diagrammed as follows:

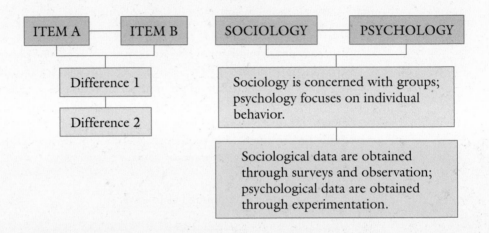

Comparison and Contrast

In many passages, writers discuss both similarities and differences. Suppose you wanted to write a paragraph discussing the similarities and differences between sociology and psychology. You could organize the paragraph in several different ways.

1. You could list all the similarities and then all the differences, as shown in this diagram:

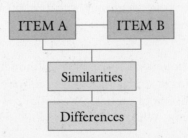

2. You could discuss Item A first, presenting both similarities and differences, and then do the same for Item B. Such a pattern would look like this:

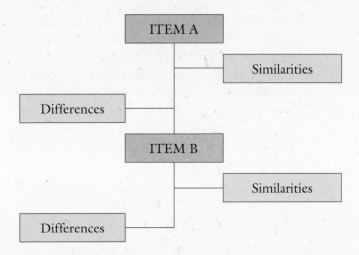

The following paragraph discusses housing in New York City. As you read it, try to visualize its pattern.

Housing in New York City differs in several ways from that in most other cities of the United States. About 60 per cent of New York's families live in apartment buildings or hotels. In other cities, most people live in one- or two-family houses. About 75 per cent of the families in New York rent their homes. In other U.S. cities, most families own their homes. About 70 per cent of the housing in New York City is more than 30 years old, and over 300,000 families live in buildings that are more than 70 years old. Most other cities have a far larger percentage of newer housing.[11]

Did you visualize the pattern like this?

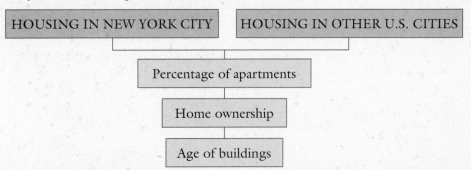

Now read the following passage and decide whether it discusses similarities, differences, or both.

A program must be written in a form that a computer can understand. Every instruction must be prepared according to specific rules. The rules form a language that we use to instruct the computer. Humans use *natural languages* such as English and Spanish to communicate with each other. When we communicate with a computer we use a *computer programming language*.

To write a sentence in a natural human language, we form words and phrases from letters and other symbols. The construction of the sentence is determined by the grammar rules of the language. The meaning of the sentence depends on what words are used and how they are organized. A computer programming language also has rules that describe how to form valid instructions. These rules are called the *syntax* of the language. The meanings or effects of the instructions are called the *semantics* of the language.[12]

This passage *compares* natural language with computer programming language. Both are means of communication and both are based on sets of rules.

<table>
<tr><td>EXERCISE
8-5</td><td>DIRECTIONS: Read each of the following passages and identify the items being compared or contrasted. Then describe the author's approach to the items. Are they compared, contrasted, or both compared and contrasted?</td></tr>
</table>

1. Perhaps it will be easier to understand the nature and function of empathic listening if we contrast it to deliberative listening. When we make a definite "deliberate" attempt to hear information, analyze it, recall it at a later time and draw conclusions from it, we are listening deliberatively. This is the way most of us listen because this is the way we have been trained. This type of listening is appropriate in a lecture-based education system where the first priority is to critically analyze the speaker's content.

   In empathic listening the objective is also understanding, but the first priority is different. Because empathic listening is transactional, the listener's first priority is to understand the communicator. We listen to what is being communicated not just by the words but by the other person's facial expressions, tone of voice, gestures, posture, and body motion.[13]

   Items Compared or Contrasted: _____

   Approach: _____

2. The term primary group, coined by Charles H. Cooley (1909), is used to refer to small, informal groups who interact in a personal, direct and intimate way. . . . A secondary group is a group whose members interact in an impersonal manner, have few emotional ties, and come together for a specific purpose.

Like primary groups, they are usually small and involve face-to-face contacts. Although the interactions may be cordial or friendly, they are more formal than primary group interactions. Sociologically, however, they are just as important. Most of our time is spent in secondary groups—committees, professional groups, sales-related groups, classroom groups, or neighborhood groups. The key difference between primary and secondary groups is in the quality of the relationships and the extent of personal intimacy and involvement. Primary groups are person-oriented, whereas secondary groups tend to be goal-oriented.[14]

Items Compared or Contrasted: _____

Approach: _____

3. The differences in the lifestyles of the city and the suburbs should be thought of as differences of degree, not kind. Suburban residents tend to be more family-oriented and more concerned about the quality of education their children receive than city dwellers. On the other hand, because the suburbs consist largely of single-family homes, most young and single people prefer city life. Suburbanites are usually more affluent than city residents and more apt to have stable career or occupational patterns. As a result, they seem to be more hardworking and achievement oriented than city residents. They may also seem to be unduly concerned with consumption, since they often buy goods and services that offer visible evidence of their financial success.[15]

Items Compared or Contrasted: _____

Approach: _____

EXERCISE 8-6

DIRECTIONS: Choose one of the topics listed below. On a separate sheet, write a paragraph in which you compare and/or contrast the two items. Then draw a diagram showing the organization of your paragraph.

1. Two restaurants

2. Two friends

3. Two musical groups

Cause/Effect

The **cause/effect** pattern is used to describe an event or action that is caused by another event or action. A cause/effect passage explains why or how something happened. For example, a description of an automobile accident would probably follow a cause/effect pattern. You would tell what caused the accident and what happened as a result. Basically, this pattern describes four types of relationships:

1. Single cause/single effect

   Example:

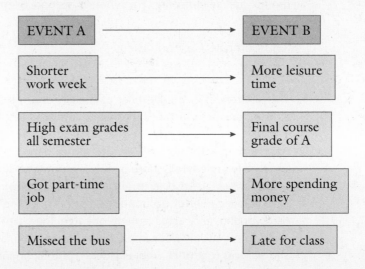

2. Single cause/multiple effects

   Examples:

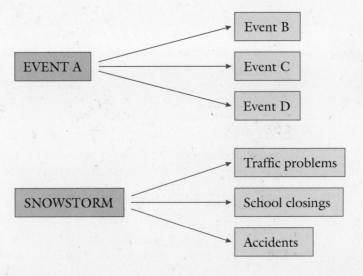

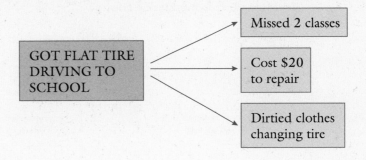

3. Multiple cause/single effect

Examples:

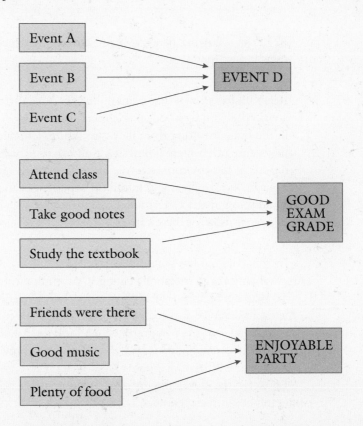

4. Multiple causes/multiple effects

Example:

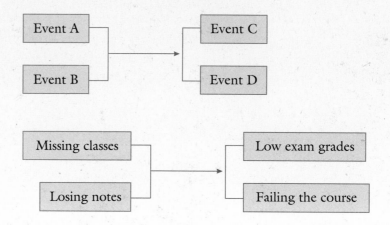

Read the following paragraph and determine which of the previous four relationships it describes.

Research has shown that mental illnesses have various causes, but the causes are not fully understood. Some mental disorders are due to physical changes in the brain resulting from illness or injury. Chemical imbalances in the brain may cause other mental illnesses. Still other disorders are mainly due to conditions in the environment that affect a person's mental state. These conditions include unpleasant childhood experiences and severe emotional stress. In addition, many cases of mental illness probably result from a combination of two or more of these causes.

In this paragraph a single effect (mental illness) is stated as having multiple causes (chemical and metabolic changes, psychological problems).

To read paragraphs that explain cause/effect relationships, pay close attention to the topic sentence. It usually states the cause/effect relationship that is detailed in the remainder of the paragraph. Then look for connections between causes and effects. What event happened as the result of a previous action? How did one event cause the other to happen?

Look for the development of the cause/effect relationship in the following paragraph about racial conflict.

Racial conflicts in New York City have had many causes. A major cause has been discrimination against blacks, Puerto Ricans, and other minority groups in jobs and housing. Many minority group members have had trouble obtaining well-paying jobs. Many also have had difficulty moving out of segregated neighborhoods and into neighborhoods where most of the people are white and of European ancestry. When members of a minority group have begun moving into such a neighborhood, the white residents often have begun moving out. In this way, segregated housing patterns have continued, and the chances for conflicts between the groups have increased.[16]

This paragraph explains why conflicts occur. It can be diagrammed as follows:

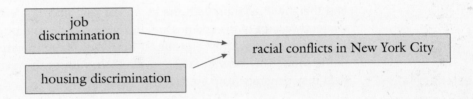

Within this paragraph, a second cause/effect relationship is introduced:

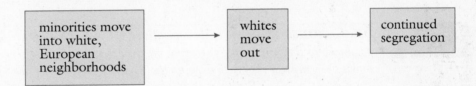

EXERCISE 8-7

DIRECTIONS: *Read each of the following paragraphs and describe the cause/effect relationship in each.*

1. By far the major cause of all business failure is inadequate management. As the Dun & Bradstreet data show, nearly 92 percent of all business failures are attributed to this one cause. What contributes to inadequate management? We see that causes of inadequate management include a lack of experience, unbalanced business experience, and incompetence.[17]

   Cause: _____

   Effect: _____

2. If a light is directed into one eye, the pupils of both eyes normally constrict. The decrease in pupil size is caused by contraction of the sphincter muscles of the iris. Constriction of the pupil in the eye in which the light was directed is known as the direct light reflex. Whereas, constriction of the pupil in the other eye is called the consensual light reflex. Both light reflexes have the typical reflex components: a sensory pathway, a motor pathway, and a central nervous system integration center.[18]

   Cause: _____

   Effect: _____

3. Snow is a poor conductor and hence is popularly said to keep the earth warm. Its flakes are formed of crystals, which collect feathery masses, imprisoning air and thereby interfering with the escape of heat from the earth's surface. The winter dwellings of the Eskimos are shielded from the cold by their snow covering. Animals in the forest find shelter from the cold in snowbanks and in holes in the snow. The snow doesn't provide them with heat; it simply prevents the heat they generate from escaping.[19]

   Cause: _____

   Effect: _____

EXERCISE 8-8

DIRECTIONS: *Choose one of the topics listed below. On a separate sheet, write a paragraph using one of the four cause/effect patterns described above to explain the topic. Then draw a diagram showing the organization of your paragraph.*

1. Why you are attending college

2. Why you chose the college you are attending

3. How a particularly frightening or tragic event happened

Classification

A common way to explain something is to divide the topic into parts and explain each part. For example, you might explain how a home computer works by describing what each major component does. You would explain the functions of the monitor (screen), the disc drives, and the central processing unit. Or you might explain the kinds of courses taken in college by dividing the courses into such categories as electives, required basic courses, courses required for a specific major, and so on and then describing each category.

Textbook writers use the classification pattern to explain a topic that can easily be divided into parts. These parts are selected on the basis of common characteristics. For example, a psychology textbook writer might explain human needs by classifying them into two categories, primary and secondary. Or in a chemistry textbook, various compounds may be grouped or classified according to common characteristics, such as the presence of hydrogen or oxygen.

The following paragraph explains horticulture. As you read, try to identify the categories into which the topic of horticulture is divided.

Horticulture, the study and cultivation of garden plants, is a large industry. Recently it has become a popular area of study. The horticulture field consists of four major divisions. First, there is pomology, the science and practice of growing and handling fruit trees. Then there is olericulture, which is concerned with growing and storing vegetables. A third field, floriculture, is the science of growing, storing, and designing flowering plants. The last category, ornamental and landscape horticulture, is concerned with using grasses, plants, and shrubs in landscaping.

This paragraph approached the topic of horticulture by describing its four areas or fields of study. You could diagram the paragraph as follows:

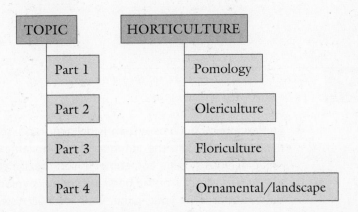

When reading textbook material that uses the classification pattern, be sure you understand *how* and *why* the topic was divided as it was. This technique will help you remember the most important parts of the topic.

Here is another example of the classification pattern:

A newspaper is published primarily to present current news and information. For large city newspapers, more than 2000 people may be involved in the distribution of this information. The staff of large city papers, headed by a publisher, is organized into departments: editorial, business, and mechanical. The editorial department, headed by an editor-in-chief, is responsible for the collection of news and preparation of written copy. The business department, headed by a business manager, handles circulation, sales, and advertising. The mechanical department is run by a production manager. This department deals with the actual production of the paper, including typesetting, layout, and printing.

You could diagram this paragraph as follows:

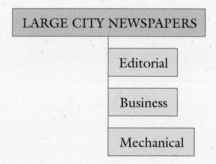

EXERCISE 8-9

DIRECTIONS: *Read each of the following passages. Then identify the topic and the parts into which it is divided.*

1. The peripheral nervous system is divided into two parts: the somatic (bodily) nervous system and the autonomic (self-governing) nervous system. The somatic nervous system, sometimes called the skeletal nervous system, controls the skeletal muscles of the body and permits voluntary action. When you turn off a light or write your name, your somatic system is active. The autonomic nervous system regulates blood vessels, glands, and internal (visceral) organs like the bladder, stomach, and heart. When you happen upon the secret object

of your desire and your heart starts to pound, your hands get sweaty, and you cheeks feel hot, you can blame your autonomic nervous system.[20]

Topics: _____

Parts: _____

2. When we communicate with others we use either verbal messages, nonverbal messages, or a combination of the two. Verbal messages are either sent or not sent, just as a light switch is either on or off. They have an all-or-nothing feature built in. Nonverbal cues are not as clear-cut.

Nonverbal communication includes such behaviors as facial expressions, posture, gestures, voice inflection, and the sequence and rhythm of the words themselves. Just as a dimmer switch on the light can be used to adjust, nonverbal cues often reveal shades or degrees of meaning. You may say, for example, "I am very upset" but *how* upset you are will be conveyed more by your facial expressions and gestures than by the actual words.[21]

Topics: _____

Parts: _____

3. The word *script* is used in this concept to mean a habitual pattern of behavior. Thomas Harris defines scripts as decisions about how life should be lived. Muriel James and Dorothy Jongeward suggest that there are various levels of scripts: (1) cultural which are dictated by society; (2) subcultural defined by geographical location, ethnic background, religious beliefs, sex, education, age and other common bonds; (3) family, the identifiable traditions and expectations for family members; and (4) psychological, people's compulsion to perform in a certain way, to live up to a specific identity, or to fulfill a destiny.[22]

Topics: _____

Parts: _____

EXERCISE 8-10

DIRECTIONS: Choose one of the topics listed below. On a separate sheet, write a paragraph explaining the topic, using the classification pattern. Then draw a diagram showing the organization of your paragraph.

1. Advertising

2. Colleges

3. Entertainment

Chronological Order/Process

The terms **chronological order** and **process** both refer to the order in which something is done. Chronological order, also called sequence of events, is one of the most obvious patterns. In a paragraph organized by chronology, the details are presented in the order in which they occur. That is, the event that happened first, or earliest in time, appears first in the paragraph, and so on. Process refers to the steps or stages in which something is done. You might expect to read a description of the events in a World War II battle presented in the order in which they happened—in chronological order. Similarly, in a computer programming manual, the steps to follow to locate an error in a computer program would be described in the order in which you should do them.

Both chronological order and process patterns can be diagrammed as follows:

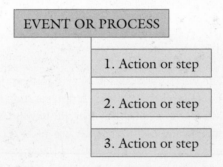

Read the following paragraph, paying particular attention to the order of the actions or steps.

> In the early 1930s, the newly established Federal Bureau of Narcotics took on a crucial role in the fight against marijuana. Under the directorship of Harry J. Anslinger, a rigorous campaign was waged against the drug and those using it. By 1937 many states had adopted a standard bill making marihuana illegal. In that same year, the federal government stepped in with the Marihuana Tax Act, a bill modeled after the Harrison "Narcotics" Act. Repressive legislation continued, and by the 1950s severe penalties were imposed on those convicted of possessing, buying, selling, or cultivating the drug.[23]

This paragraph traces the history of actions taken to limit the use of marijuana. These actions are described in chronological order, beginning with the earliest event and concluding with the most recent.

When reading text material that uses the chronological order/process pattern, pay particular attention to the order of the information presented. Both chronological order and process are concerned with the sequence of events in time.

EXERCISE
8-11

DIRECTIONS: *Read each of the following paragraphs. Identify the topic and write a list of the actions, steps, or events described in each period.*

1. These benefits of good listening occur only when the cues we give back to a speaker allow that person to know how we receive the message, permitting the speaker to adjust the message as needed. This important process is known as *feedback*. Feedback is not a simple, one-step process. First, it involves monitoring the impact or the influence of our messages on the other person. Second, it involves evaluating why the reaction or response occurred as it did. Third and finally, it involves adjustment or modification. The adjustment of our future messages reveal the process-oriented nature of communication, and, too, the impact the receiver has on the communication cycle. Feedback can provide reinforcement for the speaker if it shows if he or she is being clear, accepted, or understood.[24]

   Topic: _____

   Steps: _____

2. A geyser is a periodically erupting pressure cooker. It consists of a long, narrow, vertical hole into which underground streams seep. The column of water is heated by volcanic heat below to temperatures exceeding 100°C. This is because the vertical column of water exerts pressure on the deeper water, thereby increasing the boiling point. The narrowness of the shaft shuts off convection currents, which allows the deeper portions to become considerably hotter than the water surface. Water at the surface, of course, will boil at 100°C. The water is heated from below, so a temperature high enough to permit boiling is reached near the bottom before it is at the top. Boiling therefore begins near the bottom, the rising bubbles push out the column of water above, and the eruption starts. As the water gushes out, pressure and the remaining water is reduced. It then rapidly boils and erupts with great force.[25]

   Topic:_____

   Steps:_____

3. In spite of varied protests, the nineteenth century saw the admission of girls into elementary schools and eventually into secondary schools. In 1883, feminine education scored a victory when Oberlin College admitted women as well as men. In 1837, Mount Holyoke Seminary for Girls was established in Massachusetts, thanks to the pioneering efforts of Mary Lyon. Vassar College opened its doors in 1865, followed by Smith in 1871, Wellesley in 1877, and Bryn Mawr in 1880. The University of Michigan meanwhile had admitted women in 1870, and by the turn of the century coeducational colleges and universities were becoming commonplace. Today the great majority of the more than 2000 institutions of higher learning in the United States are coeducational, including practically all professional schools.[26]

Topic:_____

Events: _____

EXERCISE 8-12

DIRECTIONS: *On a separate sheet, write a paragraph explaining how to do something that you do well or often, such as cross-country ski, change a tire, or use a VCR to tape a TV show. Use the chronological order/process pattern. Then draw a diagram showing the organization of your paragraph.*

Diagram:

DIRECTIONS: *Read each of the following selections and identify the thought pattern used. Write the name of the pattern in the space provided. Choose from among these patterns: illustration/example, definition, comparison/contrast, cause/effect, classification, chronological order/process. Next, write a sentence explaining your choice. Then draw a diagram that shows the organization of each selection.*

1. Many wedding customs have been popular since ancient times. For example, Roman brides probably wore veils more than 2,000 years ago. Bridal veils became popular in Great Britain and the New World during the late 1700's. The custom of giving a wedding ring may also date back to the ancient Romans. The roundness of the ring probably represents eternity, and the presentation of wedding rings symbolizes that the man and woman are united forever. Wearing the wedding ring on the ring finger of the left hand is another old custom. People once thought that a vein or nerve ran directly from this finger to the heart. An old superstition says that a bride can ensure good luck by wearing "something old, something new, something borrowed, and something blue." Another superstition is that it is bad luck for a bride and groom to see each other before the ceremony on their wedding day.[27]

   Pattern: _____

   Reason: _____

      Diagram:

2. Muscle is the tough, elastic tissue that makes body parts move. All animals except the simplest kinds have some type of muscle.

People use muscles to make various movements, such as walking, jumping, or throwing. Muscles also help in performing activities necessary for growth and for maintaining a strong, healthy body. For example, people use muscles in the jaw to chew food. Other muscles help move food through the stomach and intestines, and aid in digestion. Muscles in the heart and blood vessels force the blood to circulate. Muscles in the chest make breathing possible. Muscles are found throughout the body. As a person grows, the muscles also get bigger. Muscle makes up nearly half the body weight of an adult.[28]

Pattern: _____

Reason: _____

Diagram:

3. Unless they were employed as servants, colonial women had little occupational opportunity. Even during the early 1800s, after certain types of jobs had been opened to women, female wage earners continued to be stigmatized by inferior social status.

The first large-scale influx of female workers took place in the New England factories. Most of the workers were unmarried farm girls, some hardly more than children. They were welcomed, nevertheless, because they not only were conscientious employees but would work for low wages.

During the Civil War an increasing number of occupations were opened to women, a phenomenon that was to be repeated in the First and Second World Wars. During World War II, women were employed as welders, mechanics, machinists, taxi drivers, and streetcar operators; in fact, with the exception of heavy-duty laboring jobs, females could be found in virtually every branch of industry. Also, because of their excellent record, women were made a permanent part of the armed forces.

Today there are more than 52 million women in the work force. Of those not in the labor force, the great majority are retired or have home responsibilities. From the sociological perspective it is important to note that currently even mothers with small children are likely to be employed outside the home. "Regardless of marital status or the presence of young children, labor force participation has become the norm for women." Since 1986, more than half of all women with children under three years of age have been in the labor force.[29]

Pattern: _____

Reason: _____

Diagram:

4. Mimosa is the name of a group of trees, shrubs, and herbs which have featherlike leaves. The mimosa grows chiefly in warm and tropical lands. The tree is similar to the acacia. The seed, or fruit, grows in flat pods. The small flowers may be white, pink, lavender, or purple. Mimosa grows throughout Asia, Africa, Mexico, and Australia. In the United States, it grows along the valley of the Rio Grande and in many states, including West Virginia, Virginia, Alabama, Kentucky, Louisiana, and Indiana.[30]

Pattern: _____

Reason: _____

Diagram:

5. Morphine makes severe pain bearable and moderate pain disappear. The drug also stops coughing and diarrhea, checks bleeding, and may help bring sleep.

Doctors give patients morphine only if other medicines would fail. Besides being addictive, it interferes with breathing and heart action and may cause vomiting. Small doses of morphine leave the mind fairly clear. Larger doses cloud the mind and make the user feel extremely lazy. Most morphine users feel little hunger, anger, sadness, or worry, and their sex drive is greatly reduced. Most people with mental or social problems feel happy after using morphine, even though their problems have not really been solved.[31]

Pattern: _____

Reason: _____

Diagram:

6. Personality disorders are character traits that create difficulties in personal relationships. For example, *antisocial personality disorder* is characterized by aggressive and harmful behavior that first occurs before the age of 15. Such behavior includes lying, stealing, fighting, and resisting authority. During adulthood, people with this disorder often have difficulty keeping a job or accepting other responsibilities.

Individuals with *paranoid personality disorder* are overly suspicious, cautious, and secretive. They may have delusions that people are watching them or talking about them. They often criticize others but have difficulty accepting criticism.

People who suffer from *compulsive personality disorder* attach great importance to organization. They strive for efficiency and may spend a great deal of time making lists and schedules. But they are also indecisive and seldom accomplish anything they set out to do. They often make unreasonable demands on other people and have difficulty expressing emotions.[32]

Pattern: _____

Reason: _____

Diagram:

7. Only female mosquitoes "bite," and only the females of a few species attack man and animals. They sip the victim's blood, which they need for the development of the eggs inside their bodies. Mosquitoes do not really bite because they cannot open their jaws. When a mosquito "bites," it stabs through the victim's skin with six needlelike parts called *stylets,* which form the center of the proboscis. The stylets are covered and protected by the insect's lower lip, called the *labium.* As the stylets enter the skin, the labium bends and slides upward out of the way. Then saliva flows into the wound through channels formed by the stylets. The mosquito can easily sip the blood because the saliva keeps it from clotting. Most persons are allergic to the saliva, and an itchy welt called a "mosquito bite" forms on the skin. After the mosquito has sipped enough blood, it slowly pulls the stylets out of the wound, and the labium slips into place over them. Then the insect flies away.[33]

Pattern: _____

Reason: _____

Diagram:

8. To understand the organization of long-term memory, then, we need to understand what kinds of information can be stored there. Most theories distinguish skills or habits ("knowing how") from abstract or representational knowledge ("knowing that"). Procedural memories are memories of knowing how—for example, knowing how to comb your hair, use a pencil, or swim. Declarative memories are memories of "knowing that." Declarative memories, in turn, come in two varieties. Semantic memories are internal representations of the world, independent of any particular context. They include facts, rules, and concepts. On the basis of your semantic memory of the concept *cat,* you can describe a cat as a small, furry mammal that typically spends its time eating, sleeping, and staring into space, even though a cat may not be present when you give this description and you probably won't know how or when you learned it. Episodic memories, on the other hand, are internal representations of personally experienced events. They allow you to "travel back" in time. When you remember how your furry feline once surprised you in the middle of

the night by pouncing on your face as you slept, you are retrieving an episodic memory.[34]

Pattern: _____

Reason: _____

   Diagram:

9. People turn to magic chiefly as a form of insurance—that is, they use it along with actions that actually bring results. For example, hunters may use a hunting charm. But they also use their hunting skills and knowledge of animals. The charm may give hunters the extra confidence they need to hunt even more successfully than they would without it. If they shoot a lot of game, they credit the charm for their success. Many events occur naturally without magic. Crops grow without it, and sick people get well without it. But if people use magic to bring a good harvest or to cure a patient, they may believe the magic was responsible. People also tend to forget magic's failures and to be impressed by its apparent successes. They may consider magic successful if it appears to work only 10 percent of the time. Even when magic fails, people often explain the failure without doubting the power of the magic. They may say that the magician made a mistake in reciting the spell or that another magician cast a more powerful spell against the magician.

   Many anthropologists believe that people have faith in magic because they feel a need to believe in it. People may turn to magic to reduce their fear and uncertainty if they feel they have no control over the outcome of a situation. For example, farmers use knowledge and skill when they plant their fields. But they know that weather, insects, or diseases might ruin the crops. So farmers in some societies may also plant a charm or perform a magic rite to ensure a good harvest.[35]

Pattern: _____

Reason: _____

Diagram:

10. Almost all companies realize the tremendous value of mathematics in research and planning. Many major industrial firms employ trained mathematicians. Mathematics has great importance in all engineering projects. For example, the design of a superhighway requires extensive use of mathematics. The construction of a giant dam would be impossible without first filling reams of paper with mathematical formulas and calculations. The large number of courses an engineering student must take in mathematics shows the importance of mathematics in this field.[36]

Pattern: _____

Reason: _____

Diagram:

■■■■■■■■ *WORKING TOGETHER*

Directions: Locate and mark five paragraphs in one of your textbooks or in Part 6 of this text that are clear examples of the thought patterns discussed in this chapter. Write the topic sentence of each paragraph on a separate index card. Once your instructor has formed small groups, choose a group "reader" who will collect all the cards and read each sentence aloud. Groups should discuss each and predict the pattern of the paragraph from which the sentence was taken. The "finder" of the topic sentence then confirms or rejects the choice, quoting sections of the paragraph if necessary.

■■■■■■■■ SUMMARY

How can I better comprehend and recall paragraphs I read?

Recognizing the author's thought pattern will improve comprehension and recall.

What is a thought pattern?

A thought pattern is the way in which an author organizes ideas.

What are the six common thought patterns?

The six common thought patterns are:

1. Illustration/Example—an idea is explained by providing specific instances or experiences that illustrate it.

2. Definition—an object or idea is explained by describing the general class or group to which it belongs and how the item differs from others in the same group (distinguishing features).

3. Comparison/Contrast—a new or unfamiliar idea is explained by showing how it is similar to or different from a more familiar idea.

4. Cause/Effect—connections between events are explained by showing what caused an event or what happened as a result of a particular event.

5. Classification—an object or idea is explained by dividing it into parts and describing or explaining each.

6. Chronological Order/Process—events or procedures are described in the order in which they occur in time.

Making Your Skills Work Together

Understanding Sentences and Paragraphs

Part Three focused on two units of meaning: the sentence and the paragraph. Used together with the vocabulary skills presented in Part 1, these provide the skills necessary to understand written materials. The following summary suggestions will help you understand sentences and paragraphs more easily:

1. *Search for information.* Try to sort the more important ideas from the less important ones. In sentences, sort key ideas from the information that explains them. In paragraphs, search for the main ideas and sift through the details to find the most important ones to remember.

2. *Look for relationships.* In reading sentences, try to see how parts of the sentence are connected. In reading paragraphs, discover how the details explain the main idea.

3. *Look for patterns in the way ideas are organized or put together.* In sentences, try to see whether there is one basic idea, two combined ideas, or two or more related ideas. In paragraphs, look for the thought pattern that is used to tie details together.

4. *Keep this question constantly in mind: "Do I understand this?"* The moment you feel the answer might be "no," stop and go back. Find out what is wrong. The problem may be an unknown word or words. If so, use the vocabulary skills you learned in Part 1. The problem may be a long, complicated sentence or a confusing paragraph. If so, analyze it using the techniques suggested in Part 2.

EXERCISE
1

Purpose for
reading: What
are the barriers
to effective lis-
tening?

DIRECTIONS: *The following selection, taken from a business communications textbook, has been specially marked and includes marginal notes. They call your attention to the clues that help you to find what is important and to notice patterns and relationships. Read the selection, paying attention to the special markings and notes. Then answer the questions that follow.*

Barriers to Effective Listening

—*Norman B. Sigband*

First barrier

Perhaps the most important barrier to effective listening results from the fact   1
that most of us talk at about 125–150 words per minute while we can listen
and comprehend some 600–800 words per minute. Quite obviously if the
sender talks at 125 words and the receiver listens at 600, the latter is left with
a good deal of time to think about matters other than the message; and he
does: illness, bills, cars, the baseball results, what's for dinner tonight, and so
on. This is the internal competition for attention.

Signals contrast,
new barrier

However, there is also the external competition to effective listening. These   2
are the distractions caused by clattering typewriters, ringing telephones, noisy
production lines, heated arguments, intriguing smells, captivating sights, and
dozens of other factors we all encounter in a busy, complex society.

New barrier
introduced

Time, or more accurately, the lack of it, also contributes to inefficient lis-   3
tening. Effective listening requires that we give others a block of time so they
may express their ideas as well as their feelings. Some individuals require
more time than others to do this. If we are, or we appear to be, impatient
they will either not express themselves fully or will require more time than
usual. And yet the listener possesses a limited amount of time also. In addition, there are some individuals who will monopolize *all* your listening time.
As a matter of fact, if you begin to listen to such a person at noon, you will
probably still be listening at 10:00 P.M.

That person you must turn off as tactfully as possible. However, there are   4
others with whom you work or live that you should give time to so you may
listen with undivided attention. Remember, if *you* don't listen to "them," they
will always find someone who *will*.

If an employee feels her supervisor won't listen to her, she will find an-   5
other employee or the union representative who will; if a youngster feels his
parents won't or don't listen to him, he may find a friend, gang member, or

someone whose influence might be detrimental. And if customers feel a supplier really isn't listening, they will find a competitor to the supplier who will.

There is no such thing as a vacuum in communication. 6

New barrier
Use context to
define *conditioning*

Conditioning is still another factor that contributes to poor listening. 7
Many of us have conditioned ourselves not to listen to messages that do not agree with our philosophy or that irritate, upset, or anger us. TV and radio play a role in this conditioning. If the program we see or hear doesn't entertain or intrigue us, we have been conditioned to reach over and simply change channels or stations. And this habit of changing the channel to tune a message out, we carry into our daily listening activities.

Our tendency to evaluate what we hear may constitute still another barrier. 8
So often we listen and almost immediately evaluate and reject the idea before it is completely voiced. Or we listen and then detour mentally while the individual is still talking. Of course, it is not possible *not* to evaluate, but one should continue to listen *after* evaluating. The problem is that most of us tune out as soon as we hear an idea or point of view that does not agree with ours.

New barrier

Emotions, if colored or at a high level, may also get in the way of effective listening. Surely if an individual hears ideas which are counter to his, or is involved in a confrontation, or is emotionally upset because of fear, anger, or happiness, effective listening becomes very difficult. 9

New barrier

Lack of training on how to listen is still another barrier. Most of us have 10
received much instruction on how to write more concisely and clearly, read more efficiently and rapidly, and speak more forcefully and effectively. But few of us have ever received any instruction on how to listen. Perhaps this flaw in our educational system is due to the belief on the part of many educators that if one hears, that individual is also listening. The fact remains that more effective listening *can* be taught. Fortunately more and more schools today are teaching youngsters how to listen more effectively, and there are even programs available in many universities.

New barrier

Our failure to concentrate is another barrier to effective listening. That 11
may be due to the fact that many of us have not been taught how to listen or to the simple fact that we don't *work* at listening.

All you need do is look around the room at the next meeting you attend. 12
Note how many people are sitting in a completely sprawled posture; some even have their feet stretched out on the chair next to them or on top of the meeting table or desk. How can anyone really work at listening while in a completely relaxed posture? And even if the individual does listen well in that position, think of what that posture conveys nonverbally to the speaker!

It does little good, except as items of information, to name (as we have) 13
eight reasons why many of us don't listen well. What is really of concern to us, is how we can become better listeners . . . and most of us *can* become better.[1]

1. Review the article and locate any difficult words that you don't know the meaning of. List them below. Study the context for clues. If there are no clues, analyze each word's parts and/or check the meaning in the dictionary. Write a brief definition of each.

_____

_____

_____

2. Underline the sentence in the first paragraph that best explains why our minds wander while listening.

3. Underline the main idea of each of the remaining paragraphs in the selection.

4. What thought pattern is used throughout the selection? Give a reason for your answer.

_____

_____

5. Do paragraphs 4 and 5 introduce new barriers to listening? If so, list them below. If not, explain the functions of these paragraphs.

_____

_____

6. In the last paragraph the author indicates that eight barriers to listening have been discussed. Without looking at the article, list as many barriers as you can recall. Then, check to find any you missed.

_____   _____

_____   _____

_____   _____

_____   _____

PART 4

Textbook Reading Skills

*L*et's take the case of a typical college student, Sam Sample, and see how he prepared for an exam in sociology. The exam was to cover five chapters in Sam's textbook as well as several articles assigned by the instructor. To prepare for the exam, Sam reread each of the textbook chapters. The articles were on reserve in the library, so Sam read each one. He spent a total of six hours studying, mostly on the day before the exam. A week later, when he got his graded exam paper back, he learned he had failed. Sam was angry and disappointed; he was overheard saying to a friend, "I don't know what the instructor expects. I spent six hours studying and I still failed!" Why do you think Sam failed?

The main reason Sam failed is that, although he spent time studying, he did not study *in the right way*. In fact, he used one of the *least effective* ways to study—reading and rereading. Sam's failure to review the assigned articles may also explain his poor grade. Although he could not take the articles from the library, he could have written an outline or a summary of each for review purposes. Finally, Sam limited his study to the day before the exam and did not allow himself time to think about and organize the material mentally.

Reading Textbook Chapters

■ ■

THIS CHAPTER WILL SHOW YOU HOW TO

1. *Use textbook learning aids*

2. *Follow the organization of textbook chapters*

3. *Read technical material*

■ ■

Do you ever wonder how you will be able to learn the vast amounts of information contained in each of your textbooks? Fortunately, nearly all textbook authors are college instructors. They work with students daily and understand students' difficulties. Therefore, they include in their textbooks numerous features or aids to make learning easier. They also organize chapters in ways that express their ideas as clearly as possible. This chapter will discuss textbook learning aids and the organization of textbook chapters. It will also suggest special approaches to use when reading technical material.

Textbook Learning Aids

While textbooks may seem long, difficult, and impersonal, they do contain numerous features that are intended to help you learn. By taking advantage of these features, you can make textbook reading easier.

The Preface

The **preface** is the author's introduction to the text. The preface presents basic information about the text you should know before you begin reading. It may contain such information as:

- Why and for whom the author wrote the text
- How the text is organized
- Limitations of the text (topics not covered)
- References and authorities consulted
- Major points of emphasis
- Learning aids included and how to use them

The following is an excerpt from the preface of a biology text. Read the excerpt, noting the type of information it provides.

■ ■ ■ ■ ■
Preface

Overview

Definition

I confess to a certain exuberance in presenting the fifth edition of *Biology, the World of Life*. I suspect I feel this way because I've finally completed it—it's done. At the same time I wish that I had some way to continue working, to magically update it, even while it's in your hands. This is because the story of biology is never "done." <u>Biology is the story of life and life changes.</u> Furthermore, it changes by the minute. I made a great effort to bring this book up to the minute, even making changes, updates, and adding new material at stages that must have driven my editors up the wall. (In fact, I'm sure that's the case—I have my sources.) At some point, however, I was forced to relinquish these pages and to turn them over to you. . . .

Biology, the Living Science

Examples of questions biology investigates

But biology is more than just a way to get at earthshaking problems. It's also the lively science. So there are a host of researchers out there solving all kinds of fascinating problems, such as, <u>Why do marathon runners "hit the wall?" How do pigeons know which way is home? How are new species born? How can gene splicing techniques increase crop yields? How does memory work? How does life evolve on islands?</u> And on it goes.

Because biology is both fun and critical at once, writing about it is a challenge. It seems to me, though, that precisely because the story of life is so fascinating, even compelling, the telling of it should not dampen that spirit. So, here and there you might find a lighthearted comment and I may have even let an opinion through. But if you end up liking biology, and forming your own opinions, well, that's what this is all about.

Content Features

Approach

The text moves from the micro- to the macroscopic world; that is, it takes the traditional approach of first discussing the molecular basis of life and moving toward the big picture—ecosystems. However, the format of this text is strikingly unique in that this development theme is placed in a historical context and brought home to the student by considerations of such topics as technology, ethics and human concerns. The historical information adds perspective to the discussion, allowing the student to place himself and herself in the proper position in the pageant of life. The personal and direct discussions of ethics and values are at the root of decision-making in a world where it can still make a difference.

Function of historical information

The essays, we feel, are one of the strongest features of an interesting book, simply because the topics, themselves, are so interesting. The essays have been carefully developed to augment the stories being told and to weave a certain richness into the fabric of the whole cloth.

Function of essays

The result, we feel, is the story of biology told so that it makes sense, stimulates, teaches, and so that it *invites* the student—draws the student in— by the compelling nature of the story of life, itself. . . .

Ancillaries

Learning aid

A Student Study Guide is available. This includes learning objectives, learning tips, names of note, and a study section for each chapter. Each study section contains overviews of section concepts, specific learning objectives, vocabulary checklists, and essay-type questions. Also included are self tests of multiple choice and matching questions.[1]

To the Student

Some textbooks contain a section titled "To the Student," as does this text. This section is written specifically for you. It contains practical introductory information about the text. It may, for example, explain features of the book and how to use them, or it may offer suggestions for learning and studying the text. Often, a

"To the Instructor" section precedes or follows "To the Student" and contains information useful to your instructor.

DIRECTIONS: *Read or reread the "To the Student" section on p. xvii of this book. Then answer the following questions.*

1. For what purpose was this book written?

_____

2. For whom is this book written?

_____

3. Underline the portions of the introduction that indicate the topics the text covers.

4. Underline the part(s) of the introduction that tell how the text is organized.

5. What features (learning aids) does this text contain to help you learn?

_____

_____

Table of Contents

The **table of contents** is an outline of the text. It lists all the important topics and subtopics covered. Glancing through a table of contents will give you an overview of the text and suggest its organization.

Before beginning to read a particular chapter in a textbook, refer to the table of contents again. Although chapters are intended to be separate parts of a book, it is important to see how they fit together as parts of the whole—the textbook itself.

The Opening Chapter

The first chapter of a textbook is one of the most important. Here the author sets the stage for what is to follow. At first glance, the first chapter may not seem to say much, and you may be tempted to skip it. Actually the opening chapter deserves close attention. More important, it introduces the important terminology used throughout the text.

Typically you can expect to find as many as 40 to 60 new words introduced and defined in the first chapter. These words are the language of the course, so to speak. To be successful in any new subject area, it is essential to learn to read and speak its language.

Typographical Aids

Textbooks contain various typographical aids (arrangements or types of print) that make it easy to pick out what is important to learn and remember. These include the following:

1. **Italic type** (slanted print) is often used to call attention to a particular word or phrase. Often new terms are printed in italics in the sentence in which they are defined.

   The term *drive* is used to refer to internal conditions that force an individual to work toward some goal.

2. **Enumeration** refers to the numbering or lettering of facts and ideas within a paragraph. It is used to emphasize key ideas and to make them easy to locate.

   Consumer behavior and the buying process involve five mental states: (1) awareness of the product, (2) interest in acquiring it, (3) desire or perceived need, (4) action, and (5) reaction or evaluation of the product.

3. **Headings and subheadings** divide the chapters into sections and label the major topic of each section. Basically, they tell in advance what each section will be about. When read in order, the headings and subheadings form a brief outline of the chapter.

4. **Colored print** is used in some texts to emphasize important ideas or definitions.

Chapter Questions

Many textbooks include discussion and/or review questions at the end of each chapter. Try to read these through when you preread the chapter (see Chapter 4). Then, after you have read the chapter, use the questions to review and test yourself. Since the review questions cover the factual content of the chapter, they can help you prepare for objective exams. Discussion questions often deal with interpretations or applications of the content. Use these in preparing for essay exams. Math, science, or technical courses may have problems instead of questions (see p. 196 of this chapter). Here are a few sample review and discussion questions taken from a business marketing textbook:

Review Questions

1. List some product characteristics that are of concern to marketers.
2. Distinguish between a trademark and a brand name.
3. What are some characteristics of good brand names?
4. Describe the three kinds of labels.

Discussion Questions

1. What do you think is the future of generic products?
2. Go to your local food store and look at the ways the products are packaged. Find three examples of packages that have value in themselves. Find three examples of packages that promote the products' effectiveness.
3. There is much controversy about the use of warning labels on products. Outline the pros and cons of this issue.
4. How would you go about developing a brand name for a new type of bread?

Did you notice that the review questions check your knowledge of factual information? These questions ask you to list, describe, or explain. To answer them, you have to recall the information contained in the chapter. The discussion questions, on the other hand, cannot be answered simply by looking up information in the text. Instead, you have to apply the information in the text to a practical situation or pull together and organize information.

Vocabulary List

Textbooks often contain a list of new terms introduced in the book. This list may appear at the beginning or end of individual chapters or at the back of the book. In some texts new terms are printed in the margin next to the portion of the text in which the term is introduced. Regardless of where they appear, vocabulary lists are a valuable study and review aid. Many instructors include on exams items that test mastery of new terms. Here is a sample vocabulary list taken from a financial management textbook.

Key Terms

assets
budget
cash flow statement
fixed disbursements
liabilities
money market fund
net worth
net worth statement
occasional disbursements

Notice that the author identifies the terms but does not define them. In such cases, mark new terms as you come across them in a chapter. After you have finished the chapter, review each marked term and its definition. To learn the terms, use the index card system suggested in Chapter 3.

Glossary

A **glossary** is a mini-dictionary that lists alphabetically the important vocabulary used in a book. A glossary is faster and more convenient to use than a dictionary. It does not list all the common meanings of a word as a dictionary does but instead gives only the meaning used in the text. Here is an excerpt from the glossary of an American government textbook:

pork barrel.   The list of federal projects, grants, and contracts available to cities, businesses, colleges, and institutions in a district. For members of Congress these provide a means of "servicing the constituency." See also **casework.** (11)

potential group.   Composed of all people who might be group members because they share some common interest. Potential groups are almost always larger than **actual groups.** (9)

poverty line.   According to the Bureau of the Census, this line is drawn at a sum of money that takes into account what a family would need to spend for "austere" but minimally adequate amounts of nutrition, housing, and other needs. (17)

power.   According to Robert Dahl, the capacity to get others to do something they would not otherwise do. The desire for power is one reason why people play the **politics** game. (1)

precedent.   The way similar **cases** were settled in the past that proves to be important in later decisions. (14)

presidential primary.   An election in which party voters in a state vote for a candidate (or a slate of delegates committed to the candidate) as their choice for the party's **nomination.** (8)[2]

The numbers in parentheses indicate the chapter in which the term is discussed. Look at the entry for the word *power*. First, you can see that *power* is defined only as the term is used in the field of government. The word *power* has many other meanings (see the section on multiple-meaning words in Chapter 3). Compare the glossary definition with the collegiate dictionary definition of the same word shown below.

pow•er (pou′ər) *n. Abbr.* **pwr. 1.** The ability or capacity to act or perform effectively. **2.** *Often plural.* A specific capacity, faculty, or aptitude: *his powers of concentration.* **3.** Strength or force exerted or capable of being exerted; might. **4.** The ability or official capacity to exercise control; authority. **5.** A person, group, or nation having great influence or control over others. **6.** The might of a nation, political organization, or similar group. **7.** Forcefulness; effectiveness. **8.** *Regional.* A large number or amount. **9.** *Physics.* The rate at which work is done, mathematically expressed as the first derivative of work with respect to time and commonly measured in units such as the watt and horsepower. **10.** *Electricity.* **a.** The product of applied potential difference and current in a direct-current circuit. **b.** The product of the effective values of the voltage and current with the cosine of the phase angle between current and voltage in an alternating-current circuit. **11.** *Mathematics.* **a.** An exponent *(see).* **b.** The number of elements in a finite set. **12.** *Optics.* A measure of the **magnification** *(see)* of an optical instrument, as a microscope or telescope. **13.** *Plural. Theology.* The sixth group of angels in the hierarchical order of nine. See **angel. 14.** *Archaic.* An armed force. —See Synonyms at **strength.** —*tr.v.* **powered, -ering, -ers.** To supply with power, especially mechanical power. [Middle English *pouer,* from Old French *poeir, povoir,* from *poeir,* to be able, from Old Latin *potēre* (unattested) (superseded by *posse*). See **poti-** in Appendix.*][3]

Try to pick out the definition of *power* that is closest to the one given in the glossary. Did it take time to find the right definition? You can see that a glossary is a time-saving device.

At the end of a course, a glossary can serve as a useful study aid, since it lists the important terminology introduced throughout the text. Review the glossary and test your recall of the meaning of each entry.

**EXERCISE
9-2**

DIRECTIONS: *Choose a textbook from one of your other courses. (Do not choose a workbook or book of readings.) If you do not have a textbook, use a friend's or borrow one from the library. Answer each of the following questions by referring to the textbook.*

Textbook title: _____

1. What learning aids does the book contain?

    _____

    _____

    _____

2. Of what importance is the information given in the preface?

    _____

    _____

3. Preread the opening chapter. What is its function?

    _____

    _____

4. Review the table of contents. How is the subject divided?

    _____

    _____

How Textbook Chapters are Organized

Have you ever walked into an unfamiliar supermarket and felt lost and confused? You did not know where anything was located and thought you would never find the items you needed. How did you finally locate what you needed? You probably found that signs hanging over the aisles indicated the types of products shelved in each section, which enabled you to find the right aisle. Then you no doubt found that similar products were grouped together, for example, all the cereal was in one place, all the meat was in another, and so forth.

You can easily feel lost and confused when reading textbook chapters, too. A chapter can seem like a huge, disorganized collection of facts, ideas, numbers, dates, and events to be memorized. Actually, a textbook chapter is, in one respect, much like a large supermarket. It, too, has signs that identify what is located in each section. These signs are the headings that divide the chapter into topics. Underneath each heading, similar ideas are grouped together, just as similar products are grouped together in a supermarket. Sometimes a group of similar or related ideas is labeled by a subheading (usually set in smaller type than the heading and/or indented differently). In most cases, several paragraphs come under one heading. In this way chapters take a major idea, break it into its important parts, and then break those parts into smaller parts.

You could picture the organization of the present chapter as shown in the diagram below.

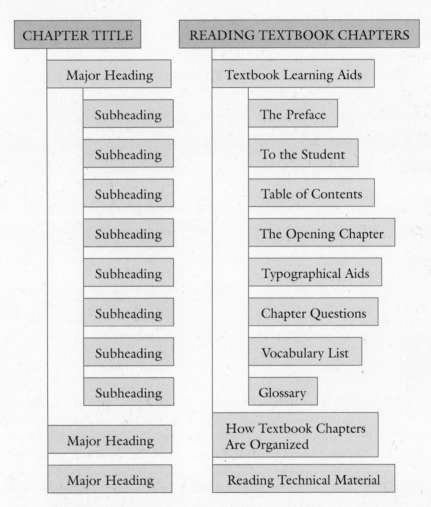

Notice that this chapter has three major headings and that the first major heading is divided into eight subheadings. Since the chapter is divided into three major headings, you know that it covers three major topics. You can also tell that the first major heading discusses eight types of textbook aids. Of course, the number of major headings, subheadings, and paragraphs under each will vary from chapter to chapter in a book.

When you know how a chapter is organized, you can use this knowledge to guide your reading. Once you are familiar with the structure, you will also begin to see how ideas are connected. The chapter will then seem orderly, moving from one idea to the next in a logical fashion.

Look at the following partial listing of headings and subheadings from a chapter of an anthropology textbook.

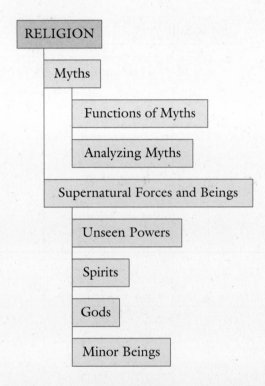

In this chapter on religion, "Myths" and "Supernatural Forces and Beings" are the first two major topics. The topic "Myths" is broken into two parts: functions and analysis. Although not shown on the diagram, each subtopic is further divided into paragraphs that list and describe particular functions and, for the second topic, present methods of analysis. If there were four paragraphs under the subheading "Functions of Myths," it would be reasonable to expect that four main points will be presented about the functions of myths.

You are probably beginning to see that titles and headings, taken together, form a brief outline of a chapter. Later, in Chapter 11, you will see how these headings can help you make a more complete outline of a chapter. For now, think of headings as a guide to reading that directs you through a chapter point by point.

EXERCISE 9-3

DIRECTIONS: *On a separate sheet, draw a diagram that shows the organization of Chapter 4 of this book.*

EXERCISE 9-4

DIRECTIONS: *Choose one of the textbooks that you are using for another course. Select a chapter you have already read and, on a separate sheet, draw an organizational diagram of its contents. Use the diagram on p. 187 as a guide.*

Reading Technical Material

If you are taking courses in the sciences, technologies, engineering, data processing, or health-related fields, you are working with a specialized type of textbook. This type of textbook is also used in courses that prepare students for specialized careers, such as food service, air conditioning and refrigeration repair, lab technology, and so forth.

In this section you will see how technical textbooks differ from those used in other classes. You will also learn several specific approaches to reading technical material.

Each of the following paragraphs describes a spice called nutmeg. Read each and decide how they differ.

Nutmeg is a spice derived by grating the kernel of the fruit produced by the nutmeg tree. This tree belongs to the nutmeg family, *Myristicacae,* genus *Myristica,* species *M. fragrans.* The tree grows to a height of seventy feet and is an evergreen. As the fruit of the tree ripens, it hardens and splits open at the top, showing a bright scarlet membrane. The spice called mace is made from this membrane.

Nutmeg is a pungent, aromatic spice often added to foods to give them a delicious tang and perfume. It adds a subtle spiciness to desserts and perks up the flavor of such bland dishes as potatoes. Nutmeg comes from a tree grown in warm climates. The nutmeg tree is tall and gracious, with long, pale leaves and beautiful yellow flowers.

Did you notice that the first paragraph presented only precise, factual information? The words used have exact meanings. Some words have technical meanings (*genus, species, Myristica*). Others are everyday words used in a special way (*evergreen, membrane*). An abbreviation, *M.,* was also used. Because of its language, the paragraph does not allow for interpretation or expression of opinion. In fact, you cannot tell whether the writer likes or has ever tasted nutmeg. The purpose of the paragraph is to give clear, detailed information about nutmeg.

The second paragraph is written quite differently. It presents fewer facts and more description. Many words—such as *delicious, beautiful, gracious,* and *subtle*—do not have a precise meaning. They allow room for interpretation and judgment. This paragraph is written to help you imagine how nutmeg tastes as well as to tell where it comes from.

Paragraph 1 is an example of technical writing. You can see that technical writing is a precise, exact, factual type of writing. This section will discuss particular features of technical writing and suggest approaches to reading technical material.

Fact Density

Technical writing is highly factual and dense (packed with ideas). A large number of facts are closely fitted together in each paragraph. Compared to other types of writing, technical writing may seem crowded with information and difficult to read. Here are a few suggestions on how to handle densely written material:

1. *Read technical material more slowly and carefully than other textbooks.* Allow more time for a technical reading assignment than for other assignments.
2. *Plan on reviewing various sections several times.* Sometimes it is useful to read a section once rather quickly to learn what key ideas it contains. Then read it a second time carefully, fitting together all the facts that explain the key ideas.
3. *Keep a notebook of important information.* In some textbooks, you can underline what is important to remember. (This method is discussed in Chapter 11.) However, since technical books are so highly factual, underlining may not work well—it may seem that everything is important, and you will end up with most of a page underlined. Instead, try using a notebook to record information you need to remember. Writing information in your own words is a good way to check whether you really understand it.

DIRECTIONS: *Refer to the two paragraphs about nutmeg on p. 189. Count how many facts (separate pieces of information) each paragraph contains. Write the number in the space provided. Then list several facts as examples.*

	Paragraph 1	Paragraph 2
Number of facts:	_____	_____
Examples:	1. _____	1. _____
	2. _____	2. _____
	3. _____	3. _____

The Vocabulary of Technical Writing

Reading a technical book is in some ways like visiting a foreign country where an unfamiliar language is spoken. You hear an occasional word you know, but, for the most part, the people are communicating in a way you cannot understand.

Technical writing is built upon a set of precise, exact word meanings in each subject area. Since each field has its own language, you must learn the language in order to understand the material. Here are a few sentences taken from several technical textbooks. As you read each sentence, note the large number of technical words used.

Engineering Materials

If the polymer is a mixture of polymers, the component homopolymers (polymers of a single monomer species) and their percentages should be stated.[4]

Auto Mechanics

Each free end of the three stator windings is connected to the leads of one negative diode and one positive diode.[5]

Data Processing

Another advantage of the PERFORM/VARYING statement is that the FROM value and the BY value may be any numeric value (except that the BY value may not be zero).[6]

In the above examples, some words are familiar ones with new, unfamiliar meanings *(FROM, BY)*. Others are words you may never have seen before *(monomer, stator)*.

TABLE 9-1
Examples of Specialized Vocabulary in Technical Writing

Field	Word	Technical Meaning
Familiar words		
chemistry	base	a chemical compound that reacts with an acid to form a salt
electrical engineering	ground	a conductor that makes an electrical connection with the earth
nursing	murmur	an abnormal sound heard from a body organ (especially the heart)
Specialized terms		
computer science	modem	an interface (connector) that allows the computer to send and receive digital signals over telephone lines or through satellites
astronomy	magnetosphere	the magnetic field that surrounds the earth or other magnetized planet
biology	cocci	spherically shaped bacteria

In technical writing, there are two types of specialized vocabulary, familiar words with new technical meanings and specialized terms. Examples of each are given in Table 9-1.

Tips for Learning Technical Vocabulary

Many of the techniques you have already learned for developing your general vocabulary also work with technical vocabulary. Here are some ways to apply these techniques:

1. Context clues (see Chapter 1) are commonly included in technical writing. A definition clue is most frequently used when a word is introduced for the first time. As each new word is introduced, mark it in your text and later transfer it to your notebook. Organize this section of your notebook by chapter. Use the card system described in Chapter 3 to learn words you are having trouble remembering.
2. Analyzing parts (see Chapter 2) is a particularly useful approach for developing technical vocabulary. The technical words in many fields are created from particular sets of prefixes, roots, and suffixes. Here are several examples from the field of medicine.

Prefix	Meaning	Example	Definition
cardi	heart	cardiogram	test that measures contractions of the heart
		cardiology	medical study of diseases and functioning of the heart
		cardiologist	physician who specializes in heart problems
hem/hema/hemo	blood	hematology	study of the blood
		hemophilia	disease in which blood fails to clot properly
		hemoglobin	protein contained in the red blood cells

Most technical fields have a core of commonly used prefixes, roots, and suffixes. As you read technical material, keep a list of common word parts in your notebook. Add to the list throughout the course. For those you have difficulty remembering, use a variation of the word card system suggested in Chapter 3. Write the word on the front and its meaning, its pronunciation, and a sample sentence on the back.

3. Learn to pronounce each new term you come across. Pronouncing a word is a good way to fix it in your memory and will also help you remember its spelling.

4. Make use of the glossary in the back of the textbook, if it has one. (See p. 185 in this chapter for further information on using a glossary.)

5. If you are majoring in a technical field, it may be worthwhile to buy a subject area dictionary (see Chapter 3). Nursing students, for example, often buy a copy of Taber's *Cyclopedic Medical Dictionary*.

Abbreviations and Notations

In many technical fields, sets of abbreviations and notations (signs and symbols) provide shortcuts to writing out complete words or meanings.

Examples:

Field	Symbol	Meaning
Chemistry	Al	aluminum
	F	fluorine
	Fe	iron
Biology	X	crossed with
	♀	female organism
	♂	male organism
Physics	M	mass
Astronomy	D	diameter
	Δ	distance

To understand technical material, you must learn the abbreviations and notation systems that are used in a specific field. Check to see whether lists of abbreviations and symbols are included in the appendix (reference section) in the back of the textbook. Make a list in your notebook of those you need to learn. Make a point of using these symbols in your class notes whenever possible. Putting them to use regularly is an excellent way to learn them.

Graphic Aids

Most technical books contain numerous drawings, charts, tables, and diagrams. These may make the text look difficult and complicated, but, actually, such graphic aids help explain and make the text easier to understand. Illustrations, for example, give a visual picture of the idea or process being explained. Here is an example of a diagram taken from a computer programming text. The text to which the diagram refers is also included. Would you find the text easy to understand without the diagram?

An *input device* is a mechanism that accepts data from outside the computer and converts it into an electronic form understandable to the computer. The data that is accepted is called *input data,* or simply *input.* For example, one common way of entering input into a computer is to type it with a typewriter-like *keyboard.*

An *output device* performs the opposite function of an input device. An output device converts data from its electronic form inside the computer to a form that can be used outside. The converted data is called *output data,* or simply *output....*

Between the input devices and the output devices is the component of the computer that does the actual computing or processing. This is the *central processing unit,* or CPU. Input data is converted into an electronic form by an input device and sent to the central processing unit where the data is stored. In the CPU the data is used in calculations or other types of processing to produce the solution to the desired problem. The central processing unit contains two basic units: the internal storage and the processor. The *internal storage* is the "memory" of the computer. The *processor* is the unit that executes instructions to the program. Among other things, the processor contains electronic circuits that do arithmetic and perform logical operations. The final component of a computer is the *auxiliary storage.* This component stores data that is not currently being processed by the computer and programs that are not currently in use.[7]

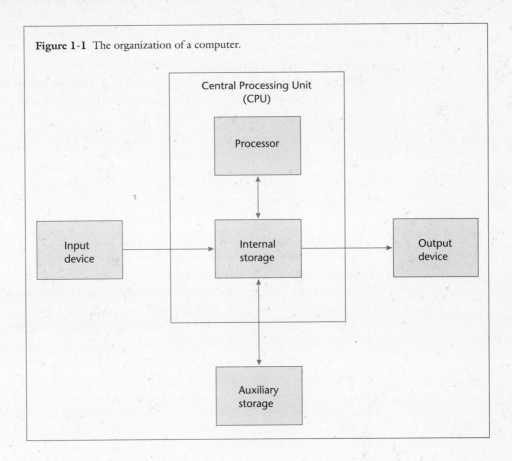

Figure 1-1 The organization of a computer.

Here are a few suggestions on how to use illustrations:

1. Go back and forth between the text and the illustrations. Illustrations are intended to be used together with the paragraphs that refer to them. You may have to stop reading several times to refer to an illustration. For example, when *input device* is mentioned in the preceding example, stop reading and find where the input device is located on the diagram. You may also have to reread parts of the explanation several times.
2. Study each illustration carefully. First, read the title or caption. These tell what the illustration is intended to show. Then look at each part of the illustration and try to see how they are connected. Notice any abbreviations, symbols, arrows, or labels. In the example given, the arrows are important. They suggest the direction or order in which the parts of the computer operate.

3. Test your understanding of illustrations by drawing and labeling an illustration of your own without looking at the one in the text. Then compare your drawing with the text. Notice whether anything is left out. If so, continue drawing and checking until your drawing is complete and correct. Include these drawings in your notebook and use them for review and study.

Examples and Sample Problems

Technical books include numerous examples and sample problems. Use the following suggestions when working with these:

1. Pay more attention to examples than you normally do in other textbooks. Examples and sample problems will often help you understand how rules, principles, theories, or formulas are actually used. Think of examples as connections between ideas on paper and practical, everyday use of those ideas.
2. Be sure to work through sample problems. Make sure you understand what was done in each step and why. For particularly difficult problems, try writing in your notebook a step-by-step list of how to solve that type of problem. Refer to sample problems as guides or models when doing problems at the end of the chapter or others assigned by the instructor.
3. Use the problems at the end of the chapter as a self-test. As you work through each problem, keep track of rules and formulas that you did not know and had to look up. Make note of the types of problems you could not solve without referring to the sample problems. You will need to do more work with each of these types.

EXERCISE 9-6

DIRECTIONS: Read the following excerpt from a textbook chapter titled "Mechanics" and answer the questions that follow.

Mechanics

Potential Energy

An object may store energy by virtue of its position. Such stored energy is called *potential energy,* for in the stored state an object has the potential for doing work. A stretched or compressed spring, for example, has potential energy. When a BB gun is cocked, energy is stored in the spring. A stretched rubber band has potential energy because of its position, for if it is part of a slingshot it is capable of doing work.

The chemical energy in fuels is potential energy, for it is actually energy of position when looked at from a microscopic point of view. This energy is available when the positions of electrical charges within and between molecules are altered, that is, when a chemical change takes place. Potential energy is possessed by any substance that can do work through chemical action. The energy of coal, gas, electric batteries, and foods is potential energy. Potential energy may be due to an elevated position of a body. Water in an elevated reservoir and the heavy ram of a pile driver when lifted have energy because of position. The energy of elevated positions is usually called *gravitational potential energy*.

The measure of the gravitational potential energy that an elevated body has is the work done against gravity in lifting it. The upward force required is equal to the weight of the body *W*, and the work done in lifting it through a height *h* is given by the product *Wh*; so we say

Gravitational potential energy = *Wh*

The potential energy of an elevated body depends only on its weight and vertical displacement *h* and is independent of the path taken to raise it (Figure 4.3).

Kinetic Energy

If we push on an object, we can set it in motion. More specifically, if we do work on an object, we can change the energy of motion of that object. If an

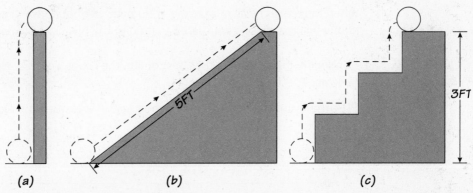

Figure 4.3 The potential energy of the 10-lb ball is the same in each case because the work done in elevating it 3 feet is the same whether it is (a) lifted with 10 lb of force, or (b) pushed with 6 lb of force up the 5-foot incline, or (c) lifted with 10 lb up each 1-foot stair—no work is done in moving it horizontally (neglecting friction).

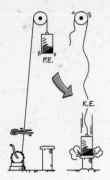

Figure 4.4 The potential energy of the elevated ram is converted to kinetic energy when released.

object is in motion, by virtue of that motion it is capable of doing work. We call energy of motion *kinetic energy.* The kinetic energy of an object is equal to half its mass multiplied by its velocity squared.

Kinetic energy = $\frac{1}{2} mv^2$

It can be shown that the kinetic energy of a moving body is equal to the work it can do in being brought to rest.*

Net force x distance = kinetic energy

or, in shorthand notation,

$Fd = \frac{1}{2} mv^2$

Accident investigators are well aware that an automobile traveling at 60 miles per hour has four times as much kinetic energy as an automobile traveling 30 miles per hour. This means that a car traveling at 60 miles per hour will skid four times as far when its brakes are locked as a car traveling 30 miles per hour. This is because the velocity is squared for kinetic energy.

Question

When the brakes of a car traveling at 90 miles per hour are locked, how much farther will the car skid compared to locking the brakes at 30 miles per hour?[8]

1. Underline the sentences that best define the terms *potential energy* and *kinetic energy.*

2. List the technical or specialized terms used in this selection. Define as many as possible.

_____

_____

*If we multiply both sides of $F = ma$ (Newton's second law) by d, we get $Fd = mad$; since $d = \frac{1}{2} at^2$, we can say $Fd = ma(\frac{1}{2} at^2) = \frac{1}{2} m(at)^2$; and substituting $v = at$, we get $Fd = \frac{1}{2} mv^2$.

3. List the abbreviations (notations) used in the article and give their meanings.

_____

_____

4. The writer uses examples as a means of explaining various ideas. List four of these examples and tell what each explains.

a. _____

b. _____

c. _____

d. _____

5. This excerpt contains two illustrations (Figures 4.3 and 4.4). The author does not discuss either in the text itself. Their use is left up to the reader. Describe when and how often you referred to each diagram.

_____

_____

6. What is Figure 4.3 intended to show?

_____

7. What is Figure 4.4 intended to show?

_____

8. What is the purpose of the question at the end of the article? To what type of energy does this question refer?

_____

_____

9. In your own words, explain the difference between potential energy and kinetic energy.

_____

_____

WORKING TOGETHER

Directions: Bring one of your textbooks to class. You may bring a textbook from another course or obtain one from the library. After your instructor forms groups, exchange texts with group members and review the learning aids in each text. Each student should evaluate the learning aid in each. Then, through discussion, make a list of the learning aids contained in each text and select the textbook that provides the "best" learning assistance. Groups may compare "winning" textbooks and choose an overall winner. Class members or the instructor may notify the course instructor(s) using the winning textbook that theirs was chosen.

SUMMARY

What types of learning aids do textbooks contain?

At the beginning of a textbook, the preface, table of contents, and opening chapter provide information on the scope and focus of the book. Within each chapter, typographical aids—italic type, enumeration, headings and sub-headings, and colored print—call attention to key information. At the end of each chapter, discussion questions and vocabulary lists provide an outline of important information and key words presented in the chapter. At the end of the textbook, the glossary provides a quick reference for important vocabulary presented in the book.

How are textbooks organized?

Textbooks are also organized so as to express ideas as clearly as possible. Through the use of headings and subheadings, chapters are divided into a number of sections that deal with different aspects of the subject covered in the chapter.

What features distinguish technical material?

The distinguishing features of technical material include fact density, specialized vocabulary, abbreviations and notations, drawings and illustrations, and examples and sample problems.

Reading Graphic Aids

THIS CHAPTER WILL SHOW YOU HOW TO

1. *Approach graphic aids*
2. *Interpret these aids*

One student was talking with a friend about her business textbook. She said, "It's difficult enough to read the chapters, but then you have to figure out all the diagrams and tables, too. And those things take time!" This student does not realize that graphic aids are designed to make the chapter itself easier to read and understand. Graphics and visuals summarize and condense information and actually save you time.

Try reading the following paragraph *without* looking at the diagram shown in Figure 10-1.

Our generalized flower is composed of four regions, each a **whorl** (or circle) of highly modified leaves. The whorls arise from a widened area, the **receptacle,** at the base of the flower. The whorl closest to the stem is the **calyx,** formed from leaflike **sepals** that were once the protective covering over the developing bud. The second whorl is the **corolla,** composed of the **petals.** In species that must attract animal pollinators (such as insects, birds, or even bats), the petals may be very bright and attractive, some with just the qualities to particularly attract certain species of pollinators. The third and fourth whorls contain the reproductive organs. The male part is the **stamen,** the female part, the **carpel.** Sometimes a carpel, or group of fused carpels (as they often appear) is called a **pistil.** Each stamen consists of a slender **filament** capped by an **anther** where, following meiosis, the male gametophyte is produced and released as **pollen.** Each carpel has three parts: the **ovary, style, and stigma.**[1]

Did you find the paragraph difficult and confusing? Now study Figure 10-1 and then reread the above paragraph.

Now the paragraph is easier to understand. You can see that graphics are a valuable aid, not a hindrance. This chapter will describe the various types of graphics commonly included in college textbooks. You will learn how to approach and interpret each kind.

A General Approach to Graphics

Graphics include tables, charts, graphs, diagrams, photographs, and maps. Here is a general step-by-step approach to reading graphics. As you read, apply each step to the graph shown in Figure 10-2 (Step 7 does not apply to this example).

1. ***Read the title or caption.*** The title will identify the subject and may suggest the relationship being described.

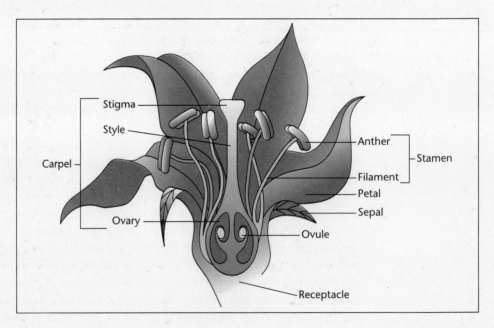

Figure 10-1 Diagram of a flower.[2]

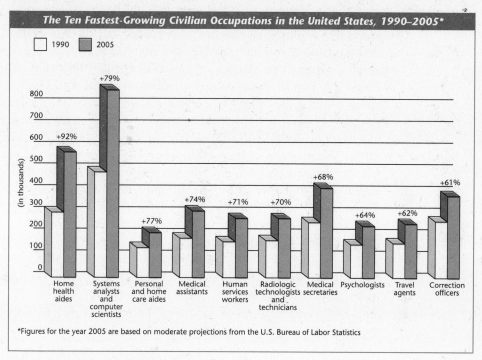

Figure 10-2 A sample graph.[3]

2. *Discover how the graphic is organized.* Read the column headings or labels on the horizontal and vertical axes.
3. *Identify the variables.* Decide what comparisons are being made or what relationship is being described.
4. *Analyze the purpose.* Based on what you have seen, predict what the graphic is intended to show. Is its purpose to show change over time, describe a process, compare costs, or present statistics?
5. *Determine scale, values, or units of measurement.* The scale is the ratio that a graphic has to the thing it represents. For example, a map may be scaled so that one inch on the map represents one mile.
6. *Study the data to identify trends or patterns.* Note changes, unusual statistics, or unexplained variations.
7. *Read the graphic along with corresponding text.* Refer to the paragraphs that discuss the graphic. These paragraphs may explain certain features of the graphic and identify trends or patterns.
8. *Make a brief summary note.* In the margin, jot a brief note summarizing the trend or pattern the graphic emphasizes. Writing will crystallize the idea in your mind and your note will be useful for reviewing.

In Figure 10-2 the title indicates the purpose of the graph: to compare the availability of jobs in various fast growth areas in 1990 and 2005. The vertical axis lists the number of jobs available. The horizontal axis lists the types of jobs. The graph compares the number of jobs available in 1990 with those projected for 2005. The unit of comparison is percentage of increase. The graph arranges the fastest growing jobs from highest to lowest percentage of increase. Each of the ten job areas examined is projected to show more than a 60 percent increase in employment by 2005. The top five areas project at least a 70 percent increase by 2005. The majority of these occupations are involved with human and medical support and services. A summary note might read "fastest growing jobs over the period of 1990–2005 will revolve around human health and well-being."

Types of Graphics

This section will describe six types of graphics: tables, graphs, charts, diagrams, maps, and photographs.

Tables

A table is an organized arrangement of facts, usually numbers or statistics. A table condenses large amounts of data to allow you to read and interpret it easily. Use the steps listed below as well as those listed on pp. 202–203 to read the table in Figure 10-3.

1. *Determine how the information is divided and arranged.* The table in Figure 10-3 is divided into two columns: magazine title and circulation (number of people who read each magazine). Note that the unit of measurement is millions of people.
2. *Make comparisons and look for trends.* Do this by surveying rows and columns, noting how each compares with the others. Look for similarities, differences, or sudden or unexpected variations. Underline or highlight unusual or outstanding figures.

   For Figure 10-3, note that some general-appeal magazines have a higher circulation than those intended for more specific audiences, such as *Woman's Day.* Also, some general-appeal magazines have a wider circulation than others. *TV Guide*'s circulation is much higher than that of *Time.*
3. *Draw conclusions.* Decide what the numbers mean and what they suggest about the subject. This table appeared in a section of an American government textbook dealing with how the public obtains information about politics and world events. You can conclude that the public does not rely heavily on newsmagazines as information sources.

```
┌─────────────────────────────────────────────┐
│  ┌───┐                                       │
│  │ 1 │  Who Reads What?                      │
│  └───┘                                       │
│                                              │
│  The Circulation of the Leading U.S. Magazines│
│                (in millions)                 │
│ ─────────────────────────────────────────── │
│                                              │
│       TV Guide                  19.9         │
│       Reader's Digest           17.7         │
│       National Geographic       10.5         │
│       Better Homes and Gardens   8.1         │
│       Family Circle              6.7         │
│       McCalls                    6.3         │
│       Woman's Day                6.2         │
│       Good Housekeeping          5.2         │
│       Ladies' Home Journal       5.2         │
│       Time                       4.6         │
│       National Enquirer          4.5         │
│       Playboy                    4.2         │
│       Star                       3.5         │
│       Penthouse                  3.2         │
│       Newsweek                   3.1         │
│       People                     3.0         │
│                                              │
└─────────────────────────────────────────────┘
```

Figure 10-3 A sample table.[4]

4. *Look for clues in corresponding text.* The textbook paragraph that corresponds to the table in Figure 10-3 is reprinted below.

Magazines—the other component of the print media—are read avidly by Americans, although the political content of our leading magazines is pretty slender. The so-called newsweeklies—mainly *Time, Newsweek,* and *U.S. News and World Report*—rank well behind such popular favorites as the *Reader's Digest, TV Guide,* and *Family Circle.* While *Time*'s circulation is a bit better than that of the *National Enquirer* (for "people with enquiring minds," its ads tell us), the *Star* and *Penthouse* edge out *Newsweek* in sales competition. Serious magazines of political news and opinion are basically reserved for the educated elite in America; such magazines as the *New Republic,* the *National Review,* and *Commentary* are greatly outsold by such American favorites as *Hot Rod, Weightwatchers Magazine,* and *Organic Gardening.*[5]

Notice the first two sentences. These reveal the author's interpretation of the graph.

DIRECTIONS: *The table in Figure 10-4 lists average daily circulation figures for the 25 largest U.S. newspapers during a six-month period in 1991. Study the table and answer the questions that follow.*

U.S. NEWSPAPERS WITH HIGHEST CIRCULATION
Circulation figures for the 25 largest newspapers in the USA for the six months ended.
Sept. 30, 22 reported gains in daily circulation form a year ago.

Newspaper	Average daily circulation Monday-Friday	Change from a year ago	Average weekend circulation	Change from a year ago
1. The Wall Street Journal	1,795,448	−3.3%	NA	NA
2. USA TODAY	1,418,477[1]	+5.3%	1,785,310	+2.1%
3. Los Angeles Times	1,770,253	−1.6%	1,529,609	+.08%
4. The New York Times	1,114,830	+0.6%	1,700,825	+0.8%
5. The Washington Post	791,289	+1.4%	1,143,145	+0.5%
6. Newsday[2]	763,972	+7.0%	875,239	+22.7%
7. (New York) Daily News	762,078	−30.6%	911,684	−34.9%
8. Chicago Tribune	723,178	+0.3%	1,107,938	+0.5%
9. Detroit Free Press Sun.: w/Detroit News	598,418	−5.9%	1,202,604	−3.0%
10. San Francisco Chronicle Sun.: w/Examiner	553,433	−1.7%	705,260	−0.7%
11. New York Post	552,227	+8.2%	NA	NA
12. Chicago Sun-Times	531,462	+0.8%	537,169	−2.0%
13. The Boston Globe	504,675	−3.2%	798,057	+0.8%
14. The Philadelphia Inquirer	503,603	−3.1%	974,697	−0.4%
15. The Atlanta Constitution/ Journal	474,578	−6.7%	688,175	+1.2%
16. The (Newark) Star Ledger	470,672	−1.2%	700,237	+1.0%
17. The Detroit News Sun.: w/Free Press	446,831	−10.8%	1,202,604	−3.0%
18. Houston Chronicle	439,574[3][4]		622,608	
19. The (Cleveland) Plain Dealer	413,678[3]	−3.4%	544,362	−1.3%
20. Minneapolis Star Tribune	408,365[3]	+0.2%	677,753	+1.6%
21. The Miami Herald	398,067[3]	−4.0%	510,549	−1.8%
22. The Dallas Morning News	393,511[5]	+2.1%	618,175	+5.5%
23. (Denver) Rocky Mountain News	355,940[3]	+1.6%	425,443	+4.9%
24. The St. Louis Post-Dispatch	350,350	−8.4%	562,700	+0.2%
25. The Orange County Register	347,675	−1.7%	400,375	−1.6%

1-Monday-Thursday. Friday-Saturday-Sunday circulation is counted on separately because ABC requires separate reporting when sales of one day exceed others by more than 15%.; 2 - total for Long Island and New York; 3 - Monday-Saturday; 4 - current publisher statement not filed. Figures for six months ended March 31; 5 - Monday-Thursday and Saturday. Friday circulation of 473,055 is counted separately because ABC requires separate reporting when sales of one day exceed others by more than 15%.

Figure 10-4 A table for use in Exercise 10-1.[6]

1. How is the table arranged?

   _____

2. Which newspaper experienced the greatest change in daily circulation from the previous year?

   _____

3. Which newspaper(s) experienced the greatest increase in average Sunday circulation in the previous year?

   _____

4. Which newspaper suffered the most dramatic loss of both daily and Sunday circulation?

   _____

Graphs

There are four types of graphs: bar, multiple bar, stacked bar, and linear. Each plots a set of points on a set of axes.

Bar Graphs

A bar graph is often used to make comparisons between quantities or amounts, and is particularly useful in showing changes that occur with passing time. Bar graphs usually are constructed to emphasize differences. The graph shown in Figure 10-5 compares the efficiency of producing five common types of meat. You can readily see that beef, which requires 16 pounds of feed to produce one pound of meat, is by far the least efficient.

Multiple Bar Graphs

A multiple bar graph makes at least two or three comparisons simultaneously. As you read them, be sure to identify exactly what comparisons are being made. Figure 10-6 compares the average (and estimated average) salaries of men and women from 1987 to 1993.

Stacked Bar Graphs

A stacked bar graph is an arrangement of data in which bars are placed one on top of another rather than side by side. This variation is often used to emphasize whole/part relationships. Stacked bar graphs show the relationship of a part to an

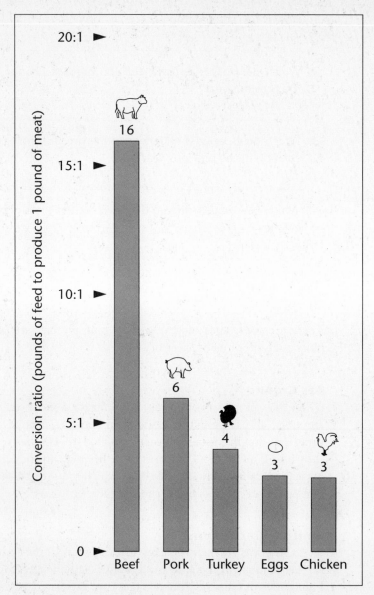

Figure 10-5 A sample bar graph.[7]

entire group or class. The graph in Figure 10-7 shows projected population figures for those over age 65 and those over age 85. Stacked bar graphs also allow numerous comparisons. The graph in Figure 10-7 compares the projected number of elderly people under and over 85 at seven time periods.

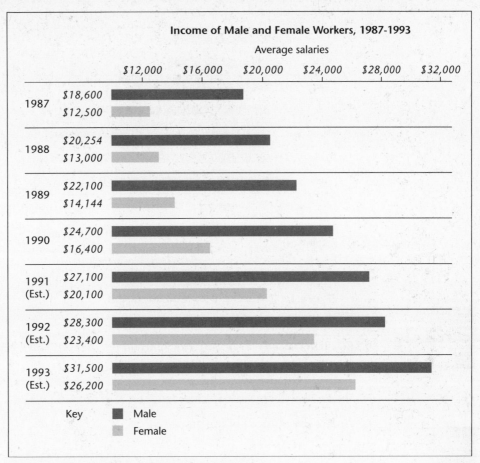

Income of Male and Female Workers, 1987-1993

Average salaries

	$12,000	$16,000	$20,000	$24,000	$28,000	$32,000
1987	$18,600	$12,500				
1988	$20,254	$13,000				
1989	$22,100	$14,144				
1990	$24,700	$16,400				
1991 (Est.)	$27,100	$20,100				
1992 (Est.)	$28,300	$23,400				
1993 (Est.)	$31,500	$26,200				

Key   ■ Male   ■ Female

Figure 10-6 A sample multiple bar graph.[8]

Linear Graphs

A linear, or line graph plots and connects points along a vertical and a horizontal axis. A linear graph allows more data points than a bar graph. Consequently, it is used to present more detailed and/or larger quantities of information. A linear graph may compare two variables; if so, then it consists of a single line. More often, however, linear graphs are used to compare relationships among several sets of variables and multiple lines are included. The graph shown in Figure 10-8 compares world population in billions of people every thousand years.

Linear graphs are usually used to display continuous data—data connected in time or events occurring in sequence. The data in Figure 10-8 are continuous, as they move from 8000 B.C. to 2000 A.D.

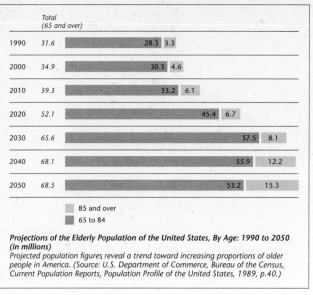

	Total (65 and over)		
1990	31.6	28.3	3.3
2000	34.9	30.3	4.6
2010	39.3	33.2	6.1
2020	52.1	45.4	6.7
2030	65.6	57.5	8.1
2040	68.1	55.9	12.2
2050	68.5	53.2	15.3

□ 85 and over
■ 65 to 84

Projections of the Elderly Population of the United States, By Age: 1990 to 2050 (in millions)
Projected population figures reveal a trend toward increasing proportions of older people in America. (Source: U.S. Department of Commerce, Bureau of the Census, Current Population Reports, Population Profile of the United States, 1989, p.40.)

Figure 10-7 A sample stacked bar graph.[9]

EXERCISE 10-2

DIRECTIONS: *Study the graphs shown in Figures 10-9 through 10-11 and answer the corresponding questions.*

Figure 10-9 Acceptable Suicide

1. What is the purpose of the graph?

   _____

   _____

2. What are the most and least acceptable reasons for suicide?

   Most: _____

   Least: _____

3. Between which two reasons is there the widest difference of opinion on acceptability?

   _____

   _____

4. What other reasons would you have liked to have seen included on the graph?

   _____

   _____

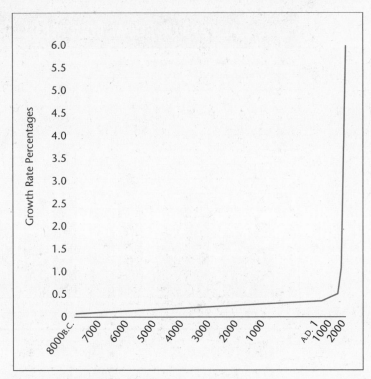

Figure 10-8 A sample linear graph.[10]

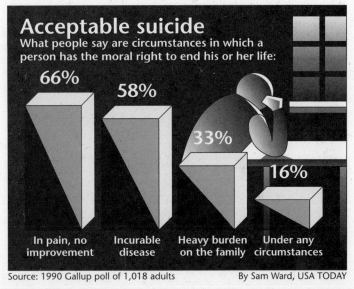

Figure 10-9 A bar graph.[11]

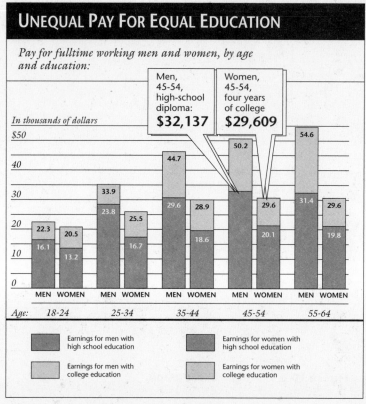

UNEQUAL PAY FOR EQUAL EDUCATION

Pay for fulltime working men and women, by age and education:

Men, 45-54, high-school diploma: **$32,137**

Women, 45-54, four years of college **$29,609**

In thousands of dollars

(bar values)

	MEN	WOMEN	MEN	WOMEN	MEN	WOMEN	MEN	WOMEN	MEN	WOMEN
high school	16.1	13.2	23.8	16.7	29.6	18.6	29.6	20.1	31.4	19.8
college (top)	22.3	20.5	33.9	25.5	44.7	28.9	50.2	29.6	54.6	29.6

Age: 18-24   25-34   35-44   45-54   55-64

Earnings for men with high school education
Earnings for women with high school education
Earnings for men with college education
Earnings for women with college education

Figure 10-10 A multiple bar graph.[12]

Figure 10-10 Unequal Pay for Education

1. What comparisons does this graph allow you to make?

_____

_____

2. How is this graph organized?

_____

_____

3. What patterns are evident?

_____

_____

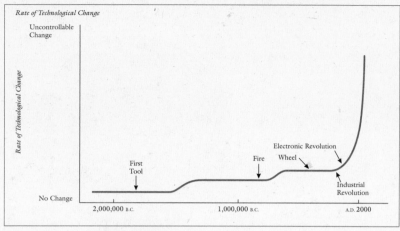

Figure 10-11 shows labels: Rate of Technological Change, Uncontrollable Change, No Change, First Tool, Fire, Wheel, Electronic Revolution, Industrial Revolution, with axis values 2,000,000 B.C., 1,000,000 B.C., A.D. 2000.

Figure 10-11 A linear graph.[13]

Figure 10-11 Rate of Technological Change

1. Describe the purpose of the graph.

   _____

   _____

2. What trend is evident?

   _____

   _____

3. Think of some examples of technological changes that have occurred over the past 50 years that may account for the dramatic upswing near the year 2000.

   _____

   _____

Charts

Four types of charts are commonly used in college textbooks: pie charts, organizational charts, flowcharts, and pictograms.

Pie Charts

Pie charts, sometimes called circle graphs, are used to show whole/part relationships or to depict how given parts of a unit have been divided or classified. They enable the reader to compare the parts to each other as well as to compare

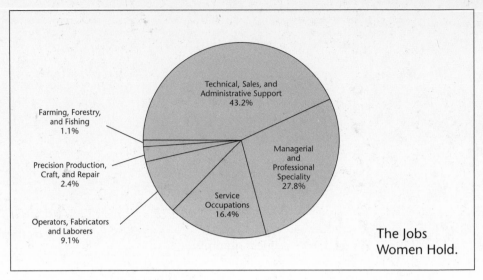

Technical, Sales, and
Administrative Support
43.2%

Farming, Forestry,
and Fishing
1.1%

Precision Production,
Craft, and Repair
2.4%

Operators, Fabricators
and Laborers
9.1%

Service
Occupations
16.4%

Managerial
and
Professional
Speciality
27.8%

The Jobs
Women Hold.

Figure 10-12 **A sample pie chart.**[14]

each part to the whole. The chart in Figure 10-12 indicates the types of jobs women hold, and the percentage who holds each.

Organizational Charts

An organizational chart divides an organization, such as a corporation, a hospital, or a university, into its administrative parts, staff positions, or lines of authority. Figure 10-13 shows the organization of the American political party. It reveals that party members belong to precinct and ward organizations. From these organizations county committees are formed. County committee members are represented on state committees and state delegates are chosen for national positions.

Flowcharts

A flowchart is a specialized type of chart that shows how a process or procedure works. Lines or arrows are used to indicate the direction (route or routes) through the procedure. Various shapes (boxes, circles, rectangles) enclose what is done at each stage or step. You could draw, for example, a flowchart to describe how to apply for and obtain a student loan or how to locate a malfunction in your car's electrical system. Refer to the flowchart shown in Figure 10-14, taken from a business management textbook. It describes the steps in the decision-making process.

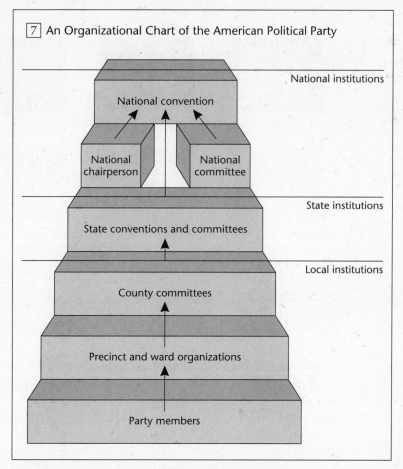

7 An Organizational Chart of the American Political Party

National institutions

National convention

National chairperson

National committee

State institutions

State conventions and committees

Local institutions

County committees

Precinct and ward organizations

Party members

Figure 10-13 A sample organizational chart.[15]

To read flowcharts effectively, use the following suggestions:

1. Decide what process the flowchart shows.
2. Next, follow the chart, using the arrows and reading each step. Start at the top or far left of the chart.
3. When you've finished, summarize the process in your own words. Try to draw the chart from memory without referring to the text. Compare your drawing with the chart and note discrepancies.

Now study the flowchart shown in Figure 10-14 and try to express each step in your own words. You might have said something like: 1. Know what has to be decided, 2. Think of all possibilities, 3. Weigh each possibility, 4. Select one, 5. Try it out, and 6. Decide if it worked.

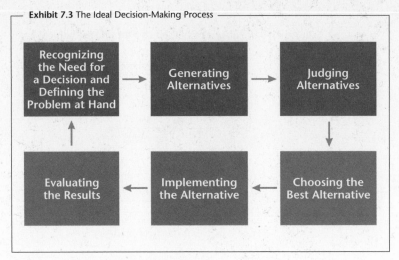

Exhibit 7.3 The Ideal Decision-Making Process

Figure 10-14 A sample flowchart.[16]

Pictograms

A pictogram uses symbols or drawings (such as books, cars, or buildings), instead of numbers, to represent specified quantities or amounts. This type of chart tends to be visually appealing, makes statistics seem realistic, and may carry an emotional impact. For example, a chart that uses knives to indicate the number of stabbing deaths each year per state may have a more significant impact than statistics presented in table form. A sample pictogram is shown in Figure 10-15. This pictogram uses human figures to represent seventh to twelfth grade students. The pictogram compares the number of drinkers with nondrinkers. It indicates the number who drink weekly and the number who purchase alcohol themselves. Patterns of drinking are described.

EXERCISE 10-3

DIRECTIONS: *Study the charts shown in Figures 10-16 through 10-18 and answer the corresponding questions.*

Figure 10-16 Race and Ethnicity Origin for the United States

1. What is the purpose of these charts?

   _____

   _____

2. What patterns are evident?

   _____

   _____

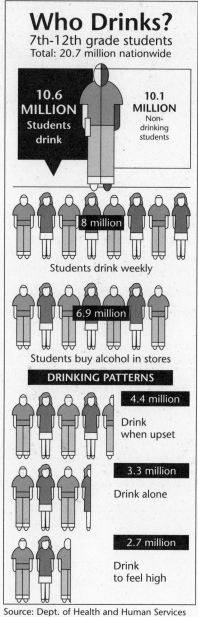

Who Drinks?
7th-12th grade students
Total: 20.7 million nationwide

10.6 MILLION Students drink

10.1 MILLION Non-drinking students

8 million
Students drink weekly

6.9 million
Students buy alcohol in stores

DRINKING PATTERNS

4.4 million
Drink when upset

3.3 million
Drink alone

2.7 million
Drink to feel high

Source: Dept. of Health and Human Services

Figure 10-15 A sample pictogram.[17]

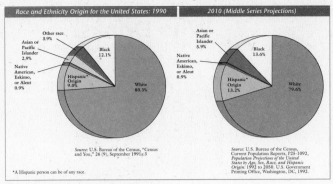

| Race and Ethnicity Origin for the United States: 1990 | 2010 (Middle Series Projections) |

Other race 3.9%
Asian or Pacific Islander 2.9%
Native American, Eskimo, or Aleut 0.9%
Hispanic* Origin 9.0%
Black 12.1%
White 80.3%

Source: U.S. Bureau of the Census, "Census and You," 26 (9), September 1991a:3

*A Hispanic person can be of any race.

Asian or Pacific Islander 5.9%
Native American, Eskimo, or Aleut 0.9%
Hispanic* Origin 13.2%
Black 13.6%
White 79.6%

Source: U.S. Bureau of the Census, Current Population Reports, P25-1092, *Population Projections of the United States by Age, Sex, Race, and Hispanic Origin: 1992 to 2050.* U.S. Government Printing Office, Washington, DC, 1992.

Figure 10-16 Pie charts.[18]

Figure 10-17 The Organization of a Medium-Market Television Station

1. What is the purpose of the chart?

   _____

   _____

2. To which person or office would the artists report directly?

   _____

   _____

3. Who is in charge of the department in which sports announcers and newscasters work?

   _____

   _____

Figure 10-18 The Components of the Criminal Justice System

1. What is the purpose of the chart?

   _____

   _____

2. Summarize its organization.

   _____

   _____

3. After a person's "Initial Appearance" what happens next if the charges against him are not dropped or dismissed?

   _____

   _____

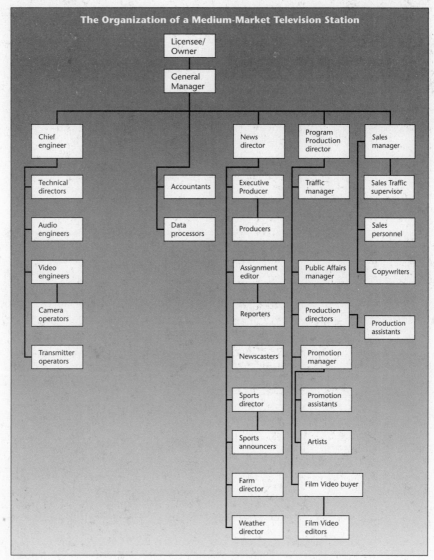

Figure 10-17 An organizational chart.[19]

Diagrams

Diagrams often are included in technical and scientific as well as many other college texts to explain processes. Diagrams are intended to help you visualize relationships between parts and understand sequences. They may also be used to illustrate ideas or concepts. Figure 10-19, taken from a biology textbook, shows the respiratory (breathing) system of an insect.

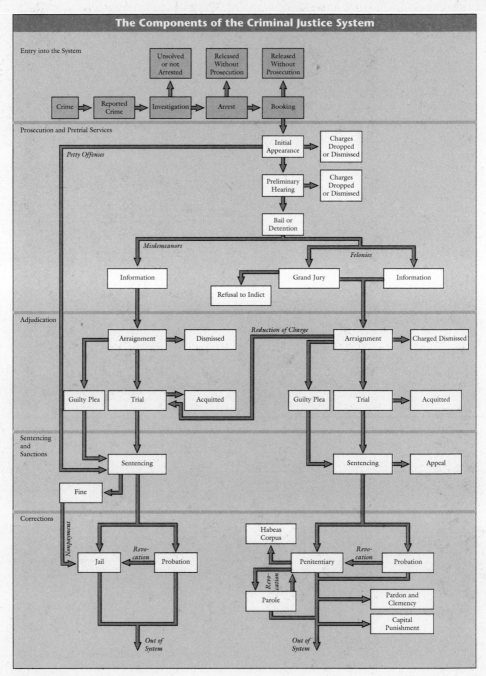

Figure 10-18 A flowchart.[20]

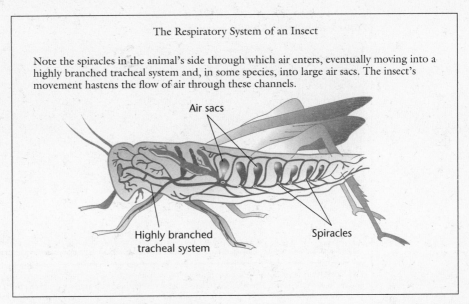

The Respiratory System of an Insect

Note the spiracles in the animal's side through which air enters, eventually moving into a highly branched tracheal system and, in some species, into large air sacs. The insect's movement hastens the flow of air through these channels.

Air sacs

Highly branched tracheal system

Spiracles

Figure 10-19 A sample diagram.[21]

Accompanying Text

Terrestrial insects generally solve the oxygen problem by breathing through a **tracheal system.** The system is comprised of tiny tubes that open to the air and permeate their body tissue. The openings to the system are called **spiracles.** As shown in Figure 19-6, oxygen enters the tracheal system directly from the air and, aided by the insect's bodily movement, moves through the tracheae (plural) deep into the body tissue. Each trachea ends amidst groups of cells or in expanded **air sacs.** The tracheal network is so extensive that no cell lies far from an oxygen source.[22]

Reading diagrams differs from reading other types of graphics in that diagrams often correspond to fairly large segments of text, requiring you to switch back and forth frequently between the text and the diagram to determine which part of the process each paragraph refers to. Figure 10-19 includes the text that accompanies the diagram.

Because diagrams of processes and their corresponding text are often difficult, complicated, or highly technical, plan on reading these sections more than once. Read first to grasp the overall process. In subsequent readings, focus on the details of the process, examining each step and understanding its progression.

One of the best ways to study a diagram is to redraw it in as much detail as possible without referring to the original. Or, test your understanding and recall of the process outlined in a diagram by explaining it, step by step in writing, using your own words.

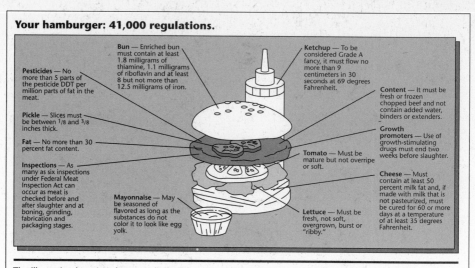

Your hamburger: 41,000 regulations.

Bun — Enriched bun must contain at least 1.8 milligrams of thiamine, 1.1 milligrams of riboflavin and at least 8 but not more than 12.5 milligrams of iron.

Pesticides — No more than 5 parts of the pesticide DDT per million parts of fat in the meat.

Pickle — Slices must be between 1/8 and 3/8 inches thick.

Fat — No more than 30 percent fat content.

Inspections — As many as six inspections under Federal Meat Inspection Act can occur as meat is checked before and after slaughter and at boning, grinding, fabrication and packaging stages.

Mayonnaise — May be seasoned of flavored as long as the substances do not color it to look like egg yolk.

Ketchup — To be considered Grade A fancy, it must flow no more than 9 centimeters in 30 seconds at 69 degrees Fahrenheit.

Content — It must be fresh or frozen chopped beef and not contain added water, binders or extenders.

Growth promoters — Use of growth-stimulating drugs must end two weeks before slaughter.

Tomato — Must be mature but not overripe or soft.

Cheese — Must contain at least 50 percent milk fat and, if made with milk that is not pasteurized, must be cured for 60 or more days at a temperature of at least 35 degrees Fahrenheit.

Lettuce — Must be fresh, not soft, overgrown, burst or "ribby."

The illustration here is only a sampling of the rules and regulations governing the burger you buy at the corner sandwich stand. The 41,000 federal and state regulations, many stemming from 200 laws and 111,000 precedent-setting court cases, touch on everything involved in meat production—grazing practices of cattle, conditions in slaughterhouses, and methods used to process meat for sale to supermarkets, restaurants, and fast-food outlets. According to a three-volume study by Colorado State University, these regulations, add an estimated 8 to 11 cents per pound to the cost of a hamburger.

Figure 10-20 A diagram.[23]

EXERCISE 10-4

DIRECTIONS: *Study the diagram and accompanying text shown in Figure 10-20 and answer the following questions:*

1. What is the purpose of the diagram?

   _____

   _____

2. How many meat inspections may have occurred before the hamburger you ordered is allowed to be served?

   _____

   _____

3. What regulations apply to farmers and/or cattle ranchers?

   _____

   _____

Maps

Maps describe relationships and provide information about location and direction. They are commonly found in geography and history texts, and also appear in ecology, biology, and anthropology texts. While most of us think of maps as describing distances and locations, maps also are used to describe the placement of geographical and ecological features such as areas of pollution, areas of population concentration, or political data (voting districts).

When reading maps, use the following steps:

1. Read the caption. This identifies the subject of the map.
2. Use the legend or key to identify the symbols or codes used.
3. Note distance scales.
4. Study the map, looking for trends or key points. Often the text that accompanies the map states the key points the map illustrates.
5. Try to visualize, or create a mental picture of, the map.
6. As a learning and study aid, write, in your own words, a statement of what the map shows.

The map in Figure 10-21 shows new countries that have emerged since World War II.

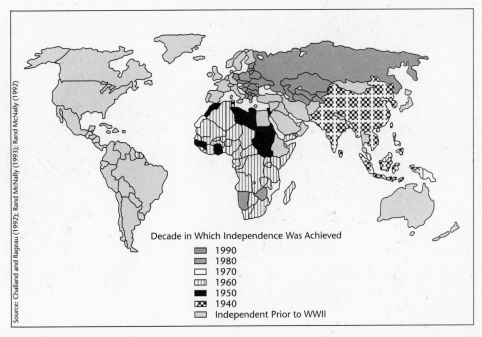

Source: Challand and Rageau (1992); Rand McNally (1993); Rand McNally (1992)

Figure 10-21 A sample map.[24]

Photographs

Although sometimes considered an art form instead of a graphic, photographs are used in place of words. Their purpose is similar to other graphics—to replace verbal descriptions in presenting information. Photographs also are used to spark interest, and, often, to draw out an emotional response or feeling. Use these suggestions when studying a photograph:

1. Read the caption. It often provides a clue to the photographer's intended meaning.
2. Ask: What is my first overall impression? What details did I notice first? These questions will lead you to discover the purpose of the photograph.

Figure 10-22 A photograph.[25]

DIRECTIONS: *Study the photograph in Figure 10-22 and answer the questions that follow.*

1. Describe what is happening in the picture.

   _____

2. Describe the feeling of each person.

   _____

3. What does this picture reveal about the causes of divorce?

   _____

■■■■■■■ WORKING TOGETHER

Directions: Bring a copy of your local newspaper or of *USA Today* to class. After your instructor forms groups, each group should select and tear out four to five graphics. For each graphic, the group should identify the type of graphic, analyze its purpose, and identify the trend or pattern it reveals. Groups should then discuss what other types of graphics could be used to accomplish the author's purpose. Each group should submit one graphic to the instructor along with a brief summary of the members' analysis.

■■■■■■■ SUMMARY

How do I read a graphic?

To read a graphic, follow these eight steps:

1. Read the title
2. Discover how the graphic is organized
3. Identify variables
4. Analyze its purpose
5. Determine the scale of measurement
6. Identify trends and patterns
7. Read corresponding text
8. Write a summary note

How many types of graphics are there, what are they, and what will they tell me?

There are six major types of graphics:

1. Tables—used to arrange and organize facts

2. Graphs—including bar, multiple bar, stacked bar, and linear graphs—are used to make comparisons between or among sets of information

3. Charts—including pie charts, organizational charts, flowcharts, and pictograms present visual displays of information

4. Diagrams—demonstrate physical relationships between parts and display sequences

5. Maps—describe information about location and direction

6. Photographs—used to spark interest or to draw out an emotional response

CHAPTER 11

Organizing and Remembering Information

THIS CHAPTER WILL SHOW YOU HOW TO

1. *Highlight and mark important information in textbook chapters*

2. *Outline information to show its organization*

3. *Summarize ideas for review purposes*

4. *Review for maximum retention*

Suppose you are planning a cross-country trip next summer. To get ready you begin to collect all kinds of information: maps, newspaper articles on various cities, places to visit, names of friends' friends, and so forth. After a while, you find that you have a great deal of information and that it is difficult to locate any one item. You begin to realize that the information you have collected will be of little or no use unless you organize it in some way. You decide to buy large envelopes and put different kinds of information into separate envelopes, such as information on individual states.

In this case, you found a practical, commonsensical solution to a problem. The rule or principle that you applied was this: when something gets confusing, organize it.

This rule also works well when applied to college textbooks. Each text contains thousands of pieces of information—facts, names, dates, theories, principles. This information quickly becomes confusing unless it is organized. Once you have organized it, you will be able to find and remember what you need more easily than if your text were still an unassorted heap of facts.

Organizing information requires sifting, sorting, and in some cases rearranging important facts and ideas. There are five common methods of organizing textbook materials:

- Highlighting
- Marking
- Outlining
- Mapping
- Summarizing

In this chapter you will learn techniques for doing each. You will also see how to study and review more effectively.

Highlighting and Marking

Highlighting and marking important facts and ideas as you read are effective methods of identifying and organizing information. They are also the biggest time-savers known to college students. Suppose it took you four hours to read an assigned chapter in sociology. One month later you need to review that chapter to prepare for an exam. If you did not highlight or mark as you read the first time, then, in order to review the chapter once, you would have to spend another four hours rereading it. However, if you had highlighted and marked as you read, you could review the chapter in an hour or less—a savings of 300 percent. By this means you can save many hours each semester. More important, the less time you spend identifying what to learn, the more thoroughly you can learn the necessary information. This strategy can help improve your grades.

Highlighting Effectively

Here are a few basic suggestions for highlighting effectively:

1. *Read a paragraph or section first.* Then go back and highlight what is important.
2. *Highlight important portions of the topic sentence* and any supporting details you want to remember (see Chapter 7).
3. *Be accurate.* Make sure your highlighting reflects the content of the passage. Incomplete or hasty highlighting can mislead you as you review the passage and can allow you to miss the main point.
4. *Use a system for highlighting.* There are several from which to choose: for instance, using two or more different colors of highlighters to distinguish between main ideas and details, or placing a bracket around the main idea and

using highlighter to mark important details. No one system is more effective than another. Try to develop a system that works well for you.

5. *Highlight as few words as possible in a sentence.* Seldom should you highlight an entire sentence. Usually highlighting the key idea along with an additional phrase or two is sufficient. Read the following paragraph. Notice that you can understand its meaning from the highlighted parts alone.

The person who smokes ==more than a pack== of cigarettes ==a day== runs nearly ==twice the risk== of ==heart attack,== and nearly ==five times the risk of stroke,== as does a nonsmoker. ==Abstaining== from smoking ==lowers== your ==risk== of heart attack ==22 percent below the norm.== Smoking ==more than a pack a day raises== your ==risk== to ==32 percent above the norm.== In addition, as explained in other chapters of this book, smoking greatly ==increases susceptibility== to ==lung cancer== and to such lung diseases as ==bronchitis== and ==emphysema.==

6. *Use headings to guide your highlighting* (see Chapter 7). Use the headings to form questions that you expect to be answered in the section (see Chapter 4). Then highlight the answer to each question.

Highlighting the Right Amount

If you highlight either too much or too little, you defeat the purpose. By highlighting too little, you miss valuable information, and your review and study of the material will be incomplete. On the other hand, if you highlight too much, you are not identifying the most important ideas and eliminating less important facts. The more you highlight, the more you will have to reread when studying and the less of a time-saver the procedure will prove to be. As a general rule of thumb, highlight no more than 20 to 30 percent of the material.

Here is a paragraph highlighted in three different ways. First read the paragraph that has not been highlighted; then look at each highlighted version. Try to decide which version would be most useful if you were rereading it for study purposes.

Outer space travel to distant planets has been limited by the human life span. Now, humans do not live long enough to reach far-away destinations. A proposed solution to this problem is human hibernation. Humans might hibernate in much the same way as certain animals do now. Scientists believe that humans who hibernate may live eight to ten times longer than if they do not. If this is so, humans might attain chronological ages of 800 years. The process is based on suspended animation. Bodily functions are slowed down to minimal levels needed to support life. Hibernation slows body time, allowing more clock time to elapse.[1]

Example 1:

Outer space travel to distant planets has been limited by the human life span. Now, humans do not live long enough to reach far-away destinations. A proposed solution to this problem is human hibernation. Humans might hibernate in much the same way as certain animals do now. Scientists believe that humans who hibernate may live eight to ten times longer than if they do not. If this is so, humans might attain chronological ages of 800 years. The process is based on suspended animation. Bodily functions are slowed down to minimal levels needed to support life. Hibernation slows body time, allowing more clock time to elapse.

Example 2:

Outer space travel to distant planets has been limited by the human life span. Now, humans do not live long enough to reach far-away destinations. A proposed solution to the problem is human hibernation. Humans might hibernate in much the same way as certain animals do now. Scientists believe that humans who hibernate may live eight to ten times longer than if they do not. If this is so, humans might attain chronological ages of 800 years. The process is based on suspended animation. Bodily functions are slowed down to minimal levels needed to support life. Hibernation slows body time, allowing more clock time to elapse.

Example 3:

Outer space travel to distant planets has been limited by the human life span. Now, humans do not live long enough to reach far-away destinations. A proposed solution to this problem is human hibernation. Humans might hibernate in much the same way as certain animals do now. Scientists believe that humans who hibernate may live eight to ten times longer than if they do not. If this is so, humans might attain chronological ages of 800 years. The process is ages of 800 years. based on suspended animation. Bodily functions are slowed down to minimal levels needed to support life. Hibernation slows body time, allowing more clock time to elapse.

The last example is the best example of effective highlighting. Only the most important information has been highlighted. In the first example, too little of the important information has been highlighted while what *has* been highlighted is either unnecessary or incomplete. The second example, on the other hand, has too much highlighting to be useful for review.

EXERCISE 11-1

DIRECTIONS: *Read and highlight the following selection, using the guidelines presented in this section.*

Tailoring the Marketing Mix for Global Markets

Marketers have several options as to the products they present in the global arena. They can sell the same product abroad that they sell at home, they can modify the product for foreign markets, or they can develop an entirely new product for foreign markets.

The simplest strategy is product extension, which involves offering the same product in all markets, domestic and foreign. This approach has worked successfully for companies including Pepsico, Coca-Cola, Kentucky Fried Chicken, and Levis. Pepsi and Coke are currently battling for market share in both Russia and Vietnam, countries with small but growing soft-drink markets. Both firms are producing and selling the same cola to the Russian and Vietnamese markets that they sell to other markets around the world. Not all companies that have attempted it, however, have found success with product extension. When Duncan Hines introduced its rich, moist American cakes to England, the British found them too messy to hold while sipping tea. Japanese consumers disliked the coleslaw produced by Kentucky Fried Chicken; it was too sweet for their tastes. KFC responded by cutting the sugar in half.

The strategy of modifying a product to meet local preferences or conditions is product adaptation. Cosmetics companies produce different colors to meet the differing preferences of European consumers. French women like bold reds while British and German women prefer pearly pink shades of lipstick and nail color. Nestle's sells varieties of coffee to suit local tastes worldwide. Unilever produces frozen versions of local delicacies such as Bami Goreng and Madras Curry for markets in Indonesia and India.

Product invention consists of developing a new product to meet a market's needs and preferences. The opportunities that exist with this strategy are great since many unmet needs exist worldwide, particularly in developing and less-developed economies. Marketers have not been quick, however, to attempt product invention. For example, despite the fact that an estimated 600 million people worldwide still scrub clothes by hand, it was the early 1980s before a company (Colgate-Palmolive) developed an inexpensive, all plastic, manual washing machine with the tumbling action of an automatic washer for use in homes without electricity.[2]

DIRECTIONS: *Read or reread and highlight Chapter 4 in this book. Follow the guidelines suggested in this chapter.*

Testing Your Highlighting

As you highlight, check to be certain your highlighting is effective and will be helpful for review purposes. To test the effectiveness of your highlighting, take any passage and reread only the highlighted portions. Then ask yourself the following questions:

- Does the highlighting tell what the passage is about?
- Does it make sense?
- Does it indicate the most important idea in the passage?

EXERCISE 11-3

DIRECTIONS: *Test the effectiveness of your highlighting for the material you highlighted in Exercises 11-1 and 11-2. Make changes, if necessary.*

Marking

When reading many types of textbooks, highlighting alone will not clearly identify and organize information. Also, highlighting does not allow you to react to or sort ideas. Try making notes in the margin in addition to highlighting. Notice how the marginal notes in the following passage organize the information in a way that underlining cannot.

4 forms of energy
1. hydraulic
2. electrical
3. geothermal
4. sun
 Radiation

 light
 energy

THE SOURCE OF ENERGY Within the biosphere itself several forms of energy are produced: <u>hydraulic</u> energy, created by <u>water in motion</u> (a river pouring over a dam, storm waves striking a shoreline); <u>electrical energy</u> (lightning); and <u>geothermal</u> energy (underground <u>water</u> converted to <u>steam</u> by <u>hot rock</u> formations). Powerful as these sources of energy can be, they are insignificant compared with the huge flow of energy that comes to earth from the <u>sun.</u>

The sun's energy begins with reactions like that of a hydrogen bomb. Nuclear fusion deep in the <u>sun's</u> <u>core</u> <u>creates</u> <u>radiation,</u> which makes its way to the sun's surface and is then radiated away—most of it as visible light, some as ultraviolet light and infrared light and X rays (see Figure 1.3). This <u>sunlight</u> is the <u>dominant</u> <u>form</u> <u>of</u> <u>energy</u> in our world, one that primitive peoples recognized eons ago as the giver of life. All the energy humans produce in a single year from our many energy sources—coal, oil, hydraulic power, nuclear power—amounts, according to our present estimates, to only two ten-thousandths of the total energy coming to us each day from the sun.[3]

Here are a few examples of useful types of marking:

1. Circle words you do not know.

   Sulfur is a yellow, solid substance that has several (allotropic) forms.

2. Mark definitions with an asterisk.

   *Chemical reactivity is the tendency of an element to participate in chemical reaction.

3. Write summary words or phrases in the margin.

   reaction w/air   Some elements, such as aluminum (Al) or Copper (Cu), tarnish just from sitting around in the air. They react with oxygen (O_2) in the air.

4. Number lists of ideas, causes, and reasons.

   Metallic properties include conductivity, luster, and ductility.

5. Place brackets around important passages.

   In Group IVA, carbon (C) is a nonmetal, silicon (Si) and germanium (Ge) are metaloids, and tin (Sn) and lead (Pb) are metals.

6. Draw arrows or diagrams to show relationships or to clarify information.

    Graphite is made up of a lot of carbon layers stacked on top of one another, like sheets of paper. The layers slide over one another, which makes it a good lubricant.

7. Make notes to yourself, such as "good test question," "reread," or "ask instructor."

   Test?   Carbon is most important to us because it is a basic element in all plant and animal structures.

8. Put question marks next to confusing passages or when you want more information.

 Sometimes an element reacts so violently with air, water, or other substances that an explosion occurs.

Try to develop your own code or set of abbreviations. Here are a few examples:

Types of Marking	Examples
ex	example
T	good test question
sum	good summary
def	important definition
RR	reread later

EXERCISE 11-4

DIRECTIONS: *Read each of the following passages and then highlight and mark each. Try various ways of highlighting and marking.*

Passage 1:

Flavors

1   "Natural flavors," "natural flavoring," "artificially flavored," "artificial flavor," "natural and artificial flavor." . . . Those are the words we will find on many food labels. What do they mean? What *is* a flavor, as the word is used to state an ingredient of a food product?

2   Flavors are the substances that impart taste and aroma to a food. The sense of taste itself detects only sweet, sour, salty, and bitter, or a blend of those. Only in its aroma, detected by the sense of smell, does a food become truly unique in its flavor.

3   To see clearly and dramatically the difference between taste and aroma, hold your nose and chew a piece of apple. Then repeat the same process, this

time with a piece of onion. Be sure to close your nostrils tightly while you do this. All you will taste is sweet—in both cases. Only the addition of the sense of smell enables you to distinguish the flavor difference between the onion and the apple.

4   The flavors present in foods such as fruits and spices can be separated from the food and used to impart the flavor to something else. The flavor is carried in what is called the essential oil, so named because it contains the flavor essence characteristic of the food. For example, the flavor of nutmeg, in the form of oil of nutmeg, can be separated from the nutmeg and added to coffee-cake dough to delicately flavor it. Similarly, essential oils of orange, lemon, grapefruit, and many other fruits can be separated and used for flavoring purposes.

5   Why do processors bother to do such a thing? Some reasons are: as a means of having the flavor available long after the source of the oil has spoiled; and to provide a source of uniform flavor, much more so than the original spice or fruit, and also in a very much more stable form.

6   These flavors are not pure chemical substances, but are a blend of many substances. We had to learn what the precise composition was that produced such strange and wonderful smells and tastes. During the nineteenth century, chemists were extraordinarily successful in analyzing the components of many natural flavors and, even more significant, learned to synthesize many of them. For example, extract of vanilla contains vanillin, the principal component of vanilla flavor; chemists soon were synthesizing and using vanillin as a flavor instead of the vanilla extract. Unfortunately, vanillin is not the only substance in vanilla flavor, and we still don't have a synthetic duplication that tastes like the real thing. But synthetic vanillin is a precise duplicate of the vanillin found in vanilla extract from the vanilla bean.

7   In some cases, the result has been ridiculous. Methyl anthranilate is the principal material responsible for typical Concord grape flavor. It is widely used as an artificial flavor in grape drinks, sodas, and ice confections. Methyl anthranilate is not the only component of grape flavor, and it has a very strong, coarse grape character. Children actually prefer grape drinks flavored with the synthetic anthranilate to the real thing, it is so much less subtle.

8   The labeling of flavors is not helpful enough to the consumer. The mere word "artificial" tells us nothing since the substance may be a synthetic duplicate of a component of natural flavor. Chances are when the label says "artificial," the overall taste sensation will not be as smooth as a naturally flavored product, but this is not inevitably so at all.

9   There are over *seven hundred* synthetic flavors permitted as food additives that are not GRAS [Generally Regarded as Safe by the Food and Drug Administration]. There are twenty-four synthetic flavors that are GRAS. The con-

sumer has no way of telling which is in the food: the GRAS product or the non-GRAS additive.

10   Do not assume that because an extract is natural that it is safe. One of the most dangerous materials is good old-fashioned oil of sassafras, out of which root beer was once made. It turned out that a natural substance in oil of sassafras, safrole, is a rather nasty cancer producer. This material is no longer permitted in foods; only safrole-free sassafras extract may now be used.

11   There is an enormous amount of ignorance on the subject of flavors. One theory presented is that *all* additives and especially artificial flavors cause hyperactivity in children, but nobody has been able to duplicate the work reported. On the other hand, nobody has ever claimed that highly flavored, artificially flavored foods are good for you, and on the general principle of moderation, especially in the presence of ignorance, it is probably a good idea to avoid eating and feeding your children a great deal of artificially flavored, or even strong naturally flavored, foods or drinks.[4]

Passage 2:

Melting Point

1   The particles (atoms or molecules) of a solid are held together by attractive forces. . . . Heating up a solid, such as a piece of ice, gives its molecules more energy and makes them move. Pretty soon they are moving fast enough to overcome the attractive forces that were holding them rigidly together in the solid. The temperature at which this happens is the *melting point* of the solid. When a liquid, such as water, is cooled, the reverse process happens. We take energy away from the molecules, and pretty soon the molecules are moving slowly enough for their attractive forces to hold them rigidly together again and form a solid. The temperature at which this happens is the *freezing point* of the liquid. Melting point and freezing point are really the same thing, approached from opposite directions. To melt a substance, we supply heat; to freeze it, we remove heat. While a solid is melting, its temperature stays constant at its melting point. Even though we keep heating a solid as it melts, we won't increase its temperature until all of the solid has changed to liquid. When a solid starts to melt, all of the heat that is put into it from then on goes into breaking up the attractive forces that hold the atoms or molecules together in the solid. When the solid is all melted, then the heat that is put in can once more go into increasing the temperature of the substance. The amount of heat that it takes to melt one gram of any substance at its melting point is called the *heat of fusion.* If we let the sub-

stance freeze, then it will give off heat in the amount of the heat of fusion. Freezing is a process that releases energy.

2

Every substance has a melting (or freezing) point except diamond, which no one has been able to melt yet. The stronger the attractive forces that hold atoms or molecules together in the solid, the higher its melting (or freezing) point will be. The forces holding a diamond together in the solid state are so strong that they can't be overcome by heating. Most elements are solids at "room temperature," a vague term meaning a range of about 20°C to 30°C. A substance that's a solid at room temperature has a melting point higher than room temperature. Some substances are borderline, and they can be either liquids or solids depending on the weather: we've all seen tar melt on a hot day. Olive oil will solidify (freeze) on a cold day. . . .[5]

Outlining

Outlining is a good way to create a visual picture of what you have read. In making an outline, you record the writer's organization and show the relative importance of and connection between ideas.

Outlining has a number of advantages:

1. It gives an overview of the topic and enables you to see how various subtopics relate to one another.
2. Recording the information in your own words tests your understanding of what you read.
3. It is an effective way to record needed information from reference books you do not own.

How to Outline

Generally, an outline follows a format like the one below.

```
I. First major idea
   A. First supporting detail
      1. Detail
      2. Detail
   B. Second supporting detail
      1. Detail
         a. Minor detail or example
         b. Minor detail or example

II. Second major idea
   A. First supporting idea
```

Notice that the most important ideas are closer to the left margin. Less important ideas are indented toward the middle of the page. A quick glance at an outline shows what is most important, what is less important, and how ideas support or explain one another.

Here are a few suggestions for using the outline format:

1. Do not be overly concerned with following the outline format exactly. As long as your outline shows an organization of ideas, it will work for you.
2. Write words and phrases rather than complete sentences.
3. Use your own words rather than lifting words from the text.
4. Do not write too much. If you need to record numerous facts and details, underlining rather than outlining might be more effective.
5. Be sure that all the information you place underneath a heading explains or supports that heading.
6. Every heading indented the same amount on the page should be of equal importance.

Now read the following passage on franchising and then study its outline.

Franchising

1 **Franchising** is an arrangement whereby a supplier, or franchiser, grants a dealer, or franchisee, the right to sell products in exchange for some type of consideration. For example, the franchiser may receive some percentage of total sales in exchange for furnishing equipment, buildings, management know-how, and marketing assistance to the franchisee. The franchisee supplies labor and capital, operates the franchised business, and agrees to abide by the provisions of the franchise agreement. In the next section we look at the major types of retail franchises, the advantages and disadvantages of franchising, and trends in retailing.

2 *Major Types of Retail Franchises*

Retail franchise arrangements can generally be classified as one of three general types. In the first arrangement, a manufacturer authorizes a number of retail stores to sell a certain brand-name item. This franchise arrangement, one of the oldest, is common in the sales of passenger cars and trucks, farm equipment, shoes, paint, earth-moving equipment, and petroleum. About 90 percent of all gasoline is sold through franchised independent retail service stations, and franchised dealers handle virtually all sales of new cars and trucks. The second type of retail franchise occurs when a producer licenses distributors to sell a given product to retailers. This franchising arrangement is common in the soft-drink industry. Most national manufacturers of soft-drink syrups—Coca-Cola, Dr Pepper, Pepsi-Cola—franchise independent bottlers, which then serve retailers. In the third type of retail franchise, a franchiser supplies brand names, techniques, or other services, instead of a complete product. The franchiser may provide certain production and distribution services, but its primary role in the arrangement is the careful development and control of marketing strategies. This approach to franchising, which is the most typical today, is used by many organizations, including Holiday Inn, AAMCO, McDonald's, Dairy Queen, Avis, Hertz, Kentucky Fried Chicken, and H&R Block.[6]

I. Franchising
   A. Arrangement betw. Franchiser (supplier) and franchisee (dealer)
      1. Right to sell products exchanged for type of consideration
      2. Franchiser may receive percentage of sales for supplying equip., Building, or services
      3. Franchisee supplies labor and capital, and operates business
   B. Types
      1. Manufacturer authorizes stores to sell brand-name items
         a. Ex: cars, shoes, gasoline
      2. Producer licenses distributors to sell product to retailers
         a. EX: soft-drink industry
      3. Franchiser supplies brand-names or services but not complete product
         a. Primary role is marketing
         b. Ex: Hertz, McDonald's
         c. Most commonly used type of franchise

EXERCISE 11-5

DIRECTIONS: *Read the following passage and the incomplete outline that follows. Fill in the missing information in the outline.*

Changing Makeup of Families and Households

1   The traditional definition of a typical U.S. household was one that contained a husband, a nonworking wife, and two or more children. That type of household accounts for only about nine percent of households today. In its place we see many single-parent households, households without children, households of one person, and other nontraditional households. A number of

trends have combined to create these changes in families and households. Americans are staying single longer—more than one-half of the women and three-quarters of the men between 20 and 24 years old in the United States are still single. Divorce rates are at an all-time high. It is predicted that almost two-thirds of first marriages may end up in divorce. There is a widening gap between the life expectancy of males and females. Currently average life expectancy in the United States is 74 years for men and 78 years for women. Widows now make up more than one-third of one-person households in the United States. These trends have produced a declining average size of household.

The impact of all these changes is significant for marketers. Nontraditional households have different needs for goods and services than do traditional households. Smaller households often have more income per person than larger households, and require smaller houses, smaller cars, and smaller package sizes for food products. Households without children often spend more on personal entertainment and respond more to fads than do traditional households. More money may be spent on travel as well.[7]

I. Typical U.S. household has changed
   A. Used to consist of
      1. husband
      2. nonworking wife
      3. two or more children
   B. _____
      1. _____
      2. _____
      3. _____

II. Trends that created this change
   A. _____
      1. _____
      2. _____
   B. Divorce rates higher
      1. maybe two-thirds of marriages
   C. _____
      1. _____
      2. _____

III. _____
   A. Different goods and services needed
   B. _____
   C. _____

D. _____

E. _____

Mapping

Mapping is a visual method of organizing information. It involves drawing diagrams to show how ideas in an article or chapter are related. Some students prefer mapping to outlining because they feel it is freer and less tightly structured.

Maps can take numerous forms. You can draw them in any way that shows the relationships of ideas. Figure 11-1 shows two sample maps. Each was drawn to show the overall organization of Chapter 4 in this book. First refer back to Chapter 4, then study each map.

MAP 1

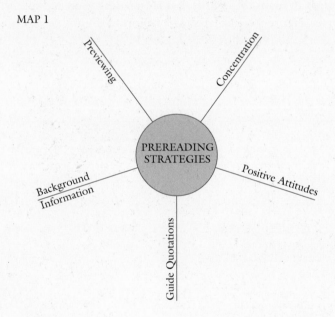

MAP 2

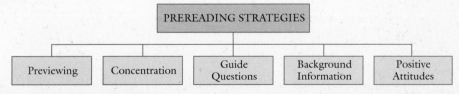

Figure 11-1 Sample maps.

How to Draw Maps

Think of a map as a picture or diagram that shows how ideas are connected. Use the following steps in drawing a map.

1. Identify the overall topic or subject and write it in the center or top of the page.
2. Identify major supporting information that relates to the topic. Draw each piece of information on a line connected to the central topic.
3. As you discover details that further explain an idea already mapped, draw a new line branching from the idea it explains.

How you arrange your map will depend on the subject matter and how it is organized. Like an outline, it can be quite detailed, or very brief, depending on your purpose. A portion of a more detailed map of Chapter 4 is shown in Figure 11-2.

Once you are skilled at drawing maps, you can become more creative, drawing different types of maps to fit what you are reading. For example, you can draw a time line (see Figure 11-3) that shows historical events, or a process diagram to show processes and procedures (see Figure 11-4).

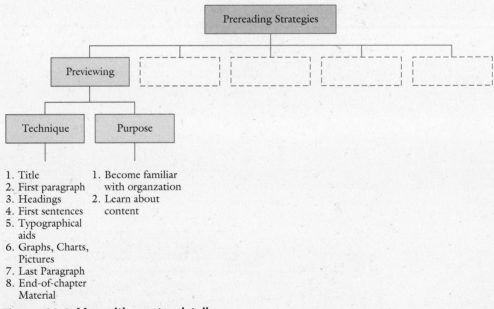

Figure 11-2 Map with greater detail.

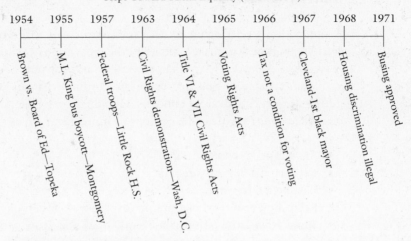

Figure 11-3 Sample time line.

EXERCISE 11-6

DIRECTIONS: *Draw a map of the excerpt "Tailoring the Marketing Mix for Global Markets" on p. 231.*

EXERCISE 11-7

DIRECTIONS: *Draw a map of the article on "Franchising" on p. 238.*

EXERCISE 11-8

DIRECTIONS: *Draw a map of Chapter 5 in this book.*

Process: Selecting a Brand Name for a New Product

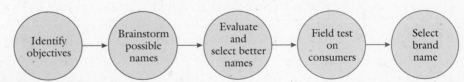

Figure 11-4 Sample process map.

Summarizing

A summary is a brief statement that reviews the major idea of something you have read. Its purpose is to make a record of the most important ideas in condensed form. A summary is much shorter than an outline and contains less detailed information.

A summary goes one step beyond recording what the writer says. It pulls together the writer's ideas by condensing and grouping them. Numerous situations in college courses require the ability to summarize, such as:

- Answering an essay question
- Reviewing a film or videotape
- Writing a term paper
- Recording results of a laboratory experiment or demonstration
- Summarizing the plot (main events) of a short story before analyzing it
- Quickly reviewing large amounts of information

How to Write a Summary

Before writing a summary, be sure you understand the material and have identified the writer's major points.

1. Write a brief outline of the material or underline each major idea.
2. Write one sentence that states the writer's overall concern or most important idea. To do this, ask yourself what one topic the material is about. Then ask what point the writer is trying to make about that topic. This sentence will be the topic sentence of your summary.
3. Be sure to use your own words rather than those of the author.
4. Next, review the major supporting information that the author gives to explain the major idea (see Chapter 7).
5. The amount of detail you include, if any, will depend on your purpose for writing the summary.
6. Normally, present ideas in the summary in the same order in which they appeared in the original materials.
7. For other than textbook material, if the writer presents a clear opinion or expresses an attitude toward the subject matter, include it in your summary.
8. If the summary is for your own use only and not to be submitted as an assignment, do not worry about sentence structure. Some students prefer to write summaries using words and phrases rather than complete sentences.

Read the following summary of "Changing Makeup of Families and Households," which appeared on p. 239.

The typical U.S. household has changed from a husband, nonworking wife, and two or more children to a smaller sized unit that might contain a single parent, no children, or even only one person. Three trends that have caused this change are: people are staying single longer, divorce rates are higher, and women are outliving men by more. Because of these changes, marketers have found that the current, smaller household needs different goods and services, has more income per person, tends to purchase smaller items, and spends more on entertainment, fads and travel than the typical household of the past.

Notice that this summary contains only the broadest, most important ideas. Details are not included. The first sentence shows how the typical household has changed, the second sentence lists the three trends that are causing this change, and the last sentence details the implications for marketers.

EXERCISE 11-9

DIRECTIONS: *On a separate sheet, write a summary of a television show you recently viewed.*

EXERCISE 11-10

DIRECTIONS: *On a separate sheet, write a summary of one of the reading selections in Part 6 of this text.*

EXERCISE 11-11

DIRECTIONS: *Write a summary of the article "Franchising" on p. 238. When you have finished, compare it with the sample summary shown in Figure 11-5 below. Then answer the following questions.*

1. How does your summary differ from the sample?

2. Did your summary begin with a topic sentence? How does it compare with the one in the sample?

3. Did your summary include ideas in the order they were given in the article?

Immediate and Periodic Review

Once you have read and organized information, the last step is to learn it. Fortunately, this is not a difficult task if you have organized the information effectively. In fact, through underlining, outlining, and/or summarizing, you have already

> franchising is an arrangement between a supplier (franchisor) and a dealer (franchisee). the franchiser supplies products or services and receives a percentage of the profits. the franchisee supplies labor and capital, and operates the business. there are three types of franchises: 1) authorized stores sell brand-name products, 2) distributors are licensed by producer to sell product to retailers, and 3) franchisor supplies brand name and/or services but does not supply the product.

Figure 11-5 Sample summary: "Franchising."

learned a large portion of the material. Review, then, is a way to fix, or store, information in your memory for later recall. There are two types of review, immediate and periodic.

How Immediate Review Works

Immediate review is done right after you have finished reading an assignment or writing an outline or summary. When you finish any of these, you may feel like breathing a sigh of relief and taking a break. However, it is worth the time and effort to spend another five minutes reviewing what you just read and refreshing your memory. The best way to do this is to go back through the chapter and reread the headings, graphic material, introduction, summary, and any underlining or marginal notes.

Immediate review works because it consolidates, or draws together, the material just read. It also gives a final, lasting impression of the content. Considerable research has been done on the effectiveness of immediate review. Results indicate that review done immediately rather than delayed until a later time makes a large difference in the amount remembered.

How Periodic Review Works

Although immediate review will increase your recall of information, it won't help you retain information for long periods of time. To remember information over time, periodically refresh your memory. This is known as **periodic review.** Go back over the material on a regular basis. Do this by looking again at those sections that carry the basic meaning and reviewing your underlining, outlining, and/or summaries. Here is an example of a schedule one student set up to periodically review assigned chapters in a psychology textbook.

Week 1—Read ch. 1
Week 2—Review ch. 1

Read ch. 2

Week 3—Review ch. 1 & 2

Read ch. 3

Week 4—Review ch. 3

Review ch. 1

Read ch. 4

Week 5—Review ch. 4

Review ch. 2

Read ch. 5

You can see that this student reviewed each chapter the week after reading it and again two weeks later. This schedule is only an example. You'll need to make a schedule for each course that fits the course requirements. For math and science courses, for example, you may need to include a review of previous homework assignments and laboratory work. In other courses, less or more frequent review of previous material may be needed.

EXERCISE 11-12

DIRECTIONS: *Choose one of your courses that involves regular textbook reading assignments. Plan a reading and periodic review schedule for the next three weeks. Assume that new chapters will be assigned as frequently as in previous weeks and that you want to review whatever has been covered over the past three weeks.*

WORKING TOGETHER

Directions: Your instructor will choose a reading from Part 6 and will then divide the class into three groups. Members of one group should outline the material, another group should draw maps, and the third should write summaries. When the groups have completed their tasks, the class members should review each other's work. Several students can read their summaries, draw maps, and write outlines on the chalkboard. Discuss which of the three methods seemed most effective for the material and how well prepared each group feels for (a) an essay exam, (b) a multiple-choice exam, and (c) a class discussion.

SUMMARY

There is so much information in textbooks, how can I organize it all?

Five methods for organizing textbook information are:

1. Highlighting—a way of sorting important information from less important information. It eliminates the need to reread entire textbook chapters in order to review their major content. It also has the advantage of helping you stay active and involved with what you are reading.

2. Marking—involves using signs, symbols, and marginal notes to react to, summarize, or comment on the material.

3. Outlining—a method of recording the most important information and showing the organization and relative importance of ideas. It is particularly useful when you need to see how ideas relate to one another or when you want to get an overview of the subject.

4. Mapping—a visual method of organizing information. It involves drawing diagrams to show how ideas in an article or chapter are related.

5. Summarizing—a way to pull together the most important ideas in condensed form. It provides a quick review of the material and forces you to explain the writer's ideas in your own words.

Making Your Skills Work Together

Building a System for Reading and Studying

Throughout Part Four and in previous sections of this book, you have seen that there is more to reading than simply opening a book, starting to read, and continuing until you finish. In Chapter 4 you learned that it is useful to preview and to form questions before you begin to read. In Chapters 5 through 10 you learned how to read to understand the writer's message and organization. Then in Chapter 11 you learned that you should highlight and mark as you read and/or outline, map, or summarize. Finally, you learned that it is important to review immediately after reading and to schedule periodic review to ensure long-term memory. These steps may at first seem to complicate your reading. However, you will find they are worth the extra effort. You will begin to understand and remember more.

Now we will put these steps together in a list:

1. PREVIEW. Become familiar with the organization and content.
2. QUESTION. Decide what you need to find out as you read.
3. READ. Look for answers to your questions.
4. HIGHLIGHT/MARK/OUTLINE/MAP/SUMMARIZE. Record and organize the information.
5. REVIEW. Go back over the important ideas.

Together these techniques form a step-by-step method. The method has been well tested and proven effective. As you try it, think of it as a way of learning while you read.

DIRECTIONS: *Read the following excerpt from a chapter on food additives in a nutrition textbook, following the steps listed.*

1. Preread the excerpt. Write a sentence describing what the chapter will be about.

   _____

2. Form several questions that you want to answer as you read. Write them in the space provided.

   _____

   _____

   _____

3. Read the excerpt, and on a separate sheet write a brief outline or draw a map.

4. Review the excerpt immediately after you finish reading. Now look at your outline or map again and make any additions or changes.

Food Additives

Why Do We Use Additives?

1. *City living:* We live in cities and suburbs, not on farms. We shop infrequently, sometimes only once a week. Since food is produced far from the consumption point and must be kept fresh and wholesome until it reaches the consumer, added preservatives are often required.

2. *Modern lifestyle:* The need and desire for refined foods and lower caloric intake require some foods to be fortified with nutritional additives to assure adequate vitamin and mineral intake.

3. *New knowledge of the relationship of food to disease*—most significantly, of saturated fats and cholesterol to heart disease—has created a need and demand for new man-made foods, which require additives to make them acceptable.

4. *High-speed processing of foods* often requires additives to make the processing economical, or even possible.

5. *More women than ever are working,* creating an enormous demand for convenience foods: prepared, ready-to-eat, or heat-and-eat foods. Addi-

tives preserve the flavor, texture, appearance, and safety of these products.

6. *Snacking* has become a national pastime. Many snacks are man-made—with additives required to make them.

What Additives Do

A food additive has been defined by the Food Protection Committee as "a substance or mixture of substances, other than a basic foodstuff, which is present in food as a result of any aspect of production, processing, storage or packaging. This term does not include chance contaminants."

Substances are added to foods in order to accomplish one or more of the following things:

1. To preserve the product; that is, to prevent its deterioration from any cause.
2. To improve the texture of the food.
3. To improve the flavor, taste, or appearance of the food.
4. To improve the nutritional quality of the food.
5. To minimize the loss of quality during processing itself.
6. To protect the food during its growth, harvest, and storage. These are the incidental, rather than the deliberate, materials, such as pesticides.

How Additives Work

Let's take a closer look at the different types of food additives and how they work.

Preservatives function to slow down or prevent the growth of bacteria, yeasts, or molds. These microorganisms may merely spoil the flavor and texture of the food or may actually produce an end product that is dangerous for human consumption. Some of the more common preservatives used are sodium benzoate, sorbic acid (or potassium sorbate), and sodium nitrate.

Antioxidants slow down or prevent the reaction of components of a food with the oxygen in the air. Such reaction can produce undesirable flavors, such as rancidity in fats; unpleasant colors; and loss of vitamin value.

Emulsifiers are used for smooth blending of liquids or batters. Mono and diglycerides are commonly used emulsifiers.

Stabilizers are often added to obtain a certain texture or to preserve a food's texture or its physical condition. For example, stabilizers are used to keep a liquid thick, to slow down the melting of ice cream, to prevent the fluid in a cheese from running off like water. Algin, xanthan gum, and other gums are stabilizers.

Sequestrants combine with trace amounts of metals that may be present in a product and prevent those metals from reacting with the foods to produce undesirable flavors or physical changes (to sequester means to keep in isolation). EDTA (ethylenediaminetetraacetic acid, a synthetically produced chemical) is a sequestrant.

Acids, alkalies, and buffers regulate the acidity of a food. We all know the difference between a tart cooking apple and a less tart (but still slightly acid) eating apple. In addition to its effect on taste, however, acidity is also very important to the preservation of food. Harmful bacteria usually do not grow in foods that are acid enough. Vitamins, including the natural vitamins present in food, tend to resist destruction more in foods that are acid, especially during the cooking process. In many foods, the preservation of the ideal flavor and color is helped by maintaining a specific acidity in the food. For these purposes, the acids make foods more acid, the alkalies make them less acid, and the buffers prevent change in acidity during storage. Citric acid is a typical acid, sodium citrate is a typical and common buffer, and sodium bicarbonate is a typical alkali.

Nutritional additives are the vitamins, minerals, and amino acids added to food either to enhance its nutritional value or to replace nutrients that might have been removed during processing. Some confusion has arisen now that vitamins are referred to by their chemical names rather than as *vitamins* in the ingredient list. It's unfortunate, but the listings of vitamins on the food label sometimes sound horrifying because their precise chemical names are given. "Vitamin B_1" is a lot more reassuring than "thiamine mononitrate."

Colors and flavors are added to make the food more appealing in appearance, smell, and taste.

Bleaching or maturing agents serve to oxidize wheat flour. While many foods must be protected against oxidation in order to preserve their quality, wheat flour used for baking must be oxidized in order to achieve the necessary quality.

Many years ago, it was possible to store flour for the necessary period of a month or longer to allow such oxidation to occur naturally with air. However, with bulk handling of flour and the massive bakeries that exist today, much flour is bleached in order to achieve artificial aging and to make the flour suitable for industrial use so that bread and cake can be produced uniformly at high speed. . . .

Non-nutritive sweeteners sweeten without calories. Until 1978, both calcium cyclamate and saccharin were used to replace sugar in foods for those people who were supposed to restrict their intake of ordinary sweets. When cyclamate was "found" to produce cancer in laboratory animals, it was prohibited under the Delaney Clause. Since 1978, saccharin alone has been used.

For years, saccharin was required to bear the statement "Contains x percent saccharin, an artificial sweetener to be used only by persons who must restrict their intake of ordinary sweets." Sometimes this statement was in type so small it could not be read without a magnifying glass.

Now, saccharin also has been "found" to produce cancer in laboratory animals. Under the Delaney Clause, it too would have been prohibited, but since it is the only usable artificial sweetener available, a delay in its prohibition has been granted, and even extended, to provide more time for confirmatory testing. (The granting of this delay actually required Congressional action.) In the meantime, saccharin must carry the warning: "Use of this product may be hazardous to your health. This product contains saccharin, which has been determined to cause cancer in laboratory animals."

The history of artificial sweeteners is an example of the seriousness with which our food labeling regulations are applied, and of the problems raised by the Delaney Clause. The rationale for the delay in the prohibition of saccharin is that the danger to people that would occur through its elimination (overweight and resultant cardiac disease and stroke) is greater than the danger of cancer. In the meantime, retesting of saccharin and cyclamates, and the testing of new substances, such as aspartame, is proceeding in the hope of finding that there is no confirmable cancer-producing hazard.

Miscellaneous materials such as leavening agents and those used for other special purposes will be explained as we go through the labels further on.

DIRECTIONS: *Choose a chapter from one of your textbooks, or use a later chapter in this book. Complete each of the following steps.*

1. Preview the chapter. Write a sentence describing what the chapter will be about.

_____

_____

2. Form several questions that you want to answer as you read. Write them in the space provided.

_____

_____

_____

3. Read the first section (major heading) of the chapter and highlight the important information.

4. Review the section immediately after you finish reading and highlighting.

5. On a separate sheet, write a brief outline or draw a map of the major ideas in the section of the chapter that you read.

PART 5

Critical Reading and Thinking:

Interpreting and Reacting

Catherine was taking a sociology course. One assignment directed her to find several articles on any controversial issue and to write a paper reacting to the writers' positions. Catherine chose the topic of legalized abortion. She easily located three articles on the topic and had no difficulty reading and taking summary notes on each article. Then she was ready to start writing her reaction paper.

After an hour or so, all Catherine had managed to create was a pile of crumpled sheets of paper. It was then she realized her problem—she had nothing to say. Although she had understood what each writer had said, she had not gone beyond the factual content to examine the author's ideas, sources, evidence, methods, or means of support. She realized that she had not only to understand the ideas, but to criticize and react to them.

College students, like many other people, accept much of what they read at face value. They assume that because something appears in print, it must be true, be worth reading, have value, and contain reliable information. They fail to step back and examine the author's argument, biases, and supporting evidence with a critical eye. Actually, much inaccurate information and many uninformed opinions appear in print every day. To be an alert, thinking, critical reader, you must approach everything you read with an open, questioning mind.

This critical approach to reading applies to literature as well. Literature is often a writer's expression of personal ideas and feelings. To understand many essays, short stories, poems, and other literary works, you must look beyond the facts and the plot line to discover the author's message.

THIS PART OF THE TEXT WILL HELP YOU

1. Understand how words can make positive or negative impressions on the reader (Chapter 12)

2. Make logical inferences (Chapter 12)

3. Understand how writers use figurative language (Chapter 12)

4. Be able to identify the author's purpose for writing (Chapter 12)

5. Become familiar with seven critical questions to ask to help evaluate what you read. (Chapter 13)

6. Apply specific strategies for reading essays, short stories, and poetry (Chapter 14)

CHAPTER 12

Interpreting:
Understanding the Writer's Message and Purpose

THIS CHAPTER WILL SHOW YOU HOW TO

1. *Recognize words that suggest positive or negative attitudes*

2. *Make inferences about what you read*

3. *Understand figurative language*

4. *Discover the author's purpose*

5. *Recognize tone*

Up to this point, we have been concerned with building vocabulary, understanding a writer's basic organizational patterns, acquiring factual information, and organizing that information for learning and recall. So far, each chapter has been concerned with understanding what the author *says*, with factual content. Now our focus must change. To read well, you must go beyond what the author says and also consider what he or she *means*.

Many writers directly state some ideas but hint at others. It is left to the reader to pick up the clues or suggestions and use logic and reasoning skills to figure out the writer's unstated message. This chapter will explain several features of writing that suggest meanings. Once you are familiar with these, you will better understand the writer's unstated message. This chapter will also discuss how to discover the author's purpose, recognize tone, and understand context.

Connotative Meanings

Which of the following would you like to be a part of: a crowd, mob, gang, audience, congregation, or class? Each of these words has the same basic meaning: "an assembled group of people." But each has a different *shade* of meaning. *Crowd* suggests a large, disorganized group. *Audience,* on the other hand, suggests a quiet, controlled group. Try to decide what meaning each of the other words in the list suggests.

This example shows that words have two levels of meaning—a literal meaning and an additional shade of meaning. These two levels of meaning are called denotative and connotative. A word's **denotative meaning** is the meaning stated in the dictionary—its literal meaning. A word's **connotative meaning** is the additional implied meanings, or nuances, that a word may take on. Often the connotative meaning carries either a positive or negative, favorable or unfavorable impression. The words *mob* and *gang* have a negative connotation because they imply a disorderly, disorganized group. *Congregation, audience,* and *class* have a positive connotation because they suggest an orderly, organized group.

Here are a few more examples. Would you prefer to be described as "slim" or "skinny"? as "intelligent" or "brainy"? as "heavy" or "fat"? as "particular" or "picky"? Notice that each pair of words has a similar literal meaning, but that each word within the pair has a different connotation.

Depending on the words they choose, writers can suggest favorable or unfavorable impressions of the person, object, or event they are describing. For example, through the writer's choice of words, the two sentences below create two entirely different impressions. As you read them, underline words that have a positive or negative connotation.

> The unruly crowd forced its way through the restraint barriers and ruthlessly attacked the rock star.

> The enthusiastic group of fans burst through the fence and rushed toward the rock star.

When reading any type of informative or persuasive material, pay attention to the writer's choice of words. Often a writer may communicate subtle or hidden messages, or he or she may encourage the reader to feel positively or negatively toward the subject.

Read the following paragraph on violence in sports and, as you read, underline words that have a strong positive or negative connotation.

> So it goes. Knifings, shootings, beatings, muggings, paralysis, and death become part of our play. Women baseball fans are warned to walk with friends

and avoid taking their handbags to games because of strong-arm robberies and purse snatchings at San Francisco's Candlestick Park. A professional football coach, under oath in a slander case, describes some of his own players as part of a "criminal element" in his sport. The commissioner of football proclaims that playing field outlaws and bullies will be punished, but to anybody with normal eyesight and a working television set the action looks rougher than ever. In Europe and South America—and, chillingly, for the first time in the United States—authorities turn to snarling attack dogs to control unruly mobs at athletic events.[1]

DIRECTIONS: *For each of the following pairs of words, underline the word with the more positive connotation.*

1. request   demand

2. overlook   neglect

3. ridicule   tease

4. glance   stare

5. display   expose

6. garment   gown

7. gaudy   showy

8. clumsy   awkward

9. artificial   fake

10. token   keepsake

DIRECTIONS: *For each word listed below, write a word that has a similar denotative meaning but a negative connotation. Then write a word that has a positive connotation. Use your dictionary or thesaurus, if necessary.*

	Negative	Positive
Example: eat	gobble	dine
1. take	_____	_____
2. ask	_____	_____

	Negative	Positive
3. look at	_____	_____
4. walk	_____	_____
5. dress	_____	_____
6. music	_____	_____
7. car	_____	_____
8. laugh	_____	_____
9. large	_____	_____
10. woman	_____	_____

Implied Meanings

An **inference** is an educated guess or prediction about something unknown based on available facts and information. It is the logical connection that you draw between what you observe or know and what you do not know.

Suppose that you arrive ten minutes late for your sociology class. All the students have papers in front of them, and everyone is busily writing. Some students have worried or concerned looks on their faces. The instructor is seated and is reading a book. What is happening? From the known information you can make an inference about what you do not know. Did you figure out that the instructor had given the class a surprise quiz? If so, then you made a logical inference.

While the inference you made is probably correct, you cannot be sure until you speak with the instructor. Occasionally a logical inference can be wrong. Although it is unlikely, perhaps the instructor has laryngitis and has written notes on the board for the students to copy. Some students may look worried because they do not understand what the notes mean.

Here are a few more everyday situations. Make an inference for each.

You are driving on an expressway and you notice a police car with flashing red lights behind you. You check your speedometer and notice that you are going ten miles over the speed limit.

A woman seated alone in a bar nervously glances at everyone who enters. Every few minutes she checks her watch.

In the first situation, a good inference might be that you are going to be stopped for speeding. However, it is possible that the officer only wants to pass you to get to an accident ahead or to stop someone driving faster than you. In the second situation, one inference is that the woman is waiting to meet someone who is late.

The following paragraphs are taken from a book by Bill Cosby titled *Time Flies*. First, read them for factual content.

When I was twenty-five, I saw a movie called *The Loneliness of the Long Distance Runner,* in which a young man running for a reform school was far ahead in a cross-country race and then suddenly stopped as an act of rebellion. That young runner had been struck by the feeling that he had to go his own way and not the way demanded by society.

That young runner was me.

I hadn't been doing time, of course, just *marking* time at Temple, where my mind was not on books but bookings; and so, I had dropped out to go into show business, a career move as sound as seeking my future as a designer of dirigibles. Although my mother and father kept telling me that I should finish college before I flopped in show business, I felt that only *I,* with the full wisdom of a north Philadelphia jock, knew what was best for me. I empathized with the hero of *The Loneliness of the Long Distance Runner,* who had said about his race, "You have to run, run, run without knowing *why.*"[2]

These paragraphs are primarily factual—they tell who did what, when, and where. However, some ideas are not directly stated and must be inferred from the information given. Here are a few examples. Some are fairly obvious inferences; others are less obvious.

1. The runner did not finish the race.
2. The runner could have won the race.
3. Cosby was *not* the young runner from reform school.
4. Cosby thought he was like the runner.
5. Temple is a university or college.
6. Cosby did not do well academically at Temple.
7. A career in show business is impractical.
8. Cosby's parents thought he would fail in show business.
9. Cosby felt it was acceptable to act without having specific reasons.
10. Cosby now realizes that he wasn't as wise as he thought he was at the time.

Although none of the above ideas are directly stated, they can be inferred from clues provided in the passage. Some of the statements could be inferred from actions, others by adding facts together, and still others by the writer's choice of words.

Now read the following passage to find out why Cindy Kane is standing on the corner of Sheridan and Sunnyside.

An oily midnight mist had settled on the city streets . . . asphalt mirrors from a ten-o'clock rain now past . . . a sleazy street-corner reflection of smog-smudged neon . . . the corner of Sheridan and, incongruously, Sunnyside . . . Chicago.

A lone lady lingers at the curb . . . but no bus will come.

She is Cindy Kane, twenty-eight. Twenty-eight hard years old. Her iridescent dress clings to her slender body. Her face is buried under a technicolor avalanche of makeup.

She is Cindy Kane.

And she has a date.

With someone she has never met . . . and may never meet again.

Minutes have turned to timelessness . . . and a green Chevy four-door pulls slowly around the corner.

The driver's window rolls down. A voice comes from the shadow . . .

"Are you working?"

Cindy nods . . . regards him with vacant eyes.

He beckons.

She approaches the passenger side. Gets in. And the whole forlorn, unromantic ritual begins all over again. With another stranger.[3]

If you made the right inferences, you realized that Cindy Kane is a prostitute and that she is standing on the corner waiting for a customer. Let us look at the kinds of clues the writer gave that led to this inference.

1. DESCRIPTION. By the way the writer describes Cindy Kane, you begin to suspect that she is a prostitute. She is described as "hard." She is wearing an iridescent, clinging dress and "a technicolor avalanche of makeup." These descriptive details convey an image of a gaudy, unconventional appearance.

2. ACTION. The actions, although few, also provide clues about what is happening. The woman is lingering on the corner. When the car approaches, she gets in.

3. CONVERSATION. The only piece of conversation, the question, "Are you working?" is one of the strongest clues the writer provides.

4. WRITER'S COMMENTARY/DETAILS. As the writer describes the situation, he slips in numerous clues. He establishes the time as around midnight ("An oily midnight mist"). His reference to a "reflection of smog-smudged neon" suggests an area of bars or night clubs. The woman's face is "buried under . . . makeup." Covering or hiding one's face is usually associated with shame or embarrassment. In the last paragraph, the reference to a "forlorn, unromantic ritual" provides a final clue.

How to Make Inferences

Making an inference is a thinking process. As you read, you are following the author's thoughts. You are also alert for ideas that are suggested but not directly stated. Because inference is a logical thought process, there is no simple, step-by-step procedure to follow. Each inference depends entirely on the situation, the facts provided, and the reader's knowledge and experience.

However, here are a few guidelines to keep in mind as you read. These will help you get in the habit of looking beyond the factual level to the inferential.

1. *Be sure you understand the literal meaning.* You should have a clear grasp of the key idea and supporting details of each paragraph.
2. *Notice details.* Often a detail provides a clue that will help you make an inference. When you spot a striking or unusual detail, ask yourself: Why did the writer include this piece of information?
3. *Add up the facts.* Consider all the facts taken together. Ask yourself: What is the writer trying to suggest from this set of facts? What do all these facts and ideas point toward?
4. *Watch for clues.* The writer's choice of words and detail often suggest his or her attitude toward the subject. Notice, in particular, descriptive words, emotionally charged words, and words with strong positive or negative connotations.
5. *Be sure your inference is supportable.* An inference must be based on fact. Make sure there is sufficient evidence to justify any inference you make.

EXERCISE 12-3

DIRECTIONS: *Read each of the following passages. Then answer the questions that follow. You will need to reason out, or infer, the answers.*

Passage 1:

Eye-to-eye contact and response are important in real-life relationships. The nature of a person's eye contact patterns, whether he or she looks another squarely in the eye or looks to the side or shifts his gaze from side to side, tells a lot about the person. These patterns also play a significant role in success or failure in human relationships. Despite its importance, eye contact is not involved in television watching. Yet children spend several hours a day in front of the television set. Certain children's programs pretend to speak directly to each individual child. (Mr. Rogers is an example, telling the child "I like you,

---

you're special," etc.) However, this is still one-way communication and no response is required of the child. How might such a distortion of real-life relationships affect a child's development of trust, or openness, of an ability to relate well to other people?[4]

a. How would the author answer the question asked in the last sentence of the paragraph?

_____

b. What is the author's attitude toward television?

_____

c. To develop a strong relationship with someone should you look directly at him or her or shift your gaze?

_____

d. What activities, other than television, do you think this author would recommend for children?

_____

Passage 2:

There is little the police or other governmental agencies can't find out about you these days.

For starters, the police can hire an airplane and fly over your backyard filming you sunbathing and whatever else is visible from above. A mail cover allows the post office, at the request of another government or police agency, to keep track of people sending you mail and organizations sending you literature through the mail. A pen register at the phone company may be installed at police request to collect the numbers dialed to and from your home telephone. Police or other governmental agencies may have access to your canceled checks and deposit records to find out who is writing checks to you and to whom you are writing checks. Library and film rental records disclose what you are reading and what you are watching. Even the trash you discard may be examined to see what you are throwing away.

No doubt by now you've realized that the accumulation of this information provides a fairly complete and accurate picture about a person, including her health, friends, lovers, political and religious activities, and even beliefs.

Figure that, if the Gillette razor company knows when it's your eighteenth birthday to send you a sample razor, your government, with its super, interconnecting computers, knows much more about you.[5]

a. What is the author's attitude toward government agencies?

_____

b. For what reason might a police agency request a pen register?

_____

c. Where do you think the author stands on the issue of right to privacy? (What rights to privacy do we or should we have?)

_____

Passage 3:

George Washington is remembered not for what he was but for what he should have been. It doesn't do any good to point out that he was an "inveterate landgrabber," and that as a young man he illegally had a surveyor stake out some prize territory west of the Alleghenies in an area decreed off limits to settlers. Washington is considered a saint, and nothing one says is likely to make him seem anything less. Though he was a wily businessman and accumulated a fortune speculating in frontier lands, he will always be remembered as a farmer—and a "simple farmer" at that.

Even his personal life is misremembered. While Washington admitted despising his mother and in her dying years saw her infrequently, others remembered his mother fondly and considered him a devoted son. While his own records show he was something of a dandy and paid close attention to the latest clothing designs, ordering "fashionable" hose, the "neatest shoes," and coats with "silver trimmings," practically no one thinks he was vain. Though he loved to drink and dance and encouraged others to join him, the first President is believed to have been something of a prude.[6]

a. Describe how Washington is usually remembered.

_____

b. Describe the author's attitude toward Washington.

_____

c. Does the author think attitudes toward Washington are likely to change?

_____

d. Explain the term "inveterate landgrabber."

_____

e. Why do you think there is such a discrepancy between what Washington did and how he is remembered?

_____

Passage 4:

> I am a peace-loving woman. But several events in the past 10 years have convinced me I'm safer when I carry a pistol. This was a personal decision, but because handgun possession is a controversial subject, perhaps my reasoning will interest others.
>
> I live in western South Dakota on a ranch 25 miles from the nearest large town; for several years I spent winters alone here. As a free-lance writer, I travel alone a lot—more than 100,000 miles by car in the last four years. With women freer than ever before to travel alone, the odds of our encountering trouble seem to have risen. And help, in the West, can be hours away. Distances are great, roads are deserted, and the terrain is often too exposed to offer hiding places.
>
> A woman who travels alone is advised, usually by men, to protect herself by avoiding bars and other "dangerous situations," by approaching her car like an Indian scout, by locking doors and windows. But these precautions aren't always enough. I spent years following them and still found myself in dangerous situations. I began to resent the idea that just because I am female, I have to be extra careful. . . .
>
> When I got my pistol, I told my husband, revising the old Colt slogan, "God made men _and women,_ but Sam Colt made them equal." Recently I have seen a gunmaker's ad with a similar sentiment. Perhaps this is an idea whose time has come, though the pacifist inside me will be saddened if the only way women can achieve equality is by carrying weapons.
>
> We must treat a firearm's power with caution. "Power tends to corrupt, and absolute power corrupts absolutely," as a man (Lord Acton) once said. A pistol is not the only way to avoid being raped or murdered in today's world, but, intelligently wielded, it can shift the balance of power and provide a measure of safety.[7]

a. Predict the author's position on the issue of gun control.

_____

b. What does the author think of the advice that women should avoid dangerous situations?

_____

c. The author lives on a ranch in South Dakota and describes the particular problems she faces there. What problems might a resident of a large city describe to justify carrying a gun?

_____

d. What was the original Colt slogan?

_____

EXERCISE 12-4

DIRECTIONS: *Read each of the following selections and answer the questions that follow.*

Selection 1:

The Father and His Daughter

1 A little girl was given so many picture books on her seventh birthday that her father, who should have run his office and let her mother run the home, thought his daughter should give one or two of her new books to a little neighbor boy named Robert, who had dropped in, more by design than by chance.

2 Now, taking books, or anything else, from a little girl is like taking candy from a baby, but the father of the little girl had his way and Robert got two of her books. "After all, that leaves you with nine," said the father, who thought he was a philosopher and a child psychologist, and couldn't shut his big fatuous mouth on the subject.

3 A few weeks later, the father went to his library to look up "father" in the Oxford English Dictionary, to feast his eyes on the praise of fatherhood through the centuries, but he couldn't find volume F-G, and then he discovered that three others were missing, too—A-B, L-M, V-Z. He began a probe of his household, and learned what had become of the four missing volumes.

4   "A man came to the door this morning," said his little daughter, "and he didn't know how to get from here to Torrington, or from Torrington to Winstead, and he was a nice man, much nicer than Robert, and so I gave him four of your books. After all, there are thirteen volumes in the Oxford English Dictionary, and that leaves you nine."

Moral

5   This truth has been known from here to Menander: what's sauce for the gosling's not sauce for the gander.[8]

1. In the first paragraph, the author gives the first clue that the father's actions are going to lead him into trouble. Underline the clue.

2. What does the writer think of the father? Support your answer with references to the article.

    _____

3. What inference did the girl make from her father's actions?

    _____

4. Do you think the father approved of his daughter's action? Explain your reasons.

    _____

5. Explain the "Moral" at the end of the selection.

    _____

Selection 2:

Private Pains

1   The damndest thing happened while I was driving down Pioneer Avenue last week. I was passing an intersection and noticed a middle-aged lady stopped in her car waiting to enter the road. There was nothing remarkable about the car, but I happened to look at just the right time and saw she was crying.

2   Her cheeks were wet and her mouth was sort of twisted in that sorrowful half-smile people sometimes get when they cry. She didn't seem to be in any kind of predicament, and I'd never seen her before, so I did what we usually do when we see people crying; I looked away and drove on.

3   I kept thinking about it as I drove down the road. What could have driven this woman to tears in the middle of the day while waiting at a stop sign? Maybe she'd just gotten some terrible news about something. Maybe a par-

ent had died or her husband left her. Perhaps a child was hurt at school and she was panicked and on her way there at that very moment. It could have been her birthday or anniversary, and her family had gone off to work and school without saying anything about it. Who could tell?

It might even have been something rather silly. She may have been coming from her hairdresser, who'd done an absolutely horrible job on her, and she didn't know how she'd face people. Or found that she'd inadvertently *not* been invited to her club luncheon that day. Maybe she was just having one of those days we all have from time to time, and trying to make a left turn onto Pioneer Avenue in lunch-hour traffic was the last straw this poor woman could bear.

I wanted to turn around and go ask her what was wrong, but I knew she'd be gone by then. Even if she wasn't, I didn't think she'd talk to a stranger about it. I had a brief vision of opening her car door and holding her, telling her it would be all right. But I knew I would never do that, and would probably get arrested if I did.

It bugged the heck outa me. [I kept] Wondering what kind of tragedy this woman was carrying with her and enduring by herself. I thought about the sadness we all carry with us every day, and take to bed with us at night. The small pains and disappointments that keep us off our mark a little. They make us snap at store clerks without meaning to, or beep our horns at a slow-poke even when we're in no particular hurry. The sadness that sits like a chip on our shoulders, daring anyone to touch it. It makes our mouths taut and our eyes steely. We move stiffly, looking at our feet when we walk, lost in our own little worlds.

This woman, all alone in her car and for no apparent reason, had let her taut mouth fold and her steely eyes fill with tears. The tears came easier with every car that rolled by and left her there, myself included.

Possibly she was the store clerk someone had snapped at, or the slow-poke that got honked at. I don't know, I'm just guessing. It seems we spend so much time torturing each other to get to the head of the line or maneuver into that last parking space. Maybe we should forget about all that stuff every once in a while and just keep our eyes peeled for the tears of a stranger.[9]

1. What inferences did the author make about the woman who was crying?

   _____

2. Which inferences seem least plausible?

   _____

3. Does the author regret not stopping to comfort the woman? Justify your answer.

_____

_____

4. Explain the meaning of the last line of the selection.

_____

_____

Figurative Language

Read each of the following statements:

The cake tasted like a moist sponge.

The wilted plants begged for water.

Jean wore her heart on her sleeve.

You know that a cake cannot really have the same taste as a sponge, that plants do not actually request water, and that a person's heart cannot really be attached to her or his sleeve. However, you know what message the writer is communicating in each sentence. The cake was soggy and tasteless, the plants were extremely dry, and Jean revealed her feelings to everyone around her.

Each of these sentences is an example of figurative language. **Figurative language** is a way of describing something that makes sense on an imaginative level but not on a factual or literal level. Notice that while none of the above expressions is literally true, each is meaningful. In many figurative expressions, one thing is compared with another for some quality they have in common. Take, for example, the familiar expression in the following sentence:

Sam eats like a horse.

The diagram below shows the comparison being made in this figurative expression:

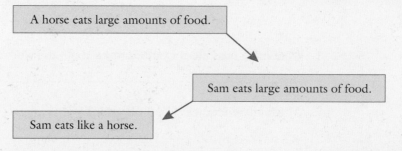

A horse eats large amounts of food.

Sam eats large amounts of food.

Sam eats like a horse.

You can see that two unlike things—Sam and a horse—are compared because they are alike in one particular way—the amount they eat.

The purpose of figurative language is to paint a word picture—to help you visualize how something looks, feels, or smells. Figurative language is a device writers use to express an idea or feeling and, at the same time, allow the reader the freedom of imagination. Since it is not factual, figurative language allows the writer to express attitudes and opinions without directly stating them. Depending on the figurative expression chosen, a writer can create a variety of impressions.

When reading an article that contains figurative language, be sure to pay close attention to the images and feelings created. Be sure you recognize that the writer is shaping your response to the topic or subject.

Figurative language is used in many types of articles and essays. It is also used in everyday speech and in slang expressions. Various types of literature, especially poetry, also use figurative language. Notice its use in the following excerpt from a poem by Emily Dickinson.

> My Life has stood—a Loaded Gun—
> In Corners—till a Day
> The Owner passed—identified—
> And carried Me away—[10]

In the opening stanza of this poem, Dickinson compares her life to a loaded gun.

Here are a few more examples from other sources. Notice how each creates a visual image of the person, object, or quality being described.

> The red sun was pasted in the sky like a wafer.
>
> (STEPHEN CRANE, THE RED BADGE OF COURAGE)

> In plucking the fruit of memory,
> one runs the risk of spoiling its bloom.
>
> (JOSEPH CONRAD)

> "I will speak daggers to her, but use none."
>
> (SHAKESPEARE, HAMLET)

> Life, like a dome of many-colored glass,
> Stains the white radiance of Eternity.
>
> (SHELLEY, "ADONAIS")

> "Float like a butterfly, sting like a bee."
>
> (MUHAMMAD ALI)

Like a bridge over troubled water,
I will lay me down.

(PAUL SIMON)

EXERCISE 12-5 **DIRECTIONS:** *Each of the following sentences includes a figurative expression. Read each sentence and explain in your own words what the expression means.*

1. My psychology quiz was a piece of cake.

   _____

   _____

2. My life is a junkyard of broken dreams.

   _____

   _____

3. Life is as tedious as a twice-told tale. (Shakespeare, *King John III*)

   _____

   _____

4. A sleeping child gives me the impression of a traveler in a very far country. (Ralph Waldo Emerson)

   _____

   _____

5. I refuse to accept the notion that nation after nation must spiral down a militaristic stairway into the hell of nuclear war. (Martin Luther King, Jr.)

   _____

   _____

DIRECTIONS: *Read each of the following articles and answer the questions that follow.*

Article 1:

Love In The Afternoon—In A Crowded Prison Hall

1   Each time I visit my man in prison, I relive the joy of reunion—and the anguish of separation.

2   We meet at the big glass door at the entrance to the small visitors' hall at Lompoc Federal Correctional Institution. We look at each other silently, then turn and walk into a room jammed with hundreds of molded fiberglass chairs lined up side by side. Finding a place in the crowded hall, we sit down, appalled that we're actually in a prison. Even now, after four months of such clocked, supervised, regulated visits, we still can't get used to the frustrations.

3   Yet, as John presses me gently to his heart, I feel warm and tender, and tears well up inside me, as they do each weekend. I have seven hours to spend with the man I love—all too brief a time for sharing a lifetime of emotion: love and longing, sympathy and tenderness, resentment and anger.

4   The guard's voice jars us: "Please keep the chairs in order!"

5   We can't keep from laughing, for we're struck by the absurdity of the scene: 60 couples, some with families, packed in a single room—each trying, somehow, to create an atmosphere of intimacy. And what's demanded by the single guard who's assigned to oversee us? *Chairs in a straight line.*

6   Nevertheless, John and I abide by the rules, holding each other as close as we can—without moving our chairs—and the loneliness of the past week gradually subsides.

7   We break our silent communion with small talk much like the kind we shared at home for the past three years. Like: *Should we have the van repaired, or sell it?*

8   Then we speak of our separate needs and fears. He feels defeated—by confinement, by prison life, by the 20 months left to serve on a two-year sentence for a drug-related charge that we think should never have come to trial. He feels deeply insecure, too, doubting my fidelity and hating himself for doubting me. He wants support and reassurance.

9   But what about me? *Doesn't he understand that this has been an ordeal for me, too?* My whole life fell apart when he went to prison. Our wedding plans were canceled; I had to quit school, sell everything, find a job, and move in with relatives.

10

Prison has become my second full-time occupation. Each weekend I spend 10 hours traveling. Always I must save money—money for my motel room in Lompoc, money for his collect phone calls to supplement the letters we write, money for his supplies at the prison commissary.

11

Worst of all, there's the almost unbearable burden of conducting my home life alone. At least in prison he has no decisions to make, no meals to worry about, no rent. So I, too, need reassurance and emotional support.[11]

1. Answer each of the following questions by making an inference.

   a. Who is visiting the man in prison?

   _____

   b. Why is she there?

   _____

   c. Does she go there often? How do you know?

   _____

   d. Why do they break the silence with small talk?

   _____

   e. Why does the guard insist that the chairs be kept in a straight line?

   _____

   f. Why did the woman have to quit school?

   _____

   g. Does the writer feel sorry for herself? How do you know?

   _____

2. List several words with negative connotations that suggest how the writer feels about the prison.

   _____

3. List several words with positive connotations that suggest how the woman feels about the man she is visiting.

   _____

4. What main point do you think the writer is trying to make?

_____

Article 2:

Stop Junk Mail Forever

1   Every American, on average, receives 677 sales pitches in his or her mailbox every year—thanks to low-cost, third-class postal rates. While the direct mailers who produce and distribute those 40 million tons of sales pitches take in over $200 billion annually, taxpayers beat the burden of some $320 million to cart their unsolicited promos, pleas, and promises to and from incinerators, garbage dumps (on land and sea), and recycling centers. Sixty-eight million trees and 28 billion gallons of water (and the animals who lived there) are used to produce each year's crop of catalogs and come-ons. Nearly half get trashed unopened.

2   Many of the environmental organizations that you'd expect to speak up for the trees, rivers, and wildlife are silent about junk mail. Why? Because they support themselves just like the other mailbox fishermen do . . . by casting an extremely wide net to catch a couple of fish. A "response rate" of 1% or 2%—that's 1 or 2 of every 100 pieces mailed—is considered typical, no matter if the mailer is a worthy charity . . . or the distributor of yet one more vegetable slicer.

3   There's another issue of great concern to us: Privacy. We think Americans should have the right to choose how personal information about them is marked, if at all. What follows are some clear instructions on how to keep your name, business, address, and other personal information private—off of those thousands upon thousands of mailing lists that are regularly bought and sold, without our approval for pennies a name.[12]

1. Underline three words in the article that carry positive or negative connotative meanings.

2. What is the author's attitude toward environmental organizations?

_____

3. What is the author's attitude toward vegetable slicers? Why does he or she use them as an example?

_____

4. Explain why the phrase "mailbox fishermen" is an example of figurative language.

Understanding the Author's Purpose

Writers have many different reasons or purposes for writing. Read the following statements and try to decide why each was written:

1. About 14,000 ocean-going ships pass through the Panama Canal each year. This averages about three ships per day.
2. *New Unsalted Dry Roasted Almonds.* Finally, a snack with a natural flavor and without salt. We simply shell the nuts and dry-roast them until they're crispy and crunchy. Try a jar this week.
3. Man is the only animal that blushes or has a need to.
4. If a choking person has fallen down, first turn him or her face up. Then knit together the fingers of both your hands and apply pressure with the heel of your bottom hand to the victim's abdomen.
5. If your boat capsizes, it is usually safer to cling to the boat than to try to swim ashore.

Statement 1 was written to give information, 2 to persuade you to buy almonds, 3 to amuse you and make a comment on human behavior, 4 to explain, and 5 to give advice.

In each of the examples, the writer's purpose was fairly clear, as it will be in most textbooks (to present information), newspaper articles (to communicate daily events), and reference books (to compile facts). However, in many other types of writing, authors have varied, sometimes less obvious, purposes. In these cases, an author's purpose must be inferred.

Often a writer's purpose is to express an opinion indirectly. Or the writer may want to encourage the reader to think about a particular issue or problem. Writers achieve their purposes by manipulating and controlling what they say and how they say it. This chapter will focus on techniques writers use and features of language that writers control to achieve the results they want.

Style and Intended Audience

Are you able to recognize a friend just by his or her voice? Can you identify family members by their footsteps? You are able to do so because each person's voice and footsteps are unique. Have you noticed that writers have unique characteristics as well? One author may use many examples; another may use few. One author may use relatively short sentences, another may use long, complicated ones. The characteristics that make a writer unique are known as **style.** By changing style, writers can create different effects.

Writers may vary their styles to suit their intended audiences. A writer may write for a general-interest audience (anyone who is interested in the subject but is not considered an expert). Most newspapers and periodicals, such as *Time* and *Newsweek,* appeal to a general-interest audience. On the other hand, a writer may have a particular interest group in mind. A writer may write for medical doctors in the *Journal of American Medicine* or for skiing enthusiasts in *Skiing Today* or for antique collectors in *The World of Antiques.* A writer may also target his or her writing for an audience with particular political, moral, or religious attitudes. Articles in the *New Republic* often appeal to the particular political viewpoint, whereas the *Catholic Digest* appeals to a specific religious group.

Depending on the group of people for whom the author is writing, he or she will change the level of language, choice of words, and method of presentation. One step toward identifying an author's purpose, then, is to ask yourself the question: Who is the intended audience? Your response will be your first clue to determining why the author wrote the article.

EXERCISE 12-7

DIRECTIONS: Read each of the following statements and decide for whom each was written. Write a sentence that describes the intended audience.

1. Chances are you're going to be putting money away over the next five years or so. You are hoping for the right things in life. Right now, a smart place to put your money is in mutual funds or bonds.

_____

2. Think about all the places your drinking water has been before you drink another drop. Most likely it has been chemically treated to remove bacteria and chemical pollutants. Soon you may begin to feel the side effects of these treatments. Consider switching to filtered, distilled water today.

_____

3. Introducing the new, high-powered Supertuner III, a stereo system guaranteed to keep your mother out of your car.

_____

4. Bright and White laundry detergent removes dirt and stains faster than any other brand.

---

5. As a driver, you're ahead if you can learn to spot car trouble before it's too late. If you can learn the difference between drips and squeaks that occur under normal conditions and those that mean big trouble is just down the road, then you'll be ahead of expensive repair bills and won't find yourself stranded on a lonely road.

Tone

The tone of a speaker's voice helps you interpret what he or she is saying. If the following sentence were read aloud, the speaker's voice would tell you how to interpret it: "Would you mind closing the door?" In print you cannot tell whether the speaker is polite, insistent, or angry. In speech you could tell by whether the speaker emphasized the word *would, door,* or *mind.*

Just as a speaker's tone of voice tells how the speaker feels, so does a writer convey a tone, or feeling, through his or her writing. **Tone** refers to the attitude or feeling a writer expresses about his or her subject. A writer may adopt a sentimental tone, an angry tone, a humorous tone, a sympathetic tone, an instructive tone, a persuasive tone, and so forth. Here are a few examples of different tones. How does each make you feel?

- Instructive

  When purchasing a piece of clothing, one must be concerned with quality as well as with price. Be certain to check for the following: double-stitched seams, matched patterns, and ample linings.

- Sympathetic

  The forlorn, frightened-looking child wandered through the streets alone, searching for someone who would show an interest in helping her find her parents.

- Persuasive

  Child abuse is a tragic occurrence in our society. Strong legislation is needed to control the abuse of innocent victims and to punish those who are insensitive to the rights and feelings of others.

- Humorous

  "As one of the most modern and well-educated citizenries in the world, you'd think we could take pretty good care of ourselves, that we could drive cars, shop in stores, and heat up a can of beans without a lot of supervision. That doesn't seem to be the case. Every place you look we are warned about things that we shouldn't need to be warned about, and reminded of things that should go without saying. Either we've all gone soft in the head, or we were among some of God's dimmer creatures in the first place."[13]

- Nostalgic

"Things change, times change, but when school starts, my little granddaughter will run up the same wooden stairs that creaked for all of the previous generations and I will still hate it when the summer ends."[14]

In the first example, the writer offers advice in a straightforward, informative style. In the second, the writer wants you to feel sorry for the child. This is done through description. In the third example, the writer tries to convince the reader that action must be taken to prevent child abuse. The use of such words as *tragic, innocent,* and *insensitive* establish this tone.

The tone of an article directly affects how the reader interprets and responds to it. If, as in the fourth example, the writer's tone is humorous and you do not recognize this, you will miss the point of the entire selection. If the writer's tone is sympathetic, it is important to know that an appeal to your feelings is being made. You can begin to suspect, then, that you may not receive an objective, unbiased treatment of the subject.

The author's tone is intended to rub off on you, so to speak. If a writer's tone is humorous, the writer hopes you will be amused. If a writer's tone is persuasive, the writer hopes you will accept his or her viewpoint. You can see how tone can be important in determining an author's purpose. Therefore, a second question to ask when trying to determine an author's purpose is: What tone does the writer use? Or: How is the writer trying to make me feel about the subject?

EXERCISE 12-8

DIRECTIONS: Read each of the following statements, paying particular attention to the tone. Then write a sentence that describes the tone. Prove your point by listing some of the words that reveal the author's feelings.

1. No one says that nuclear power is risk free. There are risks involved in all methods of producing energy. However, the scientific evidence is clear and obvious. Nuclear power is at least as safe as any other means used to generate electricity.

_____

_____

2. The condition of our city streets is outrageous. The sidewalks are littered with paper and other garbage—you could trip while walking to the store. The streets themselves are in even worse condition. Deep potholes and crumbling curbs make it unsafe to drive. Where are our city tax dollars going if not to correct these problems?

   _____

   _____

3. I am a tired American. I am tired of watching criminals walk free while they wait for their day in court. I'm tired of hearing about victims getting as much as or more hassle than criminals. I'm tired of reading about courts of law that even accept a lawsuit in which a criminal sues his or her intended victim.

   _____

   _____

4. Cross-country skis have heel plates of different shapes and materials. They may be made of metal, plastic, or rubber. Be sure that they are tacked on the ski right where the heel of your boot will fall. They will keep snow from collecting under your foot and offer some stability.

   _____

   _____

5. We in the United States have made great progress in lowering our birth rates. But now, because we have been responsible, it seems to some that we have a great surplus. There is, indeed, waste that should be eliminated, but there is not as much fat in our system as most people think. Yet we are being asked to share our resources with the hungry peoples of the world. But why should we share? The nations having the greatest needs are those that have been the least responsible in cutting down on births. Famine is one of nature's ways of telling profligate peoples that they have been irresponsible in their breeding habits.[15]

   _____

   _____

6. In July of 1986 my daughter, Lucy, was born with an underdeveloped brain. She was a beautiful little girl—at least to me and my husband—but her disabilities were severe. By the time she was two weeks old we knew that she would never walk, talk, feed herself, or even understand the concept of mother and father. It's impossible to describe the effect that her five-and-a-half-month life

had on us; suffice it to say that she was the purest experience of love and pain that we will ever have, that she changed us forever, and that we will never cease to mourn her death, even though we know that for her it was a triumphant passing.[16]

_____

_____

Language

One important feature that writers adjust to suit their purpose is the kind of language they use. There are two basic types of language: objective and subjective.

Objective and Subjective Language **Objective language** is factual, whereas **subjective language** expresses attitudes and feelings.

Read each of the following descriptions of the death penalty. As you read, decide how they differ.

> The death penalty is one of the most ancient of all types of formal punishment for crime. In early criminal codes, death was the penalty for a wide range of offenses, such as kidnapping, certain types of theft, and witchcraft. Today, in the United States, the death penalty is reserved for only the most serious of crimes—murder, kidnapping, and treason.
>
> The death penalty is a prime example of man's inhumanity to man. The death penalty violates the Eighth Amendment to the Constitution, which prohibits cruel and unusual punishment.

You probably noticed that the first paragraph gave facts about the death penalty and that the second paragraph seemed to state a case against it. These two paragraphs are examples of two different types of writing.

The first paragraph is an example of objective language. The writer reported information without showing feelings. You cannot tell whether the writer favors or is opposed to the death penalty.

The second paragraph is an example of subjective language. Here, the writer expresses freely his or her own attitudes and feelings. You know exactly how the author feels about the death penalty. Through choice of words and selection of facts, a tone of moral disapproval is evident. Such words as _inhumanity, violate,_ and _cruel_ have negative connotations.

DIRECTIONS: *Choose a topic that interests you or use one of the topics listed below. On a separate sheet, write two brief paragraphs. In the first, use only objective, factual information. In the second, try to show your feelings about the topic by using subjective language.*

1. One of your college instructors

2. Managing your time

3. Current fashion fads

Descriptive Language **Descriptive language** is a particular type of subjective language. It is the use of words that appeal to one or more of the reader's senses. Descriptive words help the reader create an imaginary picture of the object, person, or event being described. Here is a paragraph that contains numerous descriptive words and phrases. As you read, underline words and phrases that help you to imagine what the Oregon desert is like.

> You can camp in the Oregon desert for a week and see no one at all, no more than the glow of headlights hovering over a dirt road miles distant, disappearing soundlessly over the curve of the Earth. You can see, as you wander over those dry flats, that man has been there, that vast stretches of sagebrush have replaced the bunchgrass grazed off by his cattle and sheep. Against a hill you can find the dry-rotting foundation of a scuttled homestead. But the desert is not scarred by man's presence. It is still possible to be alone out there, to stare at your hands for an hour and have no one ask why. It is possible to feel the cracks in the earth, to sense the enormity of space, to roll, between the tips of your fingers, the dust of boulders gone to pieces.[17]

Through descriptive language, a writer often makes you feel a certain way about the topic. In the preceding paragraph, the writer is trying to suggest that the desert is lonely, peaceful, and a good place to think or relax. Did you notice such words and phrases as *soundlessly, enormity of space, distant, wander, vast stretches?*

DIRECTIONS: *Read each of the following articles and answer the questions that follow.*

Article 1:

Americans and the Land

I have often wondered at the savagery and thoughtlessness with which our early settlers approached this rich continent. They came at it as though it were an enemy, which of course it was. They burned the forests and changed the rainfall; they swept the buffalo from the plains, blasted the streams, set fire to the grass, and ran a reckless scythe through the virgin and noble timber. Perhaps they felt that it was limitless and could never be exhausted and that a man could move on to new wonders endlessly. Certainly there are many examples to the contrary, but to a large extent the early people pillaged the country as though they hated it, as though they held it temporarily and might be driven off at any time.[18]

1. Is this selection an objective or subjective account of the early settlement of America? Give examples to support your choice.

   _____

   _____

2. Describe the writer's tone. How does it make you feel?

   _____

   _____

3. Why do you think the author wrote this selection?

   _____

   _____

Article 2:

The Laughter Connection

Earlier in this chapter, I spoke of the role of humor in creating a relaxed and responsive environment in audiences. I had an opportunity to see this effect

1

in heightened form at the Sepulveda (California) Veterans' Administration Hospital.

I had gone to the hospital following a meeting with physicians assigned to the cancer unit. They were concerned because the mood of the cancer patients was so bleak that they feared the collective environment of treatment was being impaired.

At the suggestion of the doctors I met with the veterans in the cancer unit. There were perhaps fifty or sixty of them. They sat in rows and were every bit as glum as I had anticipated.

I reported on my conversation with their doctors, and said I doubted that they were helping them or themselves with the grim mood of the place. Certainly one could understand the reason for their feelings—and it was arrogant for anyone to lecture to them about it. But in coming to Sepulveda they were reaching out for help—and they were entitled to know what would optimize that prospect.

Any battle with serious illness, I said, involved two elements. One was represented by the ability of the physicians to make available to patients the best that medical science has to offer. The other element was represented by the ability of patients to summon all their physical and spiritual resources in fighting illness.

I said I hoped the veterans would agree that their part of the job was to create an environment in which the doctors could do their best. One thing they might do to replace the grim atmosphere was to put on performances. We could give them scripts of amusing one-act plays. Some of them might wish to produce or direct or act. If they wished, we could help them obtain videocassettes of amusing motion picture films. Ditto, audio cassettes of stand-up comics. One way or another, their part in the joint enterprise with their doctors was to create a mood conducive to the best medical treatment obtainable.

The veterans accepted the challenge. When I returned to the hospital several weeks later and spoke to the doctors I was pleased to have them describe the change not just in the general environment but in the mood of the individual patients.

When I met with the veterans, they no longer sat in rows. They sat in a large circle. They were part of a unity; they could all see one another. When they began their meeting, each veteran was obligated to tell something good that had happened to him since the previous meeting.

The first veteran spoke of his success in reaching by telephone a buddy he had not seen since the Korean War. He had tracked his buddy to Chicago and finally made the connection. They spoke for a half-hour or more. And the good news was that his buddy was coming to visit him in California.

Cheers.

The next veteran read from a letter he had received from a nephew who had just been admitted to medical school. He quoted the final sentence of the letter:

"And, Uncle Ben, I want you to know that I'm going into cancer research, and I'm going to come up with the answer, so you and your buddies just hang in there until I do."

More cheers.

And so it went, each person at the meeting taking his turn. Then I discovered that everyone was looking at me and that I was expected to report on what it was that was good that had happened to me.

I searched my recent memory and realized that something quite good had in fact happened to me only a few days earlier.

"What I have to report is better than good," I said. "It's wonderful. Actually, it's better than wonderful. It's unbelievable. And as long as I live, I don't expect that anything as magnificent as this can possibly happen to me again."

The veterans sat forward in their seats.

"What happened is that when I arrived at the Los Angeles airport last Wednesday my bag was the first off the carousel."

An eruption of applause and acclaim greeted this announcement.

"I had never even met anyone whose bag was the first off the carousel," I continued.

Again, loud expressions of delight.

"Flushed with success, I went to the nearest telephone to report my arrival to my office. That was when I lost my coin. I pondered this melancholy event for a moment or two, then decided to report it to the operator.

"'Operator,' I said, 'I put in a quarter and didn't get my number. The machine collected my coin.'

"'Sir,' she said, 'if you give me your name and address, we'll mail the coin to you.'

"I was appalled.

"'Operator,' I said, 'I think I can understand the reason behind the difficulties of A.T.&T. You're going to take the time and trouble to write down my name on a card and then you are probably going to give it to the person in charge of such matters. He will go to the cash register, punch it open and take out a quarter, at the same time recording the reason for the cash withdrawal. Then he will take a cardboard with a recessed slot to hold the coin so it won't flop around in the envelope. Then he, or someone else, will fit the cardboard with the coin into an envelope, first taking the time to write out my address on the envelope. Then the envelope will be sealed. Someone will then affix a twenty-cent stamp on the envelope. All that time and expense just to return a quarter. Now, operator, why don't you just return my coin and let's be friends.'

27   "'Sir,' she repeated in a flat voice, 'if you give me your name and address, we will mail you the refund.'

28   "Then, almost by way of afterthought, she said, 'Sir, did you remember to press the coin return plunger?'

29   "Truth to tell, I had overlooked this nicety. I pressed the plunger. To my great surprise, it worked. It was apparent that the machine had been badly constipated and I happened to have the plunger. All at once, the vitals of the machine opened up and proceeded to spew out coins of almost every denomination. The profusion was so great that I had to use my empty hand to contain the overflow.

30   "While all this was happening, the noise was registering in the telephone and was not lost on the operator.

31   "'Sir,' she said, 'what is happening?'

32   "I reported that the machine had just given up all its earnings for the past few months, at least. At a rough estimate, I said there must be close to four dollars in quarters, dimes, and nickels that had just erupted from the box.

33   "'Sir,' she said, 'will you please put the coins back in the box.'

34   "'Operator,' I said, 'if you give me your name and address I will be glad to mail you the coins.'"

35   The veterans exploded with cheers. David triumphs over Goliath. At the bottom of the ninth inning, with the home team behind by three runs, the weakest hitter in the lineup hits the ball out of the park. A mammoth business corporation is brought to its knees. Every person who had been exasperated by the loss of a coin in a public telephone booth could identify with my experience and share both in the triumph of justice and the humiliation of the mammoth and impersonal oppressor.

36   The veterans not only were having a good time; they were showing it in their relaxed expressions and in the way they moved.

37   One of the doctors stood up.

38   "Tell me," he said, "how many of you, when you came into this room a half hour or so ago, were experiencing, more or less, your normal chronic pains?"

39   More than half the veterans in the room raised their hands.

40   "Now," said the doctor, "how many of you, in the past five or ten minutes, discovered that these chronic pains receded or disappeared?"

41   The same hands, it appeared to me, went up again.

42   Why should simple laughter have produced this effect? Brain researchers with whom I have spoken have speculated that the laughter activated the release of endorphins, the body's own pain-reducing substance. The veterans were ex-

periencing the same effects that had occurred to me in my own bout with in-
flammatory joints many years earlier. The body's own morphine was at work.

In view of what is now known about the role of endorphins not only as a
painkiller but as a stimulant to the immune system, the biological value of
laughter takes on scientific validity.[19]

43

1. What is the author's main point?

   _____

   _____

2. What is the author's purpose in writing?

   _____

   _____

3. Describe the tone of the article.

   _____

   _____

4. Who is the intended audience?

   _____

   _____

5. Does the author provide an objective or subjective account of the importance
   of humor in pain reduction?

   _____

   _____

6. List several examples of descriptive language.

   _____

   _____

■ ■ ■ ■ ■ ■ ■ ■ **WORKING TOGETHER**

Directions: Bring a magazine ad to class. Working in groups of 3–4 students, make as
many inferences as possible about each ad. For example, answer questions such as
"What is happening?" "How does each person feel?" and "How will this ad sell the

product?" Group members who differ in their opinions should present evidence to support their own inferences. Each group should then state to the class, as specifically as possible, the purpose of each ad. Be specific; try to say more than "To sell the product."

■■■■■■■■ **SUMMARY**

How do authors suggest their ideas without directly stating them?

Authors use three features to state their ideas indirectly. These three features are:

1. Connotative meaning—the shades of meaning a word may have in addition to its literal meaning.

2. Implied meaning—ideas suggested based on facts and information given by the author.

3. Figurative language—a way of describing things that make sense on an imaginative level, but not on a factual level.

How can I identify the author's purpose?

There are four ways in which you can identify the author's purpose. These are

1. Style—A writer will change his or her style—level of language, choice of words, and method of presentation—to suit the intended audience.

2. Audience—Analyzing the style and identifying the intended audience are the first steps toward identifying an author's purpose.

3. Tone—A writer's tone—serious, humorous, angry, sympathetic—is a clue to how the writer wants you to feel about the topic.

4. Language—A writer's language may be objective or subjective, depending on whether the writer is simply presenting facts or expressing an opinion or feelings. This language presents one or more clue to the writer's purpose.

Evaluating:
Asking Critical Questions

■ ■

THIS CHAPTER WILL SHOW YOU HOW TO

1. *Judge the accuracy and value of what you read*

2. *Ask questions to evaluate what you read*

■ ■

If you were thinking of purchasing a used car from a private owner, you would ask questions before deciding whether to buy it. You would ask about repairs, maintenance, gas mileage, and so forth. When it comes to buying something, most of us have learned the motto "Buyer beware." We have learned to be critical, sometimes suspicious, of a product and its seller. We realize that salespeople will often tell us only what will make us want to buy the item. They will not tell what is wrong with the item or whether it compares unfavorably with a competitor's product.

Although many of us have become wise consumers, few of us have become wise, critical readers. We need to adopt a new motto: Reader beware. You can think of some writers as sellers and their written material as the product to be sold. Just as you would ask questions about a car before buying it, so should you ask questions about what you read before you accept what is said. You should ask questions about who wrote the material and where it came from. You need to decide whether the writer is selling you a one-sided, biased viewpoint. You should evaluate whether the writer provides sufficient support for his or her ideas to allow you to accept them. This chapter will discuss these critical issues and show you how to apply them to articles and essays.

What is the Source of the Material?

Just as you might check the brand label on an item of clothing before you buy it, so should you check to see where an article or essay comes from before you read it. You will often be asked to read material that is not in its original form. Many textbooks, such as this one, include excerpts or entire selections borrowed from other authors. Instructors often photocopy articles or essays and distribute them or place them on reserve in the library for students to read.

A first question to ask before you even begin to read is: What is the source—from what book, magazine, or newspaper was this taken? Knowledge of the source will help you judge the accuracy and soundness of what you read. For example, in which of the following sources would you expect to find the most accurate and up-to-date information about computer software?

- An advertisement in *Time*
- An article in *Reader's Digest*
- An article in *Software Review*

The article in *Software Review* would be the best source. This is a magazine devoted to the subject of computers and computer software. *Reader's Digest*, on the other hand, does not specialize in any one topic and often reprints or condenses articles from other sources. *Time*, a weekly newsmagazine, does contain information, but a paid advertisement is likely to provide information on only one line of software.

Knowing the source of an article will give clues to the kind of information the article will contain. For instance, suppose you went to the library to locate information for a research paper on the interpretation of dreams. You found the following sources of information. What do you expect each to contain?

- An encyclopedia entry titled "Dreams"
- An article in *Woman's Day* titled "A Dreamy Way to Predict the Future"

- An article in *Psychological Review* titled "An Examination of Research on Dreams"

You can predict that the encyclopedia entry will be a factual report. It will provide a general overview of the process of dreaming. The *Woman's Day* article will probably focus on the use of dreams to predict future events. You can expect the article to contain little research. Most likely, it will be concerned largely with individual reports of people who accurately dreamt about the future. The article from *Psychological Review*, a journal that reports research in psychology, will present a primarily factual, research-oriented discussion of dreams.

As part of evaluating a source or selecting an appropriate source, be sure to check the date of publication. For many topics, it is essential that you work with current, up-to-date information. For example, suppose you've found an article on the safety of over-the-counter, nonprescription drugs. If the article was written four or five years ago, it is already outdated. New drugs have been approved and released; new regulations have been put into effect; packaging requirements have changed. The year a book was published can be found on the copyright page. If the book has been reprinted by another publisher or has been reissued in paperback, look to see when it was first published and check the year(s) in the copyright notice.

EXERCISE 13-1

DIRECTIONS: *For each set of sources listed below, place a checkmark next to the one that would be most useful for finding information on the stated topic. Then, in the space provided, give a reason for your choice.*

1. Topic: gas mileage of American-made cars

   Sources: _____ a. A newspaper article titled "Gas-Eating American Cars"

   _____ b. An encyclopedia article on "Gas Consumption of Automobile Engines"

   _____ c. A research report in *Car and Driver* magazine on American car performance

   Reason: _____

2. Topic: viruses as a cause of cancer

   Sources: _____ a. A textbook titled *Well-Being: An Introduction to Health*

   _____ b. An article in *Scientific American* magazine on controlling viruses

        c. An issue of the *Journal of the American Medical Association* devoted to a review of current research findings on the causes of cancer

Reason: _____

3. Topic: the effects of aging on learning and memory

    Sources: _____ a. An article in *Reader's Digest* titled "Older Means Better"

              _____ b. A psychology textbook titled *A General Introduction to Psychology*

              _____ c. A textbook titled *Adult Development and Aging*

Reason: _____

What is the Authority of the Author?

The qualifications of the author to write about the subject is another clue to the reliability of the information. If the author lacks expertise in or experience with a subject, the material may not be accurate or worthwhile reading.

In textbooks, the author's credentials may appear on the title page or in the preface. In nonfiction books and general market paperbacks, a summary of the author's life and credentials may be included on the book jacket or back cover. In many other cases, however, the author's credentials are not given. You are left to rely on the judgment of the editors or publishers about an author's authority.

If you are familiar with an author's work, then you can anticipate the type of material you will be reading and predict the writer's approach and attitude toward the subject. If, for example, you found an article on world banking written by former President Carter, you could predict it will have a political point of view. If you were about to read an article on John Lennon written by Ringo Starr, one of the other Beatles, you could predict the article might possibly include details of their working relationship from Ringo's point of view.

EXERCISE 13-2

DIRECTIONS: Read each statement and place a checkmark next to the individual who would seem to be the best authority on the subject.

1. *General Hospital* is one of the best soap operas on TV.

    _____ Rick Levine, a former producer of *General Hospital*

_____ Sally Hastings, a soap-opera fan for fifteen years

_____ Frances Hailey, a TV critic for the *New York Times*

2. The president's recent news conference was a success.

   _____ Peter Jennings, a well-known news commentator

   _____ Janet Ferrick, one of the president's advisors

   _____ Howard Summers, a professor of economics

3. Kurt Vonnegut is one of the most important modern American novelists.

   _____ James Toth, producer of a TV documentary on Vonnegut's life

   _____ John Vilardo, a *Time*-magazine column writer

   _____ Cynthia Weinstein, a professor of twentieth-century literature at Georgetown University

Does the Writer make Assumptions?

An assumption is an idea, theory, or principle that the writer believes to be true. The writer then develops his or her ideas based on that assumption. Of course, if the assumption is not true or is one you disagree with, then the ideas that depend on that assumption are of questionable value. For instance, an author may believe that the death penalty is immoral and, beginning with that assumption, develop an argument for different ways to prevent crime. However, if you believe that the death penalty is moral, then from your viewpoint, the writer's argument is invalid.

Read the following paragraph. Identify the assumption the writer makes, and write it in the space provided.

> The evil of athletic violence touches nearly everyone. It tarnishes what may be our only religion. Brutality in games blasphemes play, perhaps our purest form of free expression. It blurs the clarity of open competition, obscuring our joy in victory as well as our dignity in defeat. It robs us of innocence, surprise, and self-respect. It spoils our fun.[1]
>
> Assumption: _____

Here the assumption is stated in the first sentence—the writer assumes that athletic violence exists. He makes no attempt to prove or explain that sports are violent. He assumes this and goes on to discuss its effects. You may agree or disagree with this assumption.

DIRECTIONS: *For each of the following paragraphs, identify the assumption that is made by the writer and write it in the space provided.*

1. Do you have any effective techniques that you use regularly to reduce your level of stress? If not, you may be among the many people who intellectually recognize the dangers of chronic stress—perhaps even have benefited from relaxation exercises—but somehow haven't made stress reduction part of their daily schedule. And you may be especially fascinated by a unique six-second exercise conceived and developed by Charles F. Stroebel, M.D., Ph.D., director of research at The Institute of Living in Hartford, Connecticut, and professor of psychiatry at the University of Connecticut Medical School.[2]

   Assumption: _____

2. Do boys need to rely on heroes more than girls do as sources of identity while growing up? While no one has gathered statistics, it is true that boys are more often called upon to prove themselves through performance. For example, even today, they're often still judged by how well they can kick and throw a ball. So they may have a greater *dependence* on athletes, if only as models to imitate. The baseball/football trading card ritual is still very common among elementary school-age boys; girls, however, have no equivalent for this practice, nor are they rated for their physical accomplishments the same way. Despite today's increasingly "nonsexist" child rearing, girls are still evaluated more on the basis of how they relate to other people than as solitary, achieving individuals.[3]

   Assumption: _____

Is the Author Biased?

As you evaluate any piece of writing, always try to decide whether the author is objective or one-sided (biased). Does the author present an objective view of the subject or is a particular viewpoint favored? An objective article presents all sides of an issue, while a biased one presents only one side.

You can decide whether a writer is biased by asking yourself these questions:

1. Is the writer acting as a reporter—presenting facts—or as a salesperson—providing only favorable information?
2. Are there other views toward the subject that the writer does not discuss?

Use these questions to determine whether the author of the following selection is biased:

Teachers, schools, and parent associations have become increasingly concerned about the effects of television on school performance. Based on their classroom experiences, many teachers have reported mounting incidences of fatigue, tension, and aggressive behavior, as well as lessened spontaneity and imagination.

So what have schools been doing? At Kimberton Farms School in Phoenixville, Pennsylvania, parents and teachers have been following written guidelines for five years which include no television *at all* for children through the first grade. Children in second grade through high school are encouraged to watch no television on school nights and to restrict viewing to a total of three to four hours on weekends. According to Harry Blanchard, head of the faculty, "You can observe the effects with some youngsters almost immediately. . . . Three days after they turn off the set you see a marked improvement in their behavior. They concentrate better, and are more able to follow directions and get along with their neighbors. If they go back to the set you notice it right away."

As Fiske has pointed out, "In the final analysis, the success of schools in minimizing the negative effects of television on their (children's) academic progress depends almost entirely on whether the parents share this goal."[4]

The subject of this passage is children's television viewing. It expresses concern and gives evidence that television has a negative effect on children. The other side of the issue—the positive effects or benefits—is not mentioned. There is no discussion of such positive effects as the information to be learned from educational television programs or the use of television in increasing a child's awareness of different ideas, people, and places. The author is biased and expresses only a negative attitude toward television.

Occasionally, you may come upon unintentional bias—bias that the writer is not aware of. A writer may not recognize his or her own bias on cultural, religious, or sexual issues.

Is the Writing Slanted?

Slanting refers to the selection of details that suit the author's purpose and the omission of those that do not. Suppose you were asked to write a description of a person you know. If you wanted a reader to respond favorably to the person, you might write something like this:

Alex is tall, muscular, and well built. He is a friendly person and seldom becomes angry or upset. He enjoys sharing jokes and stories with his friends.

On the other hand, if you wanted to create a less positive image of Alex, you could omit the above information and emphasize these facts instead:

> Alex has a long nose and his teeth are crooked. He talks about himself a lot and doesn't seem to listen to what others are saying. Alex wears rumpled clothes that are too big for him.

While all of these facts about Alex may be true, the writer decides which to include.

Much of what you read is slanted. For instance, advertisers tell only what is good about a product, not what is wrong with it. In the newspaper advice column, Dear Abby gives her opinion on how to solve a reader's problem, but she does not discuss all the possible solutions.

As you read material that is slanted, keep these questions in mind:

1. What types of facts has the author omitted?
2. How would the inclusion of these facts change your reaction or impression?

EXERCISE 13-4

DIRECTIONS: *Below is a list of different types of writing. For each item, decide whether it has little slant* (L), *is moderately slanted* (M), *or is very slanted* (V). *Write L, M, or V in the space provided.*

_____ 1. Help-wanted ads

_____ 2. An encyclopedia entry

_____ 3. A newspaper editorial

_____ 4. A biology textbook

_____ 5. A letter inviting you to apply for a charge account

_____ 6. A college catalog

_____ 7. An autobiography of a famous person

_____ 8. An insurance policy

_____ 9. *Time* magazine

_____10. *Catholic Digest*

How Does the Writer Support His or Her Ideas?

Suppose a friend said he thought you should quit your part-time job immediately. What would you do? Would you automatically accept his advice, or would you ask him why? No doubt you would not blindly accept the advice but would inquire why. Then, once you heard his reasons, you would decide whether they made sense.

Similarly, when you read, you should not blindly accept a writer's ideas. Instead, you should ask why by checking to see how the writer supports or explains his or her ideas. Then, once you have examined the supporting information, decide whether you accept the idea.

Evaluating the supporting evidence a writer provides involves using your judgment. The evidence you accept as conclusive may be regarded by someone else as insufficient. The judgment you make depends on your purpose and background knowledge, among other things. In judging the quality of supporting information a writer provides, you should watch for the use of (1) generalizations, (2) statements of opinion, (3) personal experience, and (4) statistics as evidence.

Generalizations

What do the following statements have in common?

Dogs are vicious and nasty.

College students are more interested in having fun than in learning.

Parents want their children to grow up to be just like them.

These sentences seem to have little in common. Although the subjects are different, the sentences do have one thing in common: each is a generalization. Each makes a broad statement about some group (dogs, college students, parents). The first statement says that dogs are vicious and nasty. Yet the writer could not be certain that this statement is true unless he or she had seen *every* existing dog. No doubt the writer felt this statement was true based on his or her observation of and experience with dogs.

A generalization is a statement that is made about an entire group or class of individuals or items based on experience with some members of that group. It necessarily involves the writer's judgment.

The question that must be asked about all generalizations is whether they are accurate. How many dogs did the writer observe and how much research did he or she do to justify the generalization? Try to think of exceptions to the generalization; in this instance, a dog that is neither vicious nor nasty.

As you evaluate the supporting evidence a writer uses, be alert for generalizations that are presented as facts. A writer may, on occasion, support a statement by offering unsupported generalizations. When this occurs, treat the writer's ideas with a critical, questioning attitude.

EXERCISE 13-5

DIRECTIONS: *Read each of the following statements and decide whether it is a generalization. Place a checkmark next to the statements that are generalizations.*

_____ 1. My sister wants to attend the University of Chicago.

_____ 2. Most engaged couples regard their wedding as one of the most important occasions in their lives.

_____ 3. Senior citizens are a cynical and self-interested group.

_____ 4. People do not use drugs unless they perceive them to be beneficial.

_____ 5. Warning signals of a heart attack include pain or pressure in the left side of the chest.

EXERCISE 13-6

DIRECTIONS: *Read the following paragraphs and underline each generalization.*

1. Teenagers need privacy; it allows them to have a life of their own. By providing privacy, we demonstrate respect. We help them disengage themselves from us and grow up. Some parents pry too much. They read their teenagers' mail and listen in on their telephone calls. Such violations may cause permanent resentment. Teenagers feel cheated and enraged. In their eyes, invasion of privacy is a dishonorable offense. As one girl said: "I am going to sue my mother for malpractice of parenthood. She unlocked my desk and read my diary."[5]

2. Farmers are interested in science, in modern methods, and in theory, but they are not easily thrown off balance and they maintain a healthy suspicion of book learning and of the shenanigans of biologists, chemists, geneticists, and other late-rising students of farm practice and management. They are, I think, impressed by education, but they have seen too many examples of the helplessness and the impracticality of educated persons to be either envious or easily budged from their position.[6]

3. Although the most commonplace reason women marry young is to "complete" themselves, a good many spirited young women gave another reason: "I did it to get away from my parents." Particularly for girls whose educations and privileges are limited, a *jailbreak marriage* is the usual thing. What might appear to be an act of rebellion usually turns out to be a transfer of dependence.[7]

Statements of Opinion

Facts are statements that can be verified. They can be proven true or false. **Opinions** are statements that express a writer's feelings, attitudes, or beliefs. They are neither true nor false. Here are a few examples of each:

Facts

1. My car insurance costs $1500.
2. The theory of instinct was formulated by Konrad Lorenz.
3. Greenpeace is an organization dedicated to preserving the sea and its animals.

Opinions

1. My car insurance is too expensive.
2. The slaughter of baby seals for their pelts should be outlawed.
3. Population growth should be regulated through mandatory birth control.

The ability to distinguish between fact and opinion is an essential part of evaluating an author's supporting information. Factual statements from reliable sources can usually be accepted as correct. Opinions, however, must be considered as one person's viewpoint that you are free to accept or reject.

EXERCISE 13-7

DIRECTIONS: *Identify and mark each of the following statements as either Fact or Opinion.*

_____ 1. Alligators provide no physical care for their young.

_____ 2. Humans should be concerned about the use of pesticides that kill insects at the bottom of the food chain.

_____ 3. There are 28 more humans living on the earth now than there were ten seconds ago.

_____ 4. We must bear greater responsibility for the environment than our ancestors did.

_____ 5. Nuclear power is the only viable solution to our dwindling natural resources.

_____ 6. Between 1850 and 1900 the death rate in Europe decreased due to industrial growth and advances in medicine.

_____ 7. Dogs make the best pets because they can be trained to obey.

_____ 8. Solar energy is available wherever sunlight reaches the earth.

_____ 9. By the year 2010, many diseases, including cancer, will be preventable.

_____10. Hormones are produced in one part of the body and carried by the blood to another part of the body where they influence some process or activity.

Personal Experience

Writers often support their ideas by describing their own personal experiences. Although a writer's experiences may be interesting and reveal a perspective on an issue, do not accept them as proof. Suppose you are reading an article on drug use and the writer uses his or her personal experience with particular drugs to prove a point. There are several reasons why you should not accept the writer's conclusions about the drugs' effects as fact. First, the effects of a drug may vary from person to person. The drug's effect on the writer may be unusual. Second, unless the writer kept careful records about times, dosages, surrounding circumstances, and so on, he or she is describing events from memory. Over time, the writer may have forgotten or exaggerated some of the effects. As you read, treat ideas supported only through personal experience as *one person's experience*. Do not make the error of generalizing the experience.

Statistics

People are often impressed by **statistics**—figures, percentages, averages, and so forth. They accept these as absolute proof. Actually, statistics can be misused, misinterpreted, or used selectively to give other than the most objective, accurate picture of a situation.

Here is an example of how statistics can be misused. Suppose you read that magazine *A* increased its readership by 50 percent, while magazine *B* had only a 10 percent increase. From this statistic, some readers might assume that magazine *A* has a wider readership than magazine *B*. The missing but crucial statistic is the total readership of each magazine prior to the increase. If magazine *A* had a readership of 20,000 and this increased by 50 percent, its readership would total 30,000. If magazine *B*'s readership was already 50,000, a 10 percent increase, bringing the new total to 55,000, would still give it the larger readership despite the smaller increase. Even statistics, then, must be read with a critical, questioning mind.

Here is another example:

Americans in the workforce are better off than ever before. The average salary of the American worker is $23,000.

At first the above statement may seem convincing. However, a closer look reveals that the statistic given does not really support the statement. The term *average* is the key to how the statistic is misused. An average includes all salaries, both high and low. It is possible that some Americans earn $4,000 while others earn $250,000. Although the average salary may be $23,000, this does not mean that everyone earns $23,000.

EXERCISE 13-8

DIRECTIONS: *Read each of the following statements and decide how the statistic is misused. Write your explanation in the space provided.*

1. Classrooms on our campus are not overcrowded. There are ten square feet of floor space for every student, faculty member, and staff member on campus.

   _____

   _____

2. More than 12,000 people have bought Lincoln Town Cars this year, so it is a popular car.

   _____

   _____

3. The average water pollution by our local industries is well below the hazardous level established by the Environmental Protection Agency.

   _____

   _____

Does the Writer make Value Judgments?

A writer who states that an idea or action is right or wrong, good or bad, desirable or undesirable is making a **value judgment.** That is, the writer is imposing his or her own judgment on the worth of an idea or action. Here are a few examples of value judgments:

Divorces should be restricted to couples who can prove incompatibility.

Abortion is wrong.

Welfare applicants should be forced to apply for any job they are capable of performing.

Premarital sex is acceptable.

You will notice that each statement is controversial. Each involves some type of conflict or idea over which there is disagreement:

1. Restriction versus freedom
2. Right versus wrong
3. Force versus choice
4. Acceptability versus nonacceptability

You may know of some people who would agree and others who might disagree with each statement. A writer who takes a position or side on a conflict is making a value judgment.

As you read, be alert for value judgments. They represent one person's view *only* and there are most likely many other views on the same topic. When you identify a value judgment, try to determine whether the author offers any evidence in support of the position.

EXERCISE 13-9

DIRECTIONS: *Read the following selection and answer the questions that follow.*

A Welfare Mother

1   I start my day here at five o'clock. I get up and prepare all the children's clothes. If there's shoes to shine, I do it in the morning. About seven o'clock I bathe the children. I leave the baby with the baby sitter and I go to work at the settlement house. I work until twelve o'clock. Sometimes I'll work longer if I have to go to welfare and get a check for somebody. When I get back, I try to make hot food for the kids to eat. In the afternoon it's pretty well on my own. I scrub and clean and cook and do whatever I have to do.

2   Welfare makes you feel like you're nothing. Like you're laying back and not doing anything and it's falling in your lap. But you must understand,

---

mothers, too, work. My house is clean. I've been scrubbing since this morning. You could check my clothes, all washed and ironed. I'm home and I'm working. I am a working mother.

A job that a woman in a house is doing is a tedious job—especially if you want to do it right. If you do it slipshod, then it's not so bad. I'm pretty much of a perfectionist. I tell my kids, hang a towel. I don't want it thrown away. That is very hard. It's a constant game of picking up this, picking up that. And putting this away, so the house'll be clean.

Some men work eight hours a day. There are mothers that work eleven, twelve hours a day. We get up at night, a baby vomits, you have to be calling the doctor, you have to be changing the baby. When do you get a break, really? You don't. This is an all-around job, day and night. Why do they say it's charity? We're working for our money. I am working for this check. It is not charity. We are giving some kind of home to these children.

I'm so busy all day I don't have time to daydream. I pray a lot. I pray to God to give me strength. If He should take a child away from me, to have the strength to accept it. It's His kid. He just borrowed him to me.

I used to get in and close the door. Now I speak up for my right. I walk with my head up. If I want to wear big earrings, I do. If I'm overweight, that's too bad. I've gotten completely over feeling where I'm little. I'm working now, I'm pulling my weight. I'm gonna get off welfare in time, that's my goal—get off.

It's living off welfare and feeling that you're taking something for nothing the way people have said. You get to think maybe you are. You get to think, Why am I so stupid? Why can't I work? Why do I have to live this way? It's not enough to live on anyway. You feel degraded.

The other day I was at the hospital and I went to pay my bill. This nurse came and gave me the green card. Green card is for welfare. She went right in front of me and gave it to the cashier. She said, "I wish I could stay home and let the money fall in my lap." I felt rotten. I was just burning inside. You hear this all the way around you. The doctor doesn't even look at you. People are ashamed to show that green card. Why can't a woman just get a check in the mail: Here, this check is for you. Forget welfare. You're a mother who works.

This nurse, to her way of thinking, she represents the working people. The ones with the green card, we represent the lazy no-goods. This is what she was saying. They're the good ones and we're the bad guys.[8]

1. What do you think is the source of this selection?

_____

_____

2. Do you consider this welfare mother to be an authority? Why or why not?

_____

_____

3. What assumptions does this welfare mother make? Do you agree or disagree? Why?

_____

_____

4. Do you think this view of a welfare mother is biased? Why or why not?

_____

_____

5. Is the writing in this article slanted? If so, give some examples.

_____

_____

6. How does this welfare mother support her ideas?

_____

_____

7. Does this welfare mother make any value judgments? If so, what are they?

_____

_____

8. Does this welfare mother make any generalizations? If so, underline them.

EXERCISE 13-10

DIRECTIONS: *Read the following article and answer the questions that follow.*

The War On Children's Culture

1

My 9-year-old daughter, Emma, and her friends have recently developed an inverse rating system. If grown-ups don't like a children's movie or TV show, it's worth considering. Anything adult critics absolutely hate is a must-see.

In recent years, as children's culture has become enormously diverse and lucrative, movie and television critics have become the disapproving voice of the adult world, transmitting to Nintendo-playing, comic book-reading, video-game playing children an unrelenting barrage of contempt.

"We don't really care for what adults see, and they don't like what we see," says Emma's friend Ben, who is 12.

No. Kids wouldn't be caught dead showing interest in grown-up movies or programs. But the adult world takes its child-rearing responsibilities seriously and *does* pay attention to what kids do and watch. The result is an undeclared and, in some ways, disturbing war on broad aspects of children's culture. . . .

Some sort of truce seems in order. It feels inappropriate to be engaged in cultural warfare with our children. When we are so relentlessly contemptuous of their culture, the signals must seem especially confusing. If this stuff is so horrible, why do all their friends like it, and how come we let them watch it? If it isn't horrible, how come everyone says it is?

Television, perhaps because it's beamed right into our living rooms, and because parents fear their inability to control it, is the target of many of these assaults. TV is portrayed as the corrupting demon, munching away at young brain cells.

Often, the media seem to find it a primary function to warn children about the very things they most enjoy, rather than to explore or explain or defend it. Dozens of newspapers and magazines ran critical reviews of one or the other of the two "Turtles" movies and many more published articles or editorials deploring their violence. Yet both movies were instant hits, smashes, with the audiences they were intended for—the young. Kids I've asked about this disparity all have the same response: adults just don't get it. . . .

If You Hate It, They Love It

Meanwhile, the list of anti-kid-culture flashpoints is growing longer all the time. From the start, "The Simpsons" on the Fox network has been criticized by some educational and parent groups—even the former Secretary of Education, William Bennett—because of its often blistering portrayals of educators, schools and parental authority.

A number of schools have banned "Underachiever and Proud of It" T-shirts with Bart's likeness. It's a tactic that can backfire. When a middle-school student in the suburb I live in was sent home because of his "I'm Bart Simpson: Who the Hell Are You?" T-shirt, Simpson-watching by my daughter and her buddies went from an occasional amusement to an almost religious ritual.

This is familiar ground for my generation. After reading an article in the 1950's warning that Buddy Holly's songs fostered disrespect for authority, my father put the offending records aside until I was older and, presumably, less impressionable. I lost none of my enthusiasm for Buddy Holly. . . .

What's a Parent To Do?

Adults might stand a better chance of helping to define their children's values by making perhaps the ultimate sacrifice—watching with them. It goes against the grain: television is one of the few things small children are happy to do by themselves and for long periods, which encourages children being left alone with it.

But children's own critical instincts might grow if, rather than sneering, parents were sitting with them in front of the VCR, comparing differences in animation, plot, character development and humor. My wife changed my daughter's perception of the early Disney movies considerably when she pointed out that the women in them seemed to always need rescuing— something my daughter hadn't noticed and was not appreciative of once she did. The two are still fighting, in fact, about whether the Little Mermaid should have left her aquatic world behind for her One True Love or made the prince come to hers.

In subsequent movies, Emma has become especially conscious of how women are portrayed. One thing she strongly disliked about the first Turtle movie, in fact, was that April O'Neill, the female (human) reporter, also needed rescuing. Meanwhile, we've largely banned the purchase of toys and products related to TV or films, arguing that a story and its characters must be appreciated—or not—on its own merits, not because of the things you can buy.

The range and diversity of children's entertainment makes it difficult to control, especially for hard-pressed parents, more of whom are working longer hours all the time. Children, like their parents, have become little entertainment moguls with access to scores of choices. If they can't access the full range of choices at home, odds are they can down the street at their buddies' houses.

Children seem to be infinitely more accepting than adults of what they see, more inclined to like a movie or television program than not. They frequently resent cultural offerings that seem preachy or stodgily educational. And they have keen noses for hypocrisy. "Makes the Turtles look like the Care Bears," sniffed Emma, when she saw a preview in a movie theater for "The Silence of the Lambs." It's not like their parents are listening to classical music all night, either. . . .

Here Today, Here Tomorrow

Whatever else happens to children's culture, parents and other adults can count on one thing: television—the things you can watch on it, the things you can plug into it, and all its other controversial offshoots—will continue to grow. Condemnation alone seems a poor strategy for responding to the technology that has given children more tantalizing choices to make than any generation in history.[9]

1. What is the main point of the article?

_____

_____

2. What is the author's attitude toward children's culture?

_____

_____

3. This article appeared in the *New York Times.* Evaluate it as source for:

   a. a sociology term paper

   b. parents who want to learn more about children's culture

_____

_____

4. Is the article biased? Explain your answer.

_____

_____

5. What types of supporting evidence does the author provide? Mark several examples of each type in the article.

_____

_____

6. What assumptions does the author make?

_____

_____

7. Describe the tone of the article.

_____

_____

WORKING TOGETHER

Directions: Bring to class a brief (2- to 3-paragraph) newspaper article, editorial, film review, etc. Working in groups of 3–4 students, each student should read his or her piece aloud. The group can then discuss and evaluate (1) assumptions, (2) bias, (3) slanted writing, (4) methods of support, and (5) value judgments for each article. Each group should choose one representative article and submit its findings to the class or instructor.

SUMMARY

How can I evaluate what I read?

In order to evaluate what you read, ask yourself seven questions:

1. What is the source of the material?

2. What is the authority of the author?

3. Does the author make assumptions?

4. Is the author biased?

5. Is the writing slanted?

6. How does the author support his or her ideas?

7. Does the author make value judgments?

Reading and Interpreting Essays and Literature

THIS CHAPTER WILL SHOW YOU HOW TO

1. Read and interpret essays and arguments
2. Read and interpret literature

Throughout most of this book we have concentrated on reading skills for textbook study. However, textbook assignments are not the only reading that you'll be asked to do in college courses. Reading assignments may include articles, essays, and stories. For example, in biology you might read an essay discussing possible outcomes of the depletion of the ozone layer. In sociology you might read an excerpt from a novel or short story as part of your study of group interaction. For health class you might read an argument that urges lighter regulation of the sale of cigarettes to minors. Also, you will probably take one or more literature courses in which you will read a wide variety of essays, poetry, and short stories. This chapter will show you how to approach articles, essays, and arguments. It will also suggest strategies for reading and interpreting short stories and poetry.

Reading and Interpreting Essays

Essays are short pieces of writing that examine a single subject. Essays follow a standard organization and have the following parts:

1. *Title.* The title usually announces the subject of the essay. For example, an essay titled "In Pursuit of the Perfect Hamburger" will probably define what the author feels the perfect hamburger is and describe his or her search to find it. Titles can also be designed to capture your interest.
2. *Introduction.* The introduction is a very important part of the essay. Read it closely. It often:
   - Defines the subject in more detail
   - Provides necessary background information
   - Builds your interest

Read only the title, author and first paragraph of the following article, "How Muzak Manipulates You." Did you notice how it introduces the subject and provides a context by establishing where and how Muzak is commonly heard?

■ ■ ■ ■ ■

How Muzak Manipulates You

—Andrea Dorfman

1   Every day, millions of people in offices and supermarkets and on assembly lines worldwide hear the bland strains of Muzak. That sound-track is more than just the homogenization of good music. <u>It has been painstakingly engineered to direct behavior—to improve employee performance by reducing on-the-job stress, boredom and fatigue or to control consumers' shopping habits.</u>

2   Background music can, indeed, enhance or interfere with business, concludes Ronald Milliman, a marketing professor at Loyola University in New Orleans. "Very few stores that play music play it for any particular purpose," he says. "But walking into an environment where music is playing apparently makes a difference."

3   Milliman measured the effects of fast- and slow-tempo music on a supermarket's traffic flow and sales. Fast music hardly affected sales when com-

pared with no music, he reported in the *Journal of Marketing,* but pieces played lento slowed shoppers and boosted receipts 38 percent above what they had been when fast music was playing.

Increases Patience

Restaurants can also use music advantageously, he found. In the evening, slow-paced music lengthens meals and increases the patience of waiting customers. When quick turnover is important—lunch, for example—lively music does the trick.

The best-known supplier of background music is a company called Muzak. But it's not the only one. In Chicago, there is Musi-Call. In California, Musicast. And in the New York area, General Background Music (GBM).

Muzak calls its product "environmental music" and has done over 100 studies—from simple surveys of employee responses to comparison of production output before and after Muzak installation—to prove its effectiveness. A recent test involved workers preparing precision parts according to exacting specifications. Overall improvement generally ranges from 5 to 10 percent to as much as 30 percent. Results are easier to obtain when routine tasks are involved; people with relatively interesting jobs, however, are also affected.

The key to Muzak's programs is something called stimulus progression. Each tune is given a stimulus code based on its tempo, instrumentation, feel and the date it was added to the firm's library. "We punch these codes into our computer, and it slots the material into fifteen-minute segments of five tunes each," music director Ralph Smith explains. "We start with a tune that has a low stimulus value—one that's slow in tempo and string-dominated— and gradually build to an up-tempo, pop sound."

After a two-minute pause, a new segment begins on a stimulus level that's higher overall than the preceding ones. In this fashion, the day's program builds to mid-morning and mid-afternoon "crescendos" designed to give workers a needed boost.

"Since Muzak's main function is in the workplace, we naturally have to program against people's normal slumps," Smith notes. "Around ten-thirty, you're running down a little, but lunch is still a distance away. So, about ten-fifteen, the stimulus value for the entire segment jumps an extra notch to bring you out of the doldrums."

"Changing the order of things produces a different effect," says psychologist William Wokoun, chairman of Muzak's scientific advisory board. "When this so-called ascending program is played in reverse, it seems to lull people to sleep. Reaction times become slower and more variable."

11   Like Muzak, GBM focuses on the mind of the nine-to-five employee. "All day long, you have ups and downs, peaks and valleys," vice-president Mel Bernstein explains. "During key periods, psychological programmers change the tempo to increase workers' adrenaline flow, which in turn increases their efficiency. The music becomes part of the surroundings. Workers no longer notice its effects on their behavior."

12   The difference between GBM and Muzak, says Bernstein, is that Muzak isn't regional; it has only one product. "But there is a very definite New York sound," he asserts, "just as there is a Midwest sound and a Los Angeles sound. And we even have rainy-day music."

13   Bernstein also says that Muzak, with its two-minute pauses every quarter hour, may help workers keep time subconsciously.[1]

3. *Thesis Statement.* The thesis statement is the one most important idea the article presents. It may also suggest the organization, purpose, and focus of the article. Just as a paragraph develops one main idea, so, too, does an article or essay. Writers usually express their thesis in one sentence near the beginning of the article, often as part of the introduction.

   Now turn back to the article on p. 310 and reread the underlined thesis statement in the first paragraph. This sentence first states the main point of the article—that Muzak is used to direct behavior. Then, in the same sentence, the writer provides several examples of the behavior Muzak controls.

4. *Supporting Information.* Essays contain supporting ideas and details that explain the thesis statement. You can expect at least one major supporting idea per paragraph.

   Most writers use various types of supporting information. Writers may support their ideas by giving descriptions, reasons, or examples; citing facts, statistics, or research findings; and/or quoting authorities. Refer to Chapter 7 for a review of the types of supporting information. Turn again to p. 310 and read the remainder of the article. Decide how the writer supports the thesis.

   The author begins by referring to research conducted by Milliman that suggests some of the effects of Muzak (see paragraphs 2–4). Then she reviews the type, use, and purpose of background music supplied by two major companies, Muzak and GBM (see paragraphs 5–12). This writer, then, uses facts, statistics, and examples to support her main points.

5. *Conclusion or Summary.* An article or essay is usually brought to a close with a summary or conclusion. Each in its own way brings together the ideas expressed in the article.

   A **summary** provides a review of important ideas. It can be thought of as an outline in paragraph form. The order in which the information appears in the summary reflects the organization of the article itself.

A **conclusion** is a final statement about the subject of the article. A conclusion does not review content as a summary does. Instead, a conclusion usually suggests a new or further direction of thought. It almost always introduces an idea that has not been stated previously or a new way of looking at what has already been stated.

Turn back to the Muzak article and reread the last paragraph, on p. 312. Is it a summary or a conclusion? Since this one-sentence paragraph does not review all the major points of the article, it is not a summary. It does suggest a new, not previously mentioned, value of Muzak, so it is a conclusion.

EXERCISE 14-1

DIRECTIONS: *Read the following essay from Annie Dillard's* The Writing Life *and answer the questions that follow.*

1 The writer studies literature, not the world. He lives in the world; he cannot miss it. If he has ever bought a hamburger, or taken a commercial airplane flight, he spares his readers a report of his experience. He is careful of what he reads, for that is what he will write. He is careful of what he learns, because that is what he will know.

2 The writer knows his field—what has been done, what could be done, the limits—the way a tennis player knows the court. And like that expert, he, too, plays the edges. That is where the exhilaration is. He hits up the line. In writing, he can push the edges. Beyond this limit, here, the reader must recoil. Reason balks, poetry snaps; some madness enters, or strain. Now, courageously and carefully, can he enlarge it, can he nudge the bounds? And enclose what wild power?

3 The body of literature, with its limits and edges, exists outside some people and inside others. Only after the writer lets literature shape her can she perhaps shape literature. In working-class France, when an apprentice got hurt, or when he got tired, the experienced workers said, "It is the trade entering his body." The art must enter the body, too. A painter cannot use paint like glue or screws to fasten down the world. The tubes of paint are like fingers; they work only if, inside the painter, the neural pathways are wide and clear to the brain. Cell by cell, molecule by molecule, atom by atom, part of the brain changes physical shape to accommodate and fit paint.

4 You adapt yourself, Paul Klee said, to the contents of the paintbox. Adapting yourself to the contents of the paintbox, he said, is more important than nature and its study. The painter, in other words, does not fit the paints to the world. He most certainly does not fit the world to himself. He fits himself to the paint. The self is the servant who bears the paintbox and its inher-

ited contents. Klee called this insight, quite rightly, "an altogether revolutionary new discovery."

5
6
7

A well-known writer got collared by a university student who asked, "Do you think I could be a writer?"

"Well," the writer said, "I don't know. . . . Do you like sentences?"

The writer could see the student's amazement. Sentences? Do I like sentences? I am twenty years old and do I like sentences? If he had liked sentences, of course, he could begin, like a joyful painter I knew. I asked him how he came to be a painter. He said, "I liked the smell of the paint."[2]

1. What is the subject of the essay?

_____

_____

2. What is Dillard's main point about writers?

_____

_____

3. What comparisons does Dillard use to explain her ideas?

_____

_____

4. Explain why painters must like the smell of paint and why writers must like sentences.

_____

_____

Narrative Essay

Narrative articles and essays tell a story. They review events that have happened. Usually the events are presented in the order in which they occurred. The story is told, however, to make a point or explain an idea. If you wrote an essay describing an important event or telling how someone influenced your life, you would use the narrative form. You would describe events as they happened, showing how or why they were important.

In addition to essays, many types of material use the narrative style—biographies, autobiographies, historical accounts, travel books. Follow these steps when reading narratives:

1. Determine when and where the events are taking place.
2. Notice the sequence of events.
3. Notice how the story is told and who is telling it.
4. Look beyond the specific events to the overall meaning. Ask yourself why the writer is telling the story. What is the point the author is trying to make?
5. Watch for the writer's commentary as he or she tells the story.

The following selection is taken from a book titled *Mortal Lessons,* written by a medical doctor. This selection tells the story of a patient who is recovering from surgery that left her face deformed.

1   I stand by the bed where a woman lies, her face postoperative, her mouth twisted in palsy, clownish. A tiny twig of the facial nerve, the one to the muscles of her mouth, has been severed. She will be thus from now on. The surgeon had followed with religious fervor the curve of her flesh; I promise you that. Nevertheless, to remove the tumor in her cheek, I had cut the little nerve.

2   Her young husband is in the room. He stands on the opposite side of the bed, and together they seem to dwell in the evening lamplight, isolated from me, private. Who are they, I ask myself, he and this wry-mouth I have made, who gaze at and touch each other so generously, greedily? The young woman speaks.

3   "Will my mouth always be like this?" she asks.

4   "Yes," I say, "it will. It is because the nerve was cut."

5   She nods, and is silent. But the young man smiles.

6   "I like it," he says. "It is kind of cute."

7   All at once I *know* who he is. I understand, and I lower my gaze. One is not bold in an encounter with a god. Unmindful, he bends to kiss her crooked mouth, and I so close I can see how he twists his own lips to accommodate to hers, to show her that their kiss still works. I remember that the gods appeared in ancient Greece as mortals, and I hold my breath and let the wonder in.[3]

The incident takes place in a hospital where a woman is recovering from surgery to remove a tumor on her cheek. The author, who is the surgeon, describes the occasion when the woman learns her mouth will be permanently twisted. The surgeon's purpose in writing becomes clear in the last paragraph. His main point is that the husband's kiss is godlike—it determines the woman's response to and acceptance of her deformity.

EXERCISE 14-2

DIRECTIONS: *Read the following narrative essay and answer the questions that follow.*

Salvation

—Langston Hughes

1   I was saved from sin when I was going on thirteen. But not really saved. It happened like this. There was a big revival at my Auntie Reed's church. Every night for weeks there had been much preaching, singing, praying, and shouting, and some very hardened sinners had been brought to Christ, and the membership of the church had grown by leaps and bounds. Then just before the revival ended, they held a special meeting for children, "to bring the young lambs to the fold." My aunt spoke of it for days ahead. That night I was escorted to the front row and placed on the mourners' bench with all the other young sinners, who had not yet been brought to Jesus.

2   My aunt told me that when you were saved you saw a light, and something happened to you inside! And Jesus came into your life! And God was with you from then on! She said you could see and hear and feel Jesus in your soul. I believed her. I had heard a great many old people say the same thing and it seemed to me they ought to know. So I sat there calmly in the hot, crowded church, waiting for Jesus to come to me.

3   The preacher preached a wonderful rhythmical sermon, all moans and shouts and lonely cries and dire pictures of hell, and then he sang a song about the ninety and nine safe in the fold, but one little lamb was left out in the cold. Then he said: "Won't you come? Won't you come to Jesus? Young lambs, won't you come?" And he held out his arms to all us young sinners there on the mourners' bench. And the little girls cried. And some of them jumped up and went to Jesus right away. But most of us just sat there.

4   A great many old people came and knelt around us and prayed, old women with jet-black faces and braided hair, old men with work-gnarled hands. And the church sang a song about the lower lights are burning, some poor sinners to be saved. And the whole building rocked with prayer and song.

5   Still I kept waiting to *see* Jesus.

6 Finally all the young people had gone to the altar and were saved, but one boy and me. He was a rounder's son named Westley. Westley and I were surrounded by sisters and deacons praying. It was very hot in the church, and getting late now. Finally Westley said to me in a whisper: "God damn! I'm tired o' sitting here. Let's get up and be saved." So he got up and was saved.

7 Then I was left all alone on the mourners' bench. My aunt came and knelt at my knees and cried, while prayers and songs swirled all around me in the little church. The whole congregation prayed for me alone, in a mighty wail of moans and voices. And I kept waiting serenely for Jesus, waiting, waiting—but he didn't come. I wanted to see him, but nothing happened to me. Nothing! I wanted something to happen to me, but nothing happened.

8 I heard the songs and the minister saying: "Why don't you come? My dear child, why don't you come to Jesus? Jesus is waiting for you. He wants you. Why don't you come? Sister Reed, what is this child's name?"

9 "Langston," my aunt sobbed.

10 "Langston, why don't you come? Why don't you come and be saved? Oh, Lamb of God! Why don't you come?"

11 Now it was really getting late. I began to be ashamed of myself, holding everything up so long. I began to wonder what God thought about Westley, who certainly hadn't seen Jesus either, but who was now sitting proudly on the platform, swinging his knickerbockered legs and grinning down at me, surrounded by deacons and old women on their knees praying. God had not struck Westley dead for taking his name in vain or for lying in the temple. So I decided that maybe to save further trouble, I'd better lie, too, and say that Jesus had come, and get up and be saved.

12 So I got up.

13 Suddenly the whole room broke into a sea of shouting, as they saw me rise. Waves of rejoicing swept the place. Women leaped in the air. My aunt threw her arms around me. The minister took me by the hand and led me to the platform.

14 When things quieted down, in a hushed silence, punctuated by a few ecstatic "Amens," all the new young lambs were blessed in the name of God. Then joyous singing filled the room.

15 That night, for the last time in my life but one—for I was a big boy twelve years old—I cried. I cried, in bed alone, and couldn't stop. I buried my head under the quilts, but my aunt heard me. She woke up and told my uncle I was crying because the Holy Ghost had come into my life, and because I had seen Jesus. But I was really crying because I couldn't bear to tell her that I had lied, that I had deceived everybody in the church, and that I hadn't seen Jesus, and that now I didn't believe there was a Jesus any more, since he didn't come to help me.[4]

1. When and where do you think the events are taking place?

   _____

   _____

2. Summarize the sequence of events this selection described.

   _____

   _____

3. Why do you think the author told this story? What point is he trying to make?

   _____

   _____

4. Underline portions of the selection in which the author shows how he feels about the events he relates.

EXERCISE 14-3

DIRECTIONS: *Choose one of the topics listed below. On a separate sheet, write at least one paragraph that uses the narrative style to explain the topics.*

1. An important event in your life

2. Your first day at college

3. One of those days when everything goes wrong

Descriptive Essay

Descriptive articles and essays present ideas by providing details about characteristics of people, places, and things. The details are intended to appeal to your senses, to help you create a mental picture, or to make you feel a certain way. For example, descriptive writing is used frequently in advertising. Notice, in the following travel ad, how the writer helps you imagine what Bermuda is like.

> For more than a century, people who value relaxation have been returning to Bermuda year after year. They appreciate the pink-tinted beaches, the flower-laden garden paths, the cozy pubs, and the clear, turquoise waters.

Now can you picture a beach in Bermuda?

In reading descriptive writing, be sure to follow these steps:

1. *Identify the subject of the essay* (ask yourself who or what is being described).

2. *Pay close attention to the writer's choice of words.* The writer often paints a picture with words. Through word choice, a writer tries to create an attitude or feeling (see the section on connotation in Chapter 12). Try to identify that feeling.

3. *Look for the overall impression the writer is trying to create.* Ask yourself: What do all these details, taken together, suggest about the subject? What is the writer trying to say? How am I supposed to feel about the subject?

4. *Pay particular attention to the first and last paragraphs.* There you are likely to find the most clues about the writer's main points and purpose for writing.

Read the following descriptive passage. It describes the first use of chemical warfare by the German army during World War I. Try to create a mental picture of the event.

1   At five o'clock, three red rockets streaked into the sky, signaling the start of a deafening artillery barrage. High explosive shells pounded into the deserted town of Ypres and the villages around it. At the same time the troops sheltering near Langemarck saw two greenish-yellow clouds rise from the enemy's lines, catch the wind, and billow forwards, gradually merging to form a single bank of blue-white mist: out of sight, in special emplacements protected by sandbags and concrete, German pioneers were opening the valves of 6,000 cylinders spread out along a four mile front. The cylinders contained liquid chlorine—the instant the pressure was released and it came into contact with the air it vaporized and hissed out to form a dense cloud. At thirty parts per million of air chlorine gas produces a rasping cough. At concentrations of one part per thousand it is fatal. The breeze stirred again, and one hundred and sixty tons of it, five feet high and hugging the ground, began to roll towards the Allied trenches.

2   Chemical warfare had begun.

3   The wave broke over the first line within a minute, enveloping tens of thousands of troops in an acrid green cloud so thick they could no longer see their neighbors in the trench. Seconds later they were clutching at the air and at their throats, fighting for breath.

4   Chlorine does not suffocate: it poisons, stripping the lining of the bronchial tubes and lungs. The inflammation produces a massive amount of fluid that blocks the windpipe, froths from the mouth and fills the lungs. In an attempt to escape the effects, some men tried to bury their mouths and nostrils in the earth; others panicked and ran. But any exertion or effort to outdistance the cloud only resulted in deeper breaths and more acute poisoning. As the tide of gas washed over the struggling men their faces turned blue from the strain of trying to breathe; some coughed so violently they ruptured their lungs. Each man, as the British casualty report was later to put it, was "being drowned in his own exudation."[5]

Do you have a picture in your mind? Can you imagine the gas rising and moving toward the trenches? Can you picture the reaction of the troops to the chlorine? Underline words in the selection that you felt were particularly helpful to you in imagining this event. Did you underline such words and phrases as *greenish-yellow clouds, billow, blue-white mist, hugging the ground, clutching at the air, turned blue?* Together these words suggest the appearance and severe effects of the chlorine gas.

Look at the selection once again and try to answer this question: How is the writer trying to make you feel about chemical warfare?

From the choice of words, you can see that the writer thinks chemical warfare is a violent form of poisoning. Also, since the writer described in detail the troops' physical reaction to the gas, you can tell that the writer wanted you to be shocked or horrified.

EXERCISE 14-4

DIRECTIONS: *Read the following descriptive essay and answer the questions that follow.*

In Idaho: Living Outside of Time

—*Gregory Jaynes*

1   Twice a week in the warm months, twice a month in the cold, a pilot named Ray Arnold ferries mail and sundries to people who live so far back in the mountains of Idaho that it sometimes seems the sun sets between them and the nearest town. To many of the people along this route, that nearest town is Cascade, where Arnold Aviation is based. There, in a cheerful office off to one side of a hangar, Arnold's wife Carol receives shopping lists from the backwoodsmen on her short-wave radio; then she does all their marketing. These goods are flown to a breed of Americans who choose to live outside of time.

2   "Now, how many was that on the pitted black olives?" Carol was saying into her radio one morning when the temperature was 10 below.

3   "Two jars. And a fifth of Christian Brothers brandy and a fifth of Dark My-ers's rum. A small container of nutmeg and two quarts of eggnog."

4   "O.K., got it." Taped to the wall above Carol's desk was a marching line of signed blank checks collected the last time Ray made the rounds. The customers trust the Arnolds, with good reason. The Arnolds are their contact, their cablehead to civilization. So intimate is this bush network, Carol can cal-

culate the state of marital relations in the mountains by the quantity of condom orders, though she chooses to push this intelligence out of mind.

In the hangar Ray was loading the plane. Four dozen eggs. A case of Old Milwaukee. A case of Budweiser. A roll of roofing tar paper. Cat Chow. Meow Mix. Grape-Nuts flakes. Bread. A broom. "Some of them out there are brand conscious," Carol said. "Some are quality conscious. Some you just know what to get. One cat at the Allison ranch, for instance, won't eat anything but Purina."

Ray had a passenger, a young bearded fellow named Hal who was going to be caretaker of a University of Idaho research station where wildlife patterns are studied. "Might as well put in another sleeping bag," Ray said. "If something happens, I sure don't want to sleep in the same bag with you."

The pilot had one last cup of coffee in the office. It is one of those offices adorned with chummy signs: DO YOU WANT TO TALK TO THE ONE IN CHARGE OR THE ONE WHO KNOWS WHAT'S GOING ON? The people of Cascade (pop. 1,000) hang around here as the people in small towns in warmer climates do around certain gas pumps. They waved Ray Arnold off as he taxied away on skis.

There have been times when the weather socked the pilot in and the mail run had to be postponed for up to five days. But this day was so clear you could almost see tomorrow. The Salmon River Mountains were below. The way the snow caught the sun, the snow looked like diamond dust. Off the starboard wing the Sawtooth Mountain Range made a ragged platinum horizon. Down canyons, through passes, over peaks, the Cessna with the skis affixed to its wheels threw a shadow that caused elk, long-horned sheep and mountain goats to bolt. On the control panel Arnold has tacked a sign: IF YOU WISH TO SMOKE, PLEASE STEP OUTSIDE.

In Idaho, skis and risk have always been a part of mail delivery. In the 1880s, carriers used 11-ft. skis to get over the high passes to reach the miners' camps. Three carriers died in avalanches. A fourth froze to death, his bag jammed with Christmas mail. Arnold has crashed twice, once when the wind shifted wildly over a jury-rigged runway and put him into the trees. The second time, a crack developed in the exhaust system, carbon monoxide leaked into the cabin, and the pilot passed out. The plane's premature landing, fortunately, was again cushioned by the trees.

Both aircraft were total losses. The pilot walked away from the first, cracked a vertebra in the second. What is more, the Federal Aviation Administration cited him 13 times for the second crash. Among his wrongdoings, said the FAA, was flying too low. That was a hard charge to dodge, since it is difficult to keep your nose up when you are unconscious and going down. In the end he enriched the FAA by $400.

11   When it is not possible to land, Arnold drops the mail, employing passengers, if he has any, as bombardiers. He orders them to open a window, makes a pass at the lowest FAA-permitted altitude of 500 ft., yells, "Get ready . . ." and then explodes with "Now!" When the drop is dead on the money, as it often is, the involuntary first-time mail bomber gets a rush not unlike the sensation one associates with having just saved the Republic.

12   Arnold's own personal rush comes from the warmth of his customers. They need him desperately, after all, and when they hear his plane they are out on their makeshift runways, pulling sleds, flashing blinding smiles. On this route the mailman is always invited inside. A couple who wish to be known only as Newt and Sharon baked him a cherry pie on this particular visit. Sharon makes her pastries with bear fat. They talked of the six otters they had seen outside in the Salmon River that morning. Newt tore through his mail, furiously writing checks as he went. "This is one of the few places where the bills are late before they get here," he explained. "Computers don't understand that."

13   At the University of Idaho research station, Ray had dropped off his first passenger and picked up Jim Akenson, who had been studying cougars and elk but was now "coming out" to visit family. People along the Salmon River, the River of No Return the pioneers called it, speak of leaving or returning as "going out" and "coming in," or "leaving the river" and "coming to the river." Jim had known Newt and Sharon by radio for 30 months but had never met them. They live 65 miles apart. "You don't look the way I pictured you," said Jim.

14   "Neither do you," said Sharon.

15   They spoke of "going out." Sharon said that this "has been a bad year. Everybody on the river has had to go to town." She said that she had had to have her teeth attended to and that Newt had got sick. "Newt hadn't been to town since December 1980. We hate to go to town."

16   The mailman left with two steelhead filets Newt wanted him to pass on to a neighbor miles away through the wilderness. He would be back that afternoon to drop off a fresh-killed elk another neighbor wanted Newt and Sharon to have. All along the route this day, he would be transferring gifts, books, food, goods and good wishes between these isolationists. It is a service not set down in his $20,000-a-year contract with the postal service. "Oh, I take it out in trade," Ray said. "The weather could ground me, and then I'd have to stay overnight with them, so I stay on their good side."

17   At the next stop, a woman named Frances Wisner, a south Texas telephone operator who settled on the river in 1940, sat waiting with her German shepherd under a lean-to. She wore more layers than a high-society wedding cake. She gave Ray Arnold a meat-loaf sandwich, a cup of steaming

coffee and a piece of her mind. She said it might help the federal deficit if they placed higher taxes on every soft drink but Coca-Cola, which she drinks, and every candy bar but Milky Way, which she favors. Around them, gathering dusk turned the day and the canyon blue, the way it does on snowy landscapes.

18   Ray Arnold flew home with a full moon rising. He had covered 550 miles. The people he had seen are not hermits in the real sense, not even xenophobic (they chatter all day on their radios; they welcome strangers who accompany Ray), so much as they are shot through with old-time ornery independence, misfits with a thing against clocks. To understand what drew them here, one need only remember those maps where population density is shown by clusters of black dots—each dot representing 100,000 people, say—on a white background.

19   On a map like that, the corridor between Washington and Boston looks like a great oil spill at sea. By contrast, Idaho, because of its configuration and lack of residents, looks like an alabaster chimney with only a few smudges. Idaho, the popular saying goes, "is what America was."[6]

1. Underline the information in the article that you feel best describes Ray Arnold.

2. What type of person is Ray Arnold? Write your own description of him. Support your description with information from the article.

   _____

   _____

   _____

   _____

3. What facts about the people who live along the Salmon River were most useful in helping you imagine what they are like? Underline them.

4. Write your own description of the backwoods people of the Salmon River area. Support your answer with references to the article.

   _____

   _____

   _____

   _____

DIRECTIONS: *Think of a topic that you could describe in as much detail as that in the article about chlorine gas or the one about life along the Salmon River. On a separate sheet, write a paragraph describing your topic.*

Expository Essays

Expository articles and essays are written to explain. They are intended to present information about a topic or to explain an idea. Most textbooks, magazine articles, and nonfiction books use the expository style. Writers use various methods to develop their subjects and present their ideas. The most common approaches include the following:

1. Illustration/example—giving examples
2. Definition—describing characteristics
3. Comparison—showing similarities
4. Contrast—showing differences
5. Cause/effect—showing relationships or connections
6. Classification—grouping ideas based on similar characteristics
7. Process—describing a procedure or giving a step-by-step list

You may have noticed that these approaches are similar to the thought patterns described in Chapter 8.

Entire articles or essays may follow one of these approaches. Often, however, you may find that a writer uses several patterns at once or moves from one to another in mid-essay. For example, a writer may use classification and then further explain the classification by giving examples. Or a narrative essay may also be descriptive.

The following questions may be used as a guide in reading expository writing:

1. What is this material about?
2. What main points is the writer making?
3. How is this material organized? How are the main points connected?
4. How much detail do I need to recall?

Persuasive Essays and Arguments

Persuasive articles and essays are written to convince the reader of something. They are usually concerned with controversial issues or those for which there is no clear-cut right and wrong. This type of writing encourages you to change your beliefs or attitudes. The two principal methods authors use to accomplish this are logical argument and emotional appeals.

Reading a persuasive article or essay involves skills of interpretation as well as basic comprehension skills. Use the following suggestions to read persuasive essays:

1. Read the entire essay through before beginning to analyze it. As you read, underline key ideas or statements.
2. Approach the article or essay with two major questions in mind:
   a. Of what is the writer trying to convince me?
   b. Does the writer provide sufficient evidence for me to accept his or her argument?
3. Pay particular attention to *how* the writer tries to persuade you. What persuasive techniques are used? Does he or she appeal to your emotions? Is a logical argument presented?
4. Notice the types of evidence the author provides. Is this evidence fact or opinion? Can it be verified as correct?
5. Does the writer present an objective view of the subject or does he or she look at only one side of an issue?
6. Identify the specific action or position the author is suggesting.
7. Evaluate the qualifications of the author to write on the subject.

Now read the following paragraph of a persuasive essay. Decide whether the writer will use a logical argument or make an emotional appeal.

My point of view is that of a cancer researcher who has been working for the last 20 years with RNA viruses that cause cancer in chickens. Since the early years of this century, it has been known that viruses cause cancer in chickens. In more recent years viruses have been shown to cause cancer not only in chickens, but also in mice, cats, and even in some primates. Therefore, it was a reasonable hypothesis that viruses might cause cancer in humans and that, if a human cancer virus existed, it could be prevented by a vaccine as so many other virus diseases have been prevented.[7]

In the first sentence, the author tells you that he is a researcher. This is your first clue that a logical argument will be presented. In the final sentence, the words *reasonable hypothesis* and *therefore* also suggest a logical presentation.

DIRECTIONS: *Read the following persuasive essay and answer the questions that follow.*

Paying to Grow a Killer

1   This country's conflicting tobacco and smoking policies defy rationality.

2   What sense does it make for surgeons general to warn that smoking kills while Agriculture secretaries spend tax dollars to produce and promote this broad-leaved killer?

3   And what logic is there in Congress voting to continue guaranteeing profits for growers of a product the Food and Drug Administration says should be regulated because it's an addictive drug?

4   We do this, of course, in response to the clash between medical facts—tobacco kills—and political reality—subsidies mean votes.

5   The result is a complex scheme that uses taxpayers' money to help 124,000 tobacco growers in a few states raise a product that, although there is declining demand, yields more money per acre than any other crop. The amount, $24 million, is slight by farm-support standards but nevertheless is real money. The point is the government is aiding an industry it says kills.

6   Tobacco lobbyists claim that withholding the government assistance would lower the price of cigarettes and thus increase smoking. That's easy to remedy: Raise tobacco taxes and use some of the money to help the farmers switch to other crops.

7   The industry also argues that tobacco supports pay for themselves. They say tobacco farmers, unlike others, receive no checks from the government. Some boast about a $30 million assessment they pay the government. And they all point to the federal, state and local taxes smokers pay.

8   But you won't hear them talk about the real costs of tobacco. Those that can't be measured in dollars—the 419,000 who die from tobacco-related cancer, heart and respiratory diseases. Or the $50 billion in health-care expenses caused by smoking, half paid by taxpayers through Medicare and Medicaid. Or the $47 billion a year in productivity lost to tobacco-related absenteeism and illness.

9   They don't want you to think about that.

10   Tobacco, of course, is a legal product. Farmers have every right to grow it, just as people have a right to smoke it. Each assumes risk. For growers, it's weather, pests, declining markets and foreign competition.

11   But the public should not be forced to spend its money to protect against those risks when all it gets in return is a threat to its health. Congress is letting an opportunity to end this madness slip away as it considers renewal of farm subsidies. Tobacco, as all farm subsidies, should be terminated.

12   There will be some withdrawal pains, of course, for the farmers and the politicians. But this is one habit they need to kick.[8]

1. What is the author's basic argument?

_____

_____

2. Summarize the main points of this argument.

_____

_____

3. What types of evidence are offered to support the argument?

_____

_____

4. Is the argument convincing? Why or why not?

_____

_____

5. The writer begins with two unanswered questions (paragraphs 2 and 3). Why were they left unanswered?

_____

_____

6. Does the writer recognize and address arguments that may be made against his or her position? If so, how?

_____

_____

EXERCISE 14-7

DIRECTIONS: *Choose one of the topics listed below. On a separate sheet, write a short essay to persuade the reader to accept your point of view on the topic.*

1. Legal drinking age

2. Gun control

---

3. Abortion

4. Animal rights

How to Approach Literature

Textbooks focus primarily on factual information; literature does not. Instead, it is concerned with the interpretation of ideas, experiences, and events. Literature can grapple with abstract ideas and universal issues such as, "What is worthwhile in life?" "What is the meaning of the human experience?" and "What is beauty?" But it can also express the innermost feelings of another person or convey day-to-day life in another time or place. You might, for example, read the diary entries of a nineteenth-century farmwoman in the Midwest.

Because literature involves the expression of personal ideas and feelings, it can be relaxing and enjoyable to read. It can also be challenging, but often you'll find that you share or have experienced some of the same fears, concerns, joys, or other emotions the writer is expressing. Literature, then, is a way to learn about life and an opportunity to reflect on your own life experiences.

The reading strategies already discussed will also help you read and understand literature, though you may need to revise them a bit. Here are a few suggestions for approaching literature:

1. *Read carefully.* Literature uses language in special ways. The use of descriptive and figurative language is common (see Chapter 12). The connotation of words is also important. You'll need to read slowly and carefully in order to pay attention to these language features. Meaning comes gradually.

2. *Establish the literal meaning first.* Look for "who did what, when, and where" (characters, action, time frame, setting, mood). Then, once you're familiar with the literal action, try to determine the author's message.

3. *Read the work several times.* Don't expect to understand a work the first time you read it. Your first reading is very much like previewing a textbook: read just to become familiar with it. On your second and third readings, focus on what the essay, story or poem means. Each time you read the piece, you'll understand it better.

4. *Make notes and underline as you read.* When you see words, descriptions, or lines that look important, mark them. Look for words and phrases that provide clues to what the work means. Be aware of words and phrases that are repeated. Write notes about your reactions or what a line means to you. Also

write questions. Here is how one student marked an African legend she was asked to read for her English class:

In the Beginning
Bantu Creation Story

= God

IN THE BEGINNING, in the dark, there was nothing but water. And Bumba was alone.

One day Bumba was in terrible pain. He retched and strained and vomited up the sun. *birth* After that light spread over everything. The heat of the sun dried up water until the black edges of the world began to show. Black sandbanks and reefs could be seen. But there were no living things.

Bumba vomited up the moon and then the stars, and after that the night had its light also. *balance*

Still Bumba was in pain. He strained again and nine living creatures came fourth: the leopard named Koy Bumba, and Pongo Bumba the crested eagle, the crocodile, Ganda Bumba, *land* and one little fish named Yo; next, old Kono Bumba, the tortoise, and Tsete, the lightning, *air water* swift, deadly, beautiful like the leopard, then the white heron, Nyanyi Bumba, also one beetle, *fire* and the goat named Budi.

mammal insect amphibian bird fish

Last of all came forth men. There were many men, but only one was white like Bumba. His name was Loko Yima.

self-creation The creatures themselves then created all the creatures. The heron created all the birds *like* of the air except the kite. He did not make the kite. The crocodile made serpents and the *make* iguana. The goat produced every beast with horns. Yo, the small fish, brought forth all the fish *like* of all the seas and waters. The beetle created insects.

Then the serpents in their turn made grasshoppers, and the iguana made the creatures without horns.

Then the three sons of Bumba said they would finish the world. The first, Nyonye Ngana, *creating is* *1st death origin* made the white ants, but he was not equal to the task, and died of it. The ants, however, *holy task* thankful for life and being, went searching for black earth in the depths of the world and covered the barren sands to bury and honor their creator.

burial ritual origin

Chonganda, the second son, brought forth a marvelous living plant from which all the trees and grasses and flowers and plants in the world have sprung. The third son, Chedi Bumba, wanted something different, but for all his trying made only a bird called the kite.

Of all the creatures, Tsetse, lightning, was the only troublemaker. She stirred up so much trouble that Bumba chased her into the sky. Then mankind was without fire until Bumba showed the people how to draw fire out of trees. "There is fire in every tree," he told them, *origin of lightning* and showed them how to make the firedrill and liberate it. Sometimes today Tsetse still leaps down and strikes the earth and causes damage.

When at least the work of creation was finished, Bumba walked through the peaceful *man owns the earth* villages and said to the people, "Behold these wonders. They belong to you." Thus from Bumba, the Creator, the First Ancestor, came forth all the wonders that we see and hold and use, and all the brotherhood of beasts and man.[9]

---

5. ***Look for themes.*** Themes are large, general ideas that are important to nearly everyone. Writers use themes to express the message they want to convey in their writing. Common themes in literature include:
   - Questions, issues, or problems raised by the story: what is right or wrong; good or bad; worthwhile or unimportant?

- Abstract ideas: love, death, heroism, honor
- Conflicts: what is versus what seems to be, freedom versus restraint, poverty versus wealth
- Common literary topics: self-realization, mortality, fall from innocence, search for the meaning of life

---

EXERCISE 14-8

DIRECTIONS: *The following is another creation story, this time taken from Quiché-Mayan civilization. Read the legend and make notes and underline as you read. Then answer the questions that follow.*

Quiché-Mayan Creation Story

1   Before the world was created, Calm and Silence were the great kings that ruled. Nothing existed, there was nothing. Things had not yet been drawn together, the face of the earth was unseen. There was only motionless sea, and a great emptiness of sky. There were no men anywhere, or animals, no birds or fish, no crabs. Trees, stones, caves, grass, forests, none of these existed yet. There was nothing that could roar or run, nothing that could tremble or cry in the air. Flatness and emptiness, only the sea, alone and breathless. It was night; silence stood in the dark.

2   In this darkness the Creators waited, the Maker, Tepeu, Gucumatz, the Forefathers. They were there in this emptiness, hidden under green and blue feathers, alone and surrounded with light. They are the same as wisdom. They are the ones who can conceive and bring forth a child from nothingness. And the time had come. The Creators were bent deep around talk in the darkness. They argued, worried, sighed over what was to be. They planned the growth of the thickets, how things would crawl and jump, the birth of man. They planned the whole creation, arguing each point until their words and thoughts crystallized and became the same thing. Heart of Heaven was there, and in the darkness the creation was planned.

3   Then let the emptiness fill! they said. Let the water weave its way downward so the earth can show its face! Let the light break on the ridges, let the sky fill up with the yellow light of dawn! Let our glory be a man walking on a path through the trees! "Earth!" the Creators called. They called only once, and it was there, from a mist, from a cloud of dust, the mountains appeared instantly. At this single word the groves of cypresses and pines sent out shoots, rivulets ran freely between the round hills. The Creators were struck by the beauty and exclaimed, "It will be a creation that will mount the darkness!"[10]

---

1. Summarize the literal meaning by briefly describing what happens in the legend.

_____

_____

2. What does the story attempt to explain?

_____

_____

3. Explain the meaning of the last sentence.

_____

_____

4. How is it similar to and different from the Bantu myth?

_____

_____

Types of Literature

In the following sections you will learn how to read and interpret two types of literature—short stories and poetry.

Reading and Interpreting Short Stories

A short story is a creative or imaginative work describing a series of events for the purpose of entertainment and/or communicating a serious message. It has five basic elements. The next section describes each. But first, read the following brief short story and then refer back to it as you read about each of the six elements.

■ ■ ■ ■ ■

Merry Christmas God

—Larry French

"Why did you say that?" she asked. "Well," he said, "don't you think he deserves one? I mean, after all he's done for us?" They had been separated for several months and she had already filed. He had come over to help put the tree up and wrap the kids' gifts. "I don't like this any better than you do,

Jim," she said. He was putting tinsel on a strand at a time. "You must have got straight out of his bed and hired the lawyer," he said. "That guy must be something in bed, huh? You must have reached right over and called the lawyer from his bedside phone." He was laying out the strings of lights and replacing the bulbs that wouldn't light. "Jim, you said you wouldn't start. You promised. I'm tired—I'm just too tired." She sighed. "I imagine you are," he said. "You might have to start taking vitamins with this new life of yours." One of the kids began crying upstairs and she went to care for it. He walked over to the record player and started an album of Bing Crosby Christmas songs. He arranged the silver and gold wrapped packages under the tree and checked to see that they all had gift tags on them. She came back down and started getting little wooden Christmas decorations out of their boxes. She hung up several then stepped back to see how they looked. He had three strands of lights connected and strung out on the floor. All the lights were working now, and he put the spares in a small brown sack. The lights flashing on and off on the floor reminded him of a disco. "Tell me, Fran," he said, "does the son-of-a-bitch dance too? Does he do it all?" She added a few more decorations and said, "I've got it too heavy on the left, don't you think?" Bing Crosby had stopped singing and their voices seemed to rise in the silence amid the flashing lights. "Vitamins," he said. "At least I'll know what to give you every Christmas—a large box of vitamins, multi-purpose vitamins. You'd like that wouldn't you?" She switched some of the decorations from the left to the right and said, "Jim, just do the damn lights, please!" He stood next to the tree and reached down and picked up a strand of the largest lights. He put a red bulb between his teeth and when it flashed on he bit down until it shattered. He did four more until he tasted blood and heard, almost unbelievably, above her screaming, the small sound of glass falling on the children's gifts.[11]

Plot The plot is the basic storyline—the sequence of events as they occur in the work. The plot focuses on conflict and often follows a predictable structure. The plot frequently begins by setting the scene, introducing the main characters, and providing the background information needed to follow the story. Next, there is often a complication or problem that arises. Suspense builds as the problem or conflict unfolds. Near the end of the story, events reach a climax—the point at which the outcome (resolution) of the conflict will be decided. A conclusion quickly follows as the story ends.

The plot of "Merry Christmas God" is: Jim helps Fran, his soon-to-be ex-wife, decorate her Christmas tree. He questions her about her relationship with another man. The story ends with Jim biting glass Christmas tree bulbs.

Setting The setting is the time, place, and circumstances under which the action occurs. The setting provides the mood or atmosphere in which the characters interact. The setting of "Merry Christmas God" is Christmas eve at Fran's home, around the Christmas tree.

Characterization Characters are the actors in a narrative story. The characters reveal themselves by what they say—the dialogue—and by their actions, appearance, thoughts, and feelings. The narrator, or person who tells the story, may also comment on or reveal information about the characters. As you read, analyze the characters' traits and motives. Also analyze their personalities and watch for character changes. Study how the characters relate to one another.

In "Merry Christmas God" there are only two characters, Jim and Fran. Jim's questions show him to be jealous, unforgiving, angry, and hurt. Fran's responses to Jim's questions show her to be evasive, tired, and resigned, a person who tries to make the best of a situation.

Point of View The point of view refers to the way the story is presented or the person from whose perspective the story is told. Often the story is not told from the narrator's perspective. The story may be told from the perspective of one of the characters, or that of an unknown narrator. In analyzing point of view, determine the role and function of the narrator. Is the narrator reliable and knowledgeable? Sometimes the narrator is able to enter the minds of some or all of the characters, knowing their thoughts and understanding their actions and motivations. In other stories, the narrator may not understand the actions or implications of the events in the story.

"Merry Christmas God" is told by a narrator not involved in the story. The narrator gives us very little background information or insight into either of the characters and does not explain their actions. The point of view of the story is very limited, perhaps to focus our attention on the action as it unfolds.

Tone The tone or mood of a story reflects the author's attitude. Like a person's tone of voice, tone suggests feelings. Many ingredients contribute to tone, including the author's choice of detail (characters, setting, etc.) and the language that is used. The tone of a story may be, for example, humorous, ironic, or tragic. The author's feelings are not necessarily those of the characters or the narrator. Instead, it is through the narrator's description of the characters and their actions that we infer tone. In "Merry Christmas God," the tone might be described as ironic. The narrator is detached and we are unable to tell how the author reacts to the characters.

Theme The theme of the story is its meaning or message. The theme of a work may also be considered its main idea or main point. Themes are often large, universal ideas dealing with life and death, human values, or existence. To establish the theme, ask yourself, "What is the author trying to say about life by telling the story?" Try to explain it in a single sentence. The theme of "Merry Christmas God" is that life does not always turn out the way we think or hope it will. Life can be frustrating, especially when it involves interpersonal relationships. Another theme at work is that of self-destruction: Jim's questions are self-defeating and his final action—biting a lightbulb—suggests he'd rather inflict violence on himself than accept the situation.

If you are having difficulty stating the theme, try the following suggestions:

1. *Study the title.* Now that you have read the story, does it take on any new meanings?
2. *Analyze the main characters.* Do they change? If so, how and in reaction to what?
3. *Look for broad general statements.* What do the characters or the narrator say about life or the problems they face?
4. *Look for symbols,* figurative expressions, meaningful names (example: Mrs. Goodheart), or objects that hint at larger ideas.

DIRECTIONS: *Read the following short story "Sunday in the Park" by Bel Kaufman and answer the questions that follow it.*

Sunday in the Park

1   It was still warm in the late-afternoon sun, and the city noises came muffled through the trees in the park. She put her book down on the bench, removed her sunglasses, and sighed contentedly. Morton was reading the *Times Magazine* section, one arm flung around her shoulder; their three-year-old son, Larry, was playing in the sandbox: a faint breeze fanned her hair softly against her cheek. It was five-thirty of a Sunday afternoon, and the small playground, tucked away in a corner of the park, was all but deserted. The swings and seesaws stood motionless and abandoned, the slides were empty, and only in the sandbox two little boys squatted diligently side by side. *How good this is,* she thought, and almost smiled at her sense of well-being. They must go out in the sun more often; Morton was so city-pale, cooped up all week inside the gray factorylike university. She squeezed his arm affectionately and glanced

at Larry, delighting in the pointed little face frowning in concentration over the tunnel he was digging. The other boy suddenly stood up and with a quick, deliberate swing of his chubby arm threw a spadeful of sand at Larry. It just missed his head. Larry continued digging; the boy remained standing, shovel raised, stolid and impassive.

"No, no, little boy." She shook her finger at him, her eyes searching for the child's mother or nurse. "We mustn't throw sand. It may get in someone's eyes and hurt. We must play nicely in the nice sandbox." The boy looked at her in unblinking expectancy. He was about Larry's age but perhaps ten pounds heavier, a husky little boy with none of Larry's quickness and sensitivity in his face. Where was his mother? The only other people left in the playground were two women and a little girl on roller skates leaving now through the gate, and a man on a bench a few feet away. He was a big man, and he seemed to be taking up the whole bench as he held the Sunday comics close to his face. She supposed he was the child's father. He did not look up from his comics, but spat once deftly out of the corner of his mouth. She turned her eyes away.

At that moment, as swiftly as before, the fat little boy threw another spadeful of sand at Larry. This time some of it landed on his hair and forehead. Larry looked up at his mother, his mouth tentative; her expression would tell him whether to cry or not.

Her first instinct was to rush to her son, brush the sand out of his hair, and punish the other child, but she controlled it. She always said that she wanted Larry to learn to fight his own battles.

"Don't *do* that, little boy," she said sharply, leaning forward on the bench. "You mustn't throw sand!"

The man on the bench moved his mouth as if to spit again, but instead he spoke. He did not look at her, but at the boy only.

"You go right ahead, Joe," he said loudly. "Throw all you want. This here is a *public* sandbox."

She felt a sudden weakness in her knees as she glanced at Morton. He had become aware of what was happening. He put his *Times* down carefully on his lap and turned his fine, lean face toward the man, smiling the shy, apologetic smile he might have offered a student in pointing out an error in his thinking. When he spoke to the man, it was with his usual reasonableness.

"You're quite right," he said pleasantly, "but just because this is a public place. . . ."

The man lowered his funnies and looked at Morton. He looked at him from head to foot, slowly and deliberately. "Yeah?" His insolent voice was edged with menace. "My kid's got just as good right here as yours, and if he feels like throwing sand, he'll throw it, and if you don't like it, you can take your kid the hell out of here."

11   The children were listening, their eyes and mouths wide open, their spades forgotten in small fists. She noticed the muscle in Morton's jaw tighten. He was rarely angry; he seldom lost his temper. She was suffused with a tenderness for her husband and an impotent rage against the man for involving him in a situation so alien and so distasteful to him.

12   "Now, just a minute," Morton said courteously, "you must realize. . . ."

13   "Aw, shut up," said the man.

14   Her heart began to pound. Morton half rose; the *Times* slid to the ground. Slowly the other man stood up. He took a couple of steps toward Morton, then stopped. He flexed his great arms, waiting. She pressed her trembling knees together. Would there be violence, fighting? How dreadful, how incredible. . . . She must do something, stop them, call for help. She wanted to put her hand on her husband's sleeve, to pull him down, but for some reason she didn't.

15   Morton adjusted his glasses. He was very pale. "This is ridiculous," he said unevenly. "I must ask you. . . ."

16   "Oh, yeah?" said the man. He stood with his legs spread apart, rocking a little, looking at Morton with utter scorn. "You and who else?"

17   For a moment the two men looked at each other nakedly. Then Morton turned his back on the man and said quietly, "Come on, let's get out of here." He walked awkwardly, almost limping with self-consciousness, to the sandbox. He stooped and lifted Larry and his shovel out.

18   At once Larry came to life; his face lost its rapt expression and he began to kick and cry. "I don't *want* to *go* home, I want to play better, I don't *want* any supper, I don't *like* supper. . . ." It became a chant as they walked, pulling their child between them, his feet dragging on the ground. In order to get to the exit gate they had to pass the bench where the man sat sprawling again. She was careful not to look at him. With all the dignity she could summon, she pulled Larry's sandy, perspiring little hand, while Morton pulled the other. Slowly and with head high she walked with her husband and child out of the playground.

19   Her first feeling was one of relief that the fight had been avoided, that no one was hurt. Yet beneath it there was a layer of something else, something heavy and inescapable. She sensed that it was more than just an unpleasant incident, more than defeat of reason by force. She felt dimly it had something to do with her and Morton, something acutely personal, familiar, and important.

20   Suddenly Morton spoke. "It wouldn't have proved anything."

21   "What?" she asked.

22   "A fight. It wouldn't have proved anything beyond the fact that he's bigger than I am."

23   "Of course," she said.

24 "The only possible outcome," he continued reasonably, "would have been—what? My glasses broken, perhaps a tooth or two replaced, a couple of days' work missed—and for what? For justice? For truth?"

25 "Of course," she repeated. She quickened her step. She wanted only to get home and to busy herself with her familiar tasks; perhaps then the feeling, glued like heavy plaster on her heart, would be gone. *Of all the stupid, despicable bullies,* she thought, pulling harder on Larry's hand. The child was still crying. Always before she had felt a tender pity for his defenseless little body, the frail arms, the narrow shoulders with sharp, winglike shoulder blades, the thin and unsure legs, but now her mouth tightened in resentment.

26 "Stop crying," she said sharply. "I'm ashamed of you!" She felt as if all three of them were tracking mud along the street. The child cried louder.

27 *If there had been an issue involved,* she thought, *if there had been something to fight for. . . . But what else could he possibly have done? Allow himself to be beaten? Attempt to educate the man? Call a policeman? "Officer, there's a man in the park who won't stop his child from throwing sand on mine. . . ."* The whole thing was as silly as that, and not worth thinking about.

28 "Can't you keep him quiet, for Pete's sake?" Morton asked irritably.

29 "What do you suppose I've been trying to do?" she said.

30 Larry pulled back, dragging his feet.

31 "If you can't discipline this child, I will," Morton snapped, making a move toward the boy.

32 But her voice stopped him. She was shocked to hear it, thin and cold and penetrating with contempt. "Indeed?" she heard herself say. "You and who else?"[12]

1. Summarize the events that take place.

   _____

   _____

2. Why is the wife in the story unnamed?

   _____

   _____

3. Are the parents "typical"? Do they respond as you would expect to the sandbox incident?

   _____

   _____

4. The tone at the beginning of the story is relaxed and peaceful. How does it change? How do you sense the change?

_____

_____

5. How is the sandbox incident similar to many other life situations?

_____

_____

6. Explain the meaning of the last paragraph.

_____

_____

Reading and Interpreting Poetry

Poetry presents ideas in a unique format. Poems are written in verse—lines and stanzas rather than paragraphs. Poetry often requires more reading time and greater concentration than other types of material. In reading a paragraph, you might miss a word, yet your comprehension might not suffer. Poetry, however, is very concentrated and precise. Every word is important and carries a meaning. You have to pay attention to each word—its sound, its meaning, its placement, and its relationship to the other words. Rhythm is also important in many poems.

A poem can relate the same ideas and feeling as other types of literature, but it does so within its own unique format. The following narrative essay and poem were written by the same author, Judith Ortiz Cofer, and describe the same situation. Read the narrative first and then the poem. After you've finished both, compare them in content and in form. Look for similarities as well as differences.

Narrative:

■ ■ ■ ■ ■

More Room

1   My grandmother's house is like a chambered nautilus; it has many rooms, yet it is not a mansion. Its proportions are small and its design simple. It is a house that has grown organically, according to the needs of its inhabitants.

To all of us in the family it is known as *la casa de Mamá*. It is the place of our origin; the stage for our memories and dreams of Island life . . .

2   Mamá slept alone on her large bed, except for the times when a sick grandchild warranted the privilege, or when a heartbroken daughter came home in need of more than herbal teas. In the family there is a story about how this came to be.

3   When one of the daughters, my mother or one of her sisters, tells the *cuento* of how Mamá came to own her nights, it is usually preceded by the qualifications that Papá's exile from his wife's room was not a result of animosity between the couple, but that the act had been Mamá's famous bloodless coup for her personal freedom. Papá was the benevolent dictator of her body and her life who had had to be banished from her bed so that Mamá could better serve her family. Before the telling, we had to agree that the old man was not to blame. We all recognized that in the family Papá was as an *alma de Dios,* a saintly, soft-spoken presence whose main pleasures in life, such as writing poetry and reading the Spanish large-type editions of *Reader's Digest,* always took place outside the vortex of Mamá's crowded realm. It was not his fault, after all, that every year or so he planted a baby-seed in Mamá's fertile body, keeping her from leading the active life she needed and desired. He loved her and the babies. Papá composed odes and lyrics to celebrate births and anniversaries and hired musicians to accompany him in singing them to his family and friends at extravagant pig-roasts he threw yearly. Mamá and the oldest girls worked for days preparing the food. Papá sat for hours in his painter's shed, also his study and library, composing the songs. At these celebrations he was also known to give long speeches in praise of God, his fecund wife, and his beloved island. As a middle child, my mother remembers these occasions as a time when the women sat in the kitchen and lamented their burdens, while the men feasted out in the patio, their rum-thickened voices rising in song and praise for each other, *compañeros* all.

4   It was after the birth of her eighth child, after she had lost three at birth or in infancy, that Mamá made her decision. They say that Mamá had had a special way of letting her husband know that they were expecting, one that had begun when, at the beginning of their marriage, he had built her a house too confining for her taste. So, when she discovered her first pregnancy, she supposedly drew plans for another room, which he dutifully executed. Every time a child was due, she would demand, *more space, more space*. Papá acceded to her wishes, child after child, since he had learned early that Mamá's renowned temper was a thing that grew like a monster along with a new belly. In this way Mamá got the house that she wanted, but with each child she lost in heart and energy. She had knowledge of her body and

perceived that if she had any more children, her dreams and her plans would have to be permanently forgotten, because she would be a chronically ill woman, like Flora with her twelve children: asthma, no teeth, in bed more than on her feet.

5   And so, after my youngest uncle was born, she asked Papá to build a large room at the back of the house. He did so in joyful anticipation. Mamá had asked him special things this time: shelves on the walls, a private entrance. He thought that she meant this room to be a nursery where several children could sleep. He thought it was a wonderful idea. He painted it his favorite color, sky blue, and made large windows looking out over a green hill and the church spires beyond. But nothing happened. Mamá's belly did not grow, yet she seemed in a frenzy of activity over the house. Finally, an anxious Papá approached his wife to tell her that the new room was finished and ready to be occupied. And Mamá, they say, replied: "Good, it's for *you*."

6   And so it was that Mamá discovered the only means of birth control available to a Catholic woman of her time: sacrifice. She gave up the comfort of Papá's sexual love for something she deemed greater: the right to own and control her body, so that she might live to meet her grandchildren—me among them—so that she could give more of herself to the ones already there, so that she could be more than a channel for other lives, so that even now that time has robbed her of the elasticity of her body and of her amazing reservoir of energy, she still emanates the kind of joy that can only be achieved by living according to the dictates of one's own heart.[13]

Poem:

■ ■ ■ ■ ■

Claims

Last time I saw her, Grandmother
had grown seamed as a bedouin tent.
She had claimed the right
to sleep alone, to own
her nights, to never bear
the weight of sex again, nor to accept
its gift of comfort, for the luxury
of stretching her bones.
She's carried eight children,
three had sunk in her belly, *náufragos,*
she called them, shipwrecked babies

drowned in her black waters.
Children are made in the night and
steal your days
for the rest of your life, amen. She said this
to each of her daughters in turn. Once she had made a pact
with man and nature and kept it. Now like the sea,
she is claiming back her territory.[14]

Did you notice that the poem describes the same situation, but in a much more compact form? The content differs, too. The narrative is filled with details. The poem, however, uses images to convey meaning. The grandmother "had grown seamed as a bedouin tent." Her miscarriages are "shipwrecked babies." The grandmother is finally compared to the sea, claiming back its territory. You can see, then, that the poem leaves much more to your imagination. You have to interpret the meaning of "shipwrecked babies," visualize the sea, and imagine the ways Grandmother reclaimed her territory.

Here are a few guidelines to help you approach poetry more effectively:

1. *Read the poem once straight through without any defined purpose.* Keep an open mind, experiencing the poem as it is written. Even if you meet an unknown word or confusing reference, continue reading.
2. *Use punctuation to guide your comprehension.* Although poetry is usually written in lines, do not expect each line to make sense by itself. Meaning often flows on from line to line, eventually forming a thought. Use the punctuation to guide you, as you do when reading paragraphs. If there is no punctuation at the end of the line, pause slightly and put an emphasis on the last word.
3. *Read the poem a second time.* Identify and address any difficulties such as an unknown word or an ambiguous thought.
4. *Notice the action (if there is any).* Who is doing what, when, and where?
5. *Analyze the intent.* Decide what the poem is meant to convey. Does it describe a feeling or a person, express a memory, present an argument?
6. *Determine who is speaking.* Poems often refer to an unidentified "I" or "we." Try to describe the speaker's viewpoint or feelings.
7. *Establish the speaker's tone.* Is he or she serious, defiant, saddened, frustrated? Read the poem aloud. Your emphasis on certain words and the rise and fall of your voice may provide clues. You may "hear" a poet's anger, desperation, or happiness.
8. *Identify to whom the poem is addressed.* Does the poem address a person, the reader, an object? Consider the possibility that the poem may be reflective, serving as an emotional outlet or helping the poet work out a problem he or she faces.

9. *Reread difficult or confusing sections.* Read them aloud several times. Copying these sections word for word may be helpful. Use context and/or your dictionary to figure out unfamiliar words.

10. *Check unfamiliar references.* A poet may refer to people, objects, or events outside the poem. These are known as *allusions.* A poet may mention Greek gods or goddesses, historical figures, or biblical characters. Often the allusion is important to the overall meaning of the poem. For example, when you see Oedipus mentioned in a poem, you'll need to find out who he was. (Paperback books on mythology and literary figures are good investments.)

11. *Analyze the language of the poem.* Consider connotative meanings and study figurative language. (See Chapter 12, p. 270.) A poet's use of language often provides the key to the meaning of the poem.

12. *Look for the poet's meaning or the poem's theme.* Paraphrase the poem: express it in your own words and connect it to your own experience. Then put each idea together to discover its overall meaning. Ask yourself: What is the poet trying to tell me? What is his or her message?

Now read the poem "Birth Right" using these guidelines.

■ ■ ■ ■ ■

Birth Right

—*Amiri Baraka*

i don't care
if my children carry the blues in their throat
i hope they do—
i hope a feeling sleeps in their stomach
it will keep them close to their people
i wanna gospel note to live on their breath
& speak black music in their voice
i don't care if my children
come from my womb
into the world of black
beautiful people
like a hundred Duke Ellington songs
sung by a million city blues singers
cause—
perhaps thats how they will survive racism[15]

"Birth Right" describes the poet's attitude toward music and its function in creating a cultural identity. Baraka hopes his children will carry and feel the blues because "it will keep them close to their people." The last line of the poem explains another function of music—to help people survive the effects of racism. The poem, then, also affirms that racism still exists and suggests that it will continue to exist, since it is Baraka's children who must survive it.

EXERCISE 14-10 **DIRECTIONS:** *Read the following poems and answer the questions that correspond to each.*

Two Look At Two

—Robert Frost

Love and forgetting might have carried them
A little further up the mountainside
With night so near, but not much further up.
They must have halted soon in any case
With thoughts of the path back, how rough it was
With rock and washout, and unsafe in darkness;
When they were halted by a tumbled wall
With barbed-wire binding. They stood facing this,
Spending what onward impulse they still had
In one last look the way they must not go,
On up the failing path, where, if a stone
Or earthslide moved at night, it moved itself;
No footstep moved it. "This is all," they sighed,
"Good-night to woods." But not so; there was more.
A doe from round a spruce stood looking at them
Across the wall, as near the wall as they.
She saw them in their field, they her in hers.
The difficulty of seeing what stood still,
Like some up-ended boulder split in two,
Was in her clouded eyes: they saw no fear there.
She seemed to think that, two thus, they were safe.

Then, as if they were something that, though strange,
She could not trouble her mind with too long,
She sighed and passed unscared along the wall.
"*This,* then, is all. What more is there to ask?"
But no, not yet. A snort to bid them wait.
A buck from round the spruce stood looking at them
Across the wall, as near the wall as they.
This was an antlered buck of lusty nostril,
Not the same doe come back into her place.
He viewed them quizzically with jerks of head,
As if to ask, "Why don't you make some motion?
Or give some sign of life? Because you can't.
I doubt if you're as living as you look."
Thus till he had them almost feeling dared
To stretch a proffering hand—and a spell-breaking.
Then he too passed unscared along the wall.
Two had seen two, whichever side you spoke from.
"This *must* be all." It was all. Still they stood,
A great wave from it going over them,
As if the earth in one unlooked-for favor
Had made them certain earth returned their love.[16]

1. Summarize the action that occurs in the poem.

   _____

   _____

2. Explain the meaning of the statements "This is all," "This, then, is all."

   _____

   _____

3. What might the tumbled wall represent?

   _____

   _____

4. What is the theme of the poem?

   _____

   _____

Do Not Go Gentle Into That Good Night

—Dylan Thomas

Do not go gentle into that good night,
Old age should burn and rave at close of day;
Rage, rage against the dying of the light.

Though wise men at their end know dark is right,
Because their words had forked no lightning they
Do not go gentle into that good night.

Good men, the last wave by, crying how bright
Their frail deeds might have danced in a green bay,
Rage, rage against the dying of the light.

Wild men who caught and sang the sun in flight,
And learn, too late, they grieved it on its way,
Do not go gentle into that good night.

Grave men, near death, who see with blinding sight
Blind eyes could blaze like meteors and be gay,
Rage, rage against the dying of the light.

And you, my father, there on the sad height,
Curse, bless, me now with your fierce tears, I pray.
Do not go gentle into that good night.
Rage, rage against the dying of the light.[17]

1. What is the poet asking his father to do?

   _____

   _____

2. What is the "good night" that the poet refers to?

   _____

   _____

3. What is the poem's theme?

   _____

   _____

Directions: Read "More Rooms" and "Claims" by Judith Ortex Cofer on pp. 338–341 before coming to class. Working in small groups, discuss how each told the same story. Then answer the question Which is more effective and why? Each group should prepare a written statement to share with the class.

■■■■■■■■ **SUMMARY**

What is literature?	Literature is concerned with the expression and interpretation of ideas, experiences, and events.
What are essays and what are the four types?	Essays are short pieces of writing that examine a single subject. They have the following parts: title, introduction, thesis statement, supporting information, and conclusion or summary. Four types of essays are narrative, descriptive, expository, and persuasive.
What is a short story and what are its elements?	A short story is an imaginative work describing a series of events for the purpose of entertainment and/or communicating a serious message. Its basic elements are plot, setting, characterization, point of view, tone and theme.
What is poetry and what does reading poetry involve?	Poetry is the condensed, concentrated expression of ideas in a unique format. Reading poetry involves rereading, analysis, and interpretation.

Making Your Skills Work Together

A Guide to Effective Reading

Now that you have completed Part Five of this book, it is time to take all the skills you have learned and see how they fit together.

At first we were concerned with understanding the writer's basic messages expressed through words, sentences, and paragraphs (Parts One, Two, and Three). Then we moved to longer materials—specifically, textbook chapters (Part Four). There, focus was on the structure of these materials and how to organize and remember the information they contain. Finally, in Part Five we were concerned with interpreting and evaluating these materials, and with reading expressive literature.

You have learned may new skills. Basically, these skills can be grouped into three levels or types of comprehension. Keep these levels in mind as you read. They will serve as a guide to help you read more effectively.

1. LITERAL LEVEL. At this level, you are concerned with understanding the writer's basic message. You are reading to find out what the writer *said*. Here you use your basic vocabulary, sentence, and paragraph structure skills.

2. INTERPRETIVE LEVEL. This second level assumes you understood the basic literal content—"Who did what, when, and where?" Here you think and reason about what you are reading. You are concerned with what the writer *means*. You look for indirect or unstated meanings. You try to see how the writer has organized his or her ideas. You are also looking for *why* the writer wrote (author's purpose) and *how* the purpose was achieved.

3. EVALUATIVE LEVEL. At this level you examine the author's ideas, organization, and approach. Your purpose is to judge the worth, use, and value of what you are reading. Here you ask critical questions.

DIRECTIONS: *Read the following selection by Eduardo Galeano and answer the questions that follow.*

If He Had Been Born a Woman

1   Of Benjamin Franklin's sixteen brothers and sisters, Jane is the one most resembling him in talent and strength of will.

2   But at the age when Benjamin leaves home to make his own way, Jane
marries a poor saddler, who accepts her without dowry, and ten months
later bears her first child. From then on, for a quarter of a century, Jane has a
child every two years. Some of them die, and each death opens a wound in
her breast. Those that live demand food, shelter, instruction, and consola-
tion. Jane spends whole nights cradling those that cry, washes mountains of
clothing, bathes stacks of children, rushes from market to kitchen, washes
piles of dishes, teaches ABC's and chores, toils elbow to elbow with her husband in his workshops, and attends to the guests whose rent helps to fill the
stewpot. Jane is a devoted wife and exemplary widow; and when the children are grown up, she takes charge of her own ailing parents and of her
unmarried daughters and her orphaned grandchildren.

3   Jane never knows the pleasure of letting herself float in a lake, drifting
over the surface hitched to the string of a kite, as Benjamin Franklin enjoys
doing despite his years. Jane never has time to think, nor allows herself to
doubt. Benjamin continues to be a fervent lover, but Jane doesn't know that
sex can produce anything except children.

4   Benjamin, founder of a nation of inventors, is a great man of all the
ages. Jane is a woman of her age, like almost all women of all the ages, who
has done her duty on this earth and expiated her share of blame in the Biblical curse. She has done all she could to keep from going mad and sought, in
vain, a little silence.

5   Her case will awaken no interest in historians.

1. Summarize the events of Jane's life.

_____

_____

2. Go beyond what Galeano says and think about what he means. What is
    Galeano's message?

_____

_____

3. What is Galeano's purpose for writing?

_____

_____

4. Explain the meaning of the last sentence.

_____

_____

5. Project what would have happened if Benjamin Franklin had been born a woman.

_____

_____

6. What words and phrases do you think are particularly descriptive? Which carry strong connotative meaning?

_____

_____

PART 6 Reading Selections

Practice is an important part of most types of learning: whether training for a sport or learning to type, cook, change a tire, or solve a math problem. The same is true of reading: *practice is important.* To read well, you must apply and practice the skills you have learned. You must try out these skills on a variety of types of reading materials.

The purpose of Part Six is to give you practice in applying the reading skills presented in Parts One through Five. Each selection gives you the opportunity to use your skills in a slightly different way on a new topic written by a different author. A set of exercises accompanies each selection. These exercises are organized in the same way. Each set has eight parts. The following is a brief introduction to each of these parts that provides some advice on how to use them to learn as much as possible.

- INTRODUCTION. Each selection begins with a brief introduction. This acquaints you with the topic of the selection and provides any background information you may need to know before you read the selection.
- VOCABULARY PREVIEW. Each selection contains some difficult words or phrases. This section lists some of these and gives a brief definition of each as used in the selection. (Words may have other meanings that are not listed.) Before you read the selection, be sure to go through this word list, noticing words you do not know and studying their meanings. Later, as you read the selection, refer back to this list to check meanings as you need them. The paragraph in which the word appears is given in parentheses following the word.

- PREREADING. Prereading (see Chapter 4) is a way of getting ready to read. This portion of the exercise directs you to preview the selection and then ask questions that are intended to focus your attention on the article and help you discover what you already know about the subject.

- CHECKING YOUR COMPREHENSION. This exercise gives you a chance to see whether you have understood what you have read. You will notice that the type of question differs for each selection. Some are true-false questions; others may ask you to write an outline or summary. Regardless of the type, each question checks your ability to understand the writer's basic message. Specifically, the questions in this section test your ability to apply the skills taught in Chapters 4–11. Often, in order to answer the question or complete the directed activity, you will apply several skills contained in these chapters.

- CRITICAL READING AND THINKING. In this exercise you are asked to interpret and react to the author's ideas. You will find a variety of questions that give you the opportunity to apply the skills taught in Part Five. Each of these questions is open ended and requires an explanation. Always answer in complete sentences. That way, you will be certain you have expressed a complete idea in a clear, understandable form.

- WORDS IN CONTEXT. Although each selection has difficult words, you can figure some of them out using context clues (see Chapter 1). This exercise contains a list of words (along with the paragraph number in which they appear). You are asked to write a brief definition of each word. To do this, go back to the paragraph in which the word is used and reread, looking for meaning clues.

- VOCABULARY REVIEW. This exercise gives you practice with all or most of the words contained in the Vocabulary Preview section. It is an opportunity to work with these words in contexts other than those used in the selection.

- WRITING EXERCISES. This exercise gives you practice expressing your own ideas in written form. Each exercise provides an opportunity for you to write about ideas discussed in the selection.

Living Life to the Fullest

MAYA ANGELOU

Are you living your life to its fullest? Read this selection to find out. Maya Angelou, a famous poet and writer, tells a story that will help you answer this question.

Vocabulary Preview

sinewy (par. 1)	lean and muscular
incurred (par. 1)	brought on; met with
tautly (par. 2)	tightly
meticulous (par. 3)	extremely careful
maven (par. 6)	expert
comradery (par. 14)	friendship
founts (par. 14)	sources
convivial (par. 14)	agreeable; cheerful
scenarios (par. 16)	plans; expected events

Prereading

DIRECTIONS: *Preview the selection and answer the following questions.*

1. What do you already know about Aunt Tee?

   _____

   _____

   _____

2. What important issues do you think this reading will be concerned with?

_____

_____

_____

1   *A*unt Tee was a Los Angeles member of our extended family. She was seventy-nine when I met her, sinewy, strong, and the color of old lemons. She wore her coarse, straight hair, which was slightly streaked with gray, in a long braided rope across the top of her head. With her high cheekbones, old gold skin, and almond eyes, she looked more like an Indian chief than an old black woman. (Aunt Tee described herself and any favored member of her race as Negroes. *Black* was saved for those who had incurred her disapproval.)

2   She had retired and lived alone in a dead, neat ground-floor apartment. Wax flowers and china figurines sat on elaborately embroidered and heavily starched doilies. Sofas and chairs were tautly upholstered. The only thing at ease in Aunt Tee's apartment was Aunt Tee.

3   I used to visit her often and perch on her uncomfortable sofa just to hear her stories. She was proud that after working thirty years as a maid, she spent the next thirty years as a live-in housekeeper, carrying the keys to rich houses and keeping meticulous accounts.

4   "Living in lets the white folks know Negroes are as neat and clean as they are, sometimes more so. And it gives the Negro maid a chance to see white folks ain't no smarter than Negroes. Just luckier. Sometimes."

5   Aunt Tee told me that once she was housekeeper for a couple in Bel Air, California, lived with them in a fourteen-room ranch house. There was a day maid who cleaned, and a gardener who daily tended the lush gardens. Aunt Tee oversaw the workers. When she had begun the job, she had cooked and served a light breakfast, a good lunch, and a full three- or four-course dinner to her employers and their guests. Aunt Tee said she watched them grow older and leaner. After a few years they stopped entertaining and ate dinner hardly seeing each other at the table. Finally, they sat in a dry silence as they ate evening meals of soft scrambled eggs, melba toast, and weak tea. Aunt Tee said she saw them growing old but didn't see herself aging at all.

6   She became the social maven. She started "keeping company" (her phrase) with a chauffeur down the street. Her best friend and her friend's husband worked in service only a few blocks away.

7   On Saturdays Aunt Tee would cook a pot of pigs' feet, a pot of greens, fry chicken, make potato salad, and bake a banana pudding. Then, that evening, her friends—the chauffeur, the other housekeeper, and her husband—would come to Aunt Tee's commodious live-in quarters. There the four would eat and drink, play records and dance. As the evening wore on, they would settle down to a serious game of bid whist.

8   Naturally, during this revelry jokes were told, fingers snapped, feet were patted, and there was a great deal of laughter.

9   Aunt Tee said that what occurred during every Saturday party startled her and her friends the first time it happened. They had been playing cards, and Aunt Tee, who had just won the bid, held a handful of trumps. She felt a cool breeze on her back and sat upright and turned around. Her employers had cracked her door open and beckoned to her. Aunt Tee, a little peeved, laid down her cards and went to the door. The couple backed away and asked her to come into the hall, and there they both spoke and won Aunt Tee's sympathy forever.

10   "Theresa, we don't mean to disturb you . . ." the man whispered, "but you all seem to be having such a good time . . ."

11   The woman added, "We hear you and your friends laughing every Saturday night, and we'd just like to watch you. We don't want to bother you. We'll be quiet and just watch."

12   The man said, "If you'll just leave your door ajar, your friends don't need to know. We'll never make a sound." Aunt Tee said she saw no harm in agreeing, and she talked it over with her company. They said it was OK with them, but it was sad that the employers owned the gracious house, the swimming pool, three cars, and numberless palm trees, but had no joy. Aunt Tee told me that laughter and relaxation had left the house; she agreed it was sad.

13   That story has stayed with me for nearly thirty years, and when a tale remains fresh in my mind, it almost always contains a lesson which will benefit me.

14   My dears, I draw the picture of the wealthy couple standing in a darkened hallway, peering into a lighted room where black servants were lifting their voices in merriment and comradery, and I realize that living well is an art which can be developed. Of course, you will need the basic talents to build upon: They are a love of life and ability to take great pleasure from small offerings, an assurance that the world owes you nothing and that every gift is exactly that, a gift. That people who may differ from you in political stance, sexual persuasion, and racial inheritance can be founts of fun, and if you are lucky, they can become even convivial comrades.

15   Living life as art requires a readiness to forgive. I do not mean that you should suffer fools gladly, but rather remember your own shortcomings, and when you encounter another with flaws, don't be eager to righteously seal yourself away from the offender forever. Take a few breaths and imagine yourself having just committed the action which has set you at odds.

16   Because of the routines we follow, we often forget that life is an ongoing adventure. We leave our homes for work, acting and even believing that we will reach our destinations with no unusual event startling us out of our set expectations. The truth is we know nothing, not where our cars will fail or when our buses will stall, whether our places of employment will be there when we arrive, or whether, in fact, we ourselves will arrive whole and alive at the end of our journeys. Life is pure adventure, and the sooner we realize that, the quicker we will be able to treat life as art: to bring all our energies to each encounter, to remain flexible enough to notice and admit when what we expected to happen did not happen. We need to remember that we are created creative and can invent new scenarios as frequently as they are needed.

17   Life seems to love the liver of it. Money and power can liberate only if they are used to do so. They can imprison and inhibit more finally than barred windows and iron chains.

Checking Your Comprehension

1. What term did Aunt Tee use to describe African Americans? Why did she prefer it?

_____

_____

2. What did her employers say that "won Aunt Tee's sympathy forever"?

_____

_____

3. How did the rich couple that Aunt Tee lived with change over the years?

_____

_____

4. According to the author, what are the requirements for good living?

_____

_____

Critical Reading and Thinking

1. What kind of a person do you think Aunt Tee was? Point out passages that support this.

   _____

   _____

2. What is the author's attitude toward Aunt Tee and her lifestyle? How can you tell?

   _____

   _____

3. The author stated that "living is an art which can be developed." Do you agree or disagree? Justify your answer.

   _____

   _____

4. Is the last paragraph of this selection a summary or a conclusion? Why?

   _____

   _____

Words in Context

DIRECTIONS: *Locate each word in the paragraph indicated and reread that paragraph. Then, based on the way the word is used, write a synonym or brief definition for each.*

1. revelry (par. 8) _____

2. beckoned (par. 9) _____

Vocabulary Review

DIRECTIONS: *Match the words in Column A with their meanings in Column B.*

Column A

_____ 1. comradery

_____ 2. meticulous

_____ 3. scenarios

_____ 4. incurred

_____ 5. maven

_____ 6. convivial

_____ 7. sinewy

_____ 8. tautly

_____ 9. founts

Column B

a. tightly

b. expert

c. sources

d. friendship

e. plans; expected events

f. brought on; met with

g. extremely careful

h. agreeable; cheerful

i. lean and muscular

Writing Exercises

1. Write a paragraph describing your "requirements for good living."

2. Write a paragraph on a favorite relative or friend and explain his or her outlook on life.

3. Maya Angelou says that "life is pure adventure." Do you agree with this? Why?

Hispanic, USA: The Conveyor-Belt Ladies

ROSE DEL CASTILLO GUILBAULT

An important part of many jobs is getting along with co-workers, as well as working with supervisors and customers. In this article a young woman describes her experiences working in a vegetable packing plant. Read the article to find out how she came to be respected by her older co-workers.

Vocabulary Preview

tedious (par. 4)	tiresome, dull
strenuous (par. 4)	requiring great physical effort or energy
sorority (par. 5)	an organization of women
irrevocably (par. 10)	impossible to change
stigmatize (par. 10)	to brand or label
gregarious (par. 12)	sociable
dyspeptic (par. 12)	having a bad disposition, grouchy
pragmatic (par. 17)	practical
melancholic (par. 18)	sad, gloomy
fatalism (par. 19)	the belief that events in life are determined by fate and cannot be changed
crescendo (par. 29)	a steady increase in volume or force
anti-climactic (par. 30)	an ordinary or commonplace event that concludes a series of important events

Prereading

DIRECTIONS: *Preview the selection and answer the following question.*

1. What do you already know about the author's co-workers?

1   The conveyor-belt ladies were the migrant women, mostly from Texas, I worked with during the summers of my teenage years. I call them conveyor-belt ladies because our entire relationship took place while sorting tomatoes on a conveyor belt.

2   We were like a cast in a play where all the action occurs on one set. We'd return day after day to perform the same roles, only this stage was a vegetable-packing shed, and at the end of the season there was no applause. The players could look forward only to the same uninspiring parts on a string of grim real-life stages.

3   The women and their families arrived in May for the carrot season, spent the summer in the tomato sheds and stayed through October for the bean harvest. After that, they emptied the town, some returning to their homes in Texas (cities like McAllen, Douglas, Brownsville), while others continued on the migrant trail, picking cotton in the San Joaquin Valley or grapefruits and oranges in the Imperial Valley.

4   Most of these women had started in the fields. The vegetable packing sheds were a step up, easier than the back-breaking, grueling work the field demanded. The work was more tedious than strenuous, paid better, provided fairly steady hours and clean bathrooms. Best of all, you weren't subjected to the elements.

5   The summer I was 16, my mother got jobs for both of us as tomato sorters. That's how I came to be included in the seasonal sorority of the conveyor belt.

6   The work consisted of standing and picking flawed tomatoes off the conveyor belt before they rolled off into the shipping boxes at the end of the line. These boxes were immediately loaded onto waiting delivery trucks, so it was crucial not to let imperfect tomatoes through.

7   The work could be slow or intense, depending on the quality of the tomatoes and how many there were. Work increased when the company's deliveries got backlogged or after rainy weather had delayed picking.

8   During those times, it was not unusual to work from 7 A.M. to midnight, playing catch-up. I never heard anyone complain about the overtime. Overtime meant desperately needed extra money.

9   I was not happy to be part of the agricultural work force. I would have preferred working in a dress shop or baby-sitting, like my friends. But I had a dream that would cost a lot of money—college. And the fact was, this was the highest-paying work I could do.

10   But it wasn't so much the work that bothered me. I was embarrassed because only Mexicans worked at packing sheds. I had heard my schoolmates joke about the "ugly, fat Mexican women" at the sheds. They ridiculed the way they dressed and laughed at the "funny way" they talked. I feared working with them would irrevocably stigmatize me, setting me further apart from my Anglo classmates.

11   At 16 I was more American than Mexican and, with adolescent arrogance, felt superior to these "uneducated" women. I might be one of them, I reasoned, but I was not like them.

12   But it was difficult not to like the women. They were a gregarious, entertaining group, easing the long, monotonous hours with bawdy humor, spicy gossip

and inventive laments. They poked fun at all the make workers and did hysterical impersonations of a dyspeptic Anglo supervisor. Although he didn't speak Spanish (other than *"Mujeres, trabajo, trabajo!"*), he seemed to sense he was being laughed at. That would account for the sudden rages when he would stamp his foot and forbid us to talk until break time.

13 "I bet he understands Spanish and just pretends so he can hear what we say," I whispered to Rosa.

14 *"Ay, no hija,* it's all the buzzing in his ears that alerts him that these *viejas* (old women) are bad-mouthing him!" Rosa giggled.

15 But it would have been easier to tie the women's tongues in a knot than to keep them quiet. Eventually the ladies had their way and their fun, and the men learned to ignore them.

16 We were often shifted around, another strategy to keep us quiet. This gave me ample opportunity to get to know everyone, listen to their life stories and absorb the gossip.

17 Pretty Rosa described her romances and her impending wedding to a handsome field worker. Bertha, a heavy-set, dark-skinned woman, told me that Rosa's marriage would cause nothing but headaches because the man was younger and too handsome. Maria, large, moon-faced and placid, described the births of each of her nine children, warning me about the horrors of childbirth. Pragmatic Minnie, a tiny woman who always wore printed cotton dresses, scoffed at Maria's stupidity, telling me she wouldn't have so many kids if she had ignored that good-for-nothing priest and gotten her tubes tied!

18 In unexpected moments, they could turn melancholic: recounting the babies who died because their mothers couldn't afford medical care; the alcoholic, abusive husbands who were their "cross to bear"; the racism they experienced in Texas, where they were branded "dirty Mexicans" or "Mexican dogs" and not allowed in certain restaurants.

19 They spoke with the detached fatalism of people with limited choices and alternatives. Their lives were as raw and brutal as ghetto streets—something they accepted with an odd grace and resignation.

20 I was appalled and deeply affected by these confidences. The injustices they endured enraged me; their personal struggles overwhelmed me. I knew I could do little but sympathize.

21 My mother, no stranger to suffering, suggested I was too impressionable when I emotionally told her the women's stories. "That's nothing," she'd say lightly. "If they were in Mexico, life would be even harder. At least there's opportunities here, you can work."

22 My icy arrogance quickly thawed, that first summer, as my respect for the conveyor-belt ladies grew.

23 I worked in the packing sheds for several summers. The last season also turned out to be the last time I lived at home. It was the end of a chapter in my life, but I

didn't know it then. I had just finished junior college and was transferring to the university. I was already over-educated for seasonal work, but if you counted the overtime, no other jobs came close to paying so well, so I went back one last time.

24 The ladies treated me with warmth and respect. I was a college student, deserving of special treatment.

25 Aguedia, the crew chief, moved me to softer and better-paying jobs within the plant. I went from the conveyor belt to shoving boxes down a chute and finally to weighing boxes of tomatoes on a scale—the highest-paying position for a woman.

26 When the union's dues collector showed up, the women hid me in the bathroom. They had decided it was unfair for me to have to join the union and pay dues, since I worked only during the summer.

27 "Where's the student?" the union rep would ask, opening the door to a barrage of complaints about the union's unfairness.

28 Maria (of the nine children) tried to feed me all summer, bringing extra tortillas, which were delicious. I accepted them guiltily, always wondering if I was taking food away from her children. Others would bring rental contracts or other documents for me to explain and translate.

29 The last day of work was splendidly beautiful, warm and sunny. If this had been a movie, these last scenes would have been shot in soft focus, with a crescendo of music in the background.

30 But real life is anti-climactic. As it was, nothing unusual happened. The conveyor belt's loud humming was turned off, silenced for the season. The women sighed as they removed their aprons. Some of them just walked off, calling "*Hasta la próxima!*" Until next time!

31 But most of the conveyor-belt ladies shook my hand, gave me a blessing or a big hug.

32 "Make us proud!" they said.

33 I hope I have.

Checking Your Comprehension

1. Who were the "conveyor-belt ladies?" What did you discover about their lives?

2. Describe the primary job of the conveyor belt ladies.

3. Why did the author choose to work at the packing shed?

4. Why was the author initially unhappy about working at the packing shed?

_____

5. Why did the ladies hide the author when the union's dues collector arrived?

_____

Reading and Critical Thinking

1. Since the author is of Mexican-American descent, why did she initially feel superior to her Mexican-American co-workers?

_____

2. In what ways did the author's attitude change toward her co-workers?

_____

3. Why did the author's attitude change toward her co-workers?

_____

4. Describe the conveyor-belt ladies' attitude toward education.

_____

5. Explain why the author's last day was anti-climactic.

_____

Vocabulary Review

DIRECTIONS: *Match the term in Column A with its correct meaning in Column B.*

Column A

_____ 1. gregarious
_____ 2. dyspeptic
_____ 3. stigmatize
_____ 4. sorority
_____ 5. pragmatic
_____ 6. tedious
_____ 7. melancholic

Column B

a. label
b. unable to change
c. practical
d. sociable
e. grouchy
f. hard physical work
g. gloomy

_____	8. irrevocably	h.	belief that life is controlled by fate
_____	9. strenuous	i.	tiresome
_____	10. fatalism	j.	steady increase in volume
_____	11. anti-climactic	k.	group of women
_____	12. crescendo	l.	commonplace event

Words in Context

DIRECTIONS: *Locate each word in the paragraph indicated and reread that paragraph. Then, based on the way the word is used, write a synonym or brief definition for each.*

1. uninspiring (par. 2) _____

2. grueling (par. 4) _____

3. impending (par.17) _____

4. scoffed (par. 17) _____

5. recounting (par. 18) _____

Writing Exercises

1. Write a paragraph describing a situation or event that changed your attitude toward a person or group.

2. The author compares her job to performing in a play. Write a paragraph comparing a job you hold or have held to a play or some other event to which it is similar.

A Guard's First Night on the Job

WILLIAM RECKTENWALD

A prison is a separate society with its own set of rules and behaviors. This selection describes one evening in a prison from the viewpoint of a new guard.

Vocabulary Preview

rookie (par. 1)	beginner or novice
cursory (par. 4)	hastily done with little attention to detail
tiers (par. 5)	groups of cells, rooms, or items arranged above or behind each other
apprehensive (par. 16)	worried, anxious, or concerned
ruckus (par. 17)	noisy confusion or disturbance
mace (par. 22)	chemical with the combined effect of tear gas and nerve gas used to stun its victims
equivalent (par. 25)	equal to

Prereading

DIRECTIONS: *Preview the selection and answer the following questions.*

What fears and feelings would you have if you were just hired as a prison guard? What problems would you expect to face?

_____

_____

1   . . . When I arrived for my first shift, 3 to 11 P.M., I had not had a minute of training except for a one-hour orientation lecture the previous day. I was a "fish," a rookie guard, and very much out of my depth.

2   A veteran officer welcomed the "fish" and told us: "Remember, these guys don't have anything to do all day, 24 hours a day, but think of ways to make you mad. No matter what happens, don't lose your cool. Don't lose your cool!"

3   I had been assigned to the segregation unit, containing 215 inmates who are the most trouble. It was an assignment nobody wanted.

4   To get there, I passed through seven sets of bars. My uniform was my only ticket through each of them. Even on my first day, I was not asked for any identification, searched, or sent through a metal detector. I could have been carrying weapons, drugs, or any other contraband. I couldn't believe this was what's meant by a maximum-security institution. In the week I worked at Pontiac, I was subjected to only one check, and that one was cursory.

5   The segregation unit consists of five tiers, or galleries. Each is about 300 feet long and has 44 cells. The walkways are about 3 1/2 feet wide, with the cells on one side and a rail and cyclone fencing on the other. As I walked along one gallery, I noticed that my elbows could touch cell bars and fencing at the same time. That made me easy pickings for anybody reaching out of a cell.

6   The first thing (they) told me was that a guard must never go out on a gallery by himself. You've got no weapons with which to defend yourself, not even a radio to summon help. All you've got is the man with whom you're working.

7   My partner that first night was Bill Hill, a soft-spoken six-year veteran who immediately told me to take the cigarettes out of my shirt pocket because the inmates would steal them. Same for my pen, he said—or "They'll grab it and stab you."

8   We were told to serve dinner on the third tier, and Hill quickly tried to fill me in on the facts of prison life. That's when I learned about cookies and the importance they have to the inmates.

9   "They're going to try and grab them, they're going to try to steal them any way they can," he said. "Remember, you only have enough cookies for the gallery, and if you let them get away, you'll have to explain to the guys at the end why there weren't any for them."

10   Hill then checked out the meal, groaning when he saw the drippy ravioli and stewed tomatoes. "We're going to be wearing this," he remarked, before deciding to simply discard the tomatoes. We served nothing to drink. In my first six days at Pontiac, I never saw an inmate served a beverage.

11   Hill instructed me to put on plastic gloves before we served the meal. In view of the trash and waste through which we'd be wheeling the food cart, I thought he was joking. He wasn't.

12   "Some inmates don't like white hands touching their food," he explained.

13 Everything went routinely as we served the first 20 cells, and I wasn't surprised when every inmate asked for extra cookies.

14 Suddenly, a huge arm shot through the bars of one cell and began swinging a metal rod at Hill. As he ducked away, the inmate snared the cookie box.

15 From the other side of the cart, I lunged to grab the cookies—and was grabbed in turn. A powerful hand from the cell behind me was pulling my arm. As I jerked away, objects began crashing about, and a metal can struck me in the back.

16 Until that moment I had been apprehensive. Now I was scared. The food cart virtually trapped me, blocking my retreat.

17 Whirling around, I noticed that mirrors were being held out of every cell so the inmates could watch the ruckus. I didn't realize the mirrors were plastic and became terrified that the inmates would start smashing them to cut me up.

18 The ordinary din of the cell house had turned into a deafening roar. For the length of the tier, arms stretched into the walkway, making grabbing motions. Some of the inmates swung brooms about.

19 "Let's get out of here—now!" Hill barked. Wheeling the food cart between us, we made a hasty retreat.

20 Downstairs, we reported what had happened. My heart was thumping, my legs felt weak. Inside the plastic gloves, my hands were soaked with sweat. Yet the attack on us wasn't considered unusual by the other guards, especially in segregation. That was strictly routine, and we didn't even file a report.

21 What was more shocking was to be sent immediately back to the same tier to pass out medication. But as I passed the cells from which we'd been attacked, the men in them simply requested their medicine. It was as if what had happened minutes before was already ancient history. From another cell, however, an inmate began raging at us. "Get my medication," he said. "Get it now, or I'm going to kill you." I was learning that whatever you're handing out, everybody wants it, and those who don't get it frequently respond by threatening to kill or maim you. Another fact of prison life.

22 Passing cell No. 632, I saw that a prisoner I had helped take to the hospital before dinner was back in his cell. When we took him out, he had been disabled by mace and was very wobbly. Hill and I had been extremely gentle, handcuffing him carefully, then practically carrying him down the stairs. As we went by his cell this time, he tossed a cup of liquid on us.

23 Back downstairs, I learned I would be going back to that tier for a third time, to finish serving dinner. This time, we planned to slip in the other side of the tier so we wouldn't have to pass the trouble cells. The plates were already prepared.

24 "Just get in there and give them their food and get out," Hill said. I could see he was nervous, which made me even more so. "Don't stop for anything. If you get hit, just back off, 'cause if they snare you or hook you some way and get you against the bars, they'll hurt you real bad."

Everything went smoothly. Inmates in the three most troublesome cells were not getting dinner, so they hurled some garbage at us. But that's something else I had learned: Getting no worse than garbage thrown at you is the prison equivalent of everything going smoothly.

Checking Your Comprehension

1. This selection describes the events that occurred during the guard's first night on the job. How is this selection organized?

   _____

   _____

2. What main point does the guard make? (Main idea: see Chapter 7)

   _____

   _____

3. Why did the guards wear gloves to serve the food?

   _____

   _____

4. Explain the prisoners' use of mirrors.

   _____

   _____

5. Does the selection end with a summary or a conclusion? (Summaries and conclusions: see Chapter 14)

   _____

   _____

6. Write a summary of the guard's experiences. (Summaries: see Chapter 14)

   _____

   _____

   _____

_____

_____

_____

Critical Reading and Thinking

1. Using evidence from the selection, show why the guard did not feel prepared to begin his first shift.

   _____

   _____

   _____

2. Do you think the new guard disagreed with how some things are done in a prison? If so, list the things with which the guard seemed dissatisfied.

   _____

   _____

3. Explain the figurative expression "I was a 'fish,' a rookie guard, and very much out of my depth." (Figurative language: see Chapter 12)

   _____

   _____

4. What did you learn from this selection about life as a prisoner?

   _____

   _____

5. Why do you think the prisoner in Cell 632, whom the guards had treated gently on the way to the hospital, threw a cup of liquid at them later in the same evening?

   _____

   _____

6. Why are cookies so important to the prisoners? What might they represent?

_____

_____

7. This selection was reprinted in a textbook titled *Introduction to Criminology*. Why do you think the author of the textbook included this selection?

_____

_____

_____

8. Decide whether this selection is a narrative or a descriptive essay. Defend your choice by referring to parts of the selection. (Types of essays: see Chapter 14)

_____

_____

9. Based on his limited experience of one evening, the guard formed some generalizations about the prisoners and prison life. Underline several of these generalizations. (Generalizations: see Chapter 13)

_____

_____

Words in Context

DIRECTIONS: *Locate each word in the paragraph indicated and reread that paragraph. Then, based on the way the word is used, write a synonym or brief definition for each.*

1. contraband (par. 4) _____

2. din (par. 18) _____

3. maim (par. 21) _____

_____

Vocabulary Review

DIRECTIONS: *Use the words listed in the Vocabulary Preview to complete each of the following sentences.*

1. A beginner on a professional hockey team is called a _____.

2. An instructor who spent little time reading essay exams could be said to have read them in a _____ manner.

3. One kilometer is _____ to .62 miles.

4. The students were _____ about their final grades in chemistry.

5. The class of kindergarten children visiting the zoo created a _____.

6. The police officer used _____ to stop the man who was attacking her.

7. The lobby of the new hotel had several _____.

Writing Exercises

1. This selection was written from the perspective of the guard describing how he felt his first night on the job. Write a paragraph that describes the guard from the perspective of one of the prisoners. (What do you think he looked like? How did he act? Was he nervous or frightened?)

2. Write a paragraph describing an experience for which you felt unprepared and how you handled it.

3. Write a paragraph explaining what you think is right or wrong with prisons today.

Angry Fathers

MELL LAZARUS

Can you recall a time in your childhood when you misbehaved so badly that you worried about the punishment you would receive for your misbehavior? In this article you will read about the outcome of a similar ordeal of three nine-year olds.

Vocabulary Preview

anonymous (par. 4)	nameless; unknown
tweak (par. 7)	tiny bit
grimly (par. 9)	seriously; solemnly
indignant (par. 9)	angry and offended
inconspicuous (par. 10)	almost hidden; not standing out
approbation (par. 11)	approval
abstractions (par. 14)	only ideas; not the real thing
reproach (par. 23)	criticism; show of disapproval
conspiracy (par. 25)	agreement or united action to do wrong
spectacle (par. 25)	show

Prereading

DIRECTIONS: *Preview the selection and answer the following questions.*

1. Do you believe in physical punishment?

_____

_____

_____

2. Do you think this story will have a happy ending?

_____

_____

_____

1   "Daddy's going to be very angry about this," my mother said.

2   It was August 1938, at a Catskill Mountains boarding house. One hot Friday afternoon three of us—9-year-old city boys—got to feeling listless. We'd done all the summer-country stuff, caught all the frogs, picked the blueberries and shivered in enough icy river water. What we needed, on this unbearably boring afternoon, was some action.

3   To consider the options, Artie, Eli and I holed up in the cool of the "casino," the little building in which the guests enjoyed their nightly bingo games and the occasional traveling magic act.

4   Gradually, inspiration came: the casino was too new, the wood frame and white Sheetrock walls too perfect. We would do it some quiet damage. Leave our anonymous mark on the place, for all time. With, of course, no thought as to consequences.

5   We began by picking up a long, wooden bench, running with it like a battering ram, and bashing it into a wall. It left a wonderful hole. But small. So we did it again. And again. . . .

6   Afterward the three of us, breathing hard, sweating the sweat of heroes, surveyed our first really big-time damage. The process had been so satisfying we'd gotten carried away; there was hardly a good square foot of Sheetrock left.

7   Suddenly, before even a tweak of remorse set in, the owner, Mr. Biolos, appeared in the doorway of the building. Furious. And craving justice: When they arrived from the city that night, he-would-tell-our-fathers!

8   Meantime, he told our mothers. My mother felt that what I had done was so monstrous she would leave my punishment to my father. "And," she said, "Daddy's going to be very angry about this."

9   By 6 o'clock Mr. Biolos was stationed out at the driveway, grimly waiting for the fathers to start showing up. Behind him, the front porch was jammed, like a sold-out bleacher section, with indignant guests. They'd seen the damage to their bingo palace, knew they'd have to endure it in that condition for the rest of the summer. They, too, craved justice.

10   As to Artie, Eli and me, we each found an inconspicuous spot on the porch, a careful distance from the other two but not too far from our respective mothers. And waited.

11   Artie's father arrived first. When Mr. Biolos told him the news and showed him the blighted casino, he carefully took off his belt and—with practiced style—viciously whipped his screaming son. With the approbation, by the way, of an ugly crowd of once-gentle people.

12   Eli's father showed up next. He was told and shown and went raving mad, knocking his son off his feet with a slam to the head. As Eli lay crying on the grass, he kicked him on the legs, buttocks and back. When Eli tried to get up he kicked him again.

13   The crowd muttered: Listen, they should have thought of this before they did the damage. They'll live, don't worry, and I bet they never do that again.

14   I wondered: What will my father do? He'd never laid a hand on me in my life. I knew about other kids, had seen bruises on certain schoolmates and even heard screams in the evenings from certain houses on my street, but they were those kids, their families, and the why and how of their bruises were, to me, dark abstractions. Until now.

15   I looked over at my mother. She was upset. Earlier she'd made it clear to me that I had done some special kind of crime. Did it mean that beatings were now, suddenly, the new order of the day?

16   My own father suddenly pulled up in our Chevy, just in time to see Eli's father dragging Eli up the porch steps and into the building. He got out of the car believing, I was sure, that whatever it was all about, Eli must have deserved it. I went dizzy with fear.

17   Mr. Biolos, on a roll, started talking. My father listened, his shirt soaked with perspiration, a damp handkerchief draped around his neck; he never did well in humid weather. I watched him follow Mr. Biolos into the casino. My dad—strong and principled, hot and bothered—what was he thinking about all this?

18   When they emerged, my father looked over at my mother. He mouthed a small "Hello." Then his eyes found me and stared for a long moment, without expression. I tried to read his eyes, but they left me and went to the crowd, from face to expectant face.

19   Then, amazingly, he got into his car and drove away! Nobody, not even my mother, could imagine where he was going.

20   An hour later he came back. Tied onto the top of his car was a stack of huge Sheetrock boards. He got out holding a paper sack with a hammer sticking out of it. Without a word he untied the Sheetrock and one by one carried the boards into the casino.

21   And didn't come out again that night.

22   All through my mother's and my silent dinner and for the rest of that Friday evening and long after we had gone to bed, I could hear—everyone could hear—

the steady bang bang bang bang of my dad's hammer. I pictured him sweating, missing his dinner, missing my mother, getting madder and madder at me. Would tomorrow be the last day of my life? It was 3 A.M. before I finally fell asleep.

23   The next morning, my father didn't say a single word about the night before. Nor did he show any trace of anger or reproach of any kind. We had a regular day, he, my mother and I, and, in fact, our usual sweet family weekend.

24   Was he mad at me? You bet he was. But in a time when many of his generation saw corporal punishment of their children as a God-given right, he knew "spanking" as beating, and beating as criminal. And that when kids were beaten, they always remembered the pain but often forgot the reason.

25   And I also realized years later that, to him, humiliating me was just as unthinkable. Unlike the fathers of my buddies, he couldn't play into a conspiracy of revenge and spectacle.

26   But my father had made his point. I never forgot that my vandalism on that August afternoon was outrageous.

27   And I'll never forget that it was also the day I first understood how deeply I could trust him.

Checking Your Comprehension

1. What did the boys do to vandalize the casino?

   _____

   _____

2. How did each boy's father react to this vandalism?

   _____

   _____

3. How did the crowd feel about the boys being publicly punished in the manner they were?

   _____

   _____

4. Why did the author's father not believe in corporal punishment?

   _____

5. How did the author feel when he and the rest of the guests could hear his father repairing the damage to the casino late at night?

_____

_____

6. Name two important things the author learned as a result of this experience.

_____

_____

Critical Reading and Thinking

1. At what point do you think the boys felt remorse for what they had done?

_____

_____

2. In your opinion, which father had the most appropriate response to his son? Justify your answer.

_____

_____

3. How could the author tell that his father was angry?

_____

_____

4. Why did the author's father respond to his anger differently than the other fathers?

_____

_____

5. Do you think Artie's and Eli's fathers were wrong to use physical punishment on their sons? Explain why or why not.

_____

_____

Words in Context

DIRECTIONS: *Locate each word in the paragraph indicated. Then, based on the way the word is used, write a synonym or brief definition of each.*

1. listless (par. 1) _____

2. holed up (par. 2) _____

3. monstrous (par. 7)_____

4. blighted (par. 10) _____

5. emerged (par. 17) _____

6. corporal (par. 23) _____

Vocabulary Review

DIRECTIONS: *Complete each of the following sentences by choosing one of the words presented in the Vocabulary Preview.*

1. These are real, everyday problems, not just _____.

2. She was _____ that her guests asked if they could help her clean the house.

3. He was glad to receive the _____ of his parents on his choice of a college.

4. Since he blended in with the crowd in the large lecture hall, he felt _____.

5. She thought there was a _____ among her neighbors to keep her awake at night.

6. She felt just a _____ of pain when the nurse gave her the injection.

7. The needy family received a gift from an _____ donor.

8. They stared _____ at the passing funeral.

9. The instructor did not _____ the students for failing the test.

10. The crying child made a _____ of himself in the mall.

Writing Exercises

1. Write a paragraph describing how you would have handled the situation if you were the parent and your child committed an act of vandalism.

2. Write a paragraph describing an incident you witnessed in which a parent could have humiliated a child, but chose not to.

Freedom From the Past

PATRICE GAINES

This article by a well-known journalist describes why she wrote an article, that revealed her past.

Vocabulary Preview

bout (par. 1)	experience; battle
slayed (par. 3)	killed
aspirations (par. 3)	goals
crafting (par. 4)	carefully making
ponder (par. 4)	think about
intimate (par. 4)	personal
treacherous (par. 7)	dangerous
redemption (par. 7)	pardon; release

Prereading

DIRECTIONS: *Preview the selection and answer the following questions.*

1. What do you think the article Gaines wrote was about?

   _____

   _____

   _____

   _____

   _____

2. Do you think she is pleased to have written it?

_____

_____

_____

1   *I* finally wrote an article that I had held inside me for years, a piece laying out in black and white some of my pseudo-secret background—hinting at my bout with heroin. I wanted to show my struggle to learn to love all of me: my crooked buck teeth; my ugly right thumb I caught in a mimeograph machine when I was high on marijuana; my self who loved so easy and so hard; the me whom I kicked and scolded and never loved half as much as I loved men barely worth a hello.

2   It was an article I had suggested writing at least five years earlier, but then an editor had told me it would be career suicide. He was probably right. But the *Post* had since hired another reporter with a background similar to mine. Nathan Mc-Call, I discovered, had been to jail and initially had not been hired by the *Post* because he had told them about his background. In talking to Nathan, I realized that between the year when the *Post* refused to hire him and the time he came to work there, the *Post* had found out about my police record and dealt with what to do with me. Could management's experience with me have helped Nathan get hired? Would our experiences help others in the future? The thought pleased me, because I can never forget how difficult it is getting a job when you have a police record.

3   Then Nathan opened a door for me. He wrote an article about his life of crime—and I saw that he wasn't hated and dismissed because of it, as the editor had predicted I would be. At first I considered that Nathan's story was more acceptable than mine because it was somehow more acceptable, macho even, for a man to write about his past crimes than for a woman to discuss hers. But then I realized the truth was that the world was different back when the editor advised me not to write such an article. Back then, we lived in a world that slayed the political aspirations of presidential candidates who were unfaithful to their wives. Then, the world never would have tolerated a president who put marijuana to his lips, even if he didn't inhale it. It was surely not a world willing to accept the truth: that we are not perfect in the way that we think, that we have never been since we entered this world and will never be until we leave again.

4   The message of the article was so important to me that I worked intensely on every word, delicately crafting a lead that would draw people into it, spending hours forming the last sentence so people would ponder it for days after they put down the paper. I wrote and rewrote, mixed in slivers of interviews with the young girls who reminded me of myself, and I was careful not to break the mood when I

switched from my story to theirs and back again. I had concentrated so much on the process of writing that I forgot how intimate the article was.

5   That Sunday when it was published, I rushed to the store to buy a newspaper, to make sure the sentences were just as I remembered. I turned to the page, read the first line: "At the D.C. jail every Saturday, young black women line up for visits, many of them toting babies on their hips." It was a scene that reminded me of my life, the next line said. But before I reached that line, I burst into tears and could not stop crying. I screamed, "This is my life! This is my fucking life!"

6   I was so surprised at my reaction that I frightened myself. I was overwhelmed by sadness. I shook and sobbed. I picked up the phone to call one of my sisters, or my best friend from work, Cindy, or someone. But I couldn't stop crying, so I put it down. I put down the article, too, and I did not read it until weeks later.

7   Waiting for me at work were messages from book agents who saw ways in which my article could become a book. I called a friend who was an agent, someone who had already been encouraging me to write a book. Five months later I had a book contract, the first major indication that my new angels were working overtime. I had only hoped to use my words to encourage people to acknowledge their imperfections and, in doing so, look less harshly at others. That included others who still made mistakes, like the people I wrote about and interviewed daily. The addicts. Juvenile delinquents. Young single mothers with five children. And teenage girls who dated hoodlums, following them down a treacherous winding road of mistakes. Whenever I interviewed one of these girls, I saw myself in her face. But now I wanted people to know when they looked at those girls, they were looking at me. When they failed to have compassion for them, they spat in my face. It wasn't a book I wanted; it was redemption from the burden of carrying this story inside me. I wanted to open my chest, rip out the past, and free myself to fly. . . .

Checking Your Comprehension

1. Why had the author's editor advised her not to write the article about her experience with heroin and prison?

   _____

   _____

2. What made the author reconsider writing her article?

   _____

   _____

3. In what ways did the author hope her experience (and Nathan's) might help others?

_____

_____

4. What was the author's immediate response to seeing her life's story in writing?

_____

_____

5. What did the author aim to accomplish by writing her life story?

_____

_____

Critical Reading and Thinking

1. The author initially thought that a man could more acceptably write about his questionable past than a woman could write about hers. Do you think this is true? Why or why not?

_____

_____

2. The author states "It was surely not a world willing to accept the truth." What truth is Gaines referring to?

_____

_____

3. Why do you think the author was so surprised at her own reaction to seeing her story in print?

_____

_____

4. Gaines says the *Post* reacted when they found out she had a police record. What do you think the reaction was? What do you think an appropriate reaction would have been?

_____

_____

5. Discuss what the author means when she says "It wasn't a book I wanted; it was redemption from the burden of carrying this story inside me."

_____

_____

Words in Context

DIRECTIONS: *Locate each word in the paragraph indicated and reread the paragraph. Then, based on the way the word is used, write a synonym or brief definition for each.*

1. initially (par. 2) _____

2. tolerated (par. 3) _____

3. toting (par. 5) _____

Vocabulary Review

DIRECTIONS: *Replace each underlined word with the best word from the Vocabulary Preview.*

1. The priest prayed for the <u>pardon</u> of the criminal's sins. _____

2. I'll have to <u>think about</u> your offer before I give you an answer. _____

3. Don't reveal the <u>personal</u> details to that big-mouth. _____

4. After his <u>battle</u> with the flu, he was weak and fraile. _____

5. The knight <u>killed</u> the dragon and rescued the fair maiden. _____

6. Many people enjoy rafting through <u>dangerous</u> river rapids. _____

7. She has <u>goals</u> to someday become a news broadcaster. _____

8. <u>Carefully building</u> model automobiles can be a very rewarding hobby. _____

Writing Exercises

1. Did you ever hold a secret inside for a long time and then feel better after you have told someone? Describe such an incident.

2. If you were in a position to hire someone with a police record, would you? Write a paragraph explaining your decision.

3. Do you know someone whose life story is an inspiration to you? Describe that person and how he or she inspired you.

Lotteries and Lightning

A. K. DEWDNEY

Do you play lotteries? What do you think your chances are of hitting the jackpot? This article gives you the odds, and more.

Vocabulary Preview

probability (par. 1)	chance; odds
analogy (par. 3)	comparison; likeness
wag (par. 5)	joker; wit
randomly (par. 6)	in no particular order; by chance alone
abandon (par. 6)	freedom

Prereading

DIRECTIONS: *Preview the selection and answer the following questions.*

1. Do you know what the odds are of your being struck by lightning? Have you ever known anyone who was struck by lightning?

   _____

   _____

   _____

2. What does the title of this article suggest about winning lotteries?

   _____

1   Anyone who has trouble grasping a red-blooded probability of 0.5 wouldn't have a hope of coming to grips with a near-vanishing probability like 0.0000000715. The problem is double-barreled because number numbness also comes into play with such a small value.

2   Does anyone truly understand how little chance he or she has of winning big in a lottery? Private and state lottery corporations, which annually part North Americans from some $30 billion of their dollars, certainly hope not.

3   Attempts to explain the fantastically small probability of winning a lottery often meet with the objection, "But what if I'm the one?" It would be fair to respond, "Don't worry, you won't be." To make the point a little more forcefully, one could drag in the old lightning analogy. "Well, what if you get hit by lightning?" Most people would answer, "Fat chance!" But what if you *are* the one to win a lottery? The bait dangles before millions of people who never fail to buy their weekly ticket.

4   To demonstrate the odds more effectively, let's look at a popular form of lottery that allows the player to select six numbers between 1 and 49, inclusive. The price of a dollar or two seems like a good value if it means a real chance at winning several million dollars. Imagine being a mere six numbers away from a new life. Six little numbers! Alas, the dream is an empty one.

5   The real chance of winning a six-number lottery, if you buy one ticket, is 1 in 13,983,816. To express this as a probability, take out your calculator and divide 1 by 13,983,816. You will get something like 0.0000000715. This is an extremely small number. How small is it? Number numbness sets in. A mathematician might say that for all practical purposes it is zero. As one wag put it, "You have the same chance of winning whether you play or not."

6   In case you still don't think this number is hopeless, think about lightning. In the United States, lightning kills between 200 and 300 people a year. The population of the United States is roughly 250,000,000. To calculate the probability of a real event, you must divide the total number of actual cases (say, 250) by the total number of potential cases (250,000,000). With the abandon of professional license, a statistician might declare, "The probability of a randomly selected American being struck and killed by lightning this year is approximately 250 divided by 250,000,000 or 0.000001." One chance in 1 million means that you are a great deal more likely to be killed by lightning sometime in the next year than you are to win the next 6-49 lottery you play. That chance, after all, is about 1 in 14 million.

Checking Your Comprehension

1. Approximately how much do North Americans spend on the lottery each year?

_____

_____

2. According to the author, what are a person's actual chances of winning the lottery?

_____

_____

3. What does the author mean by the term "number numbness"?

_____

_____

4. How likely is it that a person will be killed by lightning?

_____

_____

Critical Reading and Thinking

1. Does the author think people understand their chances of winning the lottery? How can you tell?

_____

_____

2. What does the author mean when he quotes someone else as saying: "You have the same chance of winning whether you play or not"?

_____

_____

3. What is the author's point in comparing winning the lottery to getting struck by lightning?

_____

_____

4. What was the author's purpose in writing this article? Does he accomplish it? (Author's purpose: see Chapter 12)

_____

_____

Words in Context

DIRECTIONS: *Locate each word in the paragraph indicated and reread the paragraph. Then, based on the way the word is used, write a synonym or brief definition for each.*

1. grasping (par. 1) _____

2. demonstrate (par. 4) _____

3. calculate (par. 6) _____

4. potential (par. 6) _____

Vocabulary Review

DIRECTIONS: *Complete each of the following sentences by choosing one of the words presented in the Vocabulary Preview.*

1. Our contestants today will be chosen _____ from members of the studio audience.

2. The old saying "He's as stubborn as a mule" is an example of a(an) _____.

3. The children ran through the fields with complete _____.

4. I don't want to read another smart remark about my team from that _____ who writes sports editorials.

5. What is the _____ of the Dallas Cowboys winning the Super-bowl?

Writing Exercises

1. Write a paragraph describing what you would do if you won a million-dollar lottery.

2. Write a paragraph explaining why you think so many people continually play the lottery even though their chances of winning are minimal.

3. The New York State lottery advertises that "All you need to win is a dollar and a dream." How do you think this influences people to buy tickets? What do you think this leads people to believe? How do you feel about this ad? Explain your ideas in several paragraphs.

Playing "Get The Guest"

GINIA BELLAFANTE

Have TV talk shows gone too far? This article looks at how the surprises sprung on some guests have affected them.

Vocabulary Preview

deleted (par. 1)	removed; erased
segment (par. 1)	piece; section
callous (par. 3)	uncaring; hard-hearted
humiliated (par. 4)	offended; shamed
allegedly (par. 4)	supposedly
parameters (par. 6)	guidelines; outlines
quest (par. 7)	search
confrontation (par. 7)	showdown; argument

Prereading

DIRECTIONS: *Preview the selection and answer the following questions.*

1. What does the title of this article suggest about its content?

   _____

   _____

   _____

2. Do you think talk show hosts lure guests on their shows under false pretenses?

_____

_____

_____

1   *S*hauna Miller, a 28-year-old wife and mother from Livermore, California, was intrigued by the prospect of appearing on the *Richard Bey* show. The producers had told her she would be reunited with someone from her past. Suspecting it might be an older brother whom she had never met, Miller agreed. But when she was brought onstage, Miller found herself confronting someone else: her younger brother's fiancé, Billi Burkett, with whom she had been feuding. Burkett—egged on, she says, by producers, who kept telling her, "You need to get angry"—began shouting at Miller. Among other things, she accused Miller of neglecting Burkett's daughter, who attended a daycare center Miller used to run. (Producers have since deleted that accusation from the segment, which will be broadcast this week.) "I couldn't believe what was happening," says Miller. "Looking at Bey walking up and down, I kept thinking, How can you sleep at night?'"

2   Many viewers are probably wondering the same thing about talk-show hosts in the wake of a much publicized tragedy. Three days after appearing as a guest on the *Jenny Jones* show, Scott Amedure, 32, was shot to death in front of his trailer at a mobile-home park in Michigan. His alleged killer is John Schmitz, who had appeared on the same *Jones* segment. Schmitz was told he would be confronted by a "secret admirer"; the shock of discovering that the person who had a crush on him was a man, Schmitz told police later, had "eaten away" at him. The show's producers insist that Schmitz was informed his admirer could be a man or a woman. Jones, in a statement before a taping of her show last week, expressed sympathy for the man's family but denied that the man himself had been misled. "As much as we all regret what happened," she said, "the fact is that this tragedy is about the actions of one individual."

3   The event, however, has turned the spotlight on the lengths to which talk shows such as *Jones, Jerry Springer* and *Rikki Lake* will go to catch people off guard and encourage guest warfare. Reunite the callous beau with the pregnant welfare recipient he abandoned, and let the fun begin! Bring on the male stripper, and watch the prim housewife get red-faced! In raising the pitch, are producers deceiving guests to set them up for on-camera humiliation?

4   A growing number of disgruntled guests have been humiliated enough to bring lawsuits. Yvonne Porter of Santa Clara, California, recently won a $614,000

settlement from the producers of the *Montel Williams* show who she claims lured her on the program under false pretenses. Porter was invited believing she would be reunited with past loves. Instead Williams discussed on the air the abuse that Porter was allegedly suffering at the hands of her boyfriend. Then her sister appeared on the show to reveal that she was having an affair with Porter's boyfriend.

5   Even those who don't take legal action describe talk-show horror stories. Alan Klein, an independent publicist in New York City, got a call four years ago from a producer for *9 Broadcast Plaza*, a now defunct local show. The producer, says Klein, was looking for "people with distinguished careers who had a little secret." Klein recommended a respected set designer who was gay. When the man arrived on the show, he found himself in unexpected company. The other guests included a 400-lb. Madonna impersonator in drag and a body-pierced couple dressed in leather. "When I found the segment producer and complained," recounts Klein, "she said, 'Sorry, we had to make some last-minute changes.'" His client left before the taping. Many other guests, who don't arrive with savvy publicists, remain and take the consequences.

6   Producers of these shows insist that they do not deceive guests about what is going to occur. "Guests are always given the parameters of a surprise," says host Jerry Springer. David Sittenfeld, executive producer of the *Richard Bey* show, describes the typical dialogue with a prospective guest who is going to be surprised: "We'll say, 'We want to reunite you with someone.' If they ask, 'Who is it?' we tell them we can't say because it wouldn't be a surprise. If they ask, 'Is it good?' our response is, 'It might be good, and it might be bad. We can't tell you. That's for you to decide. We don't know how you'll react.'"

7   Some press analysts point out that producers cannot be held responsible for the later actions of people who appear—voluntarily, after all—on these shows. "We're all responsible for what we do," says former CBS correspondent Marvin Kalb. "It becomes too much of a cop-out for anyone to claim that it was a television talk show that was principally responsible for a dreadful action." The question, however, is whether in their increasingly desperate quest for confrontation, these shows are making such dreadful actions ever more likely.

Checking Your Comprehension

1. What happened to Shauna Miller when she was told she would be reunited with someone from her past?

   _____

   _____

2. What happened to Scott Amedure after he appeared on the *Jenny Jones* show?

_____

_____

3. What does Shauna Miller think of the way Richard Bey handled the situation with Billi Burkett?

_____

_____

4. Why did Yvonne Porter win a lawsuit against the Montel Williams show?

_____

_____

5. What is the response of show producers to the accusations that they lure people on their shows?

_____

_____

Critical Reading and Thinking

1. Why do you think the producers deleted the Burkett accusation from the Richard Bey show?

_____

_____

2. Why do people continue to be guests on shows like these?

_____

_____

3. Explain what Jerry Springer means when he says "Guests are always given the parameter of surprise." Do you think this is fair?

_____

_____

4. Do you think the Jenny Jones show is morally responsible for the death of Scott Amedure? Why or why not?

_____

_____

5. From the way the article concluded, what can you tell about the author's attitude toward the way talk shows recruit their guests?

_____

_____

Words in Context

DIRECTIONS: *Locate each word in the paragraph indicated and reread that paragraph. Then, based on the way the word is used, write a synonym or brief definition for each.*

1. beau (par. 3) _____

2. disgruntled (par. 4) _____

3. savvy (par. 5) _____

4. prospective (par. 6) _____

5. principally (par. 7) _____

Vocabulary Review

DIRECTIONS: *Replace each underlined word in the following sentences with a word presented in the Vocabulary Preview.*

1. The <u>hard-hearted</u> killer was sentenced to life in prison. _____

2. They finally had a <u>showdown</u> over the missing rent money. _____

3. The diner was <u>offended</u> by the behavior of her waiter. _____

4. Before I accept your offer, I would like to know more about the <u>guidelines</u> of the job. _____

5. The cake didn't turn out because one of the ingredients was mistakenly <u>removed</u> from the recipe. _____

6. Lancelot was on a <u>search</u> for the holy grail. _____

7. The suspect <u>supposedly</u> held up the liquor store at 3:00 A.M. Friday. _____

8. Maria conveniently left out one <u>section</u> of the story. _____

Writing Exercises

1. Write a paragraph on whether you believe talk shows are dishonest in the way they treat their guests.

2. Do guests on TV talk shows like those mentioned in the article deserve what they get? Support your viewpoint in at least one paragraph.

Stress Management: Personally Adjusting to Stress

RICHARD L. WEAVER II

Stress, or pressure, is common in our society. Read this article to find out how to cope with stress.

Vocabulary Preview

concurrently (par. 1)	happening at the same time
intensity (par. 2)	sharpness, strength
simultaneously (par. 6)	done at the same time
retrospect (par. 9)	looking at the past
relevant (par. 11)	attentive to important things occurring
overwhelmed (par. 11)	overcome with great emotion
subjective (par. 13)	changeable according to personal views, viewed differently by different people
unrequited (par. 13)	unreturned, not mutual

Prereading

DIRECTIONS: *Preview the article and then answer the following questions:*

1. What topics do you expect the article to cover?

2. What do you already know about stress—its causes, its effects, and its control?

_____

_____

_____

1   *Stress is a state of imbalance between demands made on us from outside sources and our capabilities to meet those demands.* Often, it precedes and occurs concurrently with conflict. Stress, as you have seen, can be brought on by physical events, other people's behavior, social situations, our own behavior, feelings, thoughts, or anything that results in heightened bodily awareness. In many cases, when you experience pain, anger, fear, or depression, these emotions are a response to a stressful situation like conflict.

2   Sometimes, in highly stressful conflict situations, we must cope with the stress before we cope with the conflict. Relieving some of the intensity of the immediate emotional response will allow us to become more logical and tolerant in resolving the conflict. In this brief section, some of the ways we have for controlling our physical reactions and our thoughts will be explained.

3   People respond differently to conflict just as they respond differently to stress. Some people handle both better than others do. Individual differences are not as important as learning how to manage the stress we feel. The goal in stress management is self-control, particularly in the face of stressful events.

4   Stress reactions involve two major elements: (1) heightened physical arousal as revealed in an increased heart rate, sweaty palms, rapid breathing, and muscular tension, and (2) anxious thoughts, such as thinking you are helpless or wanting to run away. Since your behavior and your emotions are controlled by the way you think, you must acquire skills to change those thoughts.

5   Controlling physical symptoms of stress requires relaxation. Sit in a comfortable position in a quiet place where there are no distractions. Close your eyes and pay no attention to the outside world. Concentrate only on your breathing. Slowly inhale and exhale. Now, with each exhaled breath say "relax" gently and passively. Make it a relaxing experience. If you use this method to help you in conflict situations over a period of time, the word "relax" will become associated with a sense of physical calm; saying it in a stressful situation will help induce a sense of peace.

6   Another way to induce relaxation is through tension release. The theory here is that if you tense a set of muscles and then relax them, they will be more relaxed

than before you tensed them. Practice each muscle group separately. The ultimate goal, however, is to relax all muscle groups simultaneously to achieve total body relaxation. For each muscle group, in turn, tense the muscles and hold them tense for five seconds, then relax them. Repeat this tension-release sequence three times for each group of muscles. Next, tense all muscles together for five seconds, then release them. Now, take a low, deep breath and say "relax" softly and gently to yourself as you breathe out. Repeat this whole sequence three times.

7   You do not need to wait for special times to practice relaxing. If, during the course of your daily activities, you notice a tense muscle group, you can help relax this group by saying "relax" inwardly. Monitor your bodily tension. In some cases you can prepare yourself for stressful situations through relaxation *before* they occur. Practice will help you call up the relaxation response whenever needed.

8   For other ways to relax, do not overlook regular exercise. Aerobic or yoga-type exercise can be helpful. Personal fitness programs can be tied to these inner messages to "relax" for a complete relaxation response.

9   Controlling your thoughts is the second major element in stress management. Managing stress successfully requires flexibility in thinking. That is, you must consider alternative views. Your current view is causing the stress! You must also keep from attaching exaggerated importance to events. Everything seems life-threatening in a moment of panic; things dim in importance when viewed in retrospect.

10   Try to view conflict from a problem-solving approach: "Now, here is a new problem. How am I going to solve this one?" Too often, we become stressed because we take things personally. When an adverse event occurs we see it as a personal affront or as a threat to our ego. For example, when Christy told Paul she could not go to the concert with him, he felt she was letting him know she disliked him. This was a blow to Paul because he had never been turned down—rejected—before. Rather than dwell on that, however, he called Heather, she accepted his invitation, and he achieved his desired outcome—a date for the concert.

11   One effective strategy for stress management consists of talking to ourselves. We become our own manager, and we guide our thoughts, feelings, and behavior in order to cope. Phillip Le Gras suggests that we view the stress experience as a series of phases. Here, he presents the phases and some examples of coping statements:

1. *Preparing for a stressor.* [Stressors are events that result in behavioral outcomes called stress reactions.] What do I have to do? I can develop a plan to handle it. I have to think about this and not panic. Don't be negative. Think logically. Be rational. Don't worry. Maybe the tension I'm feeling is just eagerness to confront the situation.

2. *Confronting and handling a stressor.* I can do it. Stay relevant. I can psych myself up to handle this, I can meet the challenge. This tension is a cue to use my stress-management skills. Relax. I'm in control. Take a low breath.

3. *Coping with the feeling of being overwhelmed.* I must concentrate on what I have to do right now. I can't eliminate my fear completely, but I can try to keep it under control. When the fear is overwhelming, I'll just pause for a minute.

4. *Reinforcing self-statements.* Well done. I did it! It worked. I wasn't successful this time, but I'm getting better. It almost worked. Next time I can do it. When I control my thoughts I control my fear.

12   The purpose of such coping behavior is to become aware of and monitor our anxiety. In this way, we can help eliminate such self-defeating, negative statements as "I'm going to fail," or "I can't do this." Statements such as these are cues that we need to substitute positive, coping self-statements.

13   If the self-statements do not work, or if the stress reaction is exceptionally intense, then we may need to employ other techniques. Sometimes we can distract ourselves by focusing on something outside the stressful experience—a pleasant memory, a sexual fantasy—or by doing mental arithmetic. Another technique is imaging. By manipulating mental images we can reinterpret, ignore, or change the context of the experience. For example, we can put the experience of unrequited love into a soap-opera fantasy or the experience of pain into a medieval torture by the rack. The point here is that love and pain are strongly subjective and personal, and when they are causing us severe stress we can reconstruct the situation mentally to ease the stress. In both these cases the technique of imaging helps to make our response more objective—to take it *outside* ourselves. The more alternatives we have to aid us in stress reduction, the more likely we are to deal with it effectively.

Checking Your Comprehension

DIRECTIONS: *Mark each statement True or False.*

_____ 1. The tension-release method for stress management does not bring about relaxation.

_____ 2. Relaxation should only be practiced when you feel a lot of stress.

_____ 3. Exercise is an important way to relax.

_____ 4. Talking to yourself about your problems increases stress and makes it difficult to relax.

_____ 5. It is not acceptable to control fears; one must eliminate them.

_____ 6. Imaging is a means of redirecting one's attention and making one's response more objective.

_____ 7. Stress reactions include sweaty palms, rapid breathing, and wanting to run away.

_____ 8. Sometimes it is possible to prepare yourself for a stressful situation ahead of time.

_____ 9. Physical symptoms of stress cannot be controlled or reduced.

_____ 10. Fantasies usually reinforce stressful experiences.

Critical Reading and Thinking

1. Using the definition of stress given in paragraph 1, make a list of several stressful situations you have experienced. Next, from among the management techniques described, identify which might be most useful in reducing stress.

_____

_____

2. Tests and exams are often stressful for college students. What types of reinforcing self-statements might help someone handle stress caused by exams?

_____

_____

3. A college student feels stressed and overwhelmed by numerous class assignments, tests, and papers. How might he cope with this feeling? Make specific suggestions.

_____

_____

4. A student has just enrolled in a required speech communication class in which five brief speeches are required. The student is experiencing an intense stress reaction. Her instructor has recommended that she try the imaging technique. How should she use it and what should she do?

_____

_____

Words in Context

DIRECTIONS: *Locate each word in the paragraph indicated and reread that paragraph. Then, based on the way the word is used, write a synonym or brief definition for each.*

1. induce (par. 6) _____

2. flexibility (par. 9) _____

3. stressors (par. 11) _____

4. phases (par. 11) _____

5. imaging (par. 13) _____

Vocabulary Review

DIRECTIONS: *Use the words listed in the Vocabulary Preview to complete each of the following sentences.*

1. Owing to its popularity, the same movie was being shown _____ at two theatres in the movie complex.

2. When he proposed to her, she was _____ and began to cry.

3. After the patient described the _____ of the pain, the doctor decided to operate.

4. Because Ellen failed her psychology exam, she came to realize that _____ studying and watching television was not the way to succeed in college.

5. The love and respect the son showed for his father was _____.

6. In _____, Vanessa realized that putting the fragile wine glasses in the dishwasher was a mistake.

7. The student's comment about the professor's age did not seem _____.

8. Grading an essay exam is _____; two professors may give the same paper slightly different grades.

Writing Exercise

Write a paragraph describing a stressful situation that you experienced. Explain your reactions and how you managed them.

A Day on Wheels

CHERYL A. DAVIS

What should or shouldn't you say to a person who is disabled? This article describes some examples of rude behavior and the author's reactions to them.

Vocabulary Preview

meditation (par. 4)	deep thought
gratuitous (par. 5)	uncalled for
persistent (par. 5)	unrelenting
unsolicited overture (par. 7)	unasked-for response
apropos (par. 12)	relevant
comme il faut (par. 16)	as it should be, appropriate
dubious (par. 17)	doubtful
mediating (par. 25)	settling, conciliating
mortified (par. 27)	shamed, humiliated
flagellated (par. 28)	punished
adroit (par. 28)	clever
paraplegic (par. 29)	without use of the legs
haughtier (par. 31)	more contemptful
civilities (par. 39)	niceties, pleasantries
schizophrenia (par. 41)	a mental illness
conciliatory (par. 45)	soothing, friendly

DIRECTIONS: *Preview the selection and answer the following questions.*

1. What kinds of questions do people ask disabled people?

_____

_____

_____

2. How would you react if you were disabled and were asked such questions?

_____

_____

1   "Man, if I was you, I'd shoot myself," said the man on the subway platform. No one else was standing near him. I realized he was talking to me.

2   "Luckily, you're not," I said, gliding gracefully away.

3   For me, this was not an unusual encounter; indeed, it was a typical episode in my continuing true-life sitcom, "Day on Wheels."

4   A train ride can be an occasion for silent meditation in the midst of mechanical commotion. Unfortunately, I rarely get to meditate.

5   I attract attention. I pretend to ignore them, the eyes that scrutinize me and then quickly glance away. I try to avoid the gratuitous chats with loosely wrapped passengers. Usually, I fail. They may be loosely wrapped, but they're a persistent lot.

6   I use a wheelchair; I am not "confined" to one. Actually, I get around well. I drive a van equipped with a wheelchair-lift to the train station. I use a powered wheelchair with high-amperage batteries to get to work. A manual chair, light enough to carry, enables me to visit the "walkies" who live upstairs and to ride in their Volkswagens.

7   My life has been rich and varied, but my fellow passengers assume that, as a disabled person, I must be horribly deprived and so lonely that I will appreciate any unsolicited overture.

8   "Do you work?" a woman on the train asked me recently.

9   I said I did.

10   "It's nice that you have something to keep you busy, isn't it?"

11   Since we are thought of as poor invalids in need of chatting up, people are not apt to think too hard about what they are saying to us. It seems odd, since they also worry about the "right" way to talk to disabled people.

12   "How do you take a bath?" another woman asked me, apropos of nothing.

13   One day, an elderly man was staring at me as I read the newspaper.

14   "Would you like to read the sports section?" I asked him.

15   "How many miles can that thing go before you need new batteries?" he responded.

16   When I was a little girl, I once saw a woman whose teeth looked strange. "Mommy, that lady has funny teeth," I said. My mother explained that it was not *comme il faut* to offer up personal observations about other people's appearances. I thought everyone's mommy taught that, but I was wrong.

17   For many years, I was in what some of us call "the phyz-diz-biz"—developing housing and educational programs for disabled people. I was active in the disability-rights movement. I went to "special" schools offering the dubious blessing of a segregated education. As a result, I have known several thousand disabled people, at one time or another, across the United States.

18   For those whose disablement is still recent, the gratuitous remarks and unsolicited contributions can be exceptionally hurtful. It takes time to learn how to protect yourself. To learn how to do it gracefully can take a lifetime.

19   Many of us take the position that the people who bother us are to be pitied for their ignorance. We take it upon ourselves to "educate" them. We forgive them their trespasses and answer their questions patiently and try to straighten them out.

20   Others prefer to ignore the rude remarks and questions altogether. I tried that, but it didn't work. There was one woman on the train who tipped the scales for me.

21   "You're much too pretty to be in a wheelchair," she said.

22   I stared straight ahead, utterly frozen in unanticipated rage.

23   Undaunted, she grabbed my left arm below the elbow to get my attention.

24   "I said, 'You're much too pretty to be in a wheelchair.'"

25   In my fury, I lost control. Between my brain and my mouth, the mediating force of acquired tact had vanished.

26   "What do you think?" I snapped. "That God holds a beauty contest and if you come in first, you don't have to be in one?"

27   She turned away and, a moment later, was chatting with an old woman beside her as if nothing had been said at all. But I was mortified, and I moved to the other end of the train car.

28   For that one lapse, I flagellated myself all afternoon. When I got home, I telephoned one of my more socially adroit disabled friends for advice.

29   Nick is a therapist, a Ph.D. from Stanford, and paraplegic. "How do you deal with the other bozos on the bus?" I asked him.

30   "I just say, 'Grow up,'" Nick answered.

31   That was a bit haughtier than I could pull off, I told him.

32	"Well, look," he said, "if those words don't do it, find something else. The main thing is to get them to stop bothering you, right?"
33	"Yes, but—"
34	"But what?"
35	"Nick, If I'm *too* rude, they won't learn a thing. They'll just tell themselves I'm maladjusted."
36	"Then tell them their behavior is inappropriate."
37	"Inappropriate. That's marvelous!" I decided to try it next time.
38	"Next time" arrived last week. I didn't see the man coming. I was on the train platform, and he approached me from behind and tapped me on the shoulder.
39	"What's your disability?" he asked, discarding civilities.
40	I turned and looked at him. "That is not an appropriate question to ask a stranger," I said quietly.
41	"Well, *I* have schizophrenia," he said proudly.
42	"I didn't ask you."
43	"I feel rejected," he said.
44	"Well, then don't say things like that to people you don't know."
45	The train came and we got on together. I offered him a conciliatory remark, and he quieted down. Clearly he was not the best person for my new approach, but I think I'm headed in the right direction.

Checking Your Comprehension

1. What kinds of assumptions do people make about disabled people?

2. What did the author's mother teach her?

3. How did the author feel after talking back to the people who asked her questions?

4. What happened when the author tried to ignore a rude remark?

_____

_____

5. What is the author's new approach to being asked rude questions? Has it worked so far?

_____

_____

Critical Reading and Thinking

1. What kind of generalizations does the author make about people who are not disabled? (Generalizations: see Chapter 13)

_____

_____

2. What is the author's purpose? (Author's purpose: see Chapter 12)

_____

_____

3. List five words the author uses that demonstrate her feelings about being asked inappropriate questions.

_____

_____

4. Why do you think people ask the kind of questions the author mentions?

_____

_____

5. Why does the author make a distinction between using a wheelchair and being confined to one (par. 6)? What are the connotations of these terms? (Connotations: see Chapter 12)

_____

_____

Words in Context

DIRECTIONS: *Locate each word in the paragraph indicated and reread that paragraph. Then, based on the way the word is used, write a synonym or brief definition for each.*

1. commotion (par. 4) _____

2. scrutinize (par. 5) _____

3. high-amperage (par. 6) _____

4. undaunted (par. 23) _____

Vocabulary Review

DIRECTIONS: *Complete each of the following sentences by choosing one of the words presented in the Vocabulary Preview.*

1. Apologies are very _____ since they smooth things over.

2. She was _____ when her wig blew off.

3. The child's _____ comments interrupted serious adult conversation.

4. Because the attorney was very _____, the firm decided to hire her.

5. _____ are often exchanged when people run into old friends.

6. The contestant on the game show looked _____ as he gave his answer, but to his surprise, he learned it was correct.

7. Since the conversation was about museums, the comment about houseplants was not _____.

8. The child kept asking her father for candy; because she was so _____, he finally gave her some.

Writing Exercise

Describe an instance in which someone asked you an annoying, rude or ignorant question about yourself and how you responded.

Looking out for Number 1, 2, 3

STEVEN LEWIS

If you weren't raised in a big family, you may wonder how all the children in one can be loved and cared for. In this article, Steven Lewis gives us a taste of what life is like in a large family.

Vocabulary Preview

accusatory (par. 1)	blaming
à la (par. 2)	in the style of; like
logistics (par. 5)	practical details
arrogant (par. 6)	self-centered and careless of others
finite (par. 7)	limited
oppressive (par. 8)	bossy; controlling
urchins (par. 8)	irritating children
fleeting (par. 12)	passing; momentary

Prereading

DIRECTIONS: *Preview the selection and answer the following questions.*

1. What kinds of questions do people ask parents of large families?

_____

_____

_____

2. How would you respond to these questions?

_____

_____

_____

1   A lot of people tilt their heads and ask in that slightly uncomfortable, slightly accusatory voice. "How can you keep track of so many kids?"

2   They smile teasingly and want to know if I always remember their names, their birth dates, their favorite foods, their homework assignments. (Yes.) Some wonder with a wry smile if we've ever forgotten one of them à la "Home Alone." (Well, sometimes.) Others even have the temerity to ask in a whisper if each of our children has been planned. (No.)

3   What they really want to know, however, is whether it's possible to love and care for seven children—or, more to the point, whether there's enough love to go around. "Doesn't it all get used up by the time you have two or three (or at most four) kids?" It's not a question, it's a challenge.

4   I usually smile and make a joke. I tell how I sometimes call one of the kids four or five names before I get to the right one—"Hey, Cael-Nancy-Addie-Clover-what's your name?-Danny, please pass the bread." Or (for the umpteenth time this year) I recount the night we left Clover at the Vermilyes' house and didn't realize it until I counted heads in the van about 5 or 10 miles down the road. Or the afternoon when my wife, Patti, forgot that Cael was waiting for a ride at school and she, Clover and Nancy went to the mall.

5   That's what most people want to hear. They certainly don't want a lengthy monologue about the logistics of managing children after they outnumber parents three or more to one. They want affirmation that they did the right thing by stopping at one or two or three.

6   They also want to confirm their suspicions about large families. As charming as the Waltons might have been—or the Bradfords from "Eight Is Enough"—or the Bradys—everyone knows that things are out of control in big families: we're sex-crazed, we're hiding from life behind our children, we're irresponsible, we're arrogant users of the world's resources and finally, the only thing that really matters, we can't possibly provide the love necessary for that many kids.

7   Yet the truth is that loving your big family is the easy part of having seven kids. In fact, there's nothing even remotely magical or metaphysical about it. It's not like there's a finite amount of parental love doled out to each individual at birth that later gets parceled out among the children—or that you have to somehow create precious love out of base metals so that there's enough to go around. Not at all. You simply love every one of your children with all your heart. That's it. Each one gets the same

amount of love: your whole heart. (Which is not to say that you like all of them all the time—or even some of the time—you just love them without question.)

8   Last summer, Cael (25) came home to the Hudson Valley from his home in North Carolina for a quick visit. The same son who couldn't wait to escape the pesty little urchins and his oppressive parents in 1987 to go a thousand miles away to college in Florida bought a cheap flight just to come here for a few days—to see 9-year-old Bay's Little League baseball game; to watch 6-year-old Elizabeth's tap recital; to "chaperone" Danny's 15th birthday party; to pass big brotherly judgment on 17-year-old Clover's boyfriend, Jeffrey; to play a round of golf with the old man; to hang out at the local clubs with Nancy (21) and Addie (20), who had just returned from college; to eat his mother's cooking; to lay back on the couch and watch the Knicks (while Bay and Elizabeth challenged his patience by continually walking in front of the tube.

9   To be where everyone loves him no matter what.

10   After the weekend, I admit I was beat. As Cael's visit reminded me, with each additional child the house fills up not just by one but exponentially. It seemed that kids were everywhere, on all three floors of this big house—my kids, someone else's kids, kids I didn't even recognize. There were kids on the porches, kids in the refrigerator, kids in the bathrooms, kids on the phone, kids in my wallet, kids in the woods, kids in our bed; teen-age boys sneaking a smoke outside the basement door, 6-year-old girls leaving the hose running all night, 17-year-old girls returning empty juice cartons to the refrigerator, grown boys consuming the air, the couch, the TV, the CD, the cold beer, even the floor space in the living room.

11   There was no escaping all of us. Which is just the point here. A big family is profoundly different from a small or even a regular family (which we experienced for a brief time between 1969 and 1974). In this house, it's never ever about you alone; it's about everyone. Child rearing is not a piece of a grander life scheme; it's not a passage or a phase; it's not even the best part of life. In our time on earth, there will be no neat divisions for Patti and me like the infant and toddler years, then the teen-age years, then the empty nest years, then the grandparenting years. For us, it is everything all at once. There is nothing else out there for us but this big family.

12   In fact, it is so all-consuming—so inescapable—for me that I have come to understand that all my dreams of fame (vast riches, glorious adventure, etc.) are nothing more than fleeting distractions from the daily task of fathering this extraordinary brood. In the diminishing light of my 49th year, I see clearly that everything comes and everything goes except this vast inescapable family.

13   In an imploding universe where one must increasingly learn to go it alone, where survival depends upon one's ability to look out solely for No. 1, our children look out for each other. They come home because in a big family someone is always waiting for you.

Checking Your Comprehension

1. What do people really want to know when they ask personal questions of parents with large families?

_____

_____

2. What does the author think is the easiest part of having seven children?

_____

_____

3. What is the major reason Cael came home to visit?

_____

_____

4. Why did there seem to be more children than they actually had when Cael came to visit?

_____

_____

5. According to the author, how is a big family different from a small or regular family?

_____

_____

Critical Reading and Thinking

1. What is the author's purpose in writing about large families?
   (Author's purpose: see Chapter 12)

_____

_____

2. What does the author mean when he says " . . . everything comes and everything goes except this vast inescapable family"?

_____

_____

3. Why do you think people are so curious about large families?

_____

_____

4. What does the author think is the most important part of a large family?

_____

_____

5. What does the author mean when he says each child gets "the same amount of love"? Do you think this is true? Why or why not?

_____

_____

Words in Context

DIRECTIONS: *Locate each word in the paragraph indicated. Then, based on the way the word is used, write a synonym or brief definition of each.*

1. temerity (par. 2) _____

2. affirmation (par. 5) _____

3. doled (par. 7) _____

4. exponentially (par. 10) _____

5. profoundly (par. 11) _____

Vocabulary Review

DIRECTIONS: *Replace each of the underlined words or phrases with a word or phrase presented in the Vocabulary Preview.*

1. What are the <u>practical details</u> of painting a Victorian house? _____

2. "So, why are you late for work?" the manager asked in a <u>blaming</u> tone.
   _____

3. He is a soldier/politician <u>in the style of</u> Dwight Eisenhower. _____

4. I had only a <u>passing</u> glance at the hit-and-run vehicle. _____

5. The <u>irritating children</u> wouldn't stop running up and down the aisles of the theater. _____

6. You have only a <u>limited</u> number of options available to you. _____

7. Marylou canceled her engagement with her <u>bossy</u> boyfriend. _____

8. Because the king was <u>self-centered and careless of others</u>, he was the first one executed after the revolution. _____

Writing Exercises

1. Write a paragraph explaining the major advantages of belonging to a large family.

2. Write a paragraph explaining why you would or would not like to have a large family of your own.

3. The author says that some people believe the parents of large families are "irresponsible, . . . arrogant users of the world's resources." Explain your reaction to this.

Who has the Right to Name?

RICHARD APPELBAUM AND WILLIAM CHAMBLISS

This article discusses the importance of the names used for various racial and ethnic groups and why agreement about them is so difficult.

Vocabulary Preview

imposed (par. 2)	forced
vexing (par. 3)	troubling; annoying
excessive (par. 4)	too much
resurgence (par. 4)	rebirth; becoming popular again
consensus (par. 5)	agreement
obscures (par. 5)	makes unclear
contested (par. 7)	argued about

Prereading

DIRECTIONS: *Preview the selection and answer the following questions.*

1. A number of racial and ethnic groups are discussed in this article. List several.

   _____

   _____

   _____

2. Why is the name for a particular racial or ethnic group important?

   _____

1   Before Europeans came to America, one of the largest Indian nations were the *Dineh,* which, translated into English, means "the People of the Earth." No one knows exactly when or how, but the Spaniards renamed them "Navajo," the name by which they have been known for centuries.

2   Joann Toralita is a *Dineh* (Navajo). At a tribal meeting she argued that "if we change to our rightful name, we will be using the name we have always called ourselves, not the name other people imposed on us. Perhaps it will be a new beginning for our children and our grandchildren." Others disagreed. One man countered, "we know who we are. We are all "the People of the Earth." It doesn't matter if you are Navajo or African American or Cheyenne" (cited in Pressley, 1993).

3   Deciding what to be called is a particularly vexing problem for minority groups. For example, is "American Indian" preferable to "Native Americans"? Two prominent organizations—the National Congress of American Indians and the American Indian Movement—use "American Indian" to describe themselves. Yet others object to the term since, like the word "Navajo," it was given to them by Europeans. For those who object to "American Indian," the alternative "Native American" is seen as capturing the fact that they alone among ethnic groups are truly native to this continent. Yet others argue that nothing short of using the correct name for each tribe (such as Sioux, Pawnee, or Cherokee) is acceptable. Most Indian groups continue to use "American Indian" and "Native American" interchangeably, a convention we will follow in this textbook (Smithsonian, 1994).

4   African Americans, Latinos, Asian Americans, and many other minority groups have experienced similar controversies. African Americans were referred to as "Negroes" for many years, a name many associated with excessive dependence on white individuals and organizations. During the period of resurgence of black identity in the 1960s and 1970s, "Afro-American" came to be the preferred term, since it proudly pointed to their African heritage. Today, "black" and "African-American" are used interchangably. When "black" became common, however, some African-American leaders opposed the term, partly because it emphasized skin color rather than ethnic origins (it also ignored significant variations in skin pigmentation; see Janken, 1993). Yet according to a recent national poll of approximately 1,500 black adults, 37 percent preferred to be called "black," 28 percent preferred "African American," while 24 percent claimed it made "no difference" (Roper, 1993b).

5   Latinos are still sometimes referred to as "Hispanics," but there seems to be growing consensus among them that the term "Latino" is preferable, since "Hispanic" suggests that Spain is the source of their cultural heritage, rather than a mixture of Spanish and native Indian cultures (Moore and Pinderhughos, 1993). Yet even the term "Latino" obscures important ethnic differences between Spanish-speaking peoples from different regions of Mexico, different Central American countries, and elsewhere in Latin America.

6   By the same token, the term "Asian American" is commonly used to characterize immigrants from Asia, but obviously enormous cultural, linguistic, and other ethnic differences exist between people from Japan, China, the Philippines, Indonesia, Vietnam, India, and dozens of other Asian countries that together comprise more than half of the world's population.

7   The name for a particular racial or ethnic group can be highly contested, since it carries with it a great deal of information about the group's social history. The effort by many groups to "name themselves" reflects their belief that passive acceptance of the name bestowed by society's dominant group is to accept being silenced.

Checking Your Comprehension

1. What does "Dineh" actually mean in English?

_____

_____

2. Why did Joann Toralita want to change the name Navajo back to Dineh?

_____

_____

3. Why do some people object to the term "American Indian"?

_____

_____

4. Why was "Afro-American" the preferred term in the 1960s?

_____

_____

5. According to the poll cited in the reading, what do most black people prefer to be called?

_____

_____

Critical Reading and Thinking

1. In a poll of 1500 black adults, almost one-fourth said it made "no difference" whether they were called "black" or "African American". Why do you think this term doesn't matter to that 24 percent?

_____

_____

2. Many Latinos are referred to as "Hispanics." Explain why the term "Latino" is preferable to this group.

_____

_____

3. What is a clear disadvantage of the term "Latino" as opposed to "Hispanic"?

_____

_____

4. Explain the problem with the term "Asian American."

_____

_____

5. How would you summarize the author's views about racial or ethnic groups choosing their own names?

_____

_____

Words in Context

DIRECTIONS: *Locate each word in the paragraph indicated. Then, based on the way the word is used, write a synonym or brief definition of each.*

1. alternative (par. 3) _____

2. controversies (par. 4) _____

3. bestowed (par. 7) _____

Vocabulary Review

DIRECTIONS: *Answer each of the following questions.*

1. Give an example of something that has been imposed upon you.

   _____

2. If someone walks in front of your seat at a sporting event and obscures your view of the game, what has that person done?

   _____

3. When a group comes to a consensus on an issue, what have they done?

   _____

4. If there was a resurgence of crime in your neighborhood, what would be happening?

   _____

5. What are excessive taxes?

   _____

6. Name a current issue that is highly contested.

   _____

7. Give an example of a problem you face that is vexing.

   _____

Writing Exercises

1. Think of a friend who belongs to a minority group. Write a paragraph discussing what he or she prefers to be called.

2. One man in the Navajo tribal meeting said "We are all 'the People of the Earth.' It doesn't matter if you are Navajo or African American or Cheyenne." What does this statement mean to you?

3. Shakespeare wrote: "What's in a name? That which we call a rose by any other name would smell as sweet." How do you think these lines relate to the article?

"Don't Ask"

DEBORAH TANNEN

Men and women differ in many ways, including how they communicate. You'll probably recognize some of the differences Tannen describes in this excerpt taken from her book, You Just Don't Understand.

Vocabulary Preview

asymmetries (par. 1)	lack of harmony and balance
status (par. 1)	position or rank; one's standing in relation to others
paradox (par. 4)	contradiction
metamessages (par. 4)	meanings that appear beneath the surface; hidden meanings
framed (par. 5)	placed within a context
hierarchical (par. 5)	arranged in a specified order
implicit (par. 6)	not directly stated

Prereading

What differences do you notice in the ways men and women communicate?

1   Talking about troubles is just one of many conversational tasks that women and men view differently, and that consequently cause trouble in talk between them. Another is asking for information. And this difference too is traceable to the asymmetries of status and connection.

2   A man and a woman were standing beside the information booth at the Washington Folk Life Festival, a sprawling complex of booths and displays. "You ask," the man was saying to the woman. "I don't ask."

3   Sitting in the front seat of the car beside Harold, Sybil is fuming. They have been driving around for half an hour looking for a street he is sure is close by. Sybil is angry not because Harold does not know the way, but because he insists on trying to find it himself rather than stopping and asking someone. Her anger stems from viewing his behavior through the lens of her own: If she were driving, she would have asked directions as soon as she realized she didn't know which way to go, and they'd now be comfortably ensconced in their friends' living room instead of driving in circles, as the hour gets later and later. Since asking directions does not make Sybil uncomfortable, refusing to ask makes no sense to her. But in Harold's world, driving around until he finds his way is the reasonable thing to do, since asking for help makes him uncomfortable. He's avoiding that discomfort and trying to maintain his sense of himself as a self-sufficient person.

4   Why do many men resist asking for directions and other kinds of information? And, it is just as reasonable to ask, why is it that many women don't? By the paradox of independence and intimacy, there are two simultaneous and different metamessages implied in asking for and giving information. Many men tend to focus on one, many women on the other.

5   When you offer information, the information itself is the message. But the fact that you have the information, and the person you are speaking to doesn't, also sends a metamessage of superiority. If relations are inherently hierarchical, then the one who has more information is framed as higher up on the ladder, by virtue of being more knowledgeable and competent. From this perspective, finding one's own way is an essential part of the independence that men perceive to be a prerequisite for self-respect. If self-respect is bought at the cost of a few extra minutes of travel time, it is well worth the price.

6   Because they are implicit, metamessages are hard to talk about. When Sybil begs to know why Harold won't just ask someone for directions, he answers in terms of the message, the information: He says there's no point in asking, because anyone he asks may not know and may give him wrong directions. This is theoretically reasonable. There are many countries, such as, for example, Mexico, where it is standard procedure for people to make up directions rather than refuse to give requested information. But this explanation frustrates Sybil, because it doesn't make sense to her. Although she realizes that someone might give faulty directions, she believes this is relatively unlikely, and surely it cannot happen every time. Even if it did happen, they would be in no worse shape than they are in now anyway.

7   Part of the reason for their different approaches is that Sybil believes that a person who doesn't know the answer will say so, because it is easy to say, "I don't know." But Harold believes that saying "I don't know" is humiliating, so people might well take a wild guess. Because of their different assumptions, and the invisibility of framing, Harold and Sybil can never get to the bottom of this difference; they can only get more frustrated with each other. Keeping talk on the message

level is common, because it is the level we are most clearly aware of. But it is unlikely to resolve confusion since our true motivations lie elsewhere.

8   To the extent that giving information, directions, or help is of use to another, it reinforces bonds between people. But to the extent that it is asymmetrical, it creates hierarchy: Insofar as giving information frames one as the expert, superior in knowledge, and the other as uninformed, inferior in knowledge, it is a move in the negotiation of status.

9   It is easy to see that there are many situations where those who give information are higher in status. For example, parents explain things to children and answer their questions, just as teachers give information to students. An awareness of this dynamic underlies one requirement for proper behavior at Japanese dinner entertainment, according to anthropologist Harumi Befu. In order to help the highest-status member of the party to dominate the conversation, others at the dinner are expected to ask him questions that they know he can answer with authority.

10   Because of this potential for asymmetry, some men resist receiving information from others, especially women, and some women are cautious about stating information that they know, especially to men. For example, a man with whom I discussed these dynamics later told me that my perspective clarified a comment made by his wife. They had gotten into their car and were about to go to a destination that she knew well but he did not know at all. Consciously resisting an impulse to just drive off and find his own way, he began by asking his wife if she had any advice about the best way to get there. She told him the way, then added, "But I don't know. That's how I would go, but there might be a better way." Her comment was a move to redress the imbalance of power created by her knowing something he didn't know. She was also saving face in advance, in case he decided not to take her advice. Furthermore, she was reframing her directions as "just a suggestion" rather than "giving instructions."

Checking Your Comprehension

1. Explain why Harold is not comfortable asking for directions.

_____

_____

2. Why does Sybil not mind asking for directions?

_____

_____

3. Explain the relationship between an information giver and an information receiver.

_____

_____

4. Why did the wife who knew her way to a destination say she wasn't sure if it was the best way?

_____

_____

Critical Reading and Thinking

1. What is the author's purpose in writing?

_____

_____

2. This article was taken from a book titled *You Just Don't Understand*, by Deborah Tannen. Dr. Tannen is a professor of linguistics at Georgetown University and is the author of another book on communication. Evaluate the source and authority of this article.

_____

_____

3. The article discusses the different ways men and women ask for directions. What other differences do you notice in how men and women communicate?

_____

_____

4. What types of evidence does Tannen supply to make her explanation clear and understandable? (Evidence: see Chapter 13)

_____

_____

5. Do you think the article is biased? If so, is it against men or women? Justify your answer. (Bias: see Chapter 13)

_____

_____

6. Have you noticed or experienced the differences in direction seeking that Tannen describes?

_____

_____

7. Evaluate the tone of the article. (Tone: see Chapter 12)

_____

_____

Words in Context

DIRECTIONS: *Locate each word in the paragraph indicated. Then, based on the way the word is used, write a synonym or brief definition of each.*

1. self-sufficient (par. 3) _____

2. superiority (par. 5) _____

3. prerequisite (par. 5) _____

Vocabulary Review

DIRECTIONS: *Match the term in Column A with its correct meaning in Column B.*

Column A

_____ 1. status

_____ 2. implicit

_____ 3. hierarchical

_____ 4. framed

_____ 5. asymmetries

_____ 6. paradox

_____ 7. metamessage

Column B

a. lack of harmony

b. not directly stated

c. contradiction

d. position or rank

e. placed within a context

f. beneath the surface meaning

g. Arranged in a specified order

Writing Exercise

Write a paragraph explaining whether you agree or disagree with Tannen's observation that men and women differ in their willingness to ask directions. Give examples to support your ideas.

Blue Highways

WILLIAM LEAST HEAT MOON

Have you ever felt as if you needed to be alone, completely away from everything and everyone you know? This selection is taken from the first few pages of a book titled Blue Highways. *It is the story of a man, part Sioux, who tries to sort out his life by leaving everything behind and going on the road.*

Vocabulary Preview

askew (par. 1)	out of order; disorganized
remote (par. 1)	far away
jeopardy (par. 3)	great danger or peril
skeins (par. 5)	flocks of geese or birds in flight
undulating (par. 5)	moving in a wavy manner; weaving
configuration (par. 5)	arrangement; outline
vernal equinox (par. 6)	day in spring when night and day are of equal length
cartographer (par. 7)	mapmaker
contaminated (par. 13)	impure; infected; polluted
perfidious (par. 13)	not trustworthy; disloyal
rendered (par. 15)	made; caused to be
delusion (par. 15)	false belief; misleading or deceiving idea
futility (pars. 15, 16)	sense of hopelessness or uselessness

DIRECTIONS: *Preview the selection and answer the following question.*

List as many reasons as you can think of that explain why a person might want to travel through the United States alone.

_____

_____

1   *B*eware thoughts that come in the night. They aren't turned properly; they come in askew, free of sense and restriction, deriving from the most remote of sources. Take the idea of February 17, a day of canceled expectations, the day I learned my job teaching English was finished because of declining enrollment at the college, the day I called my wife from whom I'd been separated for nine months to give her the news, the day she let slip about her "friend"—Rick or Dick or Chick. Something like that.

2   That morning, before all the news started hitting the fan, Eddie Short Leaf, who worked a bottomland section of the Missouri River and plowed snow off campus sidewalks, told me if the deep cold didn't break soon the trees would freeze straight through and explode. Indeed.

3   That night, as I lay wondering whether I would get sleep or explosion, I got the idea instead. A man who couldn't make things go right could at least go. He could quit trying to get out of the way of life. Chuck routine. Live the real jeopardy of circumstance. It was a question of dignity.

4   The result: on March 19, the last night of winter, I again lay awake in the tangled bed, this time doubting the madness of just walking out on things, doubting the whole plan that would begin at daybreak—to set out on a long (equivalent to half the circumference of the earth), circular trip over the back roads of the United States. Following a circle would give a purpose—to come around again—where taking a straight line would not. And I was going to do it by living out of the back end of a truck. But how to begin a beginning?

5   A strange sound interrupted my tossing. I went to the window, the cold air against my eyes. At first I saw only starlight. Then they were there. Up in the March blackness, two entwined skeins of snow and blue geese honking north, an undulating W-shaped configuration across the deep sky, white bellies glowing eerily with the reflected light from town, necks stretched northward. Then another flock pulled by who knows what out of the south to breed and remake itself. A new season. Answer: begin by following spring as they did—darkly, with neck stuck out.

6   The vernal equinox came on gray and quiet, a curiously still morning not winter and not spring, as if the cycle paused. Because things go their own way, my daybreak departure turned to a morning departure, then to an afternoon departure. Finally, I climbed into the van, rolled down the window, looked a last time at the rented apartment. From a dead elm sparrow hawks used each year came a high *whee* as the nestlings squealed for more grub. I started the engine. When I returned a season from now—if I did return—those squabs would be gone from the nest.

7   Accompanied only by a small, gray spider crawling the dashboard (kill a spider and it will rain), I drove into the street, around the corner, through the intersection, over the bridge, onto the highway. I was heading toward those little towns that get on the map—if they get on at all—only because some cartographer has a blank space to fill: Remote, Oregon; Simplicity, Virginia; New Freedom, Pennsylvania; New Hope, Tennessee; Why, Arizona; Whynot, Mississippi; Igo, California (just down the road from Ono), here I come.

8   A pledge: I give this chapter to myself. When done with it, I will shut up about *that* topic.

9   Call me Least Heat Moon. My father calls himself Heat Moon, my elder brother Little Heat Moon. I, coming last, am therefore Least. It has been a long lesson of a name to learn.

10   To the Siouan peoples, the Moon of Heat is the seventh month, a time also known as the Blood Moon—I think because of its dusky mid-summer color.

11   I have other names: Buck, once a slur—never mind the predominant Anglo features. Also Bill Trogdon. The Christian names come from a grandfather eight generations back, one William Trogdon, an immigrant Lancashireman living in North Carolina, who was killed by the Tories for providing food to rebel patriots and thereby got his name in volume four of *Makers of America*. Yet to the red way of thinking, a man who makes peace with the new by destroying the old is not to be honored. So I hear.

12   One summer when Heat Moon and I were walking the ancestral grounds of the Osage near the river of that name in western Missouri, we talked about bloodlines. He said, "Each of the people from anywhere, when you see in them far enough, you find red blood and a red heart. There's a hope."

13   Nevertheless, a mixed-blood—let his heart be where it may—is a contaminated man who will be trusted by neither red nor white. The attitude goes back to a long history of "perfidious" half breeds, men who, by their nature, had to choose against one of their bloodlines. As for me, I will choose for heart, for spirit, but never will I choose for blood.

14   One last word about bloodlines. My wife, a woman of striking mixed-blood features, came from the Cherokee. Our battles, my Cherokee and I, we called the "Indian wars."

15   For these reasons I named my truck Ghost Dancing, a heavy-handed symbol alluding to ceremonies of the 1890s in which the Plains Indians, wearing cloth shirts they believed rendered them indestructible, danced for the return of warriors, bison, and the fervor of the old life that would sweep away the new. Ghost dances, desperate resurrection rituals, were the dying rattles of a people whose last defense was delusion—about all that remained to them in their futility.

16   A final detail: on the morning of my departure, I had seen thirty-eight Blood Moons, an age that carries its own madness and futility. With a nearly desperate sense of isolation and a growing suspicion that I lived in an alien land, I took to the open road in search of places where change did not mean ruin and where time and men and deeds connected.

Checking Your Comprehension

DIRECTIONS: *In this article, Least Heat Moon explains why he is leaving everything behind and beginning a two- to three-month trip. List below as many reasons as you can recall that explain why Least Heat Moon is beginning this trip.*

_____

_____

_____

Critical Reading and Thinking

1. What do you think Least Heat Moon means by "Chuck routine. Live the real jeopardy of circumstance"? (par. 3)

_____

_____

2. In paragraphs 4 and 5, the author asks a question and then answers it. First, underline the question and answer. Then, in your own words, explain what the answer means.

_____

_____

3. Explain Least Heat Moon's statement, "As for me, I will choose for heart, for spirit, but never will I choose for blood." (par. 13)

_____

_____

4. Why did Least Heat Moon name his truck "Ghost Dancing"?

_____

_____

5. What does the last sentence of the selection tell you about Least Heat Moon's life so far?

_____

_____

6. What do you think will be the results of Least Heat Moon's trip? Why do you think this?

_____

_____

Words in Context

DIRECTIONS: *Locate each word in the paragraph indicated and reread that paragraph. Then, based on the way the word is used, write a synonym or brief definition for each.*

1. declining (par. 1) _____

2. remake (par. 5) _____

3. pledge (par. 8) _____

4. alluding (par. 15) _____

_____

Vocabulary Review

DIRECTIONS: *Each of the following words has been formed from a root word and a suffix or verb ending. For each word, write the root word. Then, using a dictionary if necessary, write the meaning of the root word.*

Word	Root Word	Meaning of Root Word
Example: futility	futile	useless; worthless
1. undulating	_____	_____
2. contaminated	_____	_____
3. configuration	_____	_____
4. rendered	_____	_____
5. perfidious	_____	_____
6. delusion	_____	_____
7. cartographer	_____	_____

Writing Exercises

1. Have you ever felt like just getting away from everything as Least Heat Moon did? Write a paragraph describing how you felt and what you did as a result.

2. Does your ancestry affect how you behave and the decisions you make? Is being German American, Chinese American, African American, Mexican American, etc., important to your concept of yourself? Write a paragraph explaining how your ethnic or racial origin affects you.

Death on a Plate

JEREMY MACCLANCY

Would you eat something if you knew it could kill you? Read this article to find out about a Japanese delicacy that, if prepared incorrectly, could kill the person who eats it.

Vocabulary Preview

ensure (par. 2)	guarantee
desperate (par. 3)	extremely strong
dilate (par. 3)	grow larger
macabre (par. 4)	horrible; gruesome
neurological (par. 4)	of the nervous system

Prereading

DIRECTIONS: *Preview the selection and answer the following questions.*

1. What is "death on a plate"?

   _____

   _____

   _____

2. Why do you think some people eat puffer-fish?

   _____

   _____

   _____

1   A serving of the Japanese gastronomic delicacy *fugu* (puffer-fish) can be the meal to end all your meals, as it can kill you.

2   Strictly trained chefs carefully remove the fishmeat, then soak it for several hours, changing the water periodically. The meat is then cut into almost transparent slices, which are beautifully arranged on a plate in the form of a peacock. The most skillful of chefs ensure that these choice slivers contain only the merest piece of skin, ovaries, liver, or intestines, for all these parts contain tetradotoxin, a poison hundreds of times more deadly than strychnine or cyanide. As you eat, the tiny amount of the toxin makes the lips tingle. You are exhilarated, maybe even euphoric, as you flirt with death while, hopefully, avoiding its embrace.

3   What if the chef should misjudge his task by even the narrowest margin? First you will feel dizzy and your mouth will tingle, then your fingers and toes. You get cramps in your muscles, your lips go blue, you breathe with difficulty. You feel a desperate itch, as though insects are crawling all over your skin. You vomit, your pupils dilate, and you move off into a zombie-like sleep. Your meal is over and you have left your guests, and without paying the bill. Puffer-fish restaurants keep the number of an emergency doctor by the telephone. But there is little point in calling. The poison is too quick.

4   The most macabre detail of this whole process, however, is that though you may be out for the count, you are not necessarily dead. Like something out of a horror movie, tetradotoxin poisoning brings on a neurological paralysis that leaves its victim aware of what is going on, but totally unable to react. Most people then die. But some do not. The lucky few eventually wake up and return to life. From time to time cases are reported in the Japanese press of *fugu* eaters who, though conscious, were forced to attend their own funeral, only managing to arise, Lazarus-like, at the last moment.

5   Despite the demanding and lengthy training that *fugu* chefs have to undergo, puffer-fish still claim over 300 Japanese a year. For these fatalistic thrill-seekers this popular dish is not just the spice of their life, but also of their death.

Checking Your Comprehension

1. How does the diner feel immediately after eating a small amount of puffer-fish?

_____

_____

2. What will happen to the diner if the chef makes a mistake and leaves too much skin attached to the meat?

_____

_____

3. What is the most gruesome part of being poisoned by puffer-fish?

_____

_____

4. What happens to those few people who don't die from tetradotoxin poisoning?

_____

_____

Critical Reading and Thinking

1. What do you think is the author's attitude toward eating puffer-fish?

_____

_____

2. Why do you think people continue to eat puffer-fish even though it may poison them?

_____

_____

3. The author states that "puffer-fish restaurants keep the number of an emergency doctor by the telephone" even though it doesn't do much good because the poison reacts so quickly. Why do you think restaurants keep this phone number?

_____

_____

4. The article mentions that a puffer-fish chef needs to undergo special training. What do you think is involved in this kind of training?

_____

_____

5. List three other activities in which people take life-threatening risks.

_____

_____

Words in Context

DIRECTIONS: *Locate each word in the paragraph indicated and reread the paragraph. Then, based on the way the word is used, write a synonym or brief definition for each.*

1. slivers (par. 2) _____

2. merest (par. 2) _____

3. toxin (par. 2) _____

4. euphoric (par. 2) _____

5. paralysis (par. 4) _____

6. fatalistic (par. 5) _____

Vocabulary Review

DIRECTIONS: *Use the words listed in the Vocabulary Preview to complete each of the following sentences.*

1. With nothing to drink for three days, the shipwrecked sailors had a _____ thirst.

2. As a result of his head injury, the biker suffered _____ damage.

3. To _____ that you get seats at the concert, buy your tickets as early as possible.

4. After you have been in a darkened room for a while, the pupils of your eyes will _____ so you can see better.

5. The children were frightened by the _____ stories of vampires and werewolves.

Writing Exercises

1. Do you think puffer-fish could become popular in the United States? Write a paragraph supporting your position.

2. Explain why you think people take risks that place them in danger of injury or death.

How Much Are You Willing to Pay for That New-Car Smell?

ROGER LEROY MILLER

Have you ever wished you could afford to buy a new car? Many people do buy one, but without realizing how costly their purchase is. Read this article to find out how much new cars can actually cost.

Vocabulary Preview

synthetic (par. 1)	manmade
warranty (par. 2)	guarantee; agreement to repair problems
rationally (par. 3)	by thinking through carefully
acquisition (par. 4)	getting; obtaining
unique (par. 4)	unusual; one-of-a-kind
embody (par. 5)	contain; include
audio (par. 5)	sound

Prereading

DIRECTIONS: *Preview the selection and answer the following questions.*

1. What do you think the author's position is on the purchase of new cars?

_____

_____

_____

2. Do you expect this reading to be fact or opinion?

_____

_____

_____

1   *M*ost people know what it feels like to sit in a new car. Much of the feeling comes from the smell—the new-car smell—whether it comes from fine leather or less-expensive synthetic seat covers and carpets. For most people it's a good smell. They also like to know that no one else has done anything bad to the new car. It's like starting out with a clean slate. The important question, though, is how much are you really willing to pay for that new-car smell?

2   I am, of course, simplifying the issue. The purchase of a new car is more than just for the smell. In the decision to buy a new car versus a used car, you also know that with a new car you get a certain amount of increased warranty protection from the new-car dealer, and you don't have to worry about how the car was cared for previously. Additionally, you can make sure that all maintenance is carried out as it should be. Finally, you can order a new car with exactly the options you want.

3   In order to decide rationally whether you should pay for the benefits of a new rather than a used car, you have to know the marginal cost of the new-car purchase versus the used-car purchase. Otherwise stated, you have to know the true cost of, say, buying and owning a new car for one year.

4   The first cost you incur when you purchase a new car—or any asset for that matter—is the cost of acquisition. The cost of acquisition is defined as the difference between the purchase price of an asset and the *immediate* resale price. With respect to a new car, the cost of acquisition is rather dramatic. You may have to take a substantial loss of as high as 25 percent if you try to turn right around and resell your brand new car. The more unique the car, the higher is the cost of acquisition in percentage terms. For other assets, the cost of acquisition may be even higher than that of a new car. This is true for so-called high-end models of power boats, sailboats, and furniture.

5   Another important cost of owning a new car during its first year is the cost of depreciation. This can be measured by the difference between the *immediate* resale value of the car after its purchase (the purchase price minus its cost of acquisition) minus the resale value of the car at the *end of one year*. Depreciation occurs because of normal wear and tear on any machinery. Cars depreciate for another reason—they are considered relatively less desirable by car purchasers because newer cars embody improvements such as added safety features, different styling,

and better audio systems. Relatively speaking, therefore, older cars, even in the absence of physical depreciation, are relatively less desirable than newer cars.

6   The cost of operation of the automobile for the first year typically would be a minor factor in making a decision between purchasing a new and a used car. After all, the cost of operation—gas, insurance, tune-ups, etc.—should be approximately the same for a new car as for one that is one year old.

7   The two most important costs associated with purchasing a new car relative to one that is a year old are the cost of acquisition and depreciation. For a $15,000 car, these two added together can be as high as $5,000. For a $25,000 car, they can be as high as $7,500. Is that new-car smell worth it? Only you can give the answer, but at least it will be based on an understanding of the true marginal cost of a one-year difference in the age of a car that you purchase.

Checking Your Comprehension

1. What do you need to know in order to make a reasonable decision about whether to buy a new or a used car?

_____

_____

2. What is meant by the cost of acquisition?

_____

_____

3. What is the major factor that drives up the cost of acquisition of any car?

_____

_____

4. Why is the cost of operating a car during the first year only a minor factor in deciding whether to buy a new or a used car?

_____

_____

5. What are the two most important costs associated with buying a new car as opposed to a one-year-old car?

_____

_____

Critical Reading and Thinking

1. Discuss three advantages of buying a new car.

_____

_____

2. Why is the cost of depreciation an important one in owning a new car during its first year?

_____

_____

3. The author states that the cost of operating a new car should be approximately the same as the cost for operating a one-year-old car. Do you agree or disagree with the author? Justify your answer.

_____

_____

4. What is the author's purpose in writing this article? (Author's purpose: see Chapter 12)

_____

_____

5. Evaluate the completeness and usefulness of this reading. What other information, if any, do you think it should include?

_____

_____

_____

Words in Context

DIRECTIONS: *Locate each word in the paragraph indicated and reread that paragraph. Then, based on the way the word is used, write a synonym or brief definition for each.*

1. incur (par. 4) _____

2. asset (par. 4) _____

3. depreciation (par. 5) _____

Vocabulary Review

DIRECTIONS: *Use the words listed in the Vocabulary Preview to complete each of the following sentences.*

1. We knew the sound on our TV wasn't defective when we saw the message: "Experiencing _____ problems. Please do not adjust your set."

2. That is a very _____ solution for a difficult problem.

3. Nearly all new appliances come with a _____.

4. Let's stop arguing so that we can discuss this problem _____.

5. The Bill of Rights and the amendments _____ the American ideal of individual rights and responsibilities.

6. Plastic is the most common _____ material.

7. Don't let the _____ of wealth become your only reason for choosing a career.

Writing Exercises

1. Write a paragraph on whether you think it's wiser to buy a new or a used car.

2. Explain how purchasing any car fits into your current financial picture. How high does it rank among the things you need?

3. Not only the rich own expensive cars. Why are so many people attracted to them?

Nonverbal Communication

ANTHONY F. GRASHA

How do you express your feelings to and about others? The primary way we communicate with others is through words. This excerpt from a psychology textbook discusses an alternate form of communication.

Vocabulary Preview

enhance (par. 1)	make greater in value, worth, or quantity
verbal (par. 1)	concerning or associated with words; having to do with speech
violate (par. 2)	interrupt; disturb
norms (par. 2)	standard models or patterns
manipulate (par. 7)	manage or control
utterances (par. 7)	speech sounds
converse (par. 8)	talk; engage in conversation
elaborate (par. 8)	explain more fully; give details

Prereading

DIRECTIONS: *Preview the selection and answer the following questions.*

What two aspects or types of nonverbal communication does this selection discuss? What do you already know about these two forms of communication?

_____

_____

Nonverbal Messages and Interpersonal Communication

1 The way we dress, our mannerisms, how close we stand to people, eye contact, touching, and the ways we mark our personal spaces convey certain messages. *Such nonverbal behaviors communicate certain messages by themselves and also enhance the meaning of our verbal communications.* Pounding your fist on a table, for example, suggests anger without anything being spoken. Holding someone close to you conveys the message that you care. To say "I don't like you" with a loud voice or waving fists increases the intensity of the verbal message. Let us examine the concepts of *personal space* and *body language* to gain additional insights into the nonverbal side of interpersonal communication.

Nonverbal Messages: The Use of Personal Space

2 Edward Hall notes that we have personal spacial territories or zones tht allow certain types of behaviors and communications. We only allow certain people to enter or events to occur within a zone. Let us look at how some nonverbal messages can be triggered by behaviors that violate the norms of each zone. The four personal zones identified by Hall are as follows:

3 **1.** *Intimate distance.* This personal zone covers a range of distance from body contact to one foot. Relationships between a parent and child, lovers, and close friends occur within this zone. As a general rule, we only allow people we know and have some affection for to enter this zone. When someone tries to enter without our permission, they are strongly repelled by our telling them to stay away from us or by our pushing them away. Why do you think we allow a doctor to easily violate our intimate distance zone?

4 **2.** *Personal distance.* The spatial range covered by this zone extends from one to four feet. Activities like eating in a restaurant with two or three other people, sitting on chairs or the floor in small groups at parties, or playing cards occur within this zone. Violations of the zone make people feel uneasy and act nervously. When you are eating at a restaurant, the amount of table space that is considered yours is usually divided equally by the number of people present. I can remember becoming angry and generally irritated when a friend of mine placed a plate and glass in my space. As we talked I was visibly irritated, but my anger had nothing to do with the topic we discussed. Has this ever happened to you?

5 **3.** *Social distance.* Four to twelve feet is the social distance zone. Business meetings, large formal dinners, and small classroom seminars occur within the boundaries of the social distance zone. Discussions concerning everyday topics like the weather, politics, or a best seller are considered acceptable. For a husband and wife to launch into a heated argument during a party in front of ten other people would violate the accepted norms for behavior in the social zone. This once happened at a formal party I attended. The nonverbal behaviors that resulted con-

sisted of several people leaving the room, others looking angry or uncomfortable, and a few standing and watching quietly with an occasional upward glance and a rolling of their eyeballs. What would violate the social distance norms in a classroom?

6   **4.** *Public distance.* This zone includes the area beyond twelve feet. Addressing a crowd, watching a sports event, and sitting in a large lecture section are behaviors we engage in within this zone. As is true for the other zones, behaviors unacceptable for this zone can trigger nonverbal messages. At a recent World Series game a young male took his clothes off and ran around the outfield. Some watched with amusement on their faces, others looked away, and a few waved their fists at the culprit. The respective messages were, "That's funny," "I'm afraid or ashamed to look," and "How dare you interrupt the game." What would your reaction be in this situation?

Nonverbal Messages: The Use of Body Language

7   Body language refers to the various arm and hand gestures, facial expressions, tone of voice, postures, and body movements we use to convey certain messages. According to Irving Goffman, they are the things we "give off" when talking to other people. Goffman notes that our body language is generally difficult to manipulate at will. Unlike our verbal utterances, we have less conscious control over the specific body gestures or expressions we might make while talking. Unless we are acting on a stage or purposely trying to create a certain effect, they occur automatically without much thought on our part.

8   Michael Argyle notes that body language serves several functions for us. *It helps us to communicate certain emotions, attitudes, and preferences.* A hug by someone close to us lets us know we are appreciated. A friendly wave and smile as someone we know passes us lets us know we are recognized. A quivering lip tells us that someone is upset. Each of us has become quite sensitive to the meaning of various body gestures and expressions. Robert Rosenthal has demonstrated that this sensitivity is rather remarkable. When shown films of people expressing various emotions, individuals were able to identify the emotion correctly 66 percent of the time even when each frame was exposed for one twenty-fourth of a second. *Body language also supports our verbal communications.* Vocal signals of timing, pitch, voice stress, and various gestures add meaning to our verbal utterances. Argyle suggests that we may speak with our vocal organs, but we converse with our whole body. *Body language helps to control our conversations.* It helps us to decide when it is time to stop talking, to interrupt the other person, and to know when to shift topics or elaborate on something because our listeners are bored, do not understand us, or are not paying attention.

Checking Your Comprehension

DIRECTIONS: *Assume that you are enrolled in a psychology course that uses the textbook from which this selection was taken. Your next exam will cover the material presented in this excerpt as well as several other chapters. On a separate sheet, write an outline of this selection. Include information you would need to review to prepare for a multiple-choice exam.*

Critical Reading and Thinking

1. How does this author let you know what is important (make his important points stand out)?

   _____

   _____

2. Do you think that such names as Irving Goffman and Michael Argyle are important to remember? Give your reasons.

   _____

   _____

3. If an exam on this material included an essay question, what question might you predict?

   _____

   _____

4. How would you answer the questions at the end of paragraphs 3, 5, and 6?

   Par. 3: _____

   Par. 5: _____

   Par. 6: _____

5. Describe personal situations in which body language was more important than verbal communication.

   _____

   _____

Words in Context

DIRECTIONS: *Locate each word or phrase in the paragraph indicated and reread that paragraph. Then, based on the way the word is used, write a synonym or brief definition for each.*

1. intensity (par. 1) _____

2. spatial territories (par. 2) _____

3. culprit (par. 6) _____

Vocabulary Review

DIRECTIONS: *Match each word in Column A with its meaning in Column B by writing the letter of the definition next to the number of the word it defines.*

Column A

Column B

_____ 1. verbal   a. models

_____ 2. violate   b. control

_____ 3. utterances   c. increase in value

_____ 4. converse   d. talk

_____ 5. elaborate   e. explain more fully

_____ 6. norms   f. break in on

_____ 7. enhance   g. having to do with words

_____ 8. manipulate   h. sounds of someone talking

Writing Exercise

Observe someone in the hall, in a classroom, in a store, or at a party. Write a paragraph explaining what that person's body language conveyed to you.

Snack Foods

VERNON PIZER

Few of us can resist snack foods. This article discusses three popular American snacks: potato chips, popcorn, and peanuts.

Vocabulary Preview

undisputed (par. 1)	not to be argued about, certain, definite
cynical (par. 1)	always looking at the bad side of things
dubious (par. 1)	questionable, doubtful, uncertain
innovation (par. 2)	creativity, ability to create new things
domineering (par. 2)	arrogant, pushy
patronizing (par. 3)	being a customer of
burgeoning (par. 4)	rapidly growing, expanding quickly
gleaned (par. 5)	learned, discovered
apparent (par. 6)	obvious, visible
exalted (par. 8)	honored, praiseworthy, important
unassailably (par. 9)	undeniably, unable to be attacked
stalwart (par. 9)	sturdy, strong, brave
savor (par. 10)	an appetizing quality, tastefulness

Prereading

DIRECTIONS: *Preview the selection and answer the following questions.*

What is your favorite snack food? Why? Have you encountered other people eating snack foods you thought were strange? What were these foods?

1   *I*n the world of snack foods, America is the undisputed superpower, totally un-rivaled for that position by any other nation. (Only those who are mean in spirit and cynical in outlook might ask who would want to compete for such a dubious honor.) It is a position of superiority that sprouted from the humble potato.

2   The potato seemed destined to remain no more than a simple, staid, humdrum food, the kind that would always be picked out as a blue-collar intruder if it tried to move in white-collar circles. And then American innovation created a whole new dimension to the potato's personality, endowing it with a verve and sparkle it had never before enjoyed. It all took place in 1853 when a domineering industrial tycoon and a thin-skinned redskin crossed paths in Moon's Lake House, a resort in Saratoga Springs, the upstate New York spa favored by the wealthy.

3   The multimillionaire industrialist was Commodore Cornelius Vanderbilt; the Indian was George Crum, cook in the Lake House kitchen. The Lake House was not the posh sort of place Vanderbilt was accustomed to patronizing; nevertheless, he stopped in one day for lunch. When his food was served he was displeased with the fried potatoes placed before him. Complaining that they had been cut much too thick, he petulantly ordered the waiter to take them back to the kitchen and have them replaced by thinner slices.

4   Resentful of this criticism of his kitchen performance, Crum set out to teach Vanderbilt a lesson. Snatching up some potatoes, he sliced them to paper thinness, plunged them briefly in boiling oil, sprinkled them liberally with salt, and then sent them out to the table, confident that his critic would get the message. Vanderbilt looked at the unusual slivers of potato, tasted one, smiled, and praised its crispness and flavor. For the balance of the season he returned again and again to Moon's Lake House, bringing his friends along to introduce them to the pleasures of George Crum's "Saratoga chips." Though Crum was denied the satisfaction of getting even with Vanderbilt, at least he lived long enough to see the potato chip he had invented become the cornerstone of a burgeoning snack-food industry.

5   Today potato chips are established as an international favorite from Tokyo where they are flavored with seaweed, to New Delhi where they are flavored with curry, to Berlin where they are flavored with paprika. In the United States alone manufacturers send about $2 billion worth of potato chips to market each year. A feel for how many chips that amounts to can be gleaned from this awesome statistic: if all those chips were laid end to end they would encircle the globe more than 325 times. By anyone's standards, that's not small potatoes.

6   By a wide margin the potato chip is the most popular snack food to emerge from America, but it is not the first one to be launched on this side of the Atlantic. What is quite possibly the world's oldest snack, popcorn, is a New World native

with a history dating back more than 5,000 years. Popping corn was one of the initial skills the American Colonists picked up from the Indians. It has been said by some, with little apparent basis in actual fact, that as the first Thanksgiving feast was drawing to a close Quadequina, brother of Chief Massasoit, brought out a batch of popped corn to finish off the meal.

7   Popcorn is overshadowed in importance by the peanut, the snack that comes closest to rivaling potato chips in popularity. Like the others, the peanut is also a native of the Americas. It was cultivated in South America at least 3,800 years ago, was introduced to Africa by Portuguese explorers in the sixteenth century, and then was brought to North America aboard African slave ships.

8   A St. Louis doctor is credited with creating in 1890 what many consider to be the most exalted state of grace any ambitious nuts can aspire to: peanut butter. Promoting his peanut butter as a readily digestible, tasty, high-protein food, he gained a loyal circle of consumers in the St. Louis area. But it gained national exposure and national popularity when he introduced it at Chicago's Columbian Exposition of 1893. Soon grocers across the country were stocking it in bulk in large wooden tubs to satisfy customer demand. When the innovative agricultural scientist, George Washington Carver, developed an improved version of the butter, it attracted even more enthusiasts to the fold. Nowadays it takes about a third of all the peanuts grown in the United States just to satisfy the American appetite for peanut butter. How seriously Americans regard peanut butter becomes quite clear when one notes the presence in Chicago of The American Museum of Peanut Butter History.

9   Although it is unassailably true that it is in America that the snack enjoys its finest hour, fairness requires recognition that some other countries do make original contributions of their own. But it must be added, again in fairness, that from a distance some of these foreign offerings seem to suggest a form of self-abuse for consumers. A popular Spanish snack is *angulas,* miniature baby eels that look exactly like pale fishing worms and are swallowed whole in a pungent garlic oil. Japanese enjoy snacking on roasted and salted grasshoppers. The French are partial to the pulpy insides of raw sea urchins—spiny, golf ball-sized marine animals. The English are very enthusiastic about baked beans as a snack food. They consume enough baked beans to founder a less stalwart people—nearly 5 million pounds in a single day, much of it in the form of sandwiches.

10   Viewed against a backdrop of the *angulas,* grasshoppers, sea urchins, and baked bean sandwiches abroad, the American snack scene takes on added savor. Even unrelenting food snobs who profess to see nothing of merit in the American kitchen are forced to concede that when it comes to snacks Americans do seem to have an appealing, innovative touch.

Checking Your Comprehension

1. How was the potato chip invented?

_____

_____

2. What is the most popular American snack food?

_____

_____

3. What is probably the oldest snack food?

_____

_____

4. Is the story about Quadequina bringing out popcorn at the first Thanksgiving true?

_____

_____

5. Where was peanut butter invented?

_____

_____

6. What snack do the English enjoy?

_____

Critical Reading and Thinking

1. What is the author's tone? Is it heavy and serious or light and amused? Give an example that supports your answer.

_____

_____

_____

2. Is the author's writing style descriptive or dry and factual? Give two examples to support your answer.

_____

_____

3. Review paragraph 9. How does the author use descriptions of foreign snack foods to support the statement he makes in the second sentence of the paragraph?

_____

_____

4. What kind of value judgment does the author make about foreign snack foods? (pars. 9 and 10) (Value judgments: see Chapter 13)

_____

_____

Words in Context

DIRECTIONS: *Locate each word in the paragraph indicated and reread that paragraph. Then, based on the way the word is used, write a synonym or brief definition for each.*

1. unrivaled (par. 1) _____

2. staid (par. 2) _____

3. verve (par. 2) _____

4. slivers (par. 4) _____

5. rivaling (par. 7) _____

6. innovative (par. 8) _____

7. *angulas* (par. 9) _____

8. sea urchins (par. 9) _____

Vocabulary Review

DIRECTIONS: *Mark each statement True or False.*

_____ 1. If something is apparent, then it is not obvious.

_____ 2. To patronize a restaurant you must own it.

_____ 3. A stalwart person is brave and strong.

_____ 4. To burgeon means to grow quickly.

_____ 5. A dubious fact is one that is not questionable and is definitely true.

_____ 6. Innovation is a creative ability to make new things.

_____ 7. An exalted person always sees the bad side of things.

_____ 8. Someone who is domineering behaves in a quiet, lonely way.

Writing Exercises

1. Think about the way the potato chip was invented. It was an unplanned, spontaneous invention. Describe an idea you have had for an invention or a new way of doing something that came to you spontaneously. What made you think of it?

2. Write a paragraph about your favorite snack food. Describe its taste, shape, appearance, smell, and the sound it makes when you eat it. Use as many descriptive words as you can.

Acupuncture

RICK WEISS

[Xiao Ming Tian is referred to as Tian throughout this article.]

Acupuncture, the use of needles to treat physical pains and illnesses, is becoming an increasingly popular alternative to traditional medicine and surgery. Read this article to find out how it works.

Vocabulary Preview

appendectomy (par. 1)	surgery to remove the appendix
concede (par. 3)	admit; go along with
unconventional (par. 4)	nontraditional; unusual
meridians (par. 4)	lines; pathways
acute (par. 5)	sharp
chronic (par. 5)	constant
inexplicably (par. 8)	unexplainably
channels (par. 11)	routes; pathways

Prereading

DIRECTIONS: *Preview the article and then answer the following questions.*

1. Do you expect this article to be factual or persuasive?

   _____

   _____

2. Do you think the article presents a positive or negative view of acupuncture?

   _____

1   *P*erhaps no other alternative therapy has received more attention in this country or gained acceptance more quickly than acupuncture. Most Americans had never even heard of it until 1971, when *New York Times* foreign correspondent James Reston wrote a startling first person account of the painkilling effects of acupuncture following his emergency appendectomy in China. Today the needling of America is in full swing. Last year alone, Americans made some 9 to 12 million visits to acupuncturists for ailments as diverse as arthritis, bladder infections, back pain, and morning sickness.

2   In a culture that is overwhelmingly shy of needles, what could account for such popularity?

3   Safety, for one thing. There is something to be said for a medical practice that's been around for 5,000 years, with billions of satisfied patients. If acupuncture were dangerous, even its stodgiest critics concede, somebody would have noticed by now.

4   Many people are also encouraged by doctors' growing willingness to refer patients for acupuncture—or to learn the ancient art themselves—despite its unconventional claims. Acupuncturists say that health is simply a matter of tweaking into balance a mysterious life force called *qi* (pronounced chee), which is said to move through invisible meridians in the body. That's hardly a mainstream view, yet of the 9,000 practicing acupuncturists in this country, fully a third are M.D.s.

5   Most important, there's mounting evidence that acupuncture has something important to offer, especially when it comes to pain. In one big study, acupuncture offered short-term relief to 50 to 80 percent of patients with acute or chronic pain. And in the only controlled trial that followed patients for six months or more, nearly six out of ten patients with low back pain continued to show improvement, compared to a control group that showed no improvement. Other studies have shown that acupuncture may be useful in treating nausea, asthma, and a host of other common ills.

6   With success stories piling up, acupuncturists decided to approach the Food and Drug Administration, which has never officially sanctioned the practice. In November, the country's leading acupuncturists, Ming included, gathered together their best evidence and sent the 500-page document off to the agency, with a formal request that their needles be approved as safe and effective medical devices. No one can say for sure when a decision will come down, but it could be as early as May.

7   FDA approval of acupuncture needles would be big news. For starters, it would make reimbursement far more likely from Medicare, Medicaid, and the many private insurers that do not now cover acupuncture treatments. Just as important, a

nod of approval from the FDA would be a symbolic victory. It would be the first time the agency had given its stamp of approval to a medical device rooted in a theory totally outside that of mainstream medicine.

8   Ming pulls aside a curtain and strides into the cubicle where Rosenstadt is resting. A former champion discus thrower, he's a big man with a wide, kind face and balding head. With his twinkling eyes, which look inexplicably wise, and the "M.D." embroidered after his name on his white coat, he appears an almost cartoonishly perfect embodiment of Eastern and Western medicine. In many ways, he is just that. Ming is as likely as the next M.D. to prescribe antibiotics to fight a raging infection. But having studied under China's greatest masters, it is acupuncture that he relies on most. He is the first and only acupuncturist employed by the federal government, a position created for him on the recommendation of Western medical colleagues who had referred some of their patients to him as a last resort and were impressed by his results.

9   "How are you doing?" Ming asks, leaning over Rosenstadt to check on the needles he popped into her skin a few minutes ago. In addition to the one just above the bridge of her nose, there is a needle stuck in the rim of her ear, one in each temple, and five running the length of her left leg.

10   Most are not inserted very deep—perhaps a quarter of an inch—and they do not hurt. Like most patients, Rosenstadt describes the sensation as a tingling or mild buzz, especially noticeable when Ming begins to twirl the needles clockwise and counterclockwise in her skin, a technique that is said to help the needles do their job of moving qi through the body.

11   There are nearly 400 acupuncture points along the body's 14 major meridians, or energy-carrying channels, Ming says, and each has a Chinese name that describes the kind of energy or organ it affects. But to know if he is in exactly the right spot, he must twirl the needle after inserting it and be sure that he gets a response from the patient—a report of feeling a deep heaviness or numbness in the area or, more commonly, a simple "yes."

12   "That is called the *ashi* point," Ming says. "*Ashi* is Chinese for 'Oh, yes,'" he explains. "Every point, when you do it right, is an ashi point."

13   Can a simple twist of a needle really put an ailing body on the path to recovery? Consider the evidence: . . .

14   Practitioners of Chinese medicine say it is revealing that so many "cures" in Western medicine make people sick in the course of making them better. Cancer chemotherapy drugs, for example, have become so synonymous with nausea that they are now considered the standard challenge when new anti-nausea drugs are tested. And anesthesia, helpful as it is during surgery, leaves roughly a third of patients vomiting in the hours after regaining consciousness.

15   It doesn't have to be that way, acupuncturists say. To back up their claim, they offer the *neiguan* point—also known as P6—which lies about two fingers'

width above the crease on the inside of the wrist, between two tendons. For reasons that defy scientific analysis, a firm pricking of that point seems to settle the stomach.

16   Several studies during the past seven years have shown that surgical patients who receive needle stimulation of the neiguan point before getting anesthetized are far less likely than their unstuck counterparts to suffer from nausea or vomiting in the six hours after surgery. Equally good results have been obtained with cancer patients using the lifesaving but usually nauseating chemotherapy drug cisplatin. In at least two studies of more than 100 patients each, better than 90 percent of them had significantly less nausea when treated with acupuncture just before taking the drug.

17   For a nation of addicts—to cigarettes, to alcohol, to drugs—acupuncturists propose a simple antidote: a few needles in the ear, every day, for half an hour.

18   Acupuncture's habit-breaking benefits have been well documented in people hooked on heroin and crack cocaine through a program called Drug Court, in which felony drug offenders are given the chance to enter an intensive program of counseling and daily acupuncture treatments as an alternative to prison. Acupuncture stimulation of four points on the ear has a powerful calming effect, counselors and addicts say. It not only reduces the craving for a fix—perhaps by substituting the brain's own endorphins for the street-drug equivalent—but it also helps addicts relax enough to think clearly about their predicament and to resolve to change their lives.

19   The program has its roots in work by Michael Smith, a psychiatrist and acupuncturist who directs the substance abuse division of Lincoln Hospital in the rough-and-tumble South Bronx, where some 30,000 addicts have been treated with the help of acupuncture in the past 20 years.

20   All told, about half of Drug Court addicts make it through the year-long program, a graduation rate far higher than anything seen in standard residential treatment programs. And an analysis in Miami recently found that more than three quarters of the program's graduates went at least two years without another arrest, compared to the 15 to 20 percent seen with standard drug diversion programs.

21   The needle has had success against other addictions, as well. In a two-month study published in 1989, more than half the alcoholics who got acupuncture stayed sober, compared to 3 percent of those who received "sham" acupuncture treatments, in which needles were inserted in phony acupuncture points. And for a testimonial on acupuncture as an aid to quitting cigarettes, just ask the judge who administers the Drug Court program in Miami's Dade County. He smoked several packs a day for 35 years until five years ago, when he served the same sentence on himself that he had just begun serving on convicted felons: daily appointments with an acupuncturist. After ten days, he kicked the habit for good.

Checking Your Comprehension

1. Explain what *qi* is.

   _____

   _____

2. Give an example of how acupuncture controls pain.

   _____

   _____

3. According to the reading, what does an acupuncture treatment feel like?

   _____

   _____

4. What is the purpose of turning the needles during an acupuncture treatment?

   _____

   _____

5. What is meant by the *ashi* point?

   _____

   _____

Critical Reading and Thinking

1. What is the author's purpose in writing this article? (Author's purpose: see Chapter 12)

   _____

   _____

2. Why does the author consider acupuncture to be safe?

   _____

   _____

3. Why do you think the FDA has not previously sanctioned acupuncture?

   _____

   _____

4. Do you think American doctors are accepting when it comes to unconventional approaches to healing? Why?

_____

_____

5. What other forms of unconventional medical treatments do you know?

_____

_____

Words in Context

DIRECTIONS: *Locate each word in the paragraph indicated and reread that paragraph. Then, based on the way the word is used, write a synonym or brief definition of each.*

1. correspondent (par. 1) _____

2. diverse (par. 1) _____

3. stodgiest (par. 3) _____

4. tweaking (par. 4) _____

5. mainstream (par. 4) _____

6. mounting (par. 5) _____

7. sanctioned (par. 6) _____

8. embodiment (par. 8) _____

Vocabulary Review

DIRECTIONS: *Answer the following questions about the words listed in the Vocabulary Preview.*

1. What does it mean when we say someone is a <u>chronic</u> complainer?

_____

_____

2. What is the purpose of <u>appendectomy</u> surgery?

_____

3. If you were to describe a person's hairdo as <u>unconventional</u>, what would you mean?

_____

4. Give an example of an <u>acute</u> pain.

_____

5. What do we mean when we say a politician <u>conceded</u> defeat?

_____

6. If someone "went through <u>channels</u>" to get something done, what did he or she do?

_____

7. When we refer to <u>meridians</u> of longitude on a map, what do we mean?

_____

8. What do we mean when we say she was <u>inexplicably</u> absent from class?

_____

Writing Exercises

1. Write a paragraph describing your own or someone else's individual remedy for a medical condition.

2. Would you ever try acupuncture? Under what circumstances?

Kissing Customs

MICHAEL T. KAUFMAN

Hand-kissing is an ancient custom. This article describes an American's introduction to the custom.

Vocabulary Preview

feudal (par. 1)	relating to or suggesting the economic system of medieval Europe
effete (par. 1)	dandyish, weak
stammered (par. 1)	to speak in a stumbling way from excitement or embarrassment
obsequious (par. 2)	submissive, servile
proletarian (par. 3)	of the working class
sporadic (par. 9)	occasional, irregular
atavistic (par. 11)	ancestral, inherited

Prereading

DIRECTIONS: *Preview the selection and answer the following questions.*

What meanings or feelings does hand-kissing convey? How would you feel about participating in this custom?

_____

_____

1   *I*returned not long ago from a three-year assignment in Poland, where men kiss the hands of women as a matter of course when they meet. When I first arrived in Warsaw, I did not think this was such a great idea. At the time I thought of myself as a democratic kid from the streets of New York, and the notion of bending over and brushing my lips over the back of a woman's hand struck me as offensively feudal and hopelessly effete. Each time some perfectly fine woman offered me the back of her hand to kiss, I stammered my apology, saying something like, "Gosh, no offense intended, but where I come from we don't carry on like this, and while I respect you enormously, can't we make do with a simple handshake?"

2   I was at the time mindful of what my feminist friends back home might have said. I do not think they would have wanted me to kiss the hands of all women simply because they were women. They would have, rightly, seen this as a sexist custom, pointing out that not even in the grip of the most obsequious compulsions would anyone kiss the hand of a man.

3   But then I began to realize that the Polish custom had one particularly subtle and attractive aspect. After forty years of living under an unpopular Communist Government that sought to restrict society to the proletarian standard of some concocted Soviet model, the Poles were defending themselves with chivalrous customs. Instead of addressing each other with terms like "comrade citizen," as their Government had once urged them to do, Poles intuitively responded by assuming the manners of dukes and barons. In such circumstances it was pleasant and instructive to watch factory workers, mailmen, soldiers, peasants and high-school students kiss the hands held out to them while the Communist Party people, often identifiable by their wide ties and out-of-date suits, maintained stiff though ideologically correct postures.

4   Under this kind of social pressure, I kissed. At first it was tricky. There was nothing in my Upper West Side of Manhattan public-school education that prepared me for the act. I had to experiment. I think my first attempts were perhaps too noisy. They may also have been too moist. I realized that generally what I was expected to communicate was respect and not ardor, but I didn't want to appear too distant. I had observed some aristocrats take the hands extended to them and swoosh down without making real contact. I was trying for slightly more commitment.

5   Eventually, I got it right. And, to my surprise, I liked it. Each new encounter became a challenge. I found I needed to make subtle little alterations in technique as the situations demanded. For instance, if the woman was younger, I would bring her hand to my lips. If she was older, I would bring my lips to her hand. When I could not tell if she was younger or older, I went on the premise that she was younger. Sometimes you could play out little dramas. It was nothing serious or marriage-threatening, but you could, by kissing with more than normal pres-

sure, make yourself noticed—and you could notice yourself being noticed. Or you could imagine you were somebody else, which, at least in my case, can be pleasant.

6   The real advantage of hand-kissing, I came to realize, was that it provided a ritual that enriched the routine of everyday life. Whenever I returned to the West on holidays I was struck by how few such rituals existed in my own society. Hardly anyone shook hands, let alone kissed them. Instead, waiters would tell me their names before taking my order and wish me a good day as they took my money. But I never felt they really cared. I would be called by strangers who wanted to sell me something over the phone, and they would address me as Mike. I would try to squelch them with what I thought was chilling irony and say, "Make that Mr. Mike." No one got it, but some said, "That's cute; Mr. Mike."

7   In this cultural context, I doubt that the United States is ready for hand-kissing. We seem to lack the self-discipline, or perhaps the confidence, and then too, there is the real danger of insulting feminists and getting your nose broken. And, to our credit, we have limited tolerance for lah-di-dah.

8   Still, I think it would be good to have some gesture or ritual that signifies at least minimal mutual respect. The idea would be to affirm something less than intimacy but more than passing acquaintance. What I have in mind would be useful for both intersexual and intrasexual contacts. It would replace the exchange of monosyllables like "hi" and "yo."

9   My suggestion is that we shake hands every day with the people we hold in esteem. The practice, as common in Poland as hand-kissing, is, I realize, not unknown here. But in America it is sporadic and all too casual.

10   Since returning from Poland, I've renewed many acquaintances. Among them was a person whose actions had once offended my sense of ethics. We chatted civilly enough, talking of our families and our recent experiences, but I did not offer him my hand. I did this as a point of honor—and to send a message. Had I been talking to a Pole, he might have reddened, stammered or walked away. But my old acquaintance didn't even notice. In this country, the symbolism of such a small act is lost. Of course, I could have thrown a rock through one of his windows, or cursed his parentage, or even turned abruptly from him, but all that would have been overkill for the graveness of his offense.

11   As for kissing the hands of women, my reflex, unfortunately, is waning. Under the social pressures of democracy, the Polish impulses that would have me turn wrists and kiss are growing fainter and fainter. The kid from the streets of New York is reasserting himself on his home ground with authentic and atavistic boorishness. *Tant pis.**

*Literally, so much the worse; too bad.

Checking Your Comprehension

1. Why was the author uncomfortable kissing women's hands?

   _____

   _____

2. Why did he begin to kiss hands?

   _____

   _____

3. How did the author treat women of different ages?

   _____

   _____

4. What does the author like about the custom?

   _____

   _____

5. What effect did the Polish custom have on the author's behavior after he returned to America?

   _____

   _____

Critical Reading and Thinking

1. What kind of generalizations are made about feminists (pars. 2 and 7)? (Generalizations: see Chapter 13)

   _____

   _____

2. What is the author's purpose in describing this custom? (Author's purpose: see Chapter 12)

   _____

   _____

3. How does the author feel about the way people treat each other in America?

_____

_____

4. How does the author feel about hand-kissing and what effect does that have on his description?

_____

_____

5. What does the author assume about Polish attitudes toward communism?

_____

_____

6. Why does the author end his piece with a French expression?

_____

_____

Words in Context

DIRECTIONS: *Locate each word in the paragraph indicated and reread that paragraph. Then, based on the way the word is used, write a synonym or brief definition for each.*

1. chivalrous (par. 3) _____

2. ardor (par. 4) _____

3. premise (par. 5) _____

4. irony (par. 6) _____

5. esteem (par. 9) _____

6. waning (par. 11) _____

Vocabulary Review

DIRECTIONS: *Complete each of the following sentences by choosing one of the words presented in the Vocabulary Preview.*

1. The man was embarrassed when he was unable to remember an old friend's name and _____ a greeting.

2. The professor of medieval history was fascinated by the _____ system.

3. Because she often overslept, the student's attendance at the eight o'clock class was _____.

4. Because the child seemed _____, he was ridiculed and bullied by his classmates.

5. The clerk's _____ behavior to her boss revealed her hope for a promotion.

6. "A good day's work for a good day's pay" is an example of _____ values.

Writing Exercise

Describe a foreign custom you have witnessed or read about. What purpose do you think it is meant to serve? Would it be a useful addition to our culture? Why or why not?

A Degree of Detachment

BRUCE SHRAGG

Should medical doctors become emotionally involved with patients? This article describes a doctor's struggle to remain uninvolved.

Vocabulary Preview

C.T. (computed tomography) scan technologist (par. 1)	person who takes X rays so that body organs can be seen clearly without the surrounding organs, bones, or muscles appearing on the X ray.
biopsy (par. 1)	removing cells or fluids from the body for testing
pathologist (par. 3)	a medical expert dealing with disease-related changes of the body
radiologist (par. 3)	a medical doctor who reads X rays
malignant (par. 6)	cancerous
tranquil (par. 7)	calm and quiet
aspirate (par. 9)	to use suction to remove fluid from a part of the body
cavalier (par. 10)	indifferent and easy-going about important things
discernment (par. 19)	the ability to recognize clearly
havoc (par. 19)	destruction, turmoil, confusion

Prereading

DIRECTIONS: *Preview the article and then answer the following questions:*

Think about the experiences you have had with medical doctors. Are they sensitive to your needs and feelings? Why or why not?

_____

_____

1   It's 10:15 on a Tuesday morning. I'm at my desk, dictating out a stack of X-rays, when the phone rings. It's Carol, our C.T. (computed tomography) scan technologist. "Dr. Shragg, we're ready to do the biopsy."

2   "I'll be right over," I tell her.

3   A woman has a tumor in her pancreas. Her internist has asked me, the radiologist, to do a needle biopsy. A pathologist will study the biopsy under the microscope and render a final diagnosis.

4   I put on my white doctor's coat, call the pathologist, who must be in the room at the time of biopsy, and mosey on over to the C.T. room. As I'm walking, I think about all sorts of things—my forthcoming trip up the California coast, the dinner I had with a friend last night, the tires I need for the car. I'm not particularly thinking about the needle I'm about to stick into a patient's abdomen. I walk into the room smiling.

5   "Hi, Mrs. Chambers," I say to a fairly robust, fiftyish woman lying on a gurney. "How are you feeling this morning?"

6   She does her best to smile. "Fine. Well, good as can be expected, I guess." If she were more truthful, she'd probably tell me she's scared to death. She knows, from what her doctor has told her, that there's a tumor in her pancreas, and that it might be malignant.

7   I put on my sterile gloves and make reassuring small talk. She asks me if I think it's cancer. The question makes me uncomfortable. Maybe one of the reasons I chose the relatively detached and tranquil field of diagnostic radiology is that we don't have to give patients bad news very often. We let the internists and surgeons be the purveyors of doom. But I know from experience that the odds that this tumor is malignant are very high. I tell her there's no way of knowing for sure whether something is benign or malignant without looking at it under the microscope. This isn't very reassuring to her, but it gets me off the hook.

8   Mrs. Chambers is slid into the large doughnutlike machine. As the preliminary scans are taken, I think about the impact of computers on medicine, about how amazing the C.T. scanner is. It allows us to see detailed cross-sectional anatomy. C.T. scans were new 10 years ago, when I was a student. We called them

CAT scans back then. Today, we take C.T. for granted, as an indispensable tool of modern medicine.

9   As the computer processes the scans of Mrs. Chamber's abdomen, the images are painted, one by one, on the television screen. The first image reveals part of the tumor. The next one, about a centimeter away, shows more of it. On the screen, I measure the distance from the skin to the center of the tumor—seven centimeters, straight down. I mark the skin, cleanse the area, inject a local anesthetic and make a small incision. By this time, the pathologist has arrived with her glass slides and the solutions she needs to stain the cells I'm about to aspirate from the tumor.

10   It's funny how cavalier we physicians are with needles. We stick so many needles into people, we forget that needles hurt. I sometimes joke with patients as I'm about to stick them. "This won't hurt me a bit." I think I'm being funny. But I know, from having been on the receiving end, that there's nothing funny about it.

11   Biopsy needles come in all sizes. The one I'm using is nine centimeters long and very skinny. I ask Mrs. Chambers to hold her breath as I insert the needle into her abdomen. Once more, she is positioned into the scanner—this time to get a picture of the tumor with the needle in place. The scan shows the needle tip to be precisely in the center of the tumor. "Not bad," I think. I attach a syringe to the biopsy needle, aspirating as I rotate the needle, gently moving it several millimeters up and down. I pull out the needle and syringe, handing them to the pathologist. My work, I hope, is done.

12   "You all right?" I ask Mrs. Chambers.

13   "Fine," she says. "I'm surprised how little it hurt."

14   I tell her it'll take about 10 minutes for the pathologist to stain the slides, to see if we have an adequate specimen. If the slides are good, the procedure is over. If not, we may have to repeat it one or two more times.

15   "I hope the slides are good," she says.

16   Hmm, I think. A good slide. What does that mean? To me, it means that the specimen will be adequate to make the diagnosis—in this case, probably cancer. And indeed, 10 minutes later, while the pathologist and I are reviewing the freshly stained slides, she says to me: "You got it. It's definitely malignant."

17   I feel a slight rush of exhilaration at having made the diagnosis. But as I saunter back to the C.T. room, I remind myself that this woman has just been given a sentence of death. I rationalize: somebody had to make the diagnosis. Maybe I'm saving her from extensive surgery for an incurable tumor. Maybe that will allow her a better quality of life during her remaining days.

18   I walk into the room, trying to be pleasant. "We're finished," I tell her. "The specimen is adequate. After the pathologist studies the slides, she'll contact your doctor. You should have the results later this afternoon. Are you feeling O.K.?" She nods, smiles, and thanks me. I feel a twinge of guilt for not telling her the result of the biopsy. It's her body. She has a right to know. But, again, I rationalize:

It's not my job. After all, her internist has a better rapport with her. She's his patient and, if I were Mrs. Chambers, I wouldn't want someone I hardly knew to tell me I had cancer. My guilt eases a bit.

19   Yet, as I return to my desk, the conflicting emotions linger. I did my job, and I did it well, which is all a man can really hope to do. Like a judge, like a financial analyst, like a nuclear physicist, I exercised reason, discernment, skill—and like their efforts, the result of my work can sometimes create havoc in other people's lives. Maybe a certain degree of detachment is necessary in order to do an optimal job.

20   Then I think of Mrs. Chambers. She will soon be faced with the task of putting her affairs in order, saying goodbye to her husband, her two sons, her daughter, her 2-year-old granddaughter.

21   I pick up my microphone and resume dictating out my stack of 21 X-rays.

Checking Your Comprehension

1. To what profession does the author belong?

_____

_____

2. What is one of the reasons why he chose this profession?

_____

_____

3. Describe the author's reactions and feelings toward Mrs. Chambers.

_____

_____

4. How does the author justify not telling Mrs. Chambers that she has cancer?

_____

_____

5. Why is the author pleased when he learns Mrs. Chambers's diagnosis?

_____

_____

6. Does the author feel he has helped Mrs. Chambers in any way? Explain.

_____

_____

7. What message is the writer trying to communicate through the article?

_____

_____

Critical Reading and Thinking

1. Do you think a degree of detachment is necessary to be a good doctor?

_____

2. Do you think the author should have told Mrs. Chambers that she had cancer? Justify your answer.

_____

_____

3. The author compares himself to a judge and a financial analyst. Is the comparison accurate? Explain your answer.

_____

_____

4. Is the language used in this article objective or subjective? Cite examples from the article to support your answer. (Objective and Subjective: see Chapter 13)

_____

_____

5. Do you think Mrs. Chambers knows or suspects the diagnosis?

_____

_____

6. Do you feel this article is descriptive? If so, identify several particularly descriptive words. (Descriptive Language: see Chapter 13)

_____

_____

Words in Context

DIRECTIONS: *Locate each word in the paragraph indicated and reread that paragraph. Then, based on the way the word is used, write a synonym or brief definition of each word.*

1. render (par. 3) _____

2. diagnosis (par. 3) _____

3. indispensable (par. 8) _____

4. exhilaration (par. 17) _____

5. rationalize (par. 17) _____

6. rapport (par. 18) _____

7. detachment (par. 19) _____

Vocabulary Review

1. Using your knowledge of these professions, match the person with the job he or she might perform in the diagnosis of cancer.

_____ a. reads the X rays   1. C.T. scan technologist

_____ b. explains the way in which cancer affects   2. radiologist
                    the body   3. pathologist

_____ c. sets up and performs the X rays

2. Describe something you might <u>rationalize</u> about to yourself.

_____

3. What is a <u>biopsy</u>?

_____

4. If a person felt <u>tranquil</u>, how might he or she act?

_____

5. What is a <u>malignant</u> tumor?

_____

6. If a professor acted <u>cavalier</u> about your failing a class, how would you feel and why?

_____

7. Name an event that could easily be described as creating <u>havoc</u>.

_____

Writing Exercises

1. Write a paragraph describing how you would react if you learned that the doctor who did a biopsy withheld information from you.

2. How detached should doctors be? Is detachment good or bad? Whether you think it is good or bad, do you think detachment is necessary? Write a paragraph discussing these issues.

The Power of Language

NIKKI GIOVANNI

Language is our primary means of communication. Nikki Giovanni, a well-known poet, discusses function, development, and the power of language.

Vocabulary Preview

integrity (par.1)	honesty
codifiable (par. 1)	that which can be organized into a system
interchangeable (par. 3)	able to be used in each other's place
internalized (par. 3)	made part of one's way of thinking
segregation (par. 5)	the separation of people of different races
constructive (par. 5)	leading to changes and advances
anathema (par. 6)	a curse
abrogate (par. 6)	abolish, stop
devised (par. 8)	created
aggrieved (par. 8)	person who has been injured, offended
reconcile (par. 8)	to settle, make compatible

Prereading

DIRECTIONS: *Preview the selection and answer the following questions.*

Why is language important? What does it allow us to do?

_____

_____

1   The giraffe is the only species without a voice. We share with the dolphin identifiable laughter. We recognize and give integrity to the language of the apes,
baboons, orangutans and other primates though we cannot translate it. We understand and appreciate the growls and howls of the wolves, hyenas, lions, tigers, our
own pet dogs and cats. Yet human beings are the only species with codifiable language.

2   What joy that first human must have experienced when sound, reproducible
sound, came from his throat. Did he howl in imitation of the wind; did he chirp
with delight at a bird; did he laugh and gurgle like the stream? He probably
pointed and made a sound. And someone pointed and made a sound back.

3   Language builds from necessity. Only recently have we invented microwave,
electric boogie, radar, penicillin, supersonic transport, superstars. Our technology
has afforded us a new lease on life, so terms like "death with dignity," "sexual
preference," "artificial intelligence" and "single by choice" have become necessary
to explain ourselves to ourselves. Most people recognize Acquired Immunity Deficiency Syndrome or herpes, though they react to those words as if it was still B.C.
and thereby interchangeable with "leper." Mankind has learned a lot but we have
not internalized the intent.

4   We have learned that separate is never equal and therefore cannot be separate.
We have learned that quality education means young people can read, write, com-
pute, and think with some logic. We have learned we cannot expect people to pull
themselves up by their bootstraps then take the boots away; but those of us without shoes have also learned we must never cease marching forward—no matter
what hardships we encounter.

5   One of the new terms is "role model." When people do not want to do what
history requires, they say they have no "role models." I'm glad Phillis Wheatley
did not know she had no "role model" and wrote her poetry anyway. I'm glad
Harriet Tubman did not know she had no "role model" and lead the slaves to
freedom. I'm glad Frederick Douglass did not know he had no "role model" and
walked off that plantation in Maryland to become one of the great oratorical fight-
ers for freedom. I'm glad Thurgood Marshall did not say the Constitution pre-
scribes me as three fifths of a man therefore I cannot argue the Brown vs. Topeka
case before the Supreme Court. I'm glad Martin Luther King, Jr. did not say but
segregation is the law of the land and we cannot defy the law, but rather raised his
voice in constructive engagement against the segregationist practices of our generation.

6   The power of speech, the freedom to engage our hearts and our bodies in dialogue, is the most precious freedom of all. To secure all other rights granted to us
by either our religions or our laws it is necessary to raise our voices. An idea inside
our heads is, to our fellow humans, the same as no idea. It must be expressed if it
is to have power. And the voice, the pen, is far mightier than any sword, any jail,

any attempt to silence. Censorship is an anathema to a free people. We may not always like what we hear but we are always the poorer if we close down dialogue; if we abrogate free speech, and the open exchange of ideas.

7   A great part of the joy of being human is not that we think; many other mammals think. Nor that we communicate with our fellow mammals; all other mammals communicate inter- and intra-species; but that we have a history which is located in human memory and in books. We are not bound by the moment but can go back thousands of years to see how far we have progressed; and we can go forward in imagination to envision our future.

8   We with our history of slavery where native gods, language and drums were taken from us devised a language using the Christian tools available. They serve us well, giving voice to frustration; offering comfort to the aggrieved. Music is a universal language: The field hollers, the gospel calls to worship are universally recognized as a major Black contribution. Patience is universal: The faith of a mustard seed, the determination of one drop of water in the Grand Canyon, 'cause if Job waited on the Lord tell me why can't I? Love is universal because we recognize and accept the call to reconcile the irreconcilable. And books are our window to these worlds.

Checking Your Comprehension

DIRECTIONS: *Mark each statement with a T for true or F for false based on the content of the selection.*

_____   1. Other animals have language that is based on a system of sounds.

_____   2. Human language has been simplified with the development of technology.

_____   3. Many leaders and important people have accomplished great things without role models.

_____   4. Martin Luther King, Jr., did not use language to make changes in the world.

_____   5. Freedom of speech is the most important freedom, because without language and the power to speak, we cannot secure any of the other freedoms we have.

_____   6. Animals other than humans think.

_____   7. Humans are the only animals with a history preserved in words.

Critical Reading and Thinking

1. Is the author subjective or objective about her topic? (Objective and Subjective: see Chapter 13)

   _____

   _____

2. Review paragraph 4. Is the author stating facts or opinions? If they are facts, what evidence does she give? (Fact and Opinion: see Chapter 13)

   _____

   _____

3. How does the author feel about role models? (par. 5) What kind of value judgment does she make about them?

   _____

   _____

4. Review paragraph 3. Are the last two sentences facts or generalizations? (Generalizations: see Chapter 13)

   _____

   _____

5. What kind of connotation does the author suggest terms like Acquired Immune Deficiency Syndrome (AIDS) and herpes have today? (par. 3)

   _____

   _____

Words in Context

DIRECTIONS: *Locate each word in the paragraph indicated and reread that paragraph. Then, based on the way the word is used, write a synonym or brief definition for each.*

1. reproducible (par. 2) _____

2. dialogue (par. 6) _____

3. progressed (par. 7) _____

4. irreconcilable (par. 8) _____

Vocabulary Review

DIRECTIONS: *Match each word in Column A with its meaning in Column B by writing the letter of the definition next to the number of the word it defines.*

Column A

_____ 1. segregation

_____ 2. devised

_____ 3. reconcile

_____ 4. interchangeable

_____ 5. integrity

_____ 6. constructive

_____ 7. codifiable

Column B

a. settle

b. causing change

c. able to be systematized

d. made

e. can replace each other

f. separation of races

g. honesty

Writing Exercise

Describe an instance in which language gave you power or freedom. What did you say? What effect did your words have?

Characteristics of the News

ROBERT L. LINEBERRY

Who decides which news stories and events to report on radio and television and in newspapers? This article, taken from an American government textbook, discusses the factors that influence these media decisions.

Vocabulary Preview

emphasize (par. 1)	focus on, stress
instinctively (par. 2)	by an inborn tendency, naturally
procession (par. 2)	moving line, like a parade
ostensibly (par. 2)	publicly, conspicuously
preoccupation (par. 2)	being absorbed, focusing attention on one thing
satiety (par. 3)	a state of being filled
beget (par. 4)	create, give birth to
parochial (par. 4)	local, limited to a small area
miscellany (par. 5)	collection, group
calamities (par. 5)	troubles, disasters
gauge (par. 5)	to measure
unabashedly (par. 7)	without embarrassment
partisanship (par. 7)	the state of favoring one side over another
transcribing (par. 8)	writing down exactly as spoken

Prereading

DIRECTIONS: *Preview the selection and answer the following questions.*

What kinds of events do you see reported on the news? Do news programs and newspapers portray the news differently and report different stories? How?

1   American news covers a bewildering variety of subjects. Under the right circumstances, virtually any happening can qualify as news and virtually any person can make the news. But there are nevertheless standard patterns of newsworthiness. Doris Graber contends that American news tends to focus on events that are novel and entertaining, that highlight familiar people and situations, and that emphasize conflict and violence.

Partiality: Novel and Entertaining

2   News personnel instinctively favor stories that are novel and entertaining. Stories in endless procession feature political and personal misadventures, natural and human-made disasters, personal tragedies and triumphs, bizarre and unexpected events, celebrity activities, and ostensibly high-drama occurrences. Preoccupation with novelty and entertainment leads to news stories that stress the trivial aspects of serious developments and the present rather than the past. Complex issues—inflation, unemployment, poverty, disease—are often treated in terms of personal stakes and misfortunes.

3   As themes in the presentation of American news, novelty and entertainment have never been checked by a condition of popular satiety. This standard cast to news troubles critics. Consider these views from an article published in the *Saturday Evening Post* more than half a century ago (1927):

> And as affairs get harder to understand, the newspapers print relatively less about them, rather than more, because they are harder reading and their subscribers mostly want easy reading. Whatever other objects the newspaper editor may have in mind, attracting readers is his first object. If he gives them, the year through, ten columns of sports and five columns of comic strip to every quarter column of local political affairs—which is probably a very liberal estimate—it is because he has found out that their day-by-day interests run in about that proportion. There is no point in blaming the newspapers.

Partiality: Familiar People and Situations

4   Those who organize the news also prefer stories that involve familiar people and situations. One result is that coverage is circular. News about familiar people makes them even better known and thus even more newsworthy: news stories

beget news stories. Well-known politicians (and "their" agendas) thrive in this information environment, unless scandal is involved, while lesser-known ones struggle for public attention. And second, the news is more parochial than it would be otherwise. A public preoccupied with daily living does not have to work as hard to understand familiar and similar events within its own borders as it does to understand distant and foreign news.

Partiality: Conflict and Violence

5   Finally, attentiveness to certain kinds of stories is reflected in a heavy emphasis on conflict and violence. Stories of crime, bombings and rioting, assaults, assassinations and murders, investigations, indictments and convictions, and a miscellany of personal calamities crowd the pages of the typical newspaper and the format of television and radio news. Particularly in the big city media and network broadcasting, news is bad news, news is high drama. Coverage of foreign news commonly focuses on violent events. The consequences of the media's hyperattentiveness to conflict and violence are hard to gauge. Doris Graber argues that it leads to a damaging distortion of reality, to the perception that violence is an appropriate way to settle disputes. Political groups may behave violently to obtain news coverage and publicize their cause.

Neglect of Persistent Problems

6   Media leaders have never believed that public tastes are the only valid criteria for the selection of news. But it sometimes appears this way, and there is no mistaking the fact that the media place heavy emphasis on stories that entertain. Many feel that news organizations neglect the analysis of complex and persistent social, economic, and political problems. Clean water, the argument runs, becomes a news item only when there is a major oil spill, the status of prison conditions only when there is a violent riot, foreign policy only during failures such as the arms-for-hostages Iran-contra scandal. "Stories emphasize the surface appearances, the furious sounds and fiery sights of battle, the well-known or colorful personalities involved—whatever is dramatic," write David L. Paletz and Robert M. Entman. "Underlying causes and actual impacts are little known or long remembered."

Coverage of Political News by Newspapers and Network Television: Similarities and Differences

7   Both the print and broadcast media have an unabashedly practical aim: to gain and hold an audience (and thus attract advertisers). And, of course, they share other characteristics. A study of news media coverage of presidential campaigns by Michael J. Robinson and Margaret A. Sheehan found that print (represented by

the UPI wire service) and network television (represented by CBS) are quite similar in three major respects. First, both are generally committed to "objective reporting" (focusing on observable facts and events, while declining to take explicit positions on candidate qualifications or to draw conclusions or inferences about the events being covered). Second, both tend to emphasize the "horse race" (or competitiveness) aspect of campaigns; "who's winning" evaluations account for almost all of the explicit conclusions drawn by the media. And third, both the wires and networks are generally balanced and generally fair in their treatment of candidates and parties in terms of providing shares of news space and steering clear of partisanship in accounts (though "losers" and minor parties fare poorly in both print and television news).

8   Differences between the two in campaign reporting nevertheless are substantial. As contrasted with the print media, network television news is:

more personal (more inclined to focus on candidate behavior—especially blunders, gaffes, and scandals);

more mediating (more inclined to tell the audience what the candidates are "up to," not simply what they are doing—in other words, translating rather than transcribing);

more analytical (more inclined to explain and interpret events and behavior);

more political (more inclined to politicize news by portraying leaders as "politicians");

more critical (more inclined to be critical and negative in the treatment of candidates); and

more thematic (more inclined to focus on storytelling, combining various news items into overarching, and perhaps melodramatic, themes).

Checking Your Comprehension

1. What kinds of stories does the news focus on?

   _____

   _____

2. Why, according to the *Saturday Evening Post,* do newspapers print less about events as they become harder to understand?

   _____

   _____

3. Give two reasons why newswriters choose stories about familiar people and situations.

_____

_____

4. What kinds of issues do news people tend to ignore?

_____

_____

5. What is the media's primary goal?

_____

_____

6. Name two differences in campaign reporting between television news and newspapers.

_____

_____

Critical Reading and Thinking

1. What is the author's attitude toward the news?

_____

_____

2. Does the author offer any support for his conclusion that attracting advertisers is the media's aim? What other goals might people have who write and produce the news?

_____

_____

3. Review paragraph 6. Why should you or should you not accept the statement by Paletz and Entman? What would you want to know about them before you accept their opinions?

_____

_____

4. Review the information in paragraphs 7 and 8 about the study by Robinson and Sheehan. How is this information different from the quote from Paletz and Entman? What information is given about the study and how it was conducted? Of the two groups of people mentioned in the article, who would you believe more, based on the information you are given?

_____

_____

Words in Context

DIRECTIONS: *Locate each word in the paragraph indicated and reread that paragraph. Then, based on the way the word is used, write a synonym or brief definition for each.*

1. newsworthiness (par. 1) _____

2. circular (par. 4) _____

3. hyperattentiveness (par. 5) _____

4. distortion (par. 5) _____

5. observable (par. 7) _____

6. mediating (par. 8) _____

7. analytical (par. 8) _____

8. thematic (par. 8) _____

Vocabulary Review

DIRECTIONS: *Complete each of the following sentences by choosing one of the words presented in the Vocabulary Preview.*

1. Because Bill has never left his hometown, his view of the world is very _____.

2. The professor cancelled his class because of some family _____.

3. My anatomy class tomorrow will _____ the cardiovascular system.

4. After Sue quit smoking, she still had a _____ with cigarettes.

5. The car whizzed by so quickly, I could not _____ its speed.

6. Secretaries know that _____ letters from a dictaphone requires accuracy.

7. Ants crawled across the cupboard in a _____, one after the other.

8. Andrew was _____ tired—yawning and rubbing his eyes.

9. Babies _____ know how to breathe.

10. Gwen _____ entered the room and grinned at everyone.

Writing Exercise

Do you prefer reading the newspaper or watching television news? Explain your preference in a paragraph.

Exploring Virtual Reality

KEN PIMENTEL AND KEVIN TEIXEIRA

Can you imagine sitting in your own living room, traveling anywhere in the universe, and being able to see, feel, hear, and smell things as if you are really there? This is just one of the many possible uses of virtual reality technology.

Vocabulary Preview

sprawling (par. 1)	spread out
transmits (par. 2)	sends; passes on
improvisation (par. 6)	performance without preparation
evokes (par. 6)	suggests; brings out
evolving (par. 6)	changing
animation (par. 8)	movement of a screen image
synthesized (par. 8)	created electronically
spawned (par. 10)	brought about; started
disembodied (par. 14)	separate from a body; not human

Prereading

DIRECTIONS: *Preview the selection and answer the following questions.*

1. What does the term "virtual reality" mean to you?

_____

_____

_____

2. Name several uses of virtual reality presented in the article.

_____

_____

_____

1   *T*his morning, at the NASA Ames Research Center in Mountain View, California, Dr. Lew Hitchner explores the surface of Mars. He's wearing virtual reality (VR) goggles with two tiny liquid crystal display (LCD) screens inside. They give him a 3-D view of the rocky Martian landscape, Utopia Planitia, that was reconstructed from satellite data sent back by a Viking spacecraft stationed on Mars. With a change of software, he'll be flying across the sprawling canyons of Valles Marineris later this afternoon.

2   Just down the hallway in the "view lab," Dr. Stephen Ellis is remotely controlling robots, wearing VR goggles and a wired glove. The glove senses the movements of his hand and fingers, and a computer interprets and transmits them as commands for a robot arm. Ellis sees what the robot sees and the robot mimics his movements, even though he and the robot are in different rooms and can't see each other. Someday, using VR, robots will act as human eyes, arms, and ears on other planets.

3   Hitcher and Ellis are part of a NASA VR program. The goal of the program is to explore planets without physically sending people there. Instead, in the future robots will let many people visit as virtual astronauts.

4   Dr. Nomura of Matsushita, Japan, is working on a commercial VR kitchen designer, using VPL Research equipment. A Shinjuku department store is already using one of his systems to help Japanese consumers redesign their kitchens. A customer provides a drawing of his kitchen layout, which is loaded into the computer. He can then select the appliances, color, and features he wants in his kitchen using the system. After he's arranged everything, he puts on VR goggles and a wired glove to take a tour of his design. He can open drawers, turn on the water in the sink, turn the appliances on and off, and even listen to birds through the window. If everything looks, feels, and sounds the way he wants it to, the computer places the customer's order based on the layout and items selected.

5   Audiences head towards San Francisco's nightclub district, where Toon Town is getting ready to open its doors. The clubs really come alive after 2 A.M., when the "ravers" appear; engineers, accountants, artists, clerks, and data information workers dressed in wild clothes with even wilder hairstyles. They come for the music, the dancing till dawn, and the "virtual scene."

6   The owners of the club run the shows, and each night is different from the last. They use Amiga computer, PCs, video editing equipment, film, lasers, and light shows, and invite unusual musicians to entertain, such as bands with hand-made electronic instruments. Like rap music artists who build new music by sampling other recordings, they create and project their graphics, animation, and sampled video in a constant improvisation on people, screens, mirrored globes, and all interior surfaces of the building. It lasts until morning, a light show that evokes the sense of a constantly evolving environment.

7   Toon Town has found an audience hungry for new media concepts—using computers to visit, stimulate, create, and control new worlds. In a corner of the club, dozens of people line up to pay for a chance to sit down, put on goggles, and fly around in a virtual world. "They all expect to be using one at home in a couple of years," says Vince Thomas, one of the club's owners.

8   A second group of people in the club is gathered to use the Mandala Machine, where a Toon Town patron is dancing and playing imaginary musical instruments. His image is captured by a video camera and fed into a computer, where it's combined with interactive video and animation, and projected on to the wall in front of him. He controls the animation through his movements as he watches himself on the wall in the scene—with synthesized notes erupting as he slaps the virtual drums.

9   This is a very small sample of what's going on in the exploding realm of virtual reality. Don't worry if at first you feel a bit confused. VR is both a new technology and a set of ideas—concepts that are spreading faster than the hardware and software that produce them. There are several different approaches that fall under the label of *virtual reality,* though they don't all use the same effects to achieve the same results.

10   Worldwide, VR is happening in protected pockets of technology; inside giant corporations, universities, and small entrepreneurial start-ups; in Berlin and North Carolina; covering Japan; and especially in the San Francisco Bay Area. Although Silicon Valley has a lot to do with this new industry, there's more to VR than "high tech." VR has spawned a new interaction between musicians, artists, entrepreneurs, and electronic tinkerers. A rare excitement is in the air, an excitement that come from breaking through to something new. Computers are about to take the next big step—out of the lab and into the street—and the street can't wait.

11   Virtual reality is all about illusion. It's about computer graphics in the theater of the mind. It's about the use of high technology to convince yourself that you're in another reality, experiencing some event that doesn't physically exist in the world in front of you. Virtual reality is also a new media for getting your hands on information, getting inside information, and representing ideas in ways not previously possible.

12   Virtual reality is where the computer disappears and you become "the ghost in the machine." There's no little screen of symbols you must manipulate or type

commands into to get the computer to do something. Instead, the computer retreats behind the scenes and becomes invisible, leaving you free to concentrate on tasks, ideas, problems, and communications.

13   For four generations, people have experienced a type of virtual reality using the telephone. It has now been over 100 years since the introduction of the telephone, and today it's so deeply embedded in our cultural consciousness that we give it as much thought as a doorknob. As a society, we've forgotten what a shock the telephone was when it was first introduced—the strangeness of listening to a ghostly, disembodied voice.

14   Like the telephone, computers are a communications medium. Like the telescope and microscope, virtual reality is also a tool for revealing new ways of looking at information. VR gives users an efficient and effortless flow of data, details, and information in the most natural format possible—vision, sound, and sensations presented as an environment, part of the natural media of human experience and thought.

Checking Your Comprehension

1. What is the goal of the NASA virtual reality program?

   _____

   _____

2. How is the Toon Town different from traditional nightclubs?

   _____

   _____

3. Give an example of a "raver."

   _____

   _____

4. What is the Mandala Machine?

   _____

   _____

5. What type of bands do they have in Toon Town?

_____

_____

Critical Reading and Thinking

1. Explain how virtual reality allows Dr. Lew Hitchner to fly across the canyons.

_____

_____

2. Describe how Japanese consumers can redesign their kitchens with Dr. No-mura's virtual reality research equipment.

_____

_____

3. Describe how virtual reality is used in San Francisco's nightclubs.

_____

_____

4. What does the author mean by the following statement: "Computers are about to take the next big step—out of the lab and into the streets"?

_____

_____

5. How is the telephone the same as or different from the other types of virtual reality discussed in this article?

_____

_____

Words in Context

DIRECTIONS: *Locate each word in the paragraph indicated. Then, based on the way the word is used, write a synonym or brief definition of each.*

1. mimics (par. 2) _____

2. erupting (par. 7) _____

3. embedded (par. 12) _____

Vocabulary Review

DIRECTIONS: *Match the word in Column A with its meaning in Column B.*

Column A

_____ 1. evokes

_____ 2. sprawling

_____ 3. disembodied

_____ 4. spawned

_____ 5. transmits

_____ 6. animation

_____ 7. improvisation

_____ 8. synthesized

_____ 9. evolving

Column B

a. changing

b. sends; passes on

c. performance without preparation

d. suggests; brings out

e. separate from a body; not human

f. created electronically or artificially

g. brought about; started

h. movement of a screen image

i. spread out

Writing Exercises

1. Write a paragraph describing one way in which virtual reality could be useful in solving a problem.

2. Suppose you could have your own personal virtual reality set for 24 hours. Write a paragraph describing which set you would choose and how you would use it.

Night Work, Sleep, and Health

SAUL KASSIN

Do you wake up when you would rather be sleeping? Do you have difficulty staying awake late when you need to? This textbook excerpt explains how your biological clock works.

Vocabulary Preview

rotating (par. 2)	turning; taking turns
disrupted (par. 2)	upset
internal (par. 2)	built in
adverse (par. 2)	negative
inadequate (par. 3)	not enough
posed (par. 4)	presented
decline (par. 4)	decrease; lessening
realignment (par. 4)	lining up again; adjustment
circadian (par. 4)	twenty-four hour

Prereading

DIRECTIONS: *Preview the selection and answer the following questions.*

1. With which human biological function is this reading concerned?

   _____

   _____

   _____

2. What problems are caused by lack of sleep?

_____

_____

_____

We humans are diurnal creatures—active during the day and asleep at night. Thus we like to work from 9 to 5 and then play, sleep, and awaken to the light of a new day. Yet an estimated 20 percent of all Americans—including emergency-room doctors and nurses, fire-fighters, police officers, telephone operators, security guards, factory workers, interstate truckers, and power-plant operators—are forced to work late night shifts. The question is, What is the effect? Do people adapt over time to shift work, and other late-night activity, or does it compromise their health and safety?

Both biological and social clocks set the body for activity during the daytime and sleep at night, so many shift workers must struggle to stay alert. People who choose night work fare better than those who are assigned on a rotating shift basis (Baron, 1994). Still, surveys reveal that shift workers in general get fewer hours of sleep per week than day workers, complain that their sleep is significantly disrupted, and report being drowsy on the job. Often they blame their lack of sleep on environmental stimuli such as ringing phones, crying babies, honking horns, and other daytime noises. But part of the problem, too, is that the body's internal alarm clock tries to awaken the day sleeper. Either way, the adverse effects can be seen at work. In a survey of a thousand train drivers, 70 percent admitted to having dozed off at the wheel at least once and 11 percent said they do so on most night shifts. These reports are confirmed by studies in which EEG activity in train drivers was monitored. Those who operated trains in the middle of the night often took quick, two- to three-second microsleeps, which may interfere with job performance and increase the risk of accident (Carskadon, 1993).

The National Highway Transportation Safety Administration estimates that up to 200,000 traffic accidents a year are sleep related—and that 20 percent of all drivers have dozed off at least once while behind the wheel. To avoid rush-hour traffic, interstate truckers often drive late at night. The result: Due to drowsiness, truck drivers are 16 times more likely to have an accident between 4 A.M. and 6 A.M. than during the daytime hours (Chollar, 1989). Similarly disturbing are the stories told by medical interns and residents, many of whom have worked 120-hour work weeks, including 36 hours at a stretch. According to David Dinges, "Human error causes between 60 percent and 90 percent of all workplace accidents . . . and inadequate sleep is a major factor in human error" (quoted in Toufexis, 1990, pp. 78–79).

4   Can anything be done to lessen the dangers that are posed by shift work and the corresponding decline in alertness and job performance at night? Richard Coleman (1986) recommends that when rotating shifts are necessary, managers should maximize the number of days between shift changes (for example, adjustment is easier in three-week cycles than in one-week cycles) and assign workers to successively later shifts rather than earlier shifts (a person who is rotated from the 4 P.M. shift to the midnight shift will adjust more quickly than one who is rotated in the opposite direction, from midnight to 4 P.M.). Charles Czeisler and his colleagues (1990) have also found that the realignment of the circadian rhythm can be speeded up by exposing shift workers to bright, daytime levels of light in the workplace and to eight hours of total darkness at home during the day. Within a week, the body's biological clock can thus be reset and the health risks of night work reduced.

Checking Your Comprehension

1. What effect does working the night shift seem to have on those who normally work during the day?

    _____

    _____

2. How is the sleep of shift workers different from day workers?

    _____

    _____

3. When do interstate truck drivers usually drive? Why?

    _____

    _____

4. When is the worst time for truck drivers to be driving?

    _____

    _____

5. What can managers do to lessen the dangers of fatigue for shift workers?

_____

_____

Critical Reading and Thinking

1. In the second paragraph the author refers to "microsleeps." What does this mean?

_____

_____

2. The author states "we like to work from 9 to 5 and then play, sleep, and awaken to the light of a new day." Do you think this is true of everyone?

_____

_____

3. The author states that "inadequate sleep is a major factor in human error." Do you think this is true? Do you make a lot of errors due to inadequate sleep?

_____

_____

4. If you were working on the night shift, what might you do to help yourself stay awake?

_____

_____

5. What could be done to overcome the problems truck drivers experience?

_____

_____

Words in Context

DIRECTIONS: *Locate each word in the paragraph indicated. Then, based on the way the word is used, write a synonym or brief definition of each.*

1. diurnal (par. 1) _____

2. rotating (par. 2) _____

3. environmental stimuli (par. 2) _____

Vocabulary Review

DIRECTIONS: *Complete each of the following sentences by choosing one of the words presented in the Vocabulary Preview.*

1. When one student fainted the entire class was _____.

2. Eating spicy foods can have _____ affects on some people.

3. If the tires from your car are off balance, you should get a _____.

4. If you cram the night before an exam, your long-term recall of the material will probably be _____.

5. The human body operates on a _____ rhythm.

6. The instructor _____ several interesting questions.

Writing Exercises

1. Describe a time when you received less sleep than usual. What effect did this have on you the next day?

2. Write a paragraph describing whether and why you would or would not be a good candidate for working the night shift.

An Amateur Marriage

STEVE TESICH

Getting married is an important step in most people's lives. Weddings are planned for months, sometimes years, ahead. This writer presents a different, more casual attitude toward marriage.

Vocabulary Preview

mythical (par. 2)	imaginary; not real
milestones (par. 2)	important events or turning points in life
rituals of passage (par. 2)	ceremonial events signifying changes or important acts
tidal (par. 7)	naturally forceful
ludicrous (par. 8)	obviously absurd or ridiculous
endeavor (par. 10)	careful effort; honest attempt
aimlessness (par. 12)	pointlessness; the state of being without direction or purpose

Prereading

DIRECTIONS: *Preview the selection and answer the following question.*

Try to think of events that have changed your life, or that are usually thought of as important events by others. Make a list of these events.

_____

_____

1   *E*veryone told me that when I turned 16 some great internal change would oc-cur. I truly expected the lights to go down on my former life and come up again on a new, far more enchanting one. It didn't work. Nothing happened. When asked by others, I lied and said that, yes, I did feel a great change had taken place. They lied and told me that they could see it in me.

2   They lied again when I turned 18. There were rumors that I was now a "man." I noticed no difference, but I pretended to have all the rumored symp-toms of manhood. Even though these mythical milestones, these rituals of pas-sage, were not working for me, I still clung to the belief that they should, and I lied and said they were.

3   My 21st birthday was the last birthday I celebrated. The rituals weren't work-ing, and I was tired of pretending I was changing. I was merely growing—adding on rooms for all the kids who were still me to live in. At 21, I was single but a fam-ily man nevertheless.

4   All these birthday celebrations helped to prepare me for the greatest myth of all: marriage. Marriage comes with more myths attached to it than a six-volume set of ancient Greek history. Fortunately for me, by the time I decided to get mar-ried I didn't believe in myths anymore.

5   It was a very hot day in Denver, and I think Becky and I decided to get mar-ried because we knew the city hall was air-conditioned. It was a way of hanging around a cool place for a while. I had forgotten to buy a wedding ring, but Becky was still wearing the ring from her previous marriage, so we used that one. It did the job. She had to take it off and then put it back on again, but it didn't seem to bother anyone. The air-conditioners were humming.

6   I felt no great change take place as I repeated our marriage vows. I did not feel any new rush of "commitment" to the woman who was now my wife, nor did I have any plans to be married to her forever. I did love her, but I saw no reason why I should feel that I had to love her forever. I would love her for as long as I loved her. I assumed she felt the same way. The women I saw on my way out of city hall, a married man, did not look any less beautiful than the women I saw on my way in. It was still hot outside. We walked to our car carrying plastic bags con-taining little samples of mouthwash, toothpaste, shampoo and aspirin, gifts from the Chamber of Commerce to all newlyweds.

7   And so my marriage began—except that I never really felt the beginning. I had nothing against transforming myself into a married man, but I felt no tidal pull of change. I assumed Becky had married me and not somebody else, so why should I become somebody else? She married a family of kids of various ages, all of them me, and I married a family of kids of various ages, all of them her. At one time or another I assumed some of them were bound to get along.

8   Marriage, I was told, required work. This sounded all wrong to me from the start. I couldn't quite imagine the kind of "work" it required, what the hours

were, what the point was. The very idea of walking into my apartment and "working" on my marriage seemed ludicrous. My apartment was a place where I went to get away from work. The rest of life was full of work. If marriage required "work," I would have to get another apartment just for myself where I could go and rest. Since I couldn't afford that at the time, I said nothing to Becky about working on our marriage. She said nothing about it herself. We were either very wise or very lazy.

9   We are led to believe that the harder we try, the better we get. This "aerobic dancing theory" of life may apply to certain things, but I don't think marriage is one of them. You can't go to a gym and pump marriage. It can't be tuned-up like a car. It can't be trained like a dog. In this century of enormous scientific breakthroughs, there have been no major marriage breakthroughs that I know of.

10   Progress junkies find this a frustrating state of affairs. They resist the notion that marriage is essentially an amateur endeavor, not a full-time profession, and they keep trying to work on their marriages and make them better. The only way to do that is to impose a structure on the marriage and then fiddle and improve the structure. But that has nothing to do with the way you feel when the guests have left the house and it's just the two of you again. You are either glad you're there with that person or you're not. I've been both.

11   This need to improve, the belief that we can improve everything, brings to mind some of my friends who are constantly up-dating their stereo equipment until, without being aware of it, they wind up listening to the equipment and not to the music. You can do the same thing to friendship, to marriage, to life in general. Let's just say I have chosen to listen to the music, such as it is, on the equipment at hand.

12   The best trips that I have taken were always last-minute affairs, taken as a lark. When I've sent off for brochures and maps, the trips always turned into disappointments. The time I invested in planning fed my expectations, and I traveled to fulfill my expectations rather than just to go somewhere I hadn't been. I consider my marriage one of those trips taken as a lark. I have become rather fond of the sheer aimlessness of the journey. It's a choice. I know full well that people do plan journeys to the Himalayas, they hire guides, they seek advice, and when they get there, instead of being disappointed, they experience a kind of exhilaration that I never will. My kind of marriage will never reach Mount Everest. You just don't go there as a lark, nor do you get there by accident.

13   I'm neither proud nor ashamed of the fact that I've stayed married for 13 years. I don't consider it an accomplishment of any kind. I have changed; my wife has changed. Our marriage, however, for better or worse, is neither better nor worse. It has remained the same. But the climate has changed.

14   I got married on a hot day a long time ago, because it was a way of cooling off for a while. Over the years, it's also become a place where I go to warm up when the world turns cold.

Checking Your Comprehension

DIRECTIONS: *Mark each of the following statements T for true or F for false based on the content of the selection.*

_____ 1. On his eighteenth birthday, the author felt that a change had occurred in his life.

_____ 2. The author bought his wife a wedding ring before they were married.

_____ 3. When the author got married, he did not feel any new commitment or change in his feelings toward his wife.

_____ 4. The author disagrees with the idea that people have to "work" on a marriage.

_____ 5. The author believes that last-minute, unplanned trips are often the best.

_____ 6. The author was married when he was twenty.

_____ 7. The author did not love his wife at the time he married her.

Critical Reading and Thinking

1. Do you think the author gave more thought to the decision to get married than he admits in the article? Did he really get married, as he said, because the city hall was air-conditioned? If not, why did he say he did?

_____

_____

2. Did the author expect to feel different after he was married? How do you know?

_____

_____

3. Do you agree or disagree with the principle that "the harder we try, the better we get"? Are there some situations in which that statement might apply and others in which it does not? If so, give several examples.

_____

_____

4. What things about life did the author use this article to comment on or criticize?

_____

_____

5. Can you think of other events or milestones in life when everyone expects a change to occur or for you to feel or act differently?

_____

_____

6. Think of an event or milestone in your life (if you are or were married, think of the day you were married). Did people expect you to feel or act differently? Did you feel different that day?

_____

_____

7. The writer uses figurative language to express his ideas in several places in the article. Explain what Tesich means by each of the following statements. (Figurative language: see Chapter 12)

  a. I was merely growing—adding on rooms for all the kids who were still me to live in. (par. 3)

  _____

  b. At 21, I was single but a family man nevertheless. (par. 3)

  _____

  c. She married a family of kids of various ages, all of them me, . . . (par. 7)

  _____

8. Does the title reflect the content of the article? Why or why not?

_____

_____

Words in Context

DIRECTIONS: *Locate each word in the paragraph indicated and reread that paragraph. Then, based on the way the word is used, write a synonym or brief definition for each.*

1. transforming (par. 7) _____

2. lark (par. 12) _____

3. exhilaration (par. 12) _____

Vocabulary Review

1. Name a milestone in your life.

   _____

2. Give an example of something mythical.

   _____

3. Describe a ritual of passage in your family's customs or in your religion.

   _____

4. Give an example of an action or behavior you think is ludicrous.

   _____

5. Name an endeavor that has been taking a lot of your time recently.

   _____

6. Give an example of something that you have done in an aimless way.

   _____

Writing Exercise

The author explains that he did not feel any differently as he reached certain ages or when he got married. Write a paragraph discussing whether or not, and if so, how such milestones have affected you.

Why do we Grow Lawns Around our Houses?

DAVID FELDMAN

Lawns commonly surround buildings and homes. Have you ever wondered why we have them?

Vocabulary Preview

imponderable (par. 1)	unexplainable
omnipresent (par. 1)	in all places at all times
revenue (par. 2)	income
eons (par. 3)	a very long period of time
circumstantial evidence (par. 3)	evidence that does not conclusively prove something but only tends to support it
scythes (par. 4)	blades used to cut long grass
provocative (par. 5)	causing excitement or feeling
aesthetic (par. 5)	having to do with art or beauty
predilection (par. 5)	preference
foraging (par. 5)	searching for vegetables or fruits for food
savanna (par. 5)	a grassy region with a few trees in a tropical climate
emphatic (par. 7)	certain, definite

Prereading

DIRECTIONS: Preview the selection and answer the following questions.

Do you like lawns? What is it about them you like?

_____

_____

1 *A*t first blush, this Imponderable seems easily solved. Lawns are omnipresent in residential neighborhoods and even around multiunit dwellings in all but the most crowded urban areas. Lawns are pretty. Enough said.

2 But think about it again. One could look at lawns as a monumental waste of ecological resources. Today, there are approximately 55 million home lawns in the United States, covering 25 to 30 million acres. In New Jersey, the most densely populated state, *nearly one-fifth of the entire land area is covered with turfgrass,* twice as much land as is used for crop production. Although turfgrass is also used for golf courses and public parks, most is planted for lawns. The average home lawn, if used for growing fruits and vegetables, would yield two thousand dollars worth of crops. But instead of this land becoming a revenue generator, it is a "drainer": Americans spend an average of several hundred dollars a year to keep their lawns short and healthy.

3 If the purpose of lawns is solely ornamental, why has the tradition persisted for eons, when most conceptions of beauty change as often as the hem length of women's dresses? The Chinese grew lawns five thousand years ago, and circumstantial evidence indicates that the Mayans and Aztecs were lawn fanciers as well. In the Middle Ages, monarchs let their cattle run loose around their castles, not only to feed the animals, but to cut the grass so that advancing enemy forces could be spotted at a distance. Soon, aristocrats throughout Europe adopted the lawn as a symbol of prestige ("if it's good enough for the king, it's good enough for me!"). The games associated with lawns—bowls, croquet, tennis—all started as upper-class diversions.

4 The lawn quickly became a status symbol in colonial America, just as it was in Europe. Some homeowners used scythes to tend their lawns, but most let animals, particularly sheep, cows, and horses, do the work. In 1841, the lawn mower was introduced, much to the delight of homeowners, and much to the dismay of grazing animals and teenagers everywhere.

5 Dr. John Falk, who is associated with the educational research division of the Smithsonian Institution, has spent more time pondering this Imponderable than any person alive, and his speculations are provocative and convincing. Falk believes that our desire for a savannalike terrain, rather than being an aesthetic predilection, is actually a genetically encoded preference. Anthropologists agree that hu-

mankind has spent most of its history roaming the grasslands of East Africa. In order to survive against predators, humans needed trees for protection and water for drinking, but also grassland for foraging. If primitive man wandered away into rain forests, for example, he must have longed to return to the safety of his savanna home. As Falk commented in an interview in *Omni* magazine: "For more than ninety percent of human history the savanna was home. Home equals safety, and that information has to be fairly hard-wired if the animal is going to respond to danger instantaneously."

6   When we talked to Dr. Falk, he added more ammunition to support his theories. He has conducted a number of cross-cultural studies to ascertain the terrain preferences of people all over the world. He and psychologist John Balling showed subjects photographs of five different terrains—deciduous forest, coniferous forest, tropical rain forest, desert, and savanna—and asked them where they would prefer to live. The savanna terrain was chosen overwhelmingly. Falk's most recent studies were conducted in India and Nigeria, in areas where most subjects had never even seen a savanna. Yet they consistently picked the savanna as their first choice, with their native terrain usually the second preference.

7   Falk and Balling also found that children under twelve were even more emphatic in their selection of savannas, another strong, if inconclusive, indication that preference for savanna terrain is genetic.

8   In the *Omni* article, Falk also suggested that even the way we ornament our lawns mimics our East African roots. The ponds and fountains that decorate our grasses replicate the natural water formations of our homeland, and the popularity of umbrella-shaped shade trees might represent an attempt to recreate the acacia trees found in the African savanna.

9   Of course, psychologists have speculated about other reasons why we "need" lawns. The most common theory is that lawns and gardens are a way of taming and domesticating nature in an era in which affluent Westerners are virtually divorced from it. Another explanation is that lawns are a way of mapping territory, just as every other animal marks territory to let others know what property it is ready to defend. This helps explain why so many homeowners are touchy about the neighborhood kid barely scraping their lawn while trying to catch a football. As Dr. Falk told *Imponderables,* "People create extensions of themselves. When people create a lawn as an extension of themselves, they see a violation of their lawn as a violation of their space." . . .

Checking Your Comprehension

1. Why are lawns a waste of ecological energy?

_____

_____

_____

2. How did colonial Americans keep their lawns short?

_____

_____

3. What primary reason does Dr. Falk give for people liking lawns?

_____

_____

4. What type of terrain do children under 12 like best?

_____

_____

5. Why does Dr. Falk think people ornament their lawns?

_____

_____

6. What other explanations exist for why people like lawns?

_____

_____

Critical Reading and Thinking

1. What kind of evidence does the author present to support his statement that humans like lawns? What examples does he give? (Evidence: see Chapter 13)

_____

_____

2. Are the statements made by Dr. Falk fact or theory?

_____

_____

3. Do you think Falk's conclusion logically follows from the facts he offers?

_____

_____

4. Why do you think Falk feels that the fact that children definitely prefer savannas indicates that the preference is genetic?

_____

_____

5. Evaluate Dr. Falk as an authority on lawns.

_____

_____

6. In what other ways do humans mark territory?

_____

_____

Words in Context

DIRECTIONS: *Locate each word in the paragraph indicated and reread that paragraph. Then, based on the way the word is used, write a synonym or brief definition for each.*

1. monumental (par. 2) _____

2. ornamental (par. 3) _____

3. prestige (par. 3) _____

4. terrain (par. 6) _____

5. replicate (par. 8) _____

Vocabulary Review

DIRECTIONS: *Match the term in Column A with its correct meaning in Column B.*

Column A

_____ 1. provocative

_____ 2. savanna

_____ 3. omnipresent

_____ 4. predilection

_____ 5. diversions

_____ 6. imponderable

_____ 7. emphatic

Column B

a. existing everywhere all the time

b. distractions

c. definite

d. unable to be explained

e. having a particular liking for something

f. grassland

g. exciting

Writing Exercises

1. Name some activities that you think you are genetically predisposed to do? Why?

2. Describe a lawn you have seen that you really liked. What did it look like? Was it landscaped with flowers, trees, and fountains? What kind of lawn would you have if you had the time and money to make it suit your preference?

Television Addiction

MARIE WINN

We know that drugs, alcohol, and gambling can be addictive, but can television be addictive?

Vocabulary Preview

wryly (par. 1)	jokingly, kiddingly
surge (par. 1)	sudden increase
denote (par. 1)	indicate, stand for
dismaying (par. 3)	troubling, alarming
essence (par. 3)	basic quality; most important feature
pursue (par. 4)	try to obtain, strive for
sated (par. 4)	satisfied completely
passive (par. 7)	taking no active part, not involved
inchoately (par. 7)	unclearly, incompletely
enervated (par. 9)	weakened, having no strength
ruefully (par. 10)	regretfully, sadly
renders (par. 11)	makes or causes

Prereading

DIRECTIONS: *Preview the article and then write a list of 3 to 4 questions that you have about television addiction.*

_____

_____

1   The word "addiction" is often used loosely and wryly in conversation. People will refer to themselves as "mystery book addicts" or "cookie addicts." E. B. White writes of his annual surge of interest in gardening: "We are hooked and are making an attempt to kick the habit." Yet nobody really believes that reading mysteries or ordering seeds by catalogue is serious enough to be compared with addictions to heroin or alcohol. The word "addiction" is here used jokingly to denote a tendency to overindulge in some pleasurable activity.

2   People often refer to being "hooked on TV." Does this, too, fall into the lighthearted category of cookie eating and other pleasures that people pursue with unusual intensity, or is there a kind of television viewing that falls into the more serious category of destructive addiction?

3   When we think about addiction to drugs or alcohol, we frequently focus on negative aspects, ignoring the pleasures that accompany drinking or drug-taking. And yet the essence of any serious addiction is a pursuit of pleasure, a search for a "high" that normal life does not supply. It is only the inability to function without the addictive substance that is dismaying, the dependence of the organism upon a certain experience and an increasing inability to function normally without it. Thus a person will take two or three drinks at the end of the day not merely for the pleasure drinking provides, but also because he "doesn't feel normal" without them.

4   An addict does not merely pursue a pleasurable experience and need to experience it in order to function normally. He needs to *repeat* it again and again. Something about that particular experience makes life without it less than complete. Other potentially pleasurable experiences are no longer possible, for under the spell of the addictive experience, his life is peculiarly distorted. The addict craves an experience and yet he is never really satisfied. The organism may be temporarily sated, but soon it begins to crave again.

5   Finally a serious addiction is distinguished from a harmless pursuit of pleasure by its distinctly destructive elements. A heroin addict, for instance, leads a damaged life: his increasing need for heroin in increasing doses prevents him from working, from maintaining relationships, from developing in human ways. Similarly an alcoholic's life is narrowed and dehumanized by his dependence on alcohol.

6   Let us consider television viewing in the light of the conditions that define serious addictions.

7   Not unlike drugs or alcohol, the television experience allows the participant to blot out the real world and enter into a pleasurable and passive mental state. The worries and anxieties of reality are as effectively deferred by becoming absorbed in a television program as by going on a "trip" induced by drugs or alcohol. And just as alcoholics are only inchoately aware of their addiction, feeling that they control their drinking more than they really do ("I can cut it out any time I want—I just

like to have three or four drinks before dinner"), people similarly overestimate their control over television watching. Even as they put off other activities to spend hour after hour watching television, they feel they could easily resume living in a different, less passive style. But somehow or other while the television set is present in their homes, the click doesn't sound. With television pleasures available, those other experiences seem less attractive, more difficult somehow.

8
9   A heavy viewer (a college English instructor) observes:

"I find television almost irresistible. When the set is on, I cannot ignore it. I can't turn it off. I feel sapped, will-less, enervated. As I reach out to turn off the set, the strength goes out of my arms. So I sit there for hours and hours."

10   The self-confessed television addict often feels he "ought" to do other things—but the fact that he doesn't read and doesn't plant his garden or sew or crochet or play games or have conversations means that those activities are no longer as desirable as television viewing. In a way a heavy viewer's life is as imbalanced by his television "habit" as a drug addict's or an alcoholic's. He is living in a holding pattern, as it were, passing up the activities that lead to growth or development or a sense of accomplishment. This is one reason people talk about their television viewing so ruefully, so apologetically. They are aware that it is an unproductive experience, that almost any other endeavor is more worthwhile by any human measure.

11   Finally it is the adverse effect of television viewing on the lives of so many people that defines it as a serious addiction. The television habit distorts the sense of time. It renders other experiences vague and curiously unreal while taking on a greater reality for itself. It weakens relationships by reducing and sometimes eliminating normal opportunities for talking, for communicating.

Checking Your Comprehension

1. How is addiction loosely defined? How is a serious addiction defined?

   _____

   _____

2. What is the difference between often experiencing an activity that is greatly enjoyable and being addicted to that activity?

   _____

   _____

3. How does television addiction affect people's lives? Why do people become addicted to television?

_____

_____

4. Does the author seem to have any positive feelings about television viewing? If so, what are they?

_____

_____

5. How is television addiction similar to drug or alcohol addiction?

_____

_____

6. Why is the television addict never completely satisfied with his or her viewing?

_____

_____

Critical Reading

1. Does television have a negative or positive effect on your life? Explain.

_____

_____

2. What kinds of destructive addictions other than television, drugs, and alcohol can you think of?

_____

_____

3. List several words with negative connotations that are used to describe televi-sion addiction. (Connotative meanings: see Chapter 12)

_____

_____

4. Does the author present an objective or subjective description of television addiction? (Objective and subjective: see Chapter 12)

_____

_____

5. What type(s) of evidence does the writer use to support her claim that televi-sion is addictive? Evaluate the quality of this evidence. (Supporting evidence: see Chapter 13)

_____

_____

6. What negative effects of television watching have you experienced or observed in others?

_____

_____

Words in Context

DIRECTIONS: *Locate each word in the paragraph indicated and reread that para-graph. Then, based on the way the word is used, write a synonym or brief definition for each.*

1. tendency (par. 1) _____

2. craves (par. 4) _____

3. distinguished (par. 5) _____

4. deferred (par. 7) _____

5. overestimate (par. 7) _____

6. sapped (par. 9) _____

7. endeavor (par. 10) _____

8. adverse (par. 11) _____

Vocabulary Review

DIRECTIONS: *Mark each statement T for true or F for false.*

_____ 1. To do something *ruefully* is to do it slowly.

_____ 2. The word "cat" *denotes* a small four-legged animal.

_____ 3. If a student answers a question totally and clearly, he answers it *inchoately*.

_____ 4. A *surge* of sea water can cause shoreline flooding.

_____ 5. To *wryly* say something is to say it in a joking or ironic way.

_____ 6. A man who takes charge of his life is very *passive*.

_____ 7. To *pursue* a career in accounting, a student should like working with numbers.

_____ 8. If you felt *enervated*, you would feel energetic and lively.

_____ 9. Feeling *sated* is the same as feeling angry.

Writing Exercise

Write a paragraph explaining why you are or are not a television addict.

Gawk Shows

NICOLS FOX

Television talk shows continue to attract viewers. Fox argues that these shows can be more appropriately described as "gawk" shows.

Vocabulary Preview

manifestations (par. 2)	ways in which something can be shown
wizened (par. 3)	shriveled, shrunken
solicitude (par. 5, 24)	caring, concern
hypocritical (par. 8)	insincere
exploitation (par. 8)	taking advantage of
demise (par. 10)	death
virtuosos (par. 12)	persons with great skill or talent
voyeurism (par. 12)	deriving pleasure from watching
agenda (par. 18)	list of topics
paternalistic (par. 20)	fatherly control

Prereading

DIRECTIONS: *Preview the article and answer the following questions.*

1. On what topics and issues do talk shows focus?

_____

_____

2. Why are talk shows so popular?

_____

_____

1   *I* remember the dusty heat of late summer, the yellow and white tent, and the barker strutting on the platform. His voice rose above the sounds of the carnival, hinting of the wonders within the tent, wonders painted in cheap colors on the cracked backdrop: the two-headed baby, the world's fattest man, the bearded woman. I remember the sideshows. I thought they were long behind us.

2   I turn on the television and see an astonishing sight: a woman. Her soul is beautiful. It penetrates the atmosphere, even across airwaves. Her body is not. It is covered with the lumps and bumps of Elephant Man disease. Sally Jesse Raphael, wearing her trademark red spectacles, cocks her blond head and asks what the woman's life is like. A window is opened into pain. There are more victims of the disease sitting in the audience. We are treated to its various manifestations. We are horrified and amazed: We gawk.

3   Phil Donahue interviews tiny, wizened children. They have progeria, "the aging disease." With their outsize, hairless heads and huge eyes imparting solemnity and even wisdom, they offer us themselves as a sacrifice to our curiosity. We are compelled into silence, fascinated. We are back in the tent.

4   While I was living in Europe in the late '60s and early '70s, friends often asked me to tell them what to expect when they visited America. "Think of America as a carnival," I would tell them. "An unending carnival." This was the only way I knew to explain my country. Not just the quality of light and landscape but the excess, the enthusiasm, the love of excitement. We want no limitations on what we can have, on what we can do. We deny ourselves nothing—no objects, no sensations. "The pursuit of happiness": What other nation has made it an absolute right?

5   The carnival plays on, and we have returned to the sideshows—minus the honesty that made no pretense about what lay behind the curtain, the honesty that divided the world into those who were able to resist satisfying their curiosity at the expense of others and those who were not. Gawking is painted in shades of solicitude now. We justify much in the name of compassion, but we are in fact being entertained in the same ancient tradition. Gawk shows sell.

6   "I offer no apology," says Donahue. "These children have been unmercifully pressured by their very distinctive appearance." The purpose of the show? "To humanize people who have suffered. It becomes a vehicle for examining our prejudices. Just because it may be true that this kind of show draws a crowd does not condemn it," he says.

7   For Sally Jesse Raphael the rationale is the same: "Teaching the lessons of compassion. Man's triumph over adversity."

8   These are noble thoughts, and not entirely hypocritical. Compassion and understanding are always in short supply. There is an outside chance that some of each might be spread around in this exercise. We may also be witnessing exploitation. "These children are risking their lives to be here," says Sally, introducing children who will die if exposed to light. What may *she* be risking if they don't appear? As Donahue says, "If I don't draw a crowd, I could be parking cars for a living."

9   Donahue is open about the dilemma: "Americans are more interested in Madonna than Managua. The country suffers, in my opinion, from the diminished interest in serious news. Whichever way you look at it we have a culture of decay." It's tricky playing two sides at once. "It's like walking on eggs. I don't want to be a dead hero," he says.

10   We watch our cultural demise in living color.

11   Do you find yourself addicted to sex with prostitutes? Tell Oprah Winfrey and her audience all about it. Did you engage in an affair with your priest? Have your breast implants started slipping? Geraldo Rivera wants to know. Do you wish you could reverse your sex-change operation? Are you a celebrity subject to diarrhea at odd moments? Does your mother keep stealing your boyfriends? We care, we are interested. Whatever your problem, there's a television talk show that will accommodate you.

12   Donahue, Oprah, Sally, Geraldo: They are the virtuosos of voyeurism, lifting the skirts of our culture, peering into the closets, airing the national soiled linen. Sally thinks of her program as a kind of updated town meeting—the modern version of something we no longer have. Electronic gossip, in other words—the national back fence. Wishful thinking.

13   As Americans we've been indulging in an orgy of self-analysis and self-revelation—coupled with a natural curiosity now totally unbridled. We've become a society hooked on the bizarre and the astonishing—living in a perpetual state of "Can you top this?" Transvestite men marry women on Sally's show, thus proving an important point, one we all needed to know: 65 percent of all transvestites are not homosexual.

14   Nothing is sacred. There are no memories, no mysteries too precious to reveal. A woman discusses her husband's sexual addiction. Geraldo asks the husband for details—and gets them. There is nothing we won't share, or watch someone else share, with a million strangers.

15   We have invented a new social contract on the talk shows: Lay bare your body, your bed, your soul, your emotions, your worst fears, your innermost secrets, and we will give you a moment or two of fame. Every sacrifice can and should be made to the video god.

16   Are there topics too hot to talk about?

17 "How to blow up your local post office," says Donahue. He'd draw the line there.

18 There is no topic Sally wouldn't consider if it "concerns the human condition." She draws the line only at being boring. We have to want to watch it. So we set the agenda.

19 Donahue, a man obviously in conflict between his natural honesty and better instincts and his ambition, admits that his audience calls the shots. Devoting a recent show to strippers—both male and female—he says, "It must be ratings week. I don't want to do these shows . . . they make me." Sure they do. But who is making us watch?

20 Freedom of expression is not the issue here. Nobody's suggesting censorship or even paternalistic decisions based on what someone else thinks is good for us. The issue is honesty—honesty about why we watch. The talk shows are merely giving us what we want. The question is, Why do we want it?

21 In some cultures it was thought that illness or bad luck could be transferred from one person to another by magic. James G. Frazer, in his classic work *The Golden Bough,* told of one example: "To get rid of warts, take a string and make as many knots in it as you have warts. Then lay the string under a stone. Whoever treads upon the stone will get the warts, and you will be rid of them." Something like that draws us to the tent. We confirm our own normalcy because our worst fears have been manifested in someone else—the visual equivalent of burying the string. Or, if we see ourselves in someone who has survived our common plight, we are reassured; we are not alone.

22 There is no slouching into the tent today. We walk in shamelessly, casting off inhibitions in the name of openness.

23 The new openness has, in fact, turned out to be an empty promise. Are things any better than they were two decades ago? Has drug abuse or wife abuse or child abuse declined as we have learned more? Are we any happier thinking that a friend who takes a drink is a potential alcoholic, that every stranger is a child-snatcher?

24 How has this new compassion we are teaching been made evident? Ask the parents who have three HIV-positive sons and found their house burned down because of it. Ask the people who cluster over the grates of subways in our largest cities. If you were a trapped whale or a little girl down a well, solicitude would flow your way in great waves. It still helps to be cute or little or white or furry or totally nonthreatening when you're looking for compassion—or pretty, when you want a bone marrow transplant.

25 The potential is there on the TV talk shows for real entertainment—and for service. Oprah scored with a terrific show on female comics. Programs on health matters or economic questions are valuable. During the first days of the war in the Persian Gulf, Donahue aired shows that were serious and important contributions to our understanding of the conflict. "I do have a conscience," he says.

26   Geraldo, however, ever subject to the temptations of the flesh, spoiled what could have been a serious discussion of breast implants by having Jessica Hahn as the honored guest and by fondling examples of the implants interminably. Does he have it right? Are we a people who need to watch breast implants being fondled?

27   What happens when we set aside our last taboo? What happens when we've finally been titillated to a terminal numbness, incapable of shock, on the prowl for a new high? What manner of stimulation will we need next? Are we addicted? Talk show codependent?

28   Which topic affects us more: the discussion of the S & L crisis Donahue did last summer or the interviews with the strippers? Which do you think got the better ratings?

29   In a free society we get what we want. We shouldn't be surprised when we end up with what we deserve. But we can't transfer blame. It's not the hosts' fault—it's the viewers'.

Checking Your Comprehension

1. What is the essay's thesis?

   _____

   _____

2. Fox compares talk shows to the sideshows at a carnival. Explain how they are similar.

   _____

   _____

3. Summarize Phil Donahue's and Sally Jesse Raphael's justifications for the topics they address.

   _____

   _____

4. List the reason Fox gives for the popularity of talk shows.

   _____

   _____

5. According to Fox, who controls or ultimately determines the topics of talk shows?

_____

_____

Critical Reading and Thinking

1. Explain whether you agree or disagree with Fox's statement that America is "an unending carnival."

_____

_____

2. Fox describes a new social contract in paragraph 15. Explain this contract and whether you agree this is the reason people appear on talk shows.

_____

_____

3. What topics does Fox feel should be dealt with on talk shows?

_____

_____

4. What is the author's attitude toward talk show hosts? Support your answer with references to the essay.

_____

_____

5. Does Fox present an objective or biased view of talk shows? (Bias: see Chapter 13)

_____

_____

6. Explain what Fox meant in paragraph 22 when he said "There is no slouching into the tent."

_____

_____

7. What are the potential benefits of talk shows?

_____

_____

Words in Context

DIRECTIONS: *Locate each word in the paragraph indicated. Then, based on the way the word is used, write a synonym or brief definition of each.*

1. trademark (par. 2) _____

2. progeria (par. 3) _____

3. rationale (par. 7) _____

4. bizarre (par. 13) _____

5. fondled (par. 26) _____

Vocabulary Review

DIRECTIONS: *Match the words in Column A with the appropriate meaning in Column B.*

Column A

_____ 1. agenda

_____ 2. voyeurism

_____ 3. virtuoso

_____ 4. demise

_____ 5. exploitation

Column B

a. list of topics

b. ways of demonstrating

c. concern

d. insincere

e. death

_____ 6. manifestations   f. pleasure from watching

_____ 7. solicitude   g. shrunken

_____ 8. wizened   h. fatherly control

_____ 9. hypocritical   i. talented person

_____ 10. paternalistic   j. taking advantage of

Writing Exercise

Write a paragraph describing a recent talk show you've seen. Describe the topics or issues it included.

Why Confession is Good for the Soul— and the Body

CAROLE WADE AND CAROL TAVRIS

Have you found that talking about your problems or worries makes you feel better? This article, taken from a psychology textbook, explains this phenomenon.

Vocabulary Preview

obsessions (par. 1)	ever-present thoughts, desires or feelings that cannot be reasoned away
stream-of-consciousness (par. 1)	relating whatever thoughts come into the mind in a random way
accessible (par. 1)	easily approachable
lymphocytes (par. 5)	cells important in fighting disease or illness
assimilate (par. 6)	absorb and understand
therapeutic (par. 6)	healing
cognitive (par. 6)	having to do with thought
insight (par. 7)	clear understanding

Prereading

DIRECTIONS: *Preview the selection and answer the following questions.*

What happens when traumatic events are kept inside? Why do you think this occurs?

_____

_____

1     $\mathbf{N}$ow pay attention: *Don't think of a white bear*. Are you not thinking of it? Anyone who has ever tried to banish an uninvited thought knows how hard it is to erase the mental tape of worries, unhappy memories, or unwished-for obsessions. In an actual study, people who were told not to think of a white bear mentioned it nine times in a five-minute stream-of-consciousness session (Wegner et al., 1987). The reason seems to be that when you are trying to avoid a thought, you are in fact processing the thought frequently—rehearsing it and making it more accessible to consciousness.

2   According to James Pennebaker and his associates, the prolonged inhibition of thoughts and emotions requires physical effort, which is stressful to the body (Pennebaker, Hughes, & O'Heeron, 1987). Yet many people do try to inhibit secret thoughts and feelings that make them ashamed or depressed. The inability or unwillingness to confide important or traumatic events places continuing stress on the system and can lead to long-term health problems. In study after study, such individuals prove to be at greater risk of illness than people who are able to talk about their tragedies, even though disclosures of traumatic events are often painful and unpleasant at first (Pennebaker, 1988).

3   This information poses a problem: If an event is stressful and trying to stop thinking about the event is stressful, what should you do? Research from *psychoneuroimmunology,* the growing field that bridges psychology and the immune system, suggests some answers.

4   In one study, college students were assigned to write about *either* personal, traumatic experiences *or* trivial topics for 20 minutes a day, four days in a row. Those who were asked to reveal "their deepest thoughts and feelings" about a traumatic event all had something to talk about. Many told stories of sexual abuse, physical beatings, emotional humiliation, and parental abandonment. Others described upsetting changes, such as coming to college and the loneliness associated with leaving home. Yet most had never discussed these feelings with anyone.

5   The researchers took blood samples to test for the immune activity of lymphocytes; they also measured the students' physical symptoms, emotions, and visits to the health center. On every measure, the students who wrote about traumatic experiences were better off than those who did not (Pennebaker, Kiecolt-Glaser, & Glaser, 1988). Some of them showed *short-term* increases in anger and depression; writing about an unpleasant experience was not fun. But as months passed, their physical and emotional well-being improved.

6   The researchers believe that "the failure to confront a trauma forces the person to live with it in an unresolved manner." Actively writing or talking about it apparently helps people assimilate the tragedy and come to a sense of completion about it. But confession must not turn to obsession. Confessing your "deepest thoughts and feelings" is not therapeutic if you keep rehearsing and confessing them endlessly to all who will listen. The key is physiological release *and* cognitive perspective.

7   For example, several students who wrote about the same experience day after day gradually gained insight and distance. One woman, who had been molested at the age of 9 by a boy a few years older, at first wrote about her feelings of embarrassment and guilt. By the third day, she was writing about how angry she felt at the boy. By the last day, she had begun to see the whole event differently; he was young too, after all. After the experiment, she said, "Before, when I thought about it, I'd lie to myself. . . . Now, I don't feel like I even have to think about it because I got it off my chest. I finally admitted that it happened."

8   To see if the research will benefit you, why not keep a diary this year? All you have to do is jot down, from time to time, your "deepest thoughts and feelings" about school, your past, your future, anything. Pennebaker predicts that you will have fewer colds, headaches, and trips to the medical clinic next year.

Checking Your Comprehension

1. What happens when people try to avoid certain thoughts?

   _____

   _____

2. Why is the inhibition of thoughts stressful to the body?

   _____

   _____

3. What was the result of Pennebaker's study?

   _____

   _____

4. How does actively writing or talking about a trauma help people?

   _____

   _____

Critical Reading and Thinking

1. What is the author's tone? (Tone: see Chapter 12)

   _____

   _____

2. Evaluate the evidence the author provides. (Supporting Evidence: see Chapter 13)

   _____

   _____

3. Does the author definitively state as a fact that health can be improved through sharing traumatic events? Does the author believe the information he presents? How do you know?

   _____

   _____

Words in Context

DIRECTIONS: *Locate each word in the paragraph indicated and reread that paragraph. Then, based on the way the word is used, write a synonym or brief definition for each.*

1. banish (par. 1) _____

2. inhibition (par. 2) _____

3. traumatic (par. 2) _____

4. psychoneuroimmunology (par. 3) _____

5. unresolved (par. 6) _____

Vocabulary Review

DIRECTIONS: *Complete each of the following sentences by choosing one of the words presented in the Vocabulary Preview.*

1. Addicts have _____ about substances they are addicted to.

2. After a few months the Chinese student was able to _____ American culture and came to understand it well.

3. Martha's friend had _____ into her situation since she had gone through a divorce herself recently.

4. Drinking plenty of liquids is very _____ for the common cold.

5. He had a _____ acceptance of his father's death, but emotionally he was unable to deal with it.

6. Salt and pepper are _____ during most meals since they are usually left on the table.

7. The lecturer spoke in a _____, rambling wherever his thoughts led him.

Writing Exercise

Describe how you felt when you kept a disturbing experience bottled up inside you.

Drugs

GORE VIDAL

This selection offers a surprising solution to the growing drug addiction problem in the United States. It is a solution with which many people disagree. Read the selection and evaluate the author's argument.

Vocabulary Preview

heroic (par. 1)	showing great strength and courage
enslave (par. 2)	make a slave of; control
exhortation (par. 3)	plea; urgent warning; strong encouragement and advice
persecuting (par. 3)	troubling, harassing, or annoying
zombies (par. 5)	walking corpses; people who look and act more dead than alive
mainliners (par. 6)	addicts who inject drugs directly into a large vein
perennially (par. 6)	yearly; occurring again and again
moralist (par. 7)	person who tries to regulate others' morals; person who teaches, studies, or writes about right and wrong principles and behavior
repression (par. 8)	severe and strict control
vested interest (par. 10)	close involvement to promote selfish goals, usually at the expense of others
irresistible (par. 12)	unable to be resisted

Prereading

DIRECTIONS: *Preview the selection and take a few minutes to think about what you already know about drug addiction. What are its causes? How does it affect people? What possible solutions have you heard of?*

_____

_____

1   *I*t is possible to stop most drug addiction in the United States within a very short time. Simply make all drugs available and sell them at cost. Label each drug with a precise description of what effect—good and bad—the drug will have on the taker. This will require heroic honesty. Don't say that marijuana is addictive or dangerous when it is neither, as millions of people know—unlike "speed," which kills most unpleasantly, or heroin, which is addictive and difficult to kick.

2   For the record, I have tried—once—almost every drug and liked none, disproving the popular Fu Manchu theory that a single whiff of opium will enslave the mind. Nevertheless many drugs are bad for certain people to take and they should be told why in a sensible way.

3   Along with exhortation and warning, it might be good for our citizens to recall (or learn for the first time) that the United States was the creation of men who believed that each man has the right to do what he wants with his own life as long as he does not interfere with his neighbor's pursuit of happiness. (That his neighbor's idea of happiness is persecuting others does confuse matters a bit.)

4   This is a startling notion to the current generation of Americans. They reflect a system of public education which has made the Bill of Rights, literally, unacceptable to a majority of high school graduates (see the annual Purdue reports) who now form the "silent majority"—a phrase which that underestimated wit Richard Nixon took from Homer who used it to describe the dead.

5   Now one can hear the warning rumble begin: if everyone is allowed to take drugs everyone will and the GNP [Gross National Product (a measure of economic growth)] will decrease, the Commies will stop us from making everyone free, and we shall end up a race of zombies, passively murmuring "groovy" to one another. Alarming thought. Yet it seems most unlikely that any reasonably sane person will become a drug addict if he knows in advance what addiction is going to be like.

6   Is everyone reasonably sane? No. Some people will always become drug addicts just as some people will always become alcoholics, and it is just too bad. Every man, however, has the power (and should have the legal right) to kill himself if he chooses. But since most men don't, they won't be mainliners either. Nevertheless, forbidding people things they like or think they might enjoy only makes them want those things all the more. This psychological insight is, for some mysterious reason, perennially denied our governors.

7   It is a lucky thing for the American moralist that our country has always existed in a kind of time-vacuum: we have no public memory of anything that happened before last Tuesday. No one in Washington today recalls what happened during the years alcohol was forbidden to the people by a Congress that thought it had a divine mission to stamp out Demon Rum—launching, in the process, the greatest crime wave in the country's history, causing thousands of deaths from bad alcohol, and creating a general (and persisting) contempt among the citizenry for the laws of the United States.

8   The same thing is happening today. But the government has learned nothing from past attempts at prohibition, not to mention repression.

9   Last year when the supply of Mexican marijuana was slightly curtailed by the Feds, the pushers got the kids hooked on heroin and deaths increased dramatically, particularly in New York. Whose fault? Evil men like the Mafiosi? Permissive Dr. Spock? Wild-eyed Dr. Leary? No.

10   The Government of the United States was responsible for those deaths. The bureaucratic machine has a vested interest in playing cops and robbers. Both the Bureau of Narcotics and the Mafia want strong laws against the sale and use of drugs because if drugs are sold at cost there would be no money in it for anyone.

11   If there was no money in it for the Mafia, there would be no friendly playground pushers, and addicts would not commit crimes to pay for the next fix. Finally, if there was no money in it, the Bureau of Narcotics would wither away, something they are not about to do without a struggle.

12   Will anything sensible be done? Of course not. The American people are as devoted to the idea of sin and its punishment as they are to making money—and fighting drugs is nearly as big a business as pushing them. Since the combination of sin and money is irresistible (particularly to the professional politician), the situation will only grow worse.

Checking Your Comprehension

DIRECTIONS: *Vidal presents an argument for the legalization of drugs and their sale at cost. On a separate sheet, list the major points of his argument. Include the reasons and evidence he gives to support his idea that legalizing drugs will nearly eliminate the problem of drug addiction.*

Critical Reading and Thinking

1. How would you describe the tone of the article? (Tone: see Chapter 12)

    _____

    _____

2. Describe Vidal's attitude toward the U.S. government. Refer to specific parts of the article to substantiate what you say.

    _____

    _____

3. What is the basic assumption Vidal makes in building his argument? (Assumptions: see Chapter 13)

_____

_____

4. Explain why you agree or disagree with the Vidal's basic assumption.

_____

_____

5. What type of evidence does Vidal offer in support of his argument? (Supporting evidence: see Chapter 13)

_____

_____

6. Describe any other types of evidence that Vidal might have used that would have strengthened his argument.

_____

_____

7. Is there evidence that would have weakened his argument? If so, what?

_____

_____

8. Explain the expression, "We have no public memory of anything that happened before last Tuesday." Decide whether it is a literal or figurative expression and explain your reasons. (Figurative language: see Chapter 12)

_____

_____

Words in Context

DIRECTIONS: *Locate each word in the paragraph indicated and reread that paragraph. Then, based on the way the word is used, write a synonym or brief definition for each.*

1. precise (par. 1) _____

2. launching (par. 7) _____

3. contempt (par. 7) _____

4. citizenry (par. 7) _____

Vocabulary Review

DIRECTIONS: *Each of the following words has been formed from a root word and a suffix or verb ending. For each word, underline the root word. Then form a new word by adding a different or additional ending. Write a sentence using a new word.*

	New Word	**Sentence**
1. heroic	_____	_____
2. exhortation	_____	_____
3. persecuting	_____	_____
4. perennially	_____	_____
5. moralist	_____	_____
6. repression	_____	_____
7. irresistible	_____	_____

Writing Exercises

1. Write a paragraph explaining why you agree or disagree with Vidal's thesis.

2. Evaluate the evidence that Vidal offers in support of his argument. Is this evidence accurate?

Endnotes

Note: * designates entries new to the 4th ed.

Chapter 4

1. Neil J. Smelser, *Sociology* (Englewood Cliffs, N.J.: Prentice-Hall, 1991), pp. 90–91.

Chapter 5

1. Carol Wade and Carol Tavris, *Psychology* (New York: Harper & Row, 1990), p. 82.
2. Paul R. Lohnes and William W. Cooley, *Introduction to Statistical Procedures,* (New York, John Wiley & Sons, 1968), p. 11.
3. Robert Wallace, *Biology: The World of Life* (Glenview, Ill.: Scott, Foresman, 1986), p. 185.
4. William M. Pride and O.C. Ferrell, *Marketing: Concepts and Strategies* (Boston: Houghton Mifflin Company, 1991), pp. 241–243.
5. Brenda Kemp and Adele Pilliteri, *Fundamentals of Nursing* (Boston: Little, Brown, 1984), p. 776.
6. Roger Chisholm and Marilu McCarty, *Principles of Economics* (Glenview, Ill.: Scott, Foresman, 1981), pp. 483–484.
7. Knut Norstog and Andrew J. Meyerricks, *Biology* (Toronto: Charles E. Merrill, 1985), p. 193.
8. Norstog and Meyerricks, p. 315.
9. Chisholm and McCarty, p. 443.

Part Two Review

Thomas C. Kinnear, Kenneth L. Bernhardt, and Kathleen Krentler. *Principles of Marketing,* 4th ed. (NY: HarperCollins, 1995), pp. 524–525.

Chapter 6

1. Richard P. Appelbaum and William J. Chambliss, *Sociology,* (New York: HarperCollins, 1995), p. 540.
2. Edward S. Greenberg and Benjamin I. Page, *The Struggle for Democracy* (New York: HarperCollins, 1995), p. 446.
3. Greenberg and Page, p. 558.
4. Greenberg and Page, p. 540.
5. Alex Thio, *Sociology* (New York: HarperCollins, 1994) pp. 296–297.
6. Thio, p. 373.
7. Thio, p. 372.

Chapter 7

1. Bob Weinstein, *Jobs for the 21st Century* (New York: Macmillan, 1983), p. 22.
2. Richard George, *The New Consumer Survival Kit* (Boston: Little, Brown, 1978), p. 212.
3. John Dorfman et al., *Well-Being: An Introduction of Health* (Glenview, Ill.: Scott, Foresman, 1980), p. 27.
4. Dorfman, p. 263.
5. K. Warner Schaie and James Geiwitz, *Adult Development and Aging* (Boston: Little, Brown, 1972), pp. 371–372.
6. Dorfman, p. 263.
7. Wallace, p. 585.
8. Charles T. Brown, *Rock and Roll Story* (Englewood Cliffs, N.J.: Prentice-Hall, 1983), p. 109.
9. Dorfman, p. 124.
10. Weinstein, p. 118.
11. Edward S. Fox and Edward W. Wheatley, *Modern Marketing* (Glenview, Ill.: Scott, Foresman, 1978), p. 142.
12. William E. Thompson and Joseph V. Hickey. *Society in Focus* (NY: HarperCollins, 1994), p. 156.
13. Joyce Brothers, "What Dirty Words Really Mean," *Good Housekeeping,* May 1973.
14. Brown, pp. 20–21.
15. Jean L. Weirich, *Personal Financial Management* (Boston: Little, Brown, 1983) p. 155.
16. William F. Smith and Raymond D. Liedlich, *From Thought to Theme* (New York: Harcourt Brace Jovanovich, 1983), pp. 281–282.
17. Weinstein, pp. 110–111.
18. "Trees Talk to One Another," *Science Digest,* January 1984, p. 47.
19. John Naisbitt, *Megatrends* (New York: Warner Books, 1982) p. 23.
20. James Geiwitz, *Psychology,* 2nd ed. (Boston: Little, Brown 1980), p. 276.
21. Frans Gerritsen, *Theory and Practice of Color* (New York: Van Nostrand, 1975), p. 9.
22. Geiwitz, p. 512.
23. Geiwitz, p. 513.
24. Geiwitz, p. 229.
25. George, p. 114.

26. "ABC's of How a President Is Chosen," *U.S. News & World Report,* 18 February 1980, p. 45.

27. Paul G. Hewitt, *Conceptual Physics* (Boston: Little, Brown, 1985), p. 15.

28. Ross J. Eshleman and Barbara G. Cashion, *Sociology: An Introduction,* 2nd ed. (Boston: Little, Brown, 1985), p. 88.

29. Hewitt, pp. 234–235.

30. Hewitt, p. 259.

31. Edward H. Reiley and Carroll L. Shry, *Introductory Horticulture* (Albany, N.Y.: Delmar Publishers, 1979), p. 114.

32. Thio, p. 374.

Chapter 8

1. Sydney B. Newell, *Chemistry: An Introduction* (CompEditor, 1980), p. 11.

2. Hewitt, p. 21.

3. Richard L. Weaver, II, *Understanding Personal Communication* (Glenview, Ill.: Scott, Foresman and Company, 1987), p. 24.

4. Hewitt, p. 56.

5. Hewitt, p. 224.

6. *World Book* (World Book, Inc., 1985), Volume 14, p. 309.

7. Hal B. Pickle and Royce L. Abrahamson, *Introduction to Business* (Glenview, Ill.: Scott, Foresman and Company, 1987), p. 40.

8. Thompson and Hickey, p. 70.

9. Pickle and Abrahamson, p. 119.

10. Hewitt, pp. 82–84.

11. *World Book,* Volume 14, p. 270.

12. Robert C. Nickerson, *Fundamentals of Structured COBOL* (Glenview, Ill.: Scott, Foresman and Company, 1984), p. 2.

13. Weaver, p. 85.

14. Eshelman and Cashion, pp. 109–111.

15. Eshelman and Cashion, p. 583.

16. *World Book,* Volume 14, p. 271.

17. Pickle and Abrahamson, p. 123.

18. Bowman O. Davis et al., *Conceptual Human Physiology* (Columbus, Oh.: Charles E. Merrill, 1985), p. 213.

19. Hewitt, p. 233.

*20. Carole Wade and Carol Tavris. *Psychology,* 3rd ed. (NY: HarperCollins, 1993), p. 77.

21. Weaver, p. 24.

22. Weaver, p. 291.

23. Barlow, p. 332.

24. Weaver, p. 123.

25. Hewitt, p. 252.

26. William M. Kephart and Davor Jedlicka, *The Family, Society, and the Individual* (New York: HarperCollins Publishers, 1991), p. 332.

*27. *World Book,* Volume 13, p. 178.

28. Thompson and Hickey, p. 451.
29. Kephart and Jedlicka, pp. 332–333.
30. *World Book,* Volume 13, p. 474 b.
31. *World Book,* Volume 13, p. 672.
32. *World Book,* Volume 13, pp. 795–796.
33. *World Book,* Volume 13, p. 688.
*34. Wade and Travis, p. 252.
35. *World Book,* Volume 13, p. 46.
36. *World Book,* Volume 13, p. 238.

Part Three Review

Sigband, pp. 417–419.

Chapter 9

1. Wallace, preface.
2. Robert L. Lineberry, *Government in America: People, Politics, and Policy,* 2nd ed. (Glenview, Ill.: Scott, Foresman and Company, 1983), p. 668.
3. *American Heritage Dictionary of the English Language, New College Edition* (Boston: Houghton Mifflin Company, 1980).
4. Kenneth Budinski, *Engineering Materials: Properties and Selection* (Reston, Va.: Reston Publishing Co., 1979), p. 15.
5. Herbert E. Ellinger, *Auto-Mechanics,* 2nd ed. (Englewood Cliffs, N.J.: Prentice-Hall, 1977), p. 183.
6. Nickerson, p. 271.
7. Nickerson, p. 2.
8. Hewitt, pp. 54–56.

Chapter 10

1. Wallace, p. 314.
2. Wallace, p. 315.
3. Thompson and Hickey, (front cover)
4. Lineberry, p. 359.
5. Lineberry, pp. 358–359.
6. *USA Today,* November 15, 1991, p. 78.
*7. Donald G. Kaufman and Cecilia M. Franz. *Biosphere 2000.* (NY: Harper Collins, 1993), p. 172
8. William M. Pride, Robert J. Hughes, and Jack R. Kapoor, *Business* (Boston: Houghton Mifflin, 1991), p. 454.
9. Pride, Hughes, and Kapoor, p. 341.
10. Thompson and Hickey, p. 485
11. *USA Today,* November 14, 1991, p. A-1.
12. *Buffalo Evening News,* June 7, 1991.

13. Randall B. Dunham and Jon L. Pierce, *Management* (Glenview, Ill.: Scott, Foresman and Company, 1989), p. 721.
14. Smelser, p. 218.
15. Lineberry, p. 253.
16. David D. Van Fleet, *Contemporary Management* (Boston: Houghton Mifflin, 1991), p. 187.
17. *Buffalo Evening News,* June 7, 1991, p. 1.
18. Thompson and Hickey, (inside cover).
19. John C. Merrill, John Lee, and Edward Jay Friedlander. *Modern Mass Media* (New York: HarperCollins, 1994), p. 207.
20. Thompson and Hickey, p. 179
21. Wallace, p. 427.
22. Wallace, p. 426.
23. Keefe, p. 79.
24. Appelbaum and Chambliss, p. 552.
25. Kephart and Jedlicka, p. 288.

Chapter 11

1. Molly Wantz and John E. Gay, *The Aging Process: A Health Perspective* (Cambridge, Mass.: Winthrop, 1981), p. 62.
2. Kinnear, Bernhardt and Krentler, p. 132.
3. Watson M. Laetsch, *Plants: Basic Concepts in Botany* (Boston: Little, Brown, 1979), p. 8.
4. Zenas Block, *It's All on the Label* (Boston: Little, Brown, 1981), pp. 70–72.
5. Newell, pp. 47–48.
6. Pride and Ferrell, p. 380.
7. Kinnear, Bernhardt, and Krentler, pp. 39–40.

Part Four Review

Block, pp. 8–13.

Chapter 12

1. Robert C. Yeager, *Seasons of Shame: The New Violence in Sports* (New York: McGraw-Hill, 1979), p. 6.
2. Bill Cosby, *Time Flies* (New York: Doubleday, 1987), pp. 169–170.
3. Paul Arandt, *Paul Harvey's The Rest of the Story,* edited and compiled by Lynne Harvey (New York: Doubleday, 1977), p. 116.
4. Weaver, p. 291.
5. Lewis Katz, *Know Your Rights* (Cleveland: Banks Baldwin Law, 1993), p. 54
6. Richard Shenkman, *Legends, Lies, and Cherished Myths of American History* (New York: William Morrow, 1988), pp. 37–38.
7. Linda M Hasselstrom, "A Peaceful Woman Explains Why She Carries a Gun," *Utne Reader,* May/June 1991.

8. James Thurber, "The Father and His Daughter" from *Further Fables for Our Time* (New York: Simon & Schuster, 1984), pp. 51–53.

9. Tom Bodett, *As Far as You Can Go Without a Passport: The View from the End of the Road* (Reading, Mass.: Addison-Wesley, 1985), pp. 79–81.

10. Emily Dickinson, first stanza of poem #754, *The Complete Poems of Emily Dickinson* edited by Thomas E. Johnson (Boston: Little, Brown, 1960), p. 369.

11. Sara King, "Love in the Afternoon—in a Crowded Prison Hall," *Los Angeles Times,* 5 November 1976.

12. "Stop Junk Mail Forever," *Mother Earth News,* August/September, 1994, p. 18.

13. Tom Bodett, *Small Comforts* (Reading, Mass.: Addison-Wesley, 1987), p. 28.

14. Marge Thielman Hastreiter, "Not Every Mother Is Glad Kids Are Back in School," *Buffalo Evening News,* 1991.

15. Johnson C. Montgomery, "The Island of Plenty" from *The Norton Sampler: Short Essays for Composition,* Thomas Cooley, editor (New York: W. W. Norton, 1985), p. 310.

16. Bess Armstrong article, from *The Choices We Made* edited by Angela Bonavoglia (New York: Random House, 1991), p. 165.

17. Barry Lopez, "Weekend," *Audubon,* July 1973.

18. John Steinbeck, *America and Americans* (New York: Viking Press, 1966), pp. 127–128.

19. Norman Cousins, *Head First: The Biology of Hope* (New York: E. P. Dutton, 1989), pp. 141–145.

Chapter 13

1. Yeager, p. 4.

2. Barbara Stern, "Calm Down in Six Seconds," *Vogue,* October 1981.

3. Denise Fortino, "Why Kids Need Heroes," from *Parents* Magazine, November 1984.

4. Mary Gander and Harry W. Gardiner, *Child and Adolescent Development* (Boston: Little, Brown, 1981).

5. Haim Ginott, *Between Parent and Teenager* (New York: Macmillan, 1969), pp. 39–41.

6. E. B. White, *One Man's Meat* (New York: Harper & Row, 1944), pp. 305–306.

7. Gail Sheehy, *Passages* (New York: E. P. Dutton, 1976), p. 68.

8. Studs Terkel, *Working: People Talk About What They Do All Day and How They Feel About What They Do* (New York: Pantheon Books, 1974).

9. Jon Katz, "The War on Children's Culture," *New York Times,* 4 August 1991.

Chapter 14

1. Andrea Dorfan, "How Muzak Manipulates You," *Science Digest,* May 1984.

2. Annie Dillard, *The Writing Life* (New York: Harper & Row, 1989), pp. 68–70.

3. Richard Selzer, *Mortal Lessons* (New York: Simon & Schuster, 1976), pp. 45–46.

4. Langston Hughes, *The Big Sea* (New York: Farrar, Straus and Giroux, 1968).

5. Robert Harris and Jeremy Paxman, *A Higher Form of Killing* (New York: Farrar, Straus and Giroux, 1982).

6. Gregory Jaynes, "In Idaho: Living Outside of Time," *Time,* January 14, 1985, pp. 8–9.

7. Howard Temin, "A Warning to Smokers," *Wisconsin State Journal,* 3 March 1976.

8. "Paying to Grow A Killer," *USA Today,* July 27, 1995.

9. Sheena Gillespie and Robert Singleton, *Across Cultures: A Reader for Writers* (Boston: Allyn and Bacon, 1991), pp. 5–6.

10. Gillespie and Singleton, pp. 6–7.

11. Larry French, "Merry Christmas God," originally appeared in *Ascent,* 1985.

12. Bell Kaufman, "Sunday in the Park." Reprinted from *The PEN Short Story Collection,* Ballantine, 1985.

13. Judith Ortiz Cofer, *Silent Dancing: A Partial Remembrance of a Puerto Rican Childhood* (Houston: Arte Público Press, 1990), pp. 22–27.

14. Ortiz Cofer, p. 28.

15. Amiri Baraka and Amina Baraka, *The Music: Reflections on Jazz and Blues* (New York: William Morrow, 1987), p. 28.

16. Robert Frost, "Two Look at Two" from *The Poetry of Robert Frost,* E. C. Lathem, ed. Holt, Rinehart and Winston, 1923, 1969.

17. Dylan Thomas, "Do Not Go Gentle into That Good Night" from *Poems of Dylan Thomas,* Dylan Thomas, New Directions Publ. Corp. and David Higham Associates, 1952.

Part Five Review

Eduardo Galeano, *Memory of Fire: Volume II Faces and Masks,* translated by Cedric Belfrage (New York: Pantheon Books, 1987), pp. 49–50.

Credits

From William J. Keefe et al., *American Democracy,* 3rd edition, pp. 347–349. Copyright © 1989 by Harper & Row, Publishers, Inc. Reprinted by permission of HarperCollins Publishers.

Figure 10-18, from William J. Keefe et al., *American Democracy,* 3rd edition. Copyright © 1989 by Harper & Row, Publishers, Inc. Reprinted by permission of HarperCollins Publishers.

Pronunciation key, definition of "oblique": From *The American Heritage Dictionary of the English Language, New College Edition.* Copyright © 1980 by Houghton Mifflin Company. Reprinted by permission.

Chart "The components of the criminal justice system" from *The American System of Criminal Justice* by George F. Cole. Copyright © 1992. Reprinted by permission of Wadsworth Publishing Co.

From Larry French, in *Ascent.* Copyright © 1985 by Larry French. Reprinted by permission of the author.

Tom Bodett, *As Far as You can Go Without a Passport,* © 1986 by Tom Bodett. Reprinted by permission of Addison-Wesley Publishing Company, Inc.

From Bess Armstrong, *The Baltimore Evening Sun,* April 26, 1989. Reprinted by permission.

Selection in Exercise 5-1 from Robert Wallace, *Biology: The World of Life.* Copyright © 1990 by Scott, Foresman & Company.

"The earth's water environment" paragraph from Robert A. Wallace, *Biology: The World of Life,* 5th edition. Copyright © by Scott, Foresman & Company.

Figure 10-1 and paragraph from Robert A. Wallace, *Biology: The World of Life,* 5th edition. Copyright © 1990 by Scott, Foresman & Company.

Figure 10-19 and "Insects" paragraph from Robert A. Wallace, *Biology: The World of Life.* Copyright © 1990 by Scott, Foresman & Company.

Figure, "Efficiency of meat production" from *Biosphere 2000* by Kaufman and Franz. Copyright © 1996 by Kendall/Hunt Publishing Company. Used with permission.

Index

Instructor's Manual to Accompany

FOURTH EDITION

GUIDE TO College Reading

KATHLEEN T. McWHORTER

Niagara County Community College

 LONGMAN

An imprint of Addison Wesley Longman, Inc.

New York • Reading, Massachusetts • Menlo Park, California • Harlow, England
Don Mills, Ontario • Sydney • Mexico City • Madrid • Amsterdam

Contents

Chapter 1
An Introduction to the Text

This chapter discusses the need for basic reading instruction at the college level.

The Need for Developmental Reading Instruction

In both two- and four-year colleges, there is a continuing need for developmental reading instruction. Recent trends in higher education, such as the decline in verbal skills, the increased emphasis on academic standards, and the changing clientele in many institutions, have created this need.

Both the popular media and professional research have documented the decline in the verbal abilities of beginning college students. The decrease in average scores on verbal subtests of standardized achievement tests, such as the ACT (American College Testing) and the SAT (Scholastic Aptitude Test), has been well documented. Although the causes for this decline in verbal skill are debatable, colleges are forced to deal with the reality of the situation. Many students are entering college with extremely poor reading skills. They lack the ability to express their ideas in written form, and they don't have the basic comprehension skills to read textbook assignments effectively. Colleges that accept these students have recognized their responsibility to upgrade the skills of these students.

Within higher education, there is a renewed concern for academic standards and an increased interest in the establishment of general education requirements. However, in order to maintain academic standards and to require specific course groupings to fulfill general education requirements, many colleges have found that basic reading instruction is essential. That is, to continue to offer courses at previous levels of academic rigor or integrity, colleges must improve the basic skills of many students.

Finally, the change in the type of student now entering college has placed a new importance on reading instruction within the college context. In many two- and four-year colleges, an increasing number of students would be considered "nontraditional." Very different from the traditional eighteen- or nineteen-year-old student are groups such as senior citizens, mature women returning to college, unemployed workers retraining, employed adults upgrading their skills, and the handicapped. Most of these new groups have been removed from classroom learning situations for several years and are out of contact with academic skills. Their reading and writing skills, study skills, and computational skills are often poor, perhaps due to disuse. In recruiting and accepting new students, colleges have recognized the need to upgrade the skills of these students.

Basic Features of the Text

This book was written in response to a need for a developmental reading skills text that provides college students with simple, direct instruction and sufficient practice and application. Many of its distinguishing features are described below.

Integration of Reading and Writing Skills

Since reading and writing are complementary psycholinguistic processes, an effort has been made throughout the text to emphasize this relationship and to provide practice in writing as well as reading. Students are called on to respond to exercises by writing sentences or brief paragraphs. Also, some of the questions that correspond to each reading selection require composition. Many of the critical reading questions could easily be expanded into two- or three-paragraph essay assignments, if desired. A writing exercise is included for each reading selection as well.

Emphasis on Reading as Thinking

Throughout the text reading is approached as a thinking process—one in which the student interacts with the textual material and sorts, evaluates, and reacts to its organization and content. The text also facilitates comprehension monitoring—a strategy that encourages students to be aware and conscious of their levels of understanding. Numerous strategies for perceiving patterns and structure within sentences are included.

Skill Integration and Application

The text provides ample opportunity for students to integrate the skills they are learning and to apply them to articles, essays, or textbook chapter excerpts. Each of the first five sections of the text concludes with a "Making Your Skills Work Together" review unit in which the student integrates and applies the skills taught in that particular section. Part 6 of the text contains 30 reading selections chosen from a wide range of topics and sources along with questions and exercises that require the student to apply a variety of skills.

Emphasis on Critical Reading Skills

Many developmental texts focus entirely on literal comprehension or provide superficial treatment of critical reading skills. In this text, an entire section (Part 5) is devoted to critical interpretation and evaluation. Each reading selection also includes a critical reading exercise: a set of open-ended discussion or reaction questions.

Controlled Readability

Because the text is intended for students with reading deficiencies, it is written in a direct, readable style. Exercise material has also been carefully selected to be clear, understandable, and readable.

Technical Reading Skills

The text contains a unique section on techniques for reading technical material. Included in Chapter 9, "Reading Textbook Chapters," this section focuses on how technical reading differs from other types of textbook reading and offers suggestions for doing it more effectively. Specifically, the section deals with fact density, specialized vocabulary, abbreviation and notation, graphic aids, and examples of sample problems.

Sequencing of Skills

The text follows the logical progression of skill development from words to sentences and then to paragraphs, thought patterns, and textbook chapters. It also proceeds logically from literal comprehension to critical interpretation and reaction.

Reading Selections

Part Six of the text contains 30 reading selections covering a wide range of high-interest topics and chosen from a variety of sources, including textbooks, magazines, newspapers, and anthologies. The questions that accompany the selections provide application and reinforcement of skills taught in the text. The format of the questions parallels the text in skill presentation.

Chapter 2
General Suggestions for Teaching the Course

This chapter offers some general suggestions and approaches for teaching reading to beginning college students. The intended audience is instructors new to the field or those who have not previously taught developmental students.

Structuring the Course

Classroom Arrangement

A comfortable, nonthreatening classroom environment is most suitable. The arrangement, however, should have enough structure to encourage students to approach the class with the same seriousness and attentiveness as they do other college classes.

Class Scheduling

Frequent class meetings are necessary, because students require continued repetition and reinforcement of skills. At least two class sessions per week are needed; three or four per week are desirable.

Student Conferences

At the beginning of the semester, scheduling individual conferences is an effective way to become acquainted with each student and his or her needs. During the conference, you can make sure that the course is appropriate for the student and can begin to identify the student's individual problems. The conference is also a good opportunity to review with the student the results of any reading tests that may have been used in placing the student or in recommending him or her for the course.

Many instructors use the initial conference to get a verbal commitment from the student—an acknowledgment that he or she needs the course and plans to approach it seriously. A student who is committed to the course feels obligated to attend, participate in class, and apply the skills learned to other courses.

If a student has a negative or resentful attitude toward the course, the individual conference is the best place to discuss the problem. The conference allows the instructor to discuss the student's problems with or objections to the course privately, where his or her attitudes will not influence the rest of the class.

Periodic progress-check conferences are useful throughout the semester to help motivate the student, to provide feedback on his or her progress, to see whether he or she is applying newly acquired skills to other college courses, and encourage him or her to do so. An end-of-course evaluation conference can be scheduled to review the student's work, discuss any recent test results, and suggest areas for further study.

Attendance Policy

The importance of regular class attendance should be emphasized. If college policy permits, an attendance requirement or maximum number of allowable absences should be established at the beginning of the course. Students seldom can develop the skills presented and discussed in class on their own. Also, some students need the direction and structure that an attendance policy provides.

If college policy does not allow the instructor to establish an attendance requirement, an alternative is to structure the grading system so that regular class attendance is necessary to complete graded in-class assignments.

Grading Policy

A grading system is difficult to establish for a reading course. As for any college course, there are advantages and disadvantages to most grading systems. A number of options, and their pros and cons, are summarized below.

1. *Objective Quizzes and Exams.* Although these are easy to prepare, they often do not show how a student is integrating new knowledge and skills. Essay exams that require the student to understand and apply concepts derived from careful reading will reflect progress in both reading and writing skills.
2. *Skill Application Quizzes and Exams.* Exams that are constructed to measure how effectively a student can perform a skill are another option. Tests that approximate practical use situations, requiring the student to demonstrate that he or she has learned the particular skill or technique, can be devised for many skills. The skill of identifying the main idea, for instance, can be tested by asking the student to underline the main idea of a paragraph or passage. Sentence-decombining tests can be constructed to see if students can find core parts and details.
3. *The Contract System.* A contract system is frequently used in skill courses where the amount of application and practice is crucial to learning. Contracts can be established with a class as a whole or with students individually.

A class contract details the amount of work and the assignments a student must complete in order to earn a grade of A, B, or C. Generally, a class contract would cover most of the skills taught in the course, but a series of short contracts can be established to ensure that students get additional practice only where necessary.

Student Records

Many instructors find it useful to keep a manila file folder for each student. All the student's work and assignments, tests, grading contracts, and any additional handouts or worksheets distributed in class would be kept in the folder.

The folders should be distributed at the beginning of each class session. Instructors who use this system find that it is convenient to have all materials readily available to be used for reference, follow-up, or examples. If the organization of course materials is left completely to the students, instructors find that some students come to class without the materials the instructor wishes to use.

Bringing Textbook and Materials to Class

At the beginning of the semester, much frustration will be avoided if you insist that each student always bring the reading text to class. Also, tell students they should always be ready to write; they should bring papers, pens, and so on to class. You can also suggest or require students to purchase and bring a pocket dictionary and/or thesaurus to class.

Organizing the Course Content

The text is structured into self-contained sections, or parts, to permit flexibility in organizing course content. Depending on the type of student, the priority individual instructors place on particular skills, and the time during the semester the course is offered, many instructors have strong preferences about which skills should be taught first and how skills should be sequenced. Instructors are encouraged to use the text as best suits their individual needs.

For organizing and structuring course content, a number of specific suggestions are offered below.

Class Session Format

Because many students in the course may be unable to concentrate and maintain their interest in a single activity for an extended period of time, it is important to include a variety of activities within each class session. Many students would, for example, be unable to work on identifying main ideas for an entire class session of 50 to 60 minutes. It would be more effective to divide the time by working with main ideas for 20 or 30 minutes and then switch to a follow-up activity on a previously taught skill, such as context clues, for the remaining time.

Skills Orientation

It is important to establish the course clearly as skill-oriented and to emphasize that performance, not acquisition of knowledge, is the criterion of success. The overall goal of the course is to enable the student to be successful in other college courses. Many students, especially those who have experienced academic difficulty, feel that getting good grades depends primarily on preestablished abilities—intelligence and the ability to think—and that there are two types of students—good and poor, or the haves and the have-nots. Students think that there is not much they can do to improve and do not realize that how they read definitely influences their performances and grades. Students frequently need to be shown that they are capable of developing skills to increase academic success. This idea can be demonstrated by giving the students a coded set of directions to read and follow. First, have them try to break the code (they should be unable to do so). Then, offer specific instructions on how to break it. If they follow the directions, the students will be able to crack the code. Finally, discuss this situation, emphasizing that knowing how to approach the situation greatly increased their ability to perform the task at hand. Show them that this situation is similar to other situations in which knowing how to accomplish an assignment makes the task easier.

Tightly Structuring the Course

Many students enrolled in a reading course require organization and structure in order to feel comfortable. They are often confused by a loosely structured course and are not able to handle situations in which they have too many choices or decisions to make. The following suggestions may be useful in helping students understand the organization and structure of the course.

1. *Distribute a syllabus.* Before classes begin, instructors usually plan what they will teach each week throughout the semester. Students respond well if the instructor shares the semester's plan with them. They like to know what to expect and what the course will include.
2. *Distribute course requirements and a statement of the grading system.* Despite clear verbal explanations, some students do not understand or do not remember information they are given about requirements. Students are able to organize themselves more effectively if they are given a list of assignments, due dates, test dates, and a statement of how these will be used to determine grades.
3. *Relate and connect class sessions to one another.* Although a detailed syllabus clearly defines how the course is organized, it is useful to reinforce this organization almost daily by tying together the previous class session with the current one, and at the end of a session, giving a brief preview of the next class.

Collecting Student Data

It is useful to collect some basic information from each student during one of the first class sessions. In addition to such information as name, address, phone number, and Social Security number, which are useful for general recordkeeping, you might ask each student to supply such information as:

1. Curriculum or major
2. Year in college
3. Current grade point average, if any

4. Whether he or she has taken a reading course before, and if so, where and when
5. Scores on placement tests
6. Name of faculty advisor

Each of these items will help you become familiar with each student and adjust your content and approach to meet the particular needs of each class. A sample student data sheet appears on page IM-9.

Pre- and Post-testing

If students have not taken a standardized reading test before entering the course, you might consider including a reading test as part of your first week's activities.

A standardized reading test will give you an overview of the student's incoming ability. If the test reports a grade level or grade equivalency score, the results will indicate the level at which the student can function and suggest types of materials appropriate for the student. Also, depending on the test used, the test may indicate strengths and weaknesses. To the student, the test results will demonstrate the need for the course and may motivate him or her to strive for improvement.

An alternative form of the same test at the end of the course can function as a post-test, and when compared to the pre-test, can indicate the improvement a student has made. Post-tests are particularly encouraging to students because they provide clear, measurable evidence of their improvement.

Skill Application and Transfer

The immediate goal in any study skills course is to teach students skills and techniques. Teaching these skills is fairly clear-cut. However, the long-range goal of improving the students' performance in other courses is more difficult to achieve. Success in this area depends on each student's ability to transfer the skills learned in the classroom to his or her own course materials. A major task for college reading instructors is to encourage students to transfer and apply the skills they are learning to other classes.

The skill application exercises contained in the text are written to assist instructors in accomplishing this task of skill transfer. Additionally, instructors may find the following suggestions useful.

1. Early in the semester, conduct a class discussion about the utility of the skills and the importance of using them as they are learned.
2. Make specific assignments to be completed in the context of another course. For example, ask students to do a reading assignment structured around a text in another course. The text contains numerous skill application exercises, but instructors are encouraged to make additional assignments.
3. Informally spot-check the students' texts for other courses to determine whether they are using the skills taught.
4. Students are encouraged to apply a skill they have learned if they know that their content area instructors recommend or endorse the skill. Therefore, if the fac-

SAMPLE STUDENT DATA SHEET

Name: _____   Course: _____

Address: _____   Instructor: _____

Phone: _____   Semester: _____

Soc. Sec. No.: _____

Curriculum (or Major): _____

Faculty Advisor: _____

Semester: 1   2   3   4   5   6   (circle one)

Courses registered for this semester:

1. _____

2. _____

3. _____

4. _____

5. _____

6. _____

Describe any other reading courses you have taken in the past several years.

_____

Why are you taking this course?

_____

For instructor's use:

Standardized Test Scores:

ulty members who teach your students can be encouraged to reinforce the use of the skills taught in this course, student acceptance will be greatly facilitated.

Characteristics of Developmental Students and Instructional Accommodations

Developmental students exhibit unique learning characteristics, behaviors, and attitudes that must be recognized in order for the instructor to provide effective reading skill instruction. The most prevalent characteristics are described in this section, along with practical suggestions for adapting instruction to respond to these characteristics.

Negative Self-Image

Many developmental students hold a negative academic self-image and regard themselves as failures. This may be largely a result of numerous failures they have experienced in previous educational settings. Many students think of themselves as unable to learn or compete in academic situations. Consistent, then, with their past history, they expect little of themselves and demand little of those around them.

Instructional Accommodation Assignments, especially initial ones in the semester, should be designed so that the student experiences success. The first opportunity to practice a newly learned skill should also demonstrate success.

Lack of Self-Direction

Developmental students often lack goals and direction in their pursuit of a college education and in managing their lives. They have few or no longer term goals; short-term goals are often unclear and changeable. As a result, developmental students tend to lack the discipline or focus to attend class, complete assignments, or work independently on long-term projects.

Instructional Accommodation Assignments must be immediate and short-term. Due dates are essential and regular feedback is necessary. Frequent checking is needed to be sure that students complete assignments, do homework, and "stay with" the course.

Passive Approach to Learning

Partly because of their lack of experience in and success with academic environments, developmental students often exhibit a passive approach to learning. They seldom ask questions or initiate action to solve problems. Instead, they follow procedures as well as they are able to understand them, wait to be told what to do, and take little action without specific direction.

Instructional Accommodation   Class discussions that require involvement and problem solving are useful in encouraging or shaping more active learning. Often a forthright discussion of active versus passive learning characteristics is effective. Workshops or sessions conducted by a member of the counseling staff that address this issue are often useful as well.

Negative Attitudes Toward Instructors

Throughout their previous unsuccessful educational experiences, many developmental students have come to regard teachers as untrustworthy and associated with unpleasant or embarrassing situations. As a result, students are often closed, unresponsive, or evasive with their instructors.

Instructional Accommodation   Establishing a framework of trust is difficult, but necessary. Openness, directness, honesty, and patience seem effective. Careful, detailed explanations of course requirements and a willingness to listen to students are helpful. Perhaps most important is for an instructor to present him- or herself as a person—not as an authority figure—who experiences successes and failures and who has likes and dislikes, good days and bad days, just as students do.

Short Attention Span

Many developmental students exhibit very short attention spans: they are unable or unaccustomed to focusing attention at length on a particular task or assignment.

Instructional Accommodation   Lengthy lectures and extended discussions are ineffective. Rather, try to incorporate several activities into each class session. For example, a class session might be structured as follows: review and discuss answers to an assigned reading selection (20 minutes), finish exercises within a previously assigned chapter (15 minutes), and introduce a new chapter and outline its content (10 minutes).

Lack of Familiarity with College Life and Academic Procedures

More than most students, developmental students are confused and frustrated by the strangeness, formality, and seeming unfriendliness of the college environment. Many developmental students are the first in their family or among their friends to attend college. Therefore, they lack the advantage of practical advice and support that many students receive from family and peers.

Instructional Accommodation   As a means of establishing trust as well as building familiarity with college life, offer as many practical "how-to-get-around" tips as possible. Also, as events occur on campus, take a few moments to explain them. For example, when drop-and-add day begins, explain what is going on; when advance registration for the next semester begins, alert the class and explain the procedures involved.

Encourage students to get involved with social and recreational activities. At community colleges especially, where many students commute, developmental students with their passive natures tend to avoid getting involved. As a result, college means only attending classes; these students fail to make friends and develop reference groups with whom they can share their feelings, problems, and successes.

Chapter 3
Suggested Approaches to Each Section of the Text

This chapter provides a brief discussion of the skills taught in each section of the text and offers suggestions for introducing those skills.

Part One—Vocabulary: The Key to Meaning

The vocabulary of developmental students is extremely limited both in size and level of sophistication. Largely, their vocabularies consist of everyday, functional words, primarily those used in oral communication. Words used most commonly in written communication are noticeably absent, most likely due to the students' lack of experience and success with the written mode of expression. In particular, many developmental students lack the vocabulary of the academic world—those conceptual or abstract words that describe higher-level thought processes such as generalization, analysis, and inference.

The intent of Part One of the text is to provide the students with a framework of skills for improving their vocabularies. It is first in the text because vocabulary development must be a primary and continuing emphasis through the course. The following suggestions may be of use in maintaining this emphasis:

1. Require each student to purchase a paperback edition of a collegiate dictionary and to bring it to every class.
2. Make a point to discuss at least one unfamiliar or interesting word in each class session. It may be a word you used or one from the text or a reading selection. Ask students to use the dictionary to discover various meanings.
3. Encourage students to organize a system for learning new words. Some instructors build this activity into course requirements and into their grading procedure.

This section may be introduced effectively by initiating a discussion of the problems the students have with vocabulary. Often the questions "Do you think your vocabulary is good or bad?" and "Why?" are good openers. Make lists on the chalkboard of the problems students identify. Then, after the lists are completed, show how many of their problems will be addressed by topics or techniques discussed in this section of the text.

To generate interest in Chapter 1, ask students what they do when they are reading and meet an unfamiliar word. Some students will offer the answer they think you expect to hear: "Look it up in the dictionary." Students will be relieved and surprised to hear that it is the very wrong answer. (Discuss the impossibility of looking up every unfamiliar word on a difficult page.) Then, lead the discussion to alternative approaches—namely, context.

For Chapter 2, an effective introduction involves taking a simple word such as "form" from which many words can be built by adding common prefixes and suffixes and asking students to think of words that have the same root word. Write the words on the chalkboard; as the list grows, students will begin to see the value of studying word parts.

In introducing Chapter 3, you might begin by listing ten words on the chalkboard, none of which you expect the students to be able to pronounce. Then, show students how the dictionary provides pronunciation information. Most students have neither seen nor used an unabridged dictionary. If one is readily accessible, it is often worth the effort to bring one into class. Most students are interested in seeing it and comparing it with their pocket editions.

Part Two—Reading as Thinking and Learning

Many students regard reading as a passive activity requiring little or no interaction with the text or the author. The purpose of Part Two is to build and promote active reading strategies—to encourage students to approach reading not only as a process of acquiring information, but as a process of anticipating ideas, asking questions, and deciding what is important.

Chapter 4 presents prereading strategies: starting with the right attitude, building concentration, previewing, activating background knowledge, and developing guide questions. You might introduce the chapter by discussing everyday activities that require preparation or planning. Ask students to suggest activities and list them on the chalkboard. Begin by suggesting several examples: planning the route you'll take before driving to an unfamiliar destination, planning a dinner menu before starting to cook, or analyzing what is wrong with an engine before repairing it. Once the list is extensive, then suggest to students that preparation and planning are also necessary before beginning to read an assignment.

The focus of Chapter 5 is comprehension monitoring and learning style assessment. Students are taught to recognize signals of strong and weak comprehension, given several monitoring techniques, and are shown how to strengthen their comprehension. The concept of monitoring is new to many students; they assume that comprehension happens automatically as part of the reading process.

Introduce the concept of monitoring by discussing an everyday activity in which monitoring automatically occurs. Driving a car works well as an example. Explain how the driver corrects the steering wheel and adjusts speed to road conditions, speed limits, and actions of other drivers. The driver is constantly aware of his or her vehicle and its performance and position and speed and makes appropriate corrections and changes. Next, ask students to think of other situations or tasks of which monitoring is a part. Once students have grasped the concept of monitoring, introduce the idea of comprehension monitoring.

Students may experience difficulty grasping the concept of learning style. It is helpful to discuss other individual differences, such as personality, to help students understand that learning style is unique. Learning style should not be presented as a fixed, unchanging set of characteristics. Again, much like personality, it evolves, develops, and changes. If students fail to understand this, they may seize upon learning style as a reason or excuse for their inability to learn certain types of material or function in particular classes. It is also important to caution students that the learning style questionnaire is only an indicator of learning style; it is not an absolute measure. The results should be combined with the student's self-knowledge and experience in order to be used effectively.

Part Three—Comprehension Skills

Literal comprehension, the synthesis of words and ideas to understand a writer's message, is at the root of many developmental students' reading problems. Literal comprehension is also perhaps the most crucial factor in determining a student's immediate and long-term academic success. Textbook reading skill forms the core of most college courses, and developmental students must develop the literal comprehension skills to handle this.

For many developmental students, college texts are formidable because they are written at a readability level far beyond their own reading level. Many texts are written at 13th-grade level or higher, while many developmental students read below a ninth-grade level. This disparity between the level of the text and the reading ability of the student is the immediate problem to be addressed.

To introduce this section and to demonstrate the variety of problems that can interfere with understanding, you might try the following activity: Choose an extremely difficult but brief excerpt from a college text and have copies duplicated. Distribute the passage to students and ask them to read it. Create a negative attitude toward the material by saying that it is dull and will probably be boring. As the students read, make it difficult for them to concentrate by making noise, shifting papers, talking individually to students, and so forth. When the students have finished, ask whether the passage was easy or difficult to read. Then discuss why it was difficult. Point out that attitude, concentration, and difficulty of material are factors that interfere with comprehension.

A common reading problem exhibited by developmental students is that they do not perceive pattern or structure. They regard a sentence as a string of words, and a paragraph as merely a group of sentences. They fail to recognize or understand the structure of sentences and paragraphs. Therefore, they fail to grasp the relationship among ideas at both the sentence and paragraph level.

To introduce the concept of structure within a sentence, the use of a scrambled sentence is effective. Divide a sentence into several phrases and scramble their order. Ask the class to restore it to normal order. Then ask how they were able to do so, why they moved a particular phrase to the beginning, and so forth. These questions will lead to a discussion of the relationship between the parts of a sentence.

A similar exercise is useful for discussing paragraph structure. Select a paragraph and scramble the sentences, writing them in list form; have this typed and duplicated with space between each of the items. Direct students to first fold and tear the paper so that each sentence is on a separate strip of paper. Then ask students to rearrange the strips until they have formed a paragraph. Discussion that follows should focus on the clues students used to restore normal order.

Part Four—Textbook Reading Skills

The comprehension skills presented in Part Three of the text are those required for reading all types of prose material—textbooks, newspapers, nonfiction books, and magazines. They are general, high-utility skills with a wide range of applicability. It is commonly agreed that students need to be taught basic comprehension skills that can be applied to any type of material. It is equally important that they be taught specific skills and techniques for reading the types of material most frequently encountered in their college courses. The overall purpose of this section of the text is to present very specific strategies for reading and learning in college textbooks.

Students often fail to realize that different types of materials should be read differently, and, therefore, they do not vary their approach to reading in response to the material and to their purpose for reading. A second purpose of this part of the text is to focus students' attention on the particular features of textbooks that distinguish them from other types of reading material and to demonstrate how to use these features to read and study effectively.

The emphasis throughout this section is on the overall structure and organization of textbooks. Too often, students experience difficulty reading a particular chapter because they do not perceive its thought structure or progression of ideas. As a means of introducing the topic of structure and organization, an analogy is often effective. Ask students if they have ever put together a jigsaw puzzle and how they approached the task. They are likely to say that they look at the picture on the box cover. Discuss how difficult it would be to reconstruct the puzzle without seeing the picture. Explain that putting the pieces (fact) together, or making sense of the chapter without knowledge of its structure, is also a nearly impossible task. To read a chapter effectively, it is necessary to get "the big picture," or overview, of its organization and content.

A practical demonstration of the value of underlining, summarizing, and outlining is often effective in convincing students of their value. Choose two separate pages from the same source (factual material is best). Direct the students simply to read the first page. Then give either an oral or a written quiz. Next, ask the students to read and outline the second text excerpt, and then give a similar oral or a written quiz. Ask students to compare their scores on the two quizzes. Most students will score higher on the second. At this point, discuss the role of outlining in increasing recall and retention.

A chapter is devoted to strategies for reading graphics. Graphic material tends to be difficult and confusing to some students; others tend to skip over graphics, failing to realize their value in condensing and summarizing information and in presenting trends and patterns. Students often learn the value and importance of graphics by actually constructing them. As a class activity, divide the class into two groups. Present one group with a set of data in paragraph form. Ask them to draw conclusions and write a summary. Ask the second group to draw a graph, chart, or table. Then, question both groups about trends or patterns the data revealed. Discuss why the group that translated data into graphic form was better able to recognize the pattern.

As an alternative activity, have students practice drawing various graphics from sets of data you supply, discussing which form of graphic would be most effective for each set.

Part Five—Critical Reading and Thinking: Interpreting and Reacting

Part Five focuses on the interpretive and analytical skills students need to interact with and evaluate written material. Many developmental students are extremely literal—they accept what they see, hear, and read at face value and seldom question or challenge. In particular, they accept everything in print as fact or truth.

An interesting way to help students break out of this literal mode is to ask them to read two descriptions of the same event written from different points of view. Sources might include different newspapers or magazines with differing political points of view.

As an alternative, you might show the class a controversial picture or photograph and ask each student to write a paragraph describing what is occurring in the picture. Then have students exchange papers or read several aloud. No doubt, students will express differing interpretations and offer conflicting points of view. This demonstration can show that although each description is in writing (in print, so to speak), each is merely an interpretation, not necessarily factual information.

An entire chapter is devoted to reading and interpreting essays and literature. Some students report that they dislike literature. Others regard literature as difficult or different from other forms of written expression. Due to its unique format, poetry is often the genre about which students have the strongest feelings. A primary goal of Chapter 14 is to encourage positive attitudes and skilled approaches to literature.

To demonstrate that reading literature is *not* different or unique, you might begin by asking each student to write a brief biography of his or her grandmother. Then direct the students to read the narrative essay and poem included in the section titled "Reading and Interpreting Poetry" that Judith Ortiz Cofer wrote about her grandmother, asking them to compare and contrast the two. Emphasize similarities. Discuss the types of expression each genre allows. Encourage students to regard literature as a diverse, effective, and enjoyable means of expression.

Part Six—Reading Selections

The reading selections contained in Part Six were chosen from a wide range of reading materials including college texts, newspapers, anthologies, and periodicals. Selection criteria included interest, applicability to skills taught in the text, and readability. The material with each selection follows a consistent format, as follows.

Introduction

Each selection begins with a brief statement, question, or synopsis. Its purpose is to serve as an advance organizer. It is intended to capture the student's interest and focus his or her attention. Emphasize that students should read and think about the introduction before reading the selection. When you assign a selection, it is useful to read the introduction and discuss briefly its topic as a means of helping students develop an interest and purpose for reading.

Vocabulary Preview

This section lists the words and phrases with which the student is most likely to be unfamiliar, along with a brief definition of each. Encourage students to read through the list before reading the article and to refer back to it as they read.

Prereading

This activity directs the students to preview (see text Chapter 4) the article and to answer a question based on the previewing.

Checking Your Comprehension

These questions, by means of a variety of formats, check the students' literal comprehension of the article. Some exercises ask open-ended questions; others are objective; still others direct the student to outline, underline, or summarize. The format chosen depends on the type of article, its organization, and the skills it was chosen to reinforce. Answers to objective questions are included in the Answer Key section of this manual.

Critical Reading and Thinking

These open-ended questions require the student to interpret, relate to, and evaluate the author's ideas. Insist that students answer in complete sentences; this will encourage more exact and thorough responses. These questions are intended to serve as a basis for class discussion and reaction. In responding to the questions, students often tend to give their own opinions without regard to the text and the clues the author provides. Focus the students' attention on the article by asking them to support their responses by referring to specific portions of the text. Certain questions may also be selected as the basis for paragraph or essay writing assignments.

Words in Context

This section lists several words for which the context provides clues to the meaning. (Refer to text Chapter 1 for a discussion of context clues.) Students are directed to use context to provide a synonym or brief definition of each word.

Vocabulary Review

This exercise, again employing various formats, provides a review of the words listed in the Vocabulary Preview section. Several exercises ask students to analyze word parts and form new words using the root; others require the student to demonstrate understanding of the word by using or applying it to a practical situation. In other selections, the task involves more objective recall or matching of words with their meanings.

The reading selections are intended to provide an opportunity for skill application and practice. The questions are structured to focus on the skills taught within the text. Questions that focus on a particular skill are cross-referenced to the chapter in which the skill is taught. Many other questions demand a more generalized response, requiring an application or consolidation of two or more skills. This second type more closely approximates the type of questions asked in college courses and the level of understanding expected by college instructors.

Writing Exercise

This exercise encourages the student to relate his or her own ideas about the topic addressed in the reading and provides reinforcement of writing skills.

Chapter Quizzes

Chapter 1 Using Context Clues

Directions: *Each of the following sentences contains a word whose meaning can be determined from the context. Mark the choice that most clearly states the meaning of the italicized word as it is used in the sentence.*

_____ 1. Both comedians were *seasoned* performers—each had appeared before an audience over 200 times.
    (a) challenging
    (b) experienced
    (c) aged
    (d) imposing

_____ 2. The dog was *submissive*—crouching, flattening its ears, and avoiding eye contact.
    (a) friendly and excitable
    (b) yielding to the control of another
    (c) aggressive
    (d) active

_____ 3. There was a *consensus*—or unified opinion—among the students that the exam was difficult.
    (a) requirement
    (b) consequence
    (c) disagreement
    (d) agreement

_____ 4. For their own safety, household pets should be *confined* to their own yard.
    (a) controlled
    (b) restricted
    (c) surrounded
    (d) determined

_____ 5. The quarterback *sustained* numerous injuries: a fractured wrist, two broken ribs, and a hip injury.
    (a) caused
    (b) experienced
    (c) displayed
    (d) noticed

_____ 6. The child remained *demure* while the teacher scolded, but became violently angry afterwards.
(a) quiet and reserved
(b) boisterous
(c) cowardly
(d) upset and distraught

_____ 7. Your *dossier* is a record of your credentials, including college transcripts and letters of recommendation.
(a) briefcase or valise
(b) statement of account
(c) list
(d) collection of materials

_____ 8. When preparing job application letters, develop one standard letter or *prototype,* then write variations of that letter to fit the specific jobs for which you are applying.
(a) variation
(b) model
(c) detail
(d) introduction

_____ 9. Although most members of the class agreed with the instructor's evaluation of the film, several strongly *objected.*
(a) disagreed
(b) obliterated
(c) debated
(d) agreed

_____ 10. Sam's brother advised him to be *wary* of strangers he meets on the street.
(a) suspicious
(b) trusting
(c) congenial with
(d) generous toward

Chapter 2 Recognizing the Structure of Words

Directions: *Select the answer that provides the best definition for each word.*

_____ 1. multistage rocket
   (a) rocket with two stages
   (b) rocket with three stages
   (c) rocket with several stages
   (d) multipurpose rocket

_____ 2. noncommittal
   (a) unwilling to reveal attitude or feeling
   (b) unable to perform a task
   (c) unwilling to make an effort
   (d) unwilling to change

_____ 3. equidistant
   (a) specific distances
   (b) uneven distances
   (c) unlike distances
   (d) equal distances

_____ 4. triennial
   (a) lasting one year
   (b) lasting three years
   (c) lasting two years
   (d) lasting four years

_____ 5. transcultural
   (a) differences in cultures
   (b) between cultures
   (c) among cultures
   (d) extending across cultures

_____ 6. chronometer
   (a) machine to control velocity
   (b) device to control friction
   (c) instrument for measuring time
   (d) instrument for measuring speed

_____ 7. disaffiliated
   (a) not associated
   (b) partially associated
   (c) several associations
   (d) false associations

_____ 8. territory
   (a) an area of land
   (b) related to fear
   (c) upper surface area
   (d) resulting from terror

_____ 9. theology
     (a) study of the origin of gods
     (b) proposition
     (c) thermal
     (d) a type of lens

_____ 10. photosensitive cell
     (a) cell sensitive to heat
     (b) cell sensitive to light
     (c) cell sensitive to color
     (d) cell sensitive to friction

Chapter 3 Learning New Words

Directions: *Select the answer that best completes each statement.*

_____ 1. The best way to build your vocabulary is to
- (a) locate and learn new and unfamiliar words.
- (b) study word lists.
- (c) learn to use words with which you are already familiar.
- (d) learn words your professors use.

_____ 2. To check the spelling of an everyday word, such as "receive," the easiest source to use would be
- (a) an unabridged dictionary.
- (b) a subject area dictionary.
- (c) a pocket or paperback dictionary.
- (d) a thesaurus.

_____ 3. You might use a thesaurus in all of the following situations *except*
- (a) to locate a word that fits a particular situation.
- (b) to replace a word that is unclear.
- (c) to locate a word that is more descriptive.
- (d) to check the specialized or technical meaning of a word.

_____ 4. A thesaurus always lists
- (a) antonyms.
- (b) pronunciation keys.
- (c) synonyms.
- (d) variations in spelling.

_____ 5. A dictionary entry always includes all of the following *except*
- (a) part of speech.
- (b) synonyms.
- (c) pronunciation.
- (d) meanings.

_____ 6. To use the pronunciation key in the dictionary, you must know
- (a) which symbols correspond to which sounds.
- (b) how various sounds are grouped.
- (c) how to divide words into syllables.
- (d) which abbreviations correspond to which words.

_____ 7. In a dictionary entry, meanings are arranged
- (a) alphabetically.
- (b) in the order in which they were developed.
- (c) by part of speech.
- (d) by complexity.

_____ 8. Guide words are intended to
   (a) help you locate an entry rapidly.
   (b) read an entry more rapidly.
   (c) locate the right meaning quickly.
   (d) locate synonyms.

_____ 9. Which one of the following is *not* an advantage of the index card system?
   (a) it is convenient to use during spare time
   (b) it incorporates context clues and word parts
   (c) it eliminates learning words in a fixed order
   (d) you spend time learning what you do not know

_____ 10. In using the index card system you should record
   (a) all unfamiliar words you encounter each day.
   (b) the word in context.
   (c) several meanings for the same word.
   (d) words you intend to learn.

Chapter 4 Prereading Strategies

Directions: Select the one choice that best completes each statement.

____ 1. Previewing familiarizes you with
  (a) content and organization.
  (b) the writer's purpose.
  (c) inferences and conclusions.
  (d) patterns of thought.

____ 2. When previewing a textbook chapter, you should read all of the following *except*
  (a) the last paragraph.
  (b) review questions.
  (c) the introductory paragraph.
  (d) references and footnotes.

____ 3. Developing guide questions is primarily intended
  (a) to give you practice answering test questions.
  (b) to improve your retention and recall.
  (c) to force you to read.
  (d) to eliminate distractions.

____ 4. The easiest way to form a guide question is to use the
  (a) introduction.
  (b) review questions.
  (c) summary.
  (d) headings.

____ 5. Which of the following questions would be the best to ask for a section in your history text on the Revolutionary War?
  (a) When did it start?
  (b) Where did it start?
  (c) Why did it start?
  (d) Who was involved in early battles?

____ 6. To build your concentration you should
  (a) use rewards and punishments.
  (b) control your environment.
  (c) study in a comfortable place.
  (d) eliminate all time pressures.

____ 7. Recalling background information helps a student to
  (a) preview more easily.
  (b) retain content and read more easily.
  (c) write summaries and outlines.
  (d) read somewhat faster.

_____ 8. Brainstorming is the process of
    (a) asking questions.
    (b) mentally outlining reading material.
    (c) recalling personal experiences.
    (d) writing down everything about a topic that comes to mind.

_____ 9. Concentration primarily involves
    (a) asking questions.
    (b) previewing.
    (c) accepting responsibility.
    (d) focusing your attention.

_____ 10. While studying and reading you should
    (a) not take breaks.
    (b) delay pleasant activities until after you have finished.
    (c) work on one subject per night.
    (d) avoid setting time limits for yourself.

Chapter 5 Monitoring Your Comprehension and Learning

Directions: *Select the one answer that best completes each statement.*

_____ 1. Knowing where the author is leading and reading at a comfortable, consistent pace indicate that you are
(a) monitoring your comprehension.
(b) comprehending what you are reading.
(c) using checkpoints.
(d) not comprehending what you are reading.

_____ 2. The purpose of utilizing checkpoints while reading is
(a) to give yourself a rest.
(b) to look up unknown words.
(c) to assess and correct your comprehension.
(d) to preview.

_____ 3. Internal dialogue is
(a) rephrasing briefly to yourself what you have read.
(b) answering your guide questions.
(c) a method of locating topic sentences.
(d) a method of studying with a friend.

_____ 4. Which of the following techniques would be most helpful in evaluating and interpreting what you read?
(a) noticing positive and negative signals
(b) asking connection questions
(c) asking guide questions
(d) previewing

_____ 5. A student read a chapter in his economics textbook and felt he understood it. When he took a quiz on it, he realized his comprehension of it was incomplete. Which of the following is *not* an explanation of this?
(a) he read too slowly
(b) he did not recognize implied meanings
(c) he did not see more complicated relationships
(d) he understood only the facts

_____ 6. To understand a difficult paragraph, you should
(a) reread the previous paragraph.
(b) skim the material for unfamiliar words.
(c) take frequent breaks.
(d) rephrase and explain each idea in your own words.

_____ 7. Previewing and locating topic sentences are helpful strategies when
(a) everything in the material seems important.
(b) words are unfamiliar.
(c) sentences are long and confusing.
(d) you cannot answer your connection questions.

_____ 8. A student who, while reading her computer science textbook, reviews mentally each step in writing a certain type of program is using
(a) connection questions.
(b) guide questions.
(c) checkpoints.
(d) internal dialogue.

_____ 9. When you have little or no background knowledge about a topic it is sometimes necessary to
(a) write outlines.
(b) use internal dialogue.
(c) refer to other sources.
(d) preview and skim.

_____ 10. A student was having difficulty following the writer's organization in an essay assigned by his English instructor. Which of the following techniques would be _most_ helpful to him?
(a) write an outline
(b) skim read
(c) make marginal notes
(d) read aloud

Chapter 6 Understanding and Paraphrasing Sentences

_____ 1. Which of the following is a coordinate sentence that combines two equally important ideas?
   (a) They thought Jack was a sore loser, but he really was just upset with himself.
   (b) Although Pete felt tired, he went to the party.
   (c) Of course, I expected to receive a passing grade.
   (d) After Pete left the party, he walked home.

_____ 2. Which of the following is an example of a subordinate sentence that expresses one key idea and a related idea?
   (a) She wanted to stay; I wanted to leave.
   (b) The stock is selling at a price below its book value.
   (c) I left the party early, but my sister decided to stay.
   (d) While I was waiting for the bus, I finished my math assignment.

Directions: _Refer to the following sentence in answering Questions 3–6_
Trees under attack by insects release a chemical into the air.

_____ 3. The key idea of this sentence is
   (a) trees are attacked.
   (b) trees release a chemical.
   (c) chemicals are in the air.
   (d) insects attack trees.

_____ 4. The subject of the sentence is
   (a) trees.
   (b) insects.
   (c) chemicals.
   (d) air.

_____ 5. The phrase "under attack by insects"
   (a) describes which trees.
   (b) tells how trees protect themselves.
   (c) refers to chemicals.
   (d) is the subject of the sentence.

_____ 6. The phrase "into the air"
   (a) describes the chemical.
   (b) refers to trees.
   (c) tells where chemicals are released.
   (d) refers to insects.

Directions: *For each of the following questions, select the answer that is the best paraphrase (restatement) of the sentence.*

_____ 7. Because of the power of emotions and feelings and the effects they can have, they can be used destructively in numerous ways: to control, to damage, to manipulate, or to create guilt.

      (a) Feelings and emotions have powerful effects and can be harmful; they can control, injure, shape, or create guilt.

      (b) Emotions can be used destructively in many ways.

      (c) The power of emotions and feelings is destructive.

      (d) Guilt and injury often result if feelings and emotions become too powerful.

_____ 8. We often get advice from "authorities," people assumed to be knowledgeable because of their experience or position, and seldom question their advice.

      (a) Authorities are people who have many accomplishments and who give advice.

      (b) We get advice from and seldom challenge authorities, people who are experts due to their accomplishments or positions.

      (c) We respect authorities due to their accomplishments or position.

      (d) Authorities are accomplished people who give advice.

_____ 9. For most people in a society such as the United States, the most important life goal is to have a successful and dignified occupation or career that provides an adequate income and a comfortable lifestyle.

      (a) A common life goal in the United States is to have a successful career that provides income to support a comfortable way of life.

      (b) To be worthwhile, a career or occupation must provide dignity and respect.

      (c) Careers must be dignified and produce income.

      (d) A comfortable lifestyle is the most important life goal for most people in the United States.

_____ 10. Most political scientists are still uncertain about the effect of television on our values; however, its effect on our opinions is clearly established.

      (a) Political scientists know that television has a clear effect on our opinions and values.

      (b) According to political scientists, television has no effect on values but does influence opinion.

      (c) Political scientists are unsure how television affects us.

      (d) According to political scientists, television affects our opinions and may affect our values as well.

Chapter 7 Understanding Paragraphs

Directions: *Select the answer that best completes each statement.*

_____ 1. The topic of a paragraph is
    (a) the one thing that the whole paragraph is about.
    (b) the main idea of the paragraph.
    (c) the noun that is the subject of a sentence.
    (d) the object of the predicate.

_____ 2. Most of the sentences in a paragraph
    (a) restate the main idea.
    (b) explain the main idea.
    (c) provide examples.
    (d) do not connect to each other.

_____ 3. The best clue to use in identifying the topic of a paragraph is
    (a) the arrangement of the sentences.
    (b) the use of directional words.
    (c) a frequently repeated key word.
    (d) the order of details.

_____ 4. Which one of the following groups of words contains *one general* term and *three specific* terms?
    (a) *Time, Golf Digest, Newsweek, U.S. News and World Report*
    (b) students, classmates, colleagues, friends
    (c) vanilla, raspberry, chocolate, strawberry
    (d) newspapers, media, radio, television

_____ 5. In what position are you most likely to find the topic sentence in a paragraph?
    (a) first
    (b) second
    (c) last
    (d) in the middle

_____ 6. For what purpose might a writer place a topic sentence at the beginning and end of a paragraph?
    (a) repetition
    (b) emphasis
    (c) clarification
    (d) all of the above

_____ 7. If a paragraph does not have a stated topic sentence, then
    (a) the paragraph does not have a main idea.
    (b) it lacks organization and focus.
    (c) you must infer its main idea.
    (d) the details are more important.

_____ 8. A writer uses examples to support an idea to
   (a) prove that the idea is correct.
   (b) make the idea real and understandable.
   (c) create a mental picture.
   (d) emphasize similarities and differences.

_____ 9. Terms such as "on the other hand," "however," and "in contrast" indicate
   (a) a continuation of thought.
   (b) a change in thought.
   (c) a cause-effect relationship.
   (d) a list will follow.

_____ 10. Which of the following statements describes the function of transitional words in a paragraph?
   (a) they always indicate a continuation of thought
   (b) they signal a writer's direction of thought
   (c) they indicate the location of the main idea
   (d) they provide a list of key details

Chapter 8 Following the Author's Thought Patterns

Directions: *Select the answer that best completes each statement.*

_____ 1. It is useful to learn thought patterns because they
 (a) identify the author's purpose.
 (b) improve your vocabulary.
 (c) improve your comprehension.
 (d) function as a transition.

_____ 2. A paragraph that explains a technique for analyzing a poem by discussing and analyzing excerpts from several poems uses which of the following patterns?
 (a) cause-effect
 (b) illustration-example
 (c) definition
 (d) comparison-contrast

_____ 3. A definition contains which of the following parts?
 (a) general group and distribution characteristics
 (b) general class and associative features
 (c) associative features and distinguishing characteristics
 (d) general class and distinguishing characteristics

_____ 4. Which of the following patterns is most concerned with relationships between events?
 (a) classification
 (b) cause-effect
 (c) definition
 (d) illustration-example

_____ 5. In writing a paragraph describing how to load a disk into a computer, which pattern would you most likely use?
 (a) cause-effect
 (b) comparison-contrast
 (c) chronological order-process
 (d) illustration-example

_____ 6. Which of the following topics would *most* likely be developed using the cause-effect thought pattern?
 (a) the treatment of mental disorders
 (b) how to take objective exams
 (c) preparing your income tax form
 (d) limitations of context clues

_____ 7. If you wrote a paragraph explaining that there are two types of exams—objective and essay—which pattern should you use?
(a) chronological order
(b) classification
(c) cause-effect
(d) definition

_____ 8. The cause-effect pattern
(a) is always concerned with single causes and single effects.
(b) focuses on similarities among events.
(c) may express multiple causes and multiple effects.
(d) focuses on visualization skills.

_____ 9. A paragraph that discusses both similarities and differences
(a) can be organized only one way.
(b) can use one of several means of organization.
(c) usually discusses similarities and then differences.
(d) must be concerned with only one type of difference.

_____ 10. Which of the following topics would most likely be developed using the chronological order-process pattern?
(a) the psychology of humor
(b) personality theories—how they compare
(c) stages of personality development
(d) types of intimacy

Chapter 9 Reading Textbook Chapters

Directions: *Select the answer that best completes each statement.*

_____ 1. Information on the audience for whom a text is written is often included in the
(a) appendix.
(b) table of contents.
(c) first chapter.
(d) preface.

_____ 2. Typographical aids include
(a) photographs.
(b) charts.
(c) maps.
(d) headings and subheadings.

_____ 3. The first thing to read when studying an illustration is its
(a) column headings.
(b) title.
(c) scale.
(d) source.

_____ 4. Which of the following are primarily intended to organize and simplify information?
(a) italicized phrases
(b) colored print
(c) photographs
(d) diagrams

_____ 5. The glossary
(a) presents difficult everyday words alphabetically.
(b) lists technical vocabulary chapter by chapter.
(c) is a mini-dictionary of specialized vocabulary.
(d) gives all meanings of each word listed.

_____ 6. As compared to other types of textbooks, technical writing
(a) contains fewer graphs and charts.
(b) is more factually dense.
(c) uses fewer specialized words.
(d) lacks general and specific terms.

_____ 7. Which of the following strategies would be *most* useful in learning vocabulary in an anatomy and physiology course?
(a) study the glossary
(b) memorize word lists
(c) learn to pronounce each word
(d) learn key prefixes, root, suffixes

_____ 8. Which of the following would you be *most likely* to find in the first chapter of a textbook?
(a) diagrams and graphs
(b) a description of the audience for whom the text was written
(c) important terminology
(d) typographical aids

_____ 9. Which of the following pieces of information would be *least likely* to be found in a preface?
(a) the author's major points of emphasis
(b) a review of key terms used in the text
(c) a description of learning aids contained in the text
(d) information on how the text is organized

_____ 10. Which of the following learning aids would be *most useful* in preparing for an essay exam?
(a) italicized words and phrases
(b) review questions
(c) vocabulary lists
(d) discussion questions

Chapter 10 Reading Graphic Aids

Directions: Select the answer that best completes each statement.

_____ 1. The subject of a graphic is most often suggested in its
   (a) key.
   (b) footnote.
   (c) title.
   (d) legend.

_____ 2. A diagram is commonly used to
   (a) express a relationship between two or more items.
   (b) show causes or effects.
   (c) demonstrate relationships between parts of an object.
   (d) compare events over time.

_____ 3. Photographs are often included in a text to
   (a) present facts.
   (b) create an emotional response.
   (c) divide subject matter.
   (d) organize information.

_____ 4. Graphs always
   (a) describe an event.
   (b) compare at least three variables.
   (c) list information.
   (d) express a relationship.

_____ 5. Which of the following graphics could be best used to demonstrate the frequency of child abuse among various parental age groups?
   (a) a flowchart
   (b) a diagram
   (c) an organizational chart
   (d) a bar graph

_____ 6. In a sociology course Ann traced her family history. Which of the following charts would best depict her findings?
   (a) an organizational chart
   (b) a linear graph
   (c) a pictogram
   (d) a pie chart

_____ 7. If you were to use a chart showing how the heating system in your house works, the best type of chart to use would be
   (a) an organizational chart.
   (b) a linear graph.
   (c) a pictogram.
   (d) a pie chart.

_____ 8. When you write a summary note for a graphic, the note should always identify
(a) the source of the information.
(b) the unit of measurement.
(c) the trend or pattern.
(d) inconsistencies within the data.

_____ 9. Which of the following graphics could be best used to compare changes in yearly earnings of Hispanic and African-American workers over the past ten years in the following age groups: under 20, 20–40, and 40–60?
(a) diagram
(b) multiple bar graph
(c) flowchart
(d) pie chart

_____ 10. A flowchart is often used to
(a) describe distance and location.
(b) organize large amounts of statistical data.
(c) show how something is organized.
(d) explain a process.

Chapter 11 Organizing and Remembering Information

Directions: *Select the answer that best completes each selection.*

_____ 1. The *most* effective way to highlight is to
    (a) read a paragraph and then highlight what is important.
    (b) look for key words.
    (c) recognize the passage's organization.
    (d) highlight as you read.

_____ 2. As a general rule, you should highlight
    (a) less than 10 percent of a page.
    (b) 20–30 percent of a page.
    (c) 50 percent of a page.
    (d) 75 percent of a page.

_____ 3. Which of the following would be most helpful in deciding what to highlight?
    (a) chapter introductions
    (b) graphic aids
    (c) headings
    (d) summaries

_____ 4. Which of the following items might be appropriate to mark as well as highlight?
    (a) definitions
    (b) possible test questions
    (c) confusing passages
    (d) all of the above

_____ 5. Which of the following is not an advantage of outlining?
    (a) you understand how ideas are related
    (b) you can read faster
    (c) you are forced to decide what is important
    (d) you record ideas in your own words

_____ 6. In which of the following situations would summarizing be most effective?
    (a) reading the newspaper
    (b) describing the plot of a film or short story for a literature course
    (c) preparing for a multiple choice exam
    (d) showing the organization of a biology lecture

_____ 7. Immediate review is done
    (a) right after reading.
    (b) periodically throughout the semester.
    (c) as needed in preparation for exams.
    (d) after you have outlined or summarized.

_____ 8. During periodic review, you should
   (a) reread the text.
   (b) highlight key ideas.
   (c) prepare outlines.
   (d) review your highlighting or notetaking.

_____ 9. Which one of the following methods would be most effective to use when reading library reference books to complete a term paper?
   (a) highlighting and marking
   (b) outlining
   (c) periodic review
   (d) immediate review

_____ 10. In writing a summary it is always important to
   (a) include your opinion of the subject matter.
   (b) write a thesis statement.
   (c) include examples.
   (d) use the author's words as much as possible.

Chapter 12 Interpreting: Understanding the Writer's Message and Purpose

Directions: *Select the answer that best completes each selection.*

_____ 1. Which one of the following words usually carries a strong connotative meaning?
  (a) pencil
  (b) reasoning
  (c) building
  (d) abortion

_____ 2. An inference is
  (a) an expression of fact.
  (b) a broad, general statement.
  (c) something that is assumed to be true.
  (d) a prediction about the unknown based on observable evidence.

_____ 3. Which of the following statements is a figurative expression?
  (a) Walking in the rain is fun.
  (b) My dream dried up like a raisin.
  (c) Ideas are often subject to critical evaluation.
  (d) I wandered down the deserted street.

_____ 4. Suppose you were given a $1,000 bill by a stranger. Which of the following statements expresses an inference that you might make about the situation?
  (a) The stranger is wealthy.
  (b) You are his friend.
  (c) You are a student.
  (d) The stranger was wearing a black hat.

_____ 5. A figurative expression is a(n)
  (a) narrative.
  (b) sequence.
  (c) example.
  (d) comparison.

_____ 6. Which of the following describes a situation in which an inference was made?
  (a) A student in your class leaves the room in the middle of an exam.
  (b) Your instructor wears the same blue suit everyday.
  (c) The sky is darkening and you think it may rain soon.
  (d) You finished your exam in psychology before everyone else so you left the room.

_____ 7. A writer's tone can best be described as the writer's
    (a) feeling about the subject.
    (b) purpose for writing.
    (c) style.
    (d) objective content.

_____ 8. A magazine article titled "World Terrorism: A Demand for New Get Tough Policy" is _most likely_ intended to
    (a) explain.
    (b) persuade.
    (c) amuse.
    (d) entertain.

_____ 9. Which of the following statements uses subjective language?
    (a) Body language is a form of communication.
    (b) Men are hounded unmercifully by women.
    (c) Fast food is low in nutritional value.
    (d) Nuclear war may be caused by human error.

_____ 10. Which one of the following statements uses descriptive language?
    (a) Names beginning with _J_ are currently popular.
    (b) Women resent domination by men.
    (c) A kiss is intended to bring good luck.
    (d) The restaurant serves bland, colorless, thinly disguised TV-dinner style food.

Chapter 13 Evaluating: Asking Critical Questions

Directions: *Select the answer that best completes each statement.*

_____ 1. Knowledge of source is important in evaluating an article's
(a) accuracy and value.
(b) style.
(c) assumptions.
(d) generalizations.

_____ 2. An assumption is an idea that the writer
(a) proves.
(b) disagrees with.
(c) approaches logically.
(d) believes to be true.

_____ 3. Biased writing
(a) is highly descriptive.
(b) favors a particular viewpoint.
(c) is objective.
(d) contains numerous generalizations.

_____ 4. Which one of the following articles is most likely to be slanted?
(a) "Why I Am Attending College"
(b) "Repairing Foreign-Make Cars"
(c) "Careers in the Health Sciences"
(d) "Leisure Time Is Wasted Time"

_____ 5. A generalization is
(a) a broad statement about a group or class based on experience or observation.
(b) a statement of fact that is subsequently proven.
(c) a form of logical progression.
(d) a statement of right or wrong.

_____ 6. Which one of the following statements expresses a generalization?
(a) "I learned more than I ever expected in that course."
(b) "This course was my favorite."
(c) All instructors at the college are highly committed to helping students.
(d) Dr. Vilardo is a chemistry professor.

_____ 7. Which of the following statements expresses a value judgment?
(a) The engineer accepted a bribe.
(b) Accepting a bribe is wrong.
(c) This country values prestige more than defense.
(d) I expect the restaurant to be expensive.

8. In reading and evaluating a writer's value judgment, it is important to
   (a) always begin by disagreeing with the writer.
   (b) notice whether the writer makes generalizations.
   (c) take a position, either agreeing or disagreeing.
   (d) look for evidence to support the value judgment.

9. The use of statistics as evidence
   (a) is always acceptable proof.
   (b) sometimes can be misleading.
   (c) is never acceptable.
   (d) should be qualified, using additional sources.

10. Slanted writing
    (a) is based on opinion.
    (b) is objective and factual.
    (c) is always negative.
    (d) involves the selection and omission of information.

Chapter 14 Reading and Interpreting Essays and Literature

Directions: *Select the answer that best completes each statement.*

_____ 1. When reading literature it is advisable to
  (a) skip the details and focus on interpretation.
  (b) read the piece only once and work with your overall impression.
  (c) read first for interpretation, then fill in details.
  (d) first establish the literal meaning and then focus on interpretation.

_____ 2. A theme in literature is
  (a) an expression of the literal action.
  (b) the juxtaposition of appearance and reality.
  (c) the main character's purpose.
  (d) large, general ideas about an important topic or issue.

_____ 3. Essays are built around a(n)
  (a) event.
  (b) narrative.
  (c) thesis.
  (d) point of view.

_____ 4. The *purpose* of a narrative essay is to
  (a) relate a story.
  (b) paint a visual picture.
  (c) make a point by relating a series of events.
  (d) convince you to take action.

_____ 5. Point of view in a short story or novel refers to
  (a) the level of awareness of the main character.
  (b) the perspective from which the story is told.
  (c) the elements the story conveys.
  (d) the scene in which the story occurs.

_____ 6. Which one of the following strategies would be most helpful in discovering a poem's theme?
  (a) paraphrasing
  (b) skimming
  (c) underlining
  (d) outlining

_____ 7. The tone of a short story reveals
  (a) the story's theme.
  (b) the author's attitude.
  (c) the story's setting.
  (d) the author's purpose.

_____ 8. Literature is concerned primarily with
    (a) characters and their actions.
    (b) factual information.
    (c) interpretation of ideas.
    (d) opinions.

_____ 9. The conclusion of an essay is most likely to
    (a) review its main points.
    (b) provide documentation.
    (c) provide background information.
    (d) suggest a further direction of thought.

_____ 10. Expository essays
    (a) present information.
    (b) encourage you to take action.
    (c) appeal to your senses.
    (d) tell a story.

Answer Key to Chapter Quizzes 1–14

Chapter 1

| 1. b | 2. b | 3. d | 4. b | 5. b |
| 6. a | 7. d | 8. b | 9. a | 10. a |

Chapter 2

| 1. c | 2. a | 3. d | 4. b | 5. d |
| 6. c | 7. a | 8. a | 9. a | 10. b |

Chapter 3

| 1. c | 2. c | 3. d | 4. c | 5. b |
| 6. a | 7. c | 8. a | 9. b | 10. d |

Chapter 4

| 1. a | 2. d | 3. b | 4. d | 5. c |
| 6. b | 7. b | 8. d | 9. d | 10. b |

Chapter 5

| 1. b | 2. c | 3. a | 4. b | 5. a |
| 6. d | 7. a | 8. d | 9. c | 10. a |

Chapter 6

| 1. a | 2. d | 3. b | 4. a | 5. a |
| 6. c | 7. a | 8. b | 9. a | 10. d |

Chapter 7

| 1. a | 2. b | 3. c | 4. d | 5. a |
| 6. d | 7. c | 8. b | 9. b | 10. b |

Chapter 8

| 1. c | 2. b | 3. d | 4. b | 5. c |
| 6. a | 7. b | 8. c | 9. b | 10. c |

Chapter 9

| 1. d | 2. d | 3. b | 4. d | 5. c |
| 6. b | 7. d | 8. c | 9. b | 10. d |

Chapter 10

| 1. c | 2. c | 3. b | 4. d | 5. d |
| 6. a | 7. b | 8. c | 9. b | 10. d |

Chapter 11

1. a	2. b	3. c	4. d	5. b
6. b	7. a	8. d	9. b	10. b

Chapter 12

1. d	2. d	3. b	4. a	5. d
6. c	7. a	8. b	9. b	10. d

Chapter 13

1. a	2. d	3. b	4. d	5. a
6. c	7. b	8. d	9. b	10. d

Chapter 14

1. d	2. d	3. c	4. c	5. b
6. a	7. b	8. c	9. d	10. a

Answer Key to Exercises in Chapters 1–14

Note: Answers are not included in this key for those exercises that require lengthy or subjective response.

Chapter 1 Using Context Clues

Exercise 1-1
1. a Swedish hot punch
2. frankness of expression
3. a strong attractive force that holds atoms together
4. an alkali metal
5. sense of hearing
6. five-line rhyming poems
7. total market value of national output of goods and services
8. a group of animals or plants sharing similar characteristics that are able to interbreed
9. broad, flat noodles
10. periods of time between infection and appearance of a symptom

Exercise 1-2
1. drugs
2. reserved; restrained
3. seasonings for food
4. information about performance or results
5. bodily requirements
6. materials
7. forms in which water returns to the earth
8. natural, necessary, unconscious bodily activities
9. words with identical pronunciations but different spellings
10. regular, consistent shapes

Exercise 1-3
1. wealthy; well-to-do
2. doubtful
3. agreed
4. condemned; spoke against
5. prevented; blocked
6. poor people who did not own land
7. renovated; changed; updated
8. confused
9. tendency to expect the worst; practice of looking on the dark side of things
10. expressed disapproval; belittled

Exercise 1-4

1. animals that look like kangaroos
2. incorporated; absorbed
3. lacking energy; unwilling to exercise
4. inactive; involving sitting
5. financially supported
6. place of safety
7. frightened; deterred
8. moved; bumped; shoved
9. mystical; supernatural
10. future emergency

Exercise 1-5

1. change
2. freed from charges; declared blameless
3. not talkative; reserved
4. weaknesses
5. questioning
6. gruesome; gloomy; related to disease or death
7. useless
8. abandoned
9. not intended
10. limit
11. burned
12. outline of a trip; traveling plan
13. religions
14. relationship of mutual trust
15. showing off; displaying

Exercise 1-6

A. 1. change
2. doubtful
3. show
4. studied
5. colors; shades
6. prison
7. theory
8. places of confinement
9. erupt; burst out into loud or emotional activity
10. speculates; guesses; infers
11. relay station for nerve impulses
12. thinks; guesses
13. seeing
14. increases

B. 1. systematized usage of speech and hearing
   2. expressed; communicated
   3. methods of communication
   4. express; share; communicate
   5. similarity; likeness
   6. unclearly

C. 1. rules of conduct; social expectations for behavior
   2. state clearly; define
   3. dictating proper conduct
   4. dictating improper conduct
   5. set apart; separated
   6. forced; driven
   7. harshness; strictness; rigorousness
   8. infringements or breaking of rules or laws

Chapter 2 Recognizing the Structure of Words

Exercise 2-1
1. between offices
2. above natural; unusual; exceeding normal bounds
3. not making sense
4. looking within oneself
5. arrange ahead of time
6. set again
7. a topic below or of less importance than a main topic
8. to send from one place to another
9. having many dimensions
10. not perfect; flawed

Exercise 2-2
1. not typical; unusual
2. ventilate quickly; breathe quickly
3. out of the ordinary; not common
4. partially soft; not hard, yet not completely soft
5. unsocial; against the basic principles of society
6. sail around
7. three times per week; once every three weeks (most common usage)
8. not eventful; routine
9. deformed
10. breathe out

Exercise 2-3

1. bilingual
2. subscript
3. imperfect
4. irreversible
5. misinformed
6. multilingual
7. interlude
8. discontinued
9. substandard
10. retroactive
11. reacting
12. contraceptives
13. uniform
14. interviewer
15. discolored

Exercise 2-4

1. triplex
2. antiperspirant
3. illiterate
4. pseudonym
5. superhuman
6. hypercritical
7. postgraduate
8. antibacterial
9. microbiology
10. centimeter
11. millisecond
12. replay
13. disability

Exercise 2-5

1. a machine that records and transmits messages
2. a branch of medicine that is concerned with research in biology
3. a duplicate copy or reproduction
4. one who carries or transports something
5. ability to be seen
6. written evidence of one's qualifications; that which gives credit or confidence
7. to guess, reflect, take a risk
8. a tract of land; the character or quality of land
9. a trial hearing; a presentation of something heard
10. an expression of a feeling or mental disposition
11. a study of the physics of the stars
12. ability to hold or absorb
13. a record of events in time order or sequence
14. an organization or body created to govern or control itself
15. easily accomplished without effort
16. a person's signature
17. the study of human social behavior
18. an instrument that measures sound
19. the perception of sense or feeling
20. related to voice or emission of sound

Exercise 2-6

1. verdict
2. scriptures
3. visualize
4. spectators
5. prescribed
6. extensive
7. apathetic
8. synchronized
9. graphic
10. phonics
11. tendon
12. extraterrestrial
13. dictated
14. captivated
15. deduce

Exercise 2-7

1. conversation
2. assistant
3. qualifications
4. internship
5. eaten
6. audible
7. seasonable
8. permission
9. instructive
10. memory; remembrance
11. mortality
12. presidential
13. feminist
14. hazardous
15. destiny

Exercise 2-8

1. comparison, comparable, comparer, compared
2. adaptation, adaptable, adaptability, adaptational, adaptableness, adapter, adaptive
3. rightful, rightly, rightism, righteous, righteously
4. identification, identity, identical, identicalness, identifiable
5. willful, willing, willfulness, willingly, willfully
6. preferable, preferred, preferring, preference, preferential
7. noticeable, noticed, noticing, noticeably
8. likeable, likeness, likely, likelihood, likeness, liking
9. payable, payee, payment, paying, payer
10. promotion, promotable, promoter, promotive, promotional, promoted, promoting

Exercise 2-9

1. not debatable or open to dispute
2. differences; unlikeness
3. one who obtains money or information by force or intimidation
4. allowable
5. having the ability to retain or remember

6. an emotional or shocking experience
7. lack of sincerity, honesty, or truthfulness
8. displaying an excessive amount of feeling
9. deserving credit or praise
10. to make current or popular again
11. unsureness; indecision
12. not imposed by force; not carried out
13. unchangeable; not able to be reversed
14. predict; indicate beforehand
15. multiplicity of sounds
16. uncrossable; unable to be sailed
17. not respectable; disgraceful
18. not sorry; unregretful
19. not producing enough; not working at the expected level
20. opposite of clock movement

Chapter 3 Learning New Words

Exercise 3-1
1. *Dictionary of Psychology*
2. *Black's Law Dictionary*
3. *Dictionary of Statistical Terms*

Exercise 3-2
1. exciting; thrilling; scary
2. stared at; studied; observed; watched
3. generous; surprisingly large
4. delighted; elated; joyous
5. instructed; lectured; discussed with; described for

Exercise 3-3
1. having shape; line with no straight part; to move in a curved path, and so on
2. a pitched ball thrown with a spin
3. bend refers to twisting something that is normally straight

Exercise 3-4
1. transitive verb
2. less than
3. circa; about; around the time of
4. obscure
5. French
6. plural

Exercise 3-5

1. commit
2. capture
3. barometer
4. schedule
5. identification
6. indifference
7. learned
8. liquid
9. nuisance
10. pharmacy

Exercise 3-6

1. slight trace
2. a round in a race
3. courses of action; procedures
4. principal division within a musical symphony
5. a hard surfaced area in front of an airplane hangar

Exercise 3-7

1. adjective, noun
2. (ig-zas'-er-bat')
3. the second syllable
4. *American Heritage Dictionary* lists 28 meanings.

Exercise 3-8

1. yes
2. no
3. yes
4. yes
5. no

Exercise 3-9

1. pol/ka
2. pol/lute
3. or/din/al
4. hal/low
5. ju/di/ca/ture
6. in/no/va/tive
7. ob/tuse
8. ger/mi/cide
9. fu/tile
10. ex/toll
11. tan/ge/lo
12. sym/me/try
13. te/lep/a/thy
14. or/gan/ic
15. hid/e/ous
16. te/nac/i/ty
17. mes/mer/ize
18. in/tru/sive
19. in/fal/li/ble
20. fa/nat/i/cism

Part One Review: Making Your Skills Work Together

Exercise 1

1. had lost confidence; disheartened
2. not open to dispute or debate

3. close watch or observation
4. cleared of charges; proved guiltless
5. lively action; sprightliness
6. repeat or summarize
7. childish; immature
8. substances from which water has been removed
9. clumsy; awkward
10. established as compulsory; placed through use of authority

Chapter 4 Prereading Strategies

Quiz, p. 63
1. false
2. false
3. true
4. true
5. true

Exercise 4-4
1. understanding and paraphrasing sentences
2. identifying key ideas; locating details; sentences that combine ideas; reading complicated sentences

Exercise 4-7
1. What was the Black Protest? What did World War II have to do with the Black Protest?
2. What was Reagan's foreign policy?
3. Why did the number of single-parent families grow?
4. What changes have been made in optical telescopes?
5. What types of behavior are considered violent? What are the causes of violent behavior?

Exercise 4-8
1. What is the illustration/example pattern and how is it used?
2. What is the definition/example pattern and how is it used?
3. What is the comparison/contrast pattern and how is it used?
4. What is the cause/effect pattern and how is it used?
5. What is the classification pattern and how is it used?
6. What is the chronological order/process pattern and how is it used?

Exercise 4-9
1. Why do people form groups?
2. What are instrumental groups?

3. What are expressive groups?

4. How do supportive groups relieve unpleasant feelings?

Chapter 5 Monitoring Your Comprehension and Learning

Exercise 5-1

1. *Answers will vary.*
2. a. The continents used to be joined as one land mass that broke apart. Its fragments drifted northward to their present locations.
   b. South America and Africa
   c. Magnetism in ancient lava flows indicates previous positions of the continents.
   d. The Eurasian land mass moved and became the northernmost continent. The land mass that made up India and the southern continents began dividing. South America and Africa separated completely. Australia and Antarctica drifted apart, and the South and North Atlantic Oceans continued widening.

Part Two Review: Making Your Skills Work Together

1–7. Answers will vary.

8. a. Advertisers want to save money.
   b. Reasons include the cost of testing, imprecise testing methods, and time involved in testing.
   c. Focus-group interviews—a group leader conducts a discussion with members of target audience

   Folio tests—an interviewer visits a consumer's home and shows the consumer a notebook of ads while noting the person's reaction.

   In-home projector tests—an ad is shown in a consumer's home; the consumer's reaction is evaluated.

   Trailer tests—people in a waiting room are shown ads and interviewed about their response to the ads.

   Theater tests—pre- and post-viewing questionnaires are used to measure an ad's effectiveness.

Chapter 6 Understanding and Paraphrasing Sentences

Exercise 6-1

Subject	Verb
1. parents	travel
2. children	learn

3. William Faulkner   wrote
4. psychologists   are
5. patients   refuse
6. use   is increasing
7. method   is based
8. elements   exist
9. attention   may be defined
10. instructions   are written

Exercise 6-2

1. explains a condition
2. explains a circumstance
3. explains a condition
4. indicates time
5. gives a reason
6. gives a reason
7. gives a reason
8. explains a circumstance
9. gives a reason
10. gives a reason

Exercise 6-3

Answers will vary.

1. I only answered two out of three essay questions.
2. I slept.
3. I never use it then.
4. I will probably fail the course.
5. it stops until you put more gas in.
6. there are still many poor people.
7. it makes sense to develop good eating habits.
8. they may continue to be legal.
9. so has the United States.
10. they still eat junk food.

Exercise 6-4

1. c
2. s–the individual who wants to quit may find group therapy effective.
3. c
4. c
5. c
6. s—humankind has inhabited this earth for several million years.
7. s—the Cuban economy depends upon the worldwide demand for and price of sugar.
8. s—the personnel manager is well known for interviewing all likely candidates.
9. s—they fall quite differently in the presence of air.
10. c

Exercise 6-5

1. you, can relieve, how
2. instructor, expects, which
3. students, can use, which
4. shoppers, clip, why
5. I, am going, when
6. astronomers, have learned, how
7. supply, is concentrated, where
8. light, will move, where
9. cobalt, is, which
10. Ebbinghaus, studied, which

Exercise 6-6

1. a. unverified story spread among people
   b. not checked as true
   c. spreading, being passed on
   d. misrepresents, alters
   e. altered version
2. a. brief enthusiasm for a particular innovation
   b. new idea or object
   c. uniqueness, newness
   d. object

Exercise 6-7

1. urgent, means or support
2. restricts, period of time
3. clever remarks, brought
4. companionable, form, group, control
5. played, complicated

Exercise 6-8

1. Female participation in sports has increased since the 1970s.
2. There is a difference between what are typically thought to be male and female sports.
3. There are two primary reasons for shoplifting. One is being poor and the other is wanting to have the same stylish clothes worn by one's friends.
4. The United States cannot deny the right to vote to anyone who is at least 18 years old.
5. Potential violence is rarely carried out in armed robberies. However, it is this potential violence that allows the robber to attain his/her goal—generally money.
6. There are two conflicting views of what mental illness is. The pyscholsocial view identifies mental illness as an emotional problem. The medical view identifies mental illness as having a biological cause in much the same way as a physical disease.
7. According to some researchers, the cause of problem drinking lies in the part played by genetics. Other researchers perceive the cause of problem drinking as an inability to cope with stress.
8. The Supreme Court has made much of its progress primarily as a result of having been prompted by the following popular pressures. These pressures in-

clude organizations such as those concerned with civil rights and liberties, elections, popular opinion, and social movements.

9. Historically, organized crime has occurred in other parts of the world as well as in America since the 1800s. One example is the Thugs of India, who were commonly known for murdering travelers for their possessions. Another example is the Assassins in The Middle East who were publicly recognized for killing Christians.

10. Although much progress has been made in increasing the limits of rights and liberties of Americans in the twentieth century, much more work still needs to be done.

Chapter 7 Understanding Paragraphs

Exercise 7-1
1. *Answers will vary.*
2. flowers
3. *Answers will vary.*
4. music, painting, drawing, dance
5. dramas, Westerns, romantic comedies, thrillers

Exercise 7-2
1. weights
2. beverage
3. TV programs
4. home furnishings
5. social sciences

Exercise 7-3
1. age discrimination
2. loss of job and self-esteem
3. exercise and effort
4. mental illness
5. sleep

Exercise 7-4
1. first sentence
2. first sentence
3. third sentence
4. first sentence
5. last sentence

Exercise 7-5
Answers will vary.

1. Immigration has contributed to population growth, the shift to an urban economy, and an increased mortality rate.

2. Trees have communication and protective systems that shield them from attack by insects or animals.
3. Speed of communication has changed dramatically since Lincoln's time.
4. Several attempts have been made to teach chimpanzees the English language, all resulting in only minimal success.
5. Color is used as a code or signal in a variety of situations.

Exercise 7-6
1. Tolerance means. . . .
   Withdrawal means. . . .
2. Caffeine is. . . .
   Nicotine is. . . .
3. In psychotherapy. . . .
   Sufferers of. . . .
4. absorptive glasses. . . .
   Polarizing sunglasses. . . .
   Coated sunglasses. . . .
   photochromatic . . . Their chemical composition. . . .
5. First, . . .
   After. . . .
   The candidate must. . . .

Exercise 7-7
1. examples; reasons; descriptions
2. facts; reasons
3. examples; facts; statistics
4. description; reasons
5. steps or procedures

Exercise 7-8
1. when; for example
2. therefore; one of
3. for example
4. but; so
5. first; after

Exercise 7-9
1. an example of the valuable services that pharmacies provide
2. one suggestion for preventing a home burglary
3. information that suggests some mail order businesses are not honest and reliable
4. a second advantage of a compact stereo system
5. what happens when your hormonal balance is affected or how you should take medication carefully

6. the next step in choosing the candidate you will vote for
7. a negative effect of eating only vegetables
8. what has happened as a result of this finding
9. examples of cars or trucks created for specific purposes
10. examples of other planets surrounded by moons

Exercise 7-10
1. Later
2. like; such as; for example
3. Next; Secondly; Then
4. Also; In addition
5. But; On the other hand; In contrast; However
6. Also; Similarly; Likewise
7. since; because
8. For example; For instance; To illustrate
9. For example; For instance; To illustrate
10. because; since

Chapter 8 Following the Author's Thought Pattern

Exercise 8-1
1. First sentence examples: seeing a movie, third week of class
2. Second sentence examples: walking across the floor, tires of a car, swimming, person or car on ice
3. Last sentence examples: onions and squash, apple pie filling, frozen dinner covering, toast, soup

Exercise 8-3
1. *Term:* partnership
   Class: small business
   Features: two owners, endless variation of firms, partners establish conditions and contributions, authority, duties, liability
2. *Term:* language
   Class: complex system
   Features: symbols are used for communication, includes verbal, non-verbal and written symbols
3. *Term:* Small Business Administration
   Class: independent federal agency
   Features: created through the Small Business Act, its administrator is appointed by and reports to the President, assists people in getting into business, helps them stay in business, helps small firms win federal contracts, acts as a strong advocate for small business

Exercise 8-5

1. *Items:* emphatic listening, deliberative listening
   Approach: contrasted
2. *Items:* primary groups, secondary groups
   Approach: compared and contrasted
3. *Items:* city lifestyles, suburban lifestyles
   Approach: contrasted

Exercise 8-7

1. *Causes:* inadequate management, lack of experience, unbalanced business experience, incompetence
   Effect: business failure
2. *Cause:* light
   Effect: contraction of sphincter muscles of the iris, constriction of pupils
   Effect: decrease in pupil size
3. *Cause:* snow and its crystals which collect in feathery masses and imprison air
   Effects: keep the earth warm, interferes with the escape of heat from the earth's surface

Exercise 8-9

1. *Topic:* peripheral nervous system
   Parts: somatic nervous system, autonomic nervous system
2. *Topic:* communication
   Parts: verbal messages, nonverbal messages, combinations of the two
3. *Topic:* scripts
   Parts: cultural, subcultural, family, psychological

Exercise 8-11

1. *Topic:* feedback
   Steps: monitoring impact or influence of messages on the other person, evaluating why the reaction or response occurred as it did, adjustment or modification
2. *Topic:* eruption of a geyser
   Steps: vertical column of water exerts pressure on deeper water increasing its boiling point, convection currents are shut off by shaft narrowness allowing the deeper portions to become hotter than the surface, boiling begins at the bottom, rising bubbles push out the column of water, eruption starts, pressure and the remaining water is reduced and it rapidly boils and erupts
3. *Topic:* admission of women into colleges
   Events: 1883 Oberlin College admitted women; 1837 Mount Holyoke Seminary established; 1865 Vassar College opened; Smith in 1871, Wellesley in 1877, Bryn Mawr in 1880; 1870 University of Michigan admitted women;

1900 coeducation commonplace; today majority of institutions coeducational.

Exercise 8-13
1. illustration/example
2. definition or classification
3. chronological order
4. comparison/contrast or definition
5. illustration/example
6. classification
7. chronological order/process
8. classification
9. illustration/example
10. illustration/example

Part Three Review: Making Your Skills Work Together

Exercise 1
2. second sentence in paragraph 1
4. The illustration/example thought pattern, because the selection gives examples of the barriers to listening. Or the classification pattern, because listening barriers are broken down into categories.
5. *No.* These paragraphs give more information about the barrier identified in paragraph 3, not listening because of lack of time.
6. internal competition
   external distractions
   lack of time
   conditioning
   evaluations
   emotions
   lack of training
   poor concentration

Chapter 9 Reading Textbook Chapters

Exercise 9-1
1. The text was written to help students get the most out of college and take advantage of the opportunities it offers.
2. The book is written for beginning college students.
3. Refer to the capitalized comment following the responses to the quiz.
4. Refer to the first paragraph on page xx.
5. Refer to the list on page xx.

Exercise 9-6

1. See the first and the fifth paragraphs.
2. Kinetic energy, potential energy, gravitational energy
3. W = weight
   h = height
   wh = gravitational potential energy
   m = mass
   v = velocity
   F = force
   d = distance
4. A spring, a cocked BB gun, a stretched rubber band, gas, coal, and batteries are examples of potential energy. A car in motion is an example of kinetic energy.
5. *Answers will vary.*
6. Figure 4-3 illustrates the formula *weight times height equals potential energy.*
7. Figure 4-4 indicates how potential energy is converted to kinetic energy.
8. The question is meant to illustrate how to calculate kinetic energy.
9. Kinetic energy refers to the energy of motion whereas potential energy refers to stored energy or a potential for doing work.

Chapter 10 Reading Graphic Aids

Exercise 10-1

1. It is arranged from high to low average daily circulation.
2. *(New York) Daily News*
3. *Newsday*
4. *(New York) Daily News*

Exercise 10-2

Figure 10-9

1. To compare acceptability of reasons for suicide
2. most: pain; least: family burden
3. in pain vs. any circumstance
4. *Answers will vary.*

Figure 10-10

1. The graph compares pay of full-time working men and women by age and education.
2. The graph is organized by age and income (in thousands of dollars).
3. High school-educated men earn more than high school-educated women. College educated-women earn less than college-educated men. There is a greater discrepancy between men and women's salaries with increasing age.

Figure 10-11
1. The graph traces the rate of technological change.
2. The graph reveals a dramatic increase following the Industrial Revolution.
3. *Answers will vary:* Lasers, computers, and microchips, etc.

Exercise 10-3

Figure 10-16
1. To compare race and ethnic origin in the U.S. in 1990 with projections for 2010.
2. Trends:
    a. There will be an increase in the number of residents of Hispanic origin.
    b. There will be a decrease in the number of whites.
    c. There will be a decrease in the number of blacks.

Figure 10-17
1. The chart depicts the organization of a medium-size television station.
2. They would report to the promotion manager.
3. The news director.

Figure 10-18
1. The chart explains the components of the criminal justice system.
2. It is organized in the order in which events occur.
3. A preliminary hearing is held.

Exercise 10-4
1. The diagram illustrates the rules and regulations that govern production of a hamburger.
2. As many as six inspections.
3. The use of growth-stimulating drugs must end two weeks before slaughter.

Exercise 10-5
1. The man and woman have had a disagreement or argument.
2. The man appears angry, the woman appears upset.
3. Disagreements, disputes, and arguments may cause divorce.

Chapter 11 Organizing and Remembering Information

Exercise 11-5
I. Typical U.S. household has changed
    A. Used to consist of
        1. husband
        2. nonworking wife
        3. two or more children

B. Now might be
1. single parent
2. no children
3. only one person
II. Trends that created this change
A. Americans stay single longer
1. one-half of women age 20–24
2. three-quarters of men age 20–24
B. Divorce rates higher
1. maybe two-thirds of marriages
C. Gap between male and female life expectancies
1. Women (78 years) live longer than men (74)
2. Widows one-third of one-person households
III. Impact of changes for marketers
A. Different goods and services needed
B. More income per person
C. Need smaller houses, cars, food packages
D. Spend more on entertainment and fads
E. Spend more on travel

Part Four Review: Making Your Skills Work Together

Exercise 1

1–2. *Answers will vary.*
  3. *Outline should have the following major headings:*
      I. Food Additives
          A. Reasons for Using Additives
          B. Functions of Additives
          C. Types of Food Additives

Chapter 12 Interpreting: Understanding The Writer's Message And Purpose

Exercise 12-1

1. request
2. overlook
3. tease
4. glance
5. display
6. gown
7. showy
8. awkward
9. artificial
10. keepsake

Exercise 12-2

Answers may vary.

Negative	Positive
1. snatch	grasp
2. interrogate	inquire
3. inspect	observe
4. stumble	stroll
5. smock	gown
6. ditty	composition
7. jalopy	limousine
8. guffaw	chuckle
9. oversized	massive
10. gal	lady

Exercise 12-3

1. a. A distortion of real-life relationships would affect a child negatively. It would hinder development of ability to relate and be open and provide an incorrect idea of trust (a child would not learn how to tell if he or she can trust someone). The child would not learn how to appropriately respond in real relationships.

   b. negative

   c. look directly at him or her

   d. conversations, games, playing with other children

2. a. The author may be suspicious or distrustful of government agencies

   b. A pen register might be requested to verify an alibi.

   c. The author is a right-to-privacy advocate.

3. a. Washington is usually thought of as saintlike—a simple farmer and a devoted son.

   b. The author regards Washington as dishonest and vain.

   c. No.

   d. The term refers to someone who acquires land illegally or dishonestly for personal profit.

   e. Washington is the founding father of our country, and he is remembered in a way that is consistent with that role.

4. a. The author would oppose restrictions or limitations on her right to carry a gun.

   b. The author feels these precautions to avoid them are insufficient. She may feel that reference to "dangerous situations" is stereotypical and doesn't give women credit to use their common sense to avoid danger.

   c. high crime rates; closeness to other people; drug-related crimes; limited police protection

   d. God made men, but Sam Colt made them equal.

Exercise 12-4

Selection 1: The Father and His Daughter

1. who should have run his office and let her mother run the home
2. The author dislikes the father and considers him meddlesome and overbearing.

   Clues: shut his big fatuous mouth; thought he was a philosopher and child psychologist
3. The girl inferred that it was acceptable to give away items of which one has many.
4. No, because he began to "probe" the household to locate the missing volumes.
5. The father was not happy that the rules he made for his daughter were applied to him.

Selection 2: Private Pains

1. The author made inferences about why she was crying. For example, he thought one of her parents had died or that her husband left her.
2. The silly ones: hairdresser; club luncheon
3. Yes. He seems to regret not stopping because he says we should "keep our eyes peeled for the tears of a stranger."
4. We should be less concerned with unimportant details of life and pay more attention to the needs of those around us.

Exercise 12-5

1. The quiz was simple or easy.
2. My life is a series of disappointments.
3. Parts of life are dull and repetitious.
4. A sleeping child looks distant and unfamiliar.
5. I refuse to accept the idea that nations are headed for nuclear war.

Exercise 12-6

Article 1: Love in the Afternoon

1. a. The man is visited by the woman who plans to marry him.
   b. She visits him regularly during visiting hours.
   c. Yes; see paragraph 10.
   d. They feel awkward and uncomfortable.
   e. To keep the people under control; to prevent intimacy.
   f. She quit in order to support herself.
   g. Yes; see paragraphs 9–11.
2. clocked, supervised, regulated visits, absurdity of the scene
3. joy of reunion, feel warm and tender, loving and longing, sympathy and tenderness

4. The writer believes the prison system creates unnecessary hardships on the inmates as well as their relatives.

Article 2: Stop Junk Mail Forever
1. pitches, burden, pleas, come-ons, trashed
2. The author is disappointed that environmental organizations do not oppose junk mail.
3. Vegetable slicers are a worthless product. The author uses them as an example of a product that is advertised frequently.
4. The author compares fishermen catching fish to retailers who hope to catch customers through catalog advertising.

Exercise 12-7
1. a person or couple with a high income
2. an environmentalist or a person concerned about his or her health
3. a teenager who owns a car
4. someone who does laundry
5. a car owner who is unfamiliar with a car's operation

Exercise 12-8
1. logical, persuasive
2. angry, disturbed
3. disgusted, disenchanted with the legal system
4. instructive
5. coldly logical, impersonal
6. tragic, emotional

Exercise 12-10

Article 1: Americans and the Land
1. subjective
2. amazed, disgusted
3. to describe how the early settlers abused and destroyed their natural surroundings

Article 2: The Laughter Connection
1. Laughter plays a role in pain control.
2. To describe a situation that demonstrates the use of laughter in pain control.
3. The tone is informal. It is humorous, at points. The tone of the last few paragraphs is informational.
4. The article is intended for readers interested in the effects of laughter.
5. subjective
6. *Answers will vary.*

Chapter 13 Evaluating: Asking Critical Questions

Exercise 13-1
1. c
2. c
3. c

Exercise 13-2
1. Frances Hailey
2. Peter Jennings
3. Cynthia Weinstein

Exercise 13-3
1. The writer assumes the reader is under stress.
2. The writer assumes that children do rely on heroes.

Exercise 13-4
1. M or V
2. L
3. V
4. L
5. V
6. L or M
7. V
8. L
9. M
10. M or V

Note: Answers may vary.

Exercise 13-5
Generalizations: 2, 3, 4

Exercise 13-6
1. sentences 1, 4, and 7
2. sentences 1 and 2
3. sentences 1 and 2

Exercise 13-7
1. Fact
2. Opinion
3. Fact
4. Opinion
5. Opinion
6. Fact
7. Opinion
8. Fact
9. Opinion
10. Fact

Exercise 13-8
1. Statistics are not given about numbers of students who must use the same fa-

cilities at the same time—that is, classrooms, lecture halls, cafeterias—nor about the sizes of these facilities.

2. Statistics are not given for sales of other cars.

3. Pollution statistics for individual industries are not given (some may be well above the hazardous level).

Exercise 13-9

1. *Answers will vary.* Actual source is a book by Studs Terkel titled *Working: People Talk About What They Do All Day and How They Feel About It.*

2. *Answers will vary.*

3. People think that welfare recipients are "taking something for nothing." Also, see last paragraph.

4. *Answers will vary.*

5. *Answers will vary.*

6. She uses personal experience.

7. "Welfare makes you feel like you're nothing."

8. "A job that a woman in a house is doing is a tedious job."

Exercise 13-10

1. The age-old gap between adult and children's tastes in entertainment continues today.

2. The author regards children's culture as diverse and lucrative, but inevitably in dispute with adult preferences.

3. For a sociology term paper, this source by itself would be inadequate and insufficient. The article would be helpful to parents.

4. Yes. It is written from an adult viewpoint.

5. Types of supporting evidence include: personal experience, examples, and description.

6. The author assumes (does not prove) that adults dislike children's entertainment; that television will continue to grow; that adults do not watch children's entertainment; and that children are more accepting than adults.

7. The tone is informative with an element of humor.

Chapter 14 Reading and Interpreting Literature

Exercise 14-1

1. The essay focuses on what writers study and write about.

2. Writers study literature, not the world.

3. Dillard compares the writer to a tennis player. She also compares the writer to a painter.

4. Painters must like paint, and writers must like sentences because they are the medium of expression, or the tools with which each works.

Exercise 14-2

1. *Answers will vary.* The story may have taken place in a small town in the early twentieth century.
2. At a church revival meeting, Langston Hughes was forced to pretend he was saved and felt guilty about it afterward and questioned Jesus' existence.
3. Hughes told the story to relate a very personal, traumatic experience and to comment upon the nature of religious experience.
4. *Answers will vary.*

Exercise 14-4

1. *Answers will vary.*
2. Ray Arnold is friendly, trustworthy, adventuresome, and self-reliant.
3. *Answers will vary.*
4. *Answers will vary.*

Exercise 14-6

1. The author argues that tobacco farmers should not receive tax support.
2. While growing and selling tobacco is legal, taxes should not be paid to support the tobacco industry, which causes addiction, illness, time lost from employment, and death.
3. The author offers facts and statistics to support the argument.
4. Yes—because the argument implies that lives and money will be saved if tax support for tobacco farmers is eliminated and the argument is logical in terms of consistency and common sense.
5. The writer intends to demonstrate to the reader that the government is illogical in promoting taxes and profits for tobacco while opposing smoking.

Exercise 14-8

1. The creators talked and argued about how the world should be created. Their thoughts and ideas crystallized, or took shape. Then creation began. As they called out each word, that aspect of the world appeared.
2. The story explains the creation of the earth.
3. The last sentence indicates the Creators were pleased with their creation and felt it would surpass the darkness.
4. Both explain creation; in the beginning nothing but darkness and water existed. The Quiché-Mayan creation was planned; the Bantu creation seemed more spontaneous. In the Quiché-Mayan myth, the Creators created everything; in the Bantu, creatures were created, and they created others.

Exercise 14-9

1. Morton and his wife and their child, Larry, are in a city park on a Sunday afternoon. Another child, Joe, throws sand at Larry. The mother reprimands Joe, but he does not stop. Joe's father does not reprimand Joe; instead, he en-

courages him. Morton approaches Joe and they argue. Joe threatens Morton. Morton and his wife and Larry leave the park. The child throws a temper tantrum. Morton and his wife argue.

2. The wife may be left unnamed because her character is not as fully developed as Morton's or Joe's.
3. They appear to be typical parents. Morton and his wife respond typically at the sandbox; their behavior as they return home is not.
4. The tone becomes tense as the story progresses.
5. *Answers will vary.*
6. The wife uses Joe's expression to express her contempt for and disappointment in her husband.

Exercise 14-10

"Two Look at Two"
1. A couple, as they are walking a mountainous path, meet a doe and a buck. They stand motionless, observing one another.
2. The statements reveal the couple's continuing surprise and revelation about what nature has to offer.
3. The tumbled wall may represent the distance or separation between man and nature.
4. The poem's theme is separation, coexistence, and compatibility of humans and nature.

"Do Not Go Gentle into That Good Night"
1. The poet asks his father to continue to fight for life.
2. death
3. The poem argues that life is valuable and worthwhile and should always be fought for, even when one is elderly or near death.

Part Five Review: Making Your Skills Work Together

Exercise 1

1. Jane marries and bears a child ten months later. For the next twenty-five years, she has a child every two years. She spends her life caring for the children and her husband. Later she cares for her parents, unmarried daughters or orphaned grandchildren.
2. Jane has spent her life burdened with the care of others. She has not had the opportunity to develop intellectually or creatively.
3. Galeano wrote the essay to comment upon the role of women in our society at that time period.
4. The last line contrasts Jane's life to that of her brother, Benjamin, who commands great historical attention.
5. If Benjamin Franklin had been born a woman, she may not have made the discoveries that he did.

Answer Key to Exercises in Reading Selections 1–30

Note: Since many of the open-ended questions require full sentence answers for which a variety of responses are acceptable, this key includes answers for only objective or fill-in-the-blank questions.

Selection 1 Living Life to the Fullest

Words in Context
1. cheerful and noisy party
2. got her attention by gesturing

Vocabulary Review
1. d   6. h
2. g   7. i
3. e   8. a
4. f   9. c
5. b

Selection 2 Hispanic, USA: The Conveyor-Belt Ladies

Words in Context
1. not interesting, not stimulating
2. physically demanding
3. about to happen
4. made fun of
5. telling a story about

Vocabulary Review
1. d   7. g
2. e   8. b
3. a   9. f
4. k   10. h
5. c   11. l
6. i   12. j

Selection 3 A Guard's First Night on the Job

Words in Context
1. illegal or forbidden goods
2. noise
3. do permanent bodily injury

Vocabulary Review
1. rookie
2. cursory
3. equivalent
4. apprehensive
5. ruckus
6. mace
7. tiers

Selection 4 Angry Fathers

Words in Context
1. bored and restless
2. hid
3. extremely bad; shocking
4. ruined; destroyed
5. came out
6. physical

Vocabulary Review
1. abstractions
2. indignant
3. approbation
4. inconspicuous
5. conspiracy
6. tweak
7. anonymous
8. grimly
9. reproach
10. spectacle

Selection 5 Freedom From the Past

Words in Context
1. at first
2. allowed; accepted
3. carrying

Vocabulary Review
1. redemption
2. ponder
3. intimate
4. bout
5. slayed
6. treacherous
7. aspirations
8. crafting

Selection 6 Lotteries and Lightning

Words in Context

1. understanding
2. show; explain
3. figure out; work out
4. possible; that could happen

Vocabulary Review

1. randomly
2. analogy
3. abandon
4. wag
5. probability

Selection 7 Playing "Get The Guest"

Words in Context

1. boyfriend
2. unhappy; angry; upset
3. quick thinking; smart
4. likely to be; probable
5. mainly; primarily

Vocabulary Review

1. callous
2. confrontation
3. humiliated
4. parameters
5. deleted
6. quest
7. allegedly
8. segment

Selection 8 Stress Management: Personally Adjusting to Stress

Checking Your Comprehension

1. F
2. F
3. T
4. F
5. F
6. T
7. T
8. T
9. F
10. F

Words in Context

1. bring on; cause
2. ability to change or alter
3. events that cause stress reactions
4. steps; stages
5. mentally manipulating images

Vocabulary Review

1. concurrently; simultaneously
2. overwhelmed
3. intensity
4. simultaneously; concurrently
5. unrequited
6. retrospect
7. relevant
8. subjective

Selection 9 A Day on Wheels

Words in Context

1. confusion
2. to look at closely
3. high-powered
4. without hesitation

Vocabulary Review

1. apropos
2. mortified
3. gratuitous
4. adroit
5. Civilities
6. dubious
7. comme il faut
8. persistent

Selection 10 Looking out for Number 1, 2, 3

Words in Context

1. nerve; boldness
2. proof; support; assurance
3. handed out; measured out
4. by multiples; by larger numbers
5. extremely; vastly

Vocabulary Review

1. logistics
2. an accusatory
3. à la
4. fleeting
5. urchins
6. finite
7. oppressive
8. arrogant

Selection 11 Who has the Right to Name?

Words in Context

1. other choice; substitute
2. disagreements; arguments
3. given

Vocabulary Review

1. taxes; laws; fines for speeding
2. blocks your view; prevents you from seeing it well
3. they agree on it
4. increasing again; reappearance
5. more than you can afford; more than is right
6. abortion
7. "making ends meet"; finding enough time to do everything

Selection 12 Don't Ask

Words in Context

1. able to provide for one's self without help from others
2. surpassing others in rank or quality
3. required as a prior condition

Vocabulary Review

1. d
2. b
3. g
4. e

5. a
6. c
7. f

Selection 13 Blue Highways

Words in Context

1. diminishing
2. to make again; renew

3. promise
4. referring to

Vocabulary Review

Root Word	Meaning
1. undulate	to move in waves
2. contaminate	to corrupt or make impure
3. configure	to shape or form
4. render	give; make available; present
5. perfidy	breach of faith; violation of trust
6. delude	mislead, or deceive
7. cartography	technique of mapmaking

Selection 14 Death on a Plate

Words in Context
1. small pieces
2. slightest
3. poison
4. blissful; feeling great happiness
5. inability to move
6. believing you cannot change what will happen to you

Vocabulary Review
1. desperate
2. neurological
3. ensure
4. dilate
5. macabre

Selection 15 How Much Are You Willing to Pay for That New-Car Smell

Words in Context
1. get; run into
2. valuable item you own
3. difference between original cost and resale value later; gradual decrease in what something is worth

Vocabulary Review
1. audio
2. unique
3. warranty
4. rationally
5. embody
6. synthetic
7. acquisition

Selection 16 Nonverbal Communication

Words in Context
1. strength
2. areas of space
3. person guilty of a crime

Vocabulary Review
1. g
2. f
3. h
4. d
5. e
6. a
7. c
8. b

Selection 17 Snack Foods

Words in Context
1. unequaled, supreme
2. permanent, fixed
3. vigor, enthusiasm
4. slender pieces
5. equaling or surpassing, competing with
6. creative, introducing new ideas
7. miniature baby eels
8. spiny, golf-ball sized marine animals

Vocabulary Review
1. F	5. F
2. F	6. T
3. T	7. F
4. T	8. F

Selection 18 Acupuncture

Words in Context
1. reporter
2. different
3. most traditional; stuffiest
4. adjusting; carefully bringing
5. usual; most accepted
6. growing
7. approved of
8. image; best example

Vocabulary Review
1. they complain all the time
2. to remove the appendix
3. it is unusual or different
4. a toothache
5. admitted that he or she lost
6. did it the proper way; followed the correct procedure
7. lines
8. we can't explain why

Selection 19 Kissing Customs

Words in Context
1. gallant, courteous, honorable
2. passion, eagerness
3. assumption
4. opposite of the intended meaning
5. high regard
6. fading, diminishing

Vocabulary Review
1. stammered
2. feudal
3. sporadic
4. effete
5. obsequious
6. proletarian

Selection 20 A Degree of Detachment

Words in Context
1. give; present
2. decision and description of the nature of a condition
3. absolutely necessary
4. extreme joy
5. justify; convince oneself
6. close relationship
7. impartiality

Vocabulary Review
1. a. 2
   b. 3
   c. 1
2. *Answers will vary.*
3. removal of cells or fluid from the body for tests
4. calm; quiet; relaxed
5. one that is cancerous
6. upset because he acted indifferently
7. *Answers will vary.*

Selection 21 The Power of Language

Checking Your Comprehension

1. T
2. F
3. T
4. F

5. T
6. T
7. T

Words in Context

1. able to be made again
2. exchange of ideas
3. moved forward, advanced
4. cannot be brought into agreement

Vocabulary Review

1. f
2. d
3. a
4. e

5. g
6. b
7. c

Selection 22 Characteristics of the News

Words in Context

1. having quality of news; degree to which it warrants press coverage
2. moving in a circle, coming around to where something began
3. paying special or excessive attention to
4. being twisted out of shape; change in the usual appearance
5. able to be seen
6. functioning as a go-between or interpreter
7. examining functions, relationships, causes, effects
8. focusing on trends or patterns, or continuing sequence of ideas

Vocabulary Review

1. parochial
2. calamities
3. emphasize

6. transcribing
7. procession
8. unabashedly

4. preoccupation
5. gauge

9. instinctively
10. ostensibly

Selection 23 Exploring Virtual Reality

Words in Context
1. acts like; repeats
2. exploding; pouring out
3. buried; included

Vocabulary Review
1. d
2. i
3. e
4. g
5. b

6. h
7. c
8. f
9. a

Selection 24 Night Work, Sleep, and Health

Words in Context
1. active during the daytime
2. going from one to another; changing
3. events that occur in one's surroundings

Vocabulary Review
1. disrupted
2. adverse
3. realignment

4. inadequate
5. circadian
6. posed

Selection 25 An Amateur Marriage

Checking Your Comprehension
1. F
2. F
3. T
4. T

5. T
6. F
7. F

Words in Context
1. changing
2. playful, nonserious action
3. a lively, invigorating feeling

Selection 26 Why do we Grow Lawns Around our Houses?

Words in Context

1. enormous; extremely large
2. decorative
3. importance; status
4. surface of the earty
5. copy

Vocabulary Review

1. g
2. f
3. a
4. e
5. b
6. d
7. c

Selection 27 Television Addiction

Words in Context

1. inclination; predisposition
2. desires; wants
3. set aside; made different
4. postponed
5. hold too high an opinion of; overvalue
6. drained; without energy
7. activity
8. harmful

Vocabulary Review

1. F
2. T
3. F
4. T
5. T
6. F
7. T
8. F
9. F

Selection 28 Gawk Shows

Words in Context

1. symbol of identification; distinctive sign
2. aging disease
3. reasons, logical basis
4. unconventional, odd, farfetched
5. caressed, stroked lovingly

Vocabulary Review

1. a	6. b
2. f	7. c
3. i	8. g
4. e	9. d
5. j	10. h

Selection 29 Why Confession is Good for the Soul— and the Body

Words in Context

1. dismiss, send away
2. psychological process of suppressing action, emotion, or thought
3. emotional or shocking experience
4. field of study connecting psychology and medical research of the immune system
5. undecided, unsettled

Vocabulary Review

1. obsessions
2. assimilate
3. insight
4. therapeutic
5. cognitive
6. accessible
7. stream-of-consciousness

Selection 30 Drugs

Words in Context

1. exact
2. setting in motion
3. hatred
4. groups of citizens

Vocabulary Review

Root Word	*New Word*
1. hero	heroism
2. exhort	exhortative
3. persecute	persecution
4. perennial	perennials
5. moral	morality
6. repress	repressive
7. resist	resistance

Sentences will vary.